THE MAKING OF
AN ARCHITECT
1881–1981

THE MAKING OF AN ARCHITECT·1881–1981

Columbia University in the City of New York

Edited by Richard Oliver

RIZZOLI
NEW YORK

The Graduate School of Architecture and Planning is grateful to the following contributors whose generous gifts have helped make this book a reality.

Mr. and Mrs. Charles Agee Atkins
Temple Hoyne Buell Foundation
Mary Duke Biddle Foundation
The Durst Foundation
Equitable Life Assurance Society of the United States
Ford Foundation
JEWISH COMMUNAL FUND OF NEW YORK –
Daniel and Joanna S. Rose Philanthropic Fund
J.M. Kaplan Fund, Inc.
Knoll International
Phyllis Lambert and Gene R. Summers
Morse-Diesel, Inc.
NEW YORK COMMUNITY TRUST –
Mr. and Mrs. Robert M. Pennoyer
New York State Council on the Arts
Park Tower Realty Corporation
Rockefeller Center, Inc.
Skidmore, Owings and Merrill Foundation
Sheldon H. Solow
Starrett Housing Corporation
Fred C. Trump Foundation
Vinmont Foundation, Inc.
The School is deeply indebted to its alumni for their generous support.

Published in the United States of America in 1981 by
RIZZOLI INTERNATIONAL PUBLICATIONS, INC.,
712 Fifth Avenue, New York, NY 10019

LC 81-51717
ISBN: 0-8478-0416-X

Design by Abby Goldstein
Type composition by Candice Odell
Printed and bound by Kingsport Press, Kingsport, Tennessee

Contents

The structure of this book arose out of discussions among the Faculty who have written the thematic essays, and myself, with the idea that the particular history of the Graduate School of Architecture and Planning at Columbia University — here presented in serial form as seven chapters — should be seen against a backdrop of events in the profession of architecture, in New York City, and in the world at large. Thus, the more personal thematic essays thrust the School into a relationship with larger ideas and events while the more dispassionate historical essays carry the reader through the evolution of the School itself. Not only was this structure a felicitous way to make a scholarly history also engaging reading, but it proved ideal as a way to distribute among many people a large amount of work which had to be accomplished in a short time. I am grateful to the Faculty authors for these discussions.

In organizing this history, it quickly became apparent that the tenures of the various administrative heads of the School formed the logical divisions of time. The appointment of a Dean proved not to be an isolated administrative event, but one that was embedded in discussions among various interested parties about the structure, content, and direction of the School itself, its obligations to the profession of architecture, and its relationship to New York City. Thus, it should be clearly stated that this book is not about administrative appointments per se, but about them as a reflection of ideas about architectural education itself, which is the essential subject of this book.

This history was aided by two earlier efforts: Theodor Rohdenburg's *A History of the School of Architecture,* written in 1954 upon the occasion of the bicentennial of the founding of the University; and the research completed by Dennis McFadden in the first half of 1980. Rohdenburg also generously made available for use his complete personal archive on the history of the School. The general research for this history was begun by Steven M. Bedford and Judith Oberlander under my direction in the fall of 1980. It quickly became apparent to me that these graduate students were capable of much more than research, and each was asked to become the author of one of the historical essays. They were later joined by Diane Boas and Susan M. Strauss, each of whom also undertook research and wrote individual essays for the book. I am grateful to these four individuals not only for their dedicated work, but for the collegial atmosphere in which it was accomplished. Other individuals completed research for the thematic essays, and they are acknowledged in the respective footnotes.

The School and I wish to thank the many Alumni, Faculty, and Staff who agreed to be inteviewed as part of the research. These interviews are cited in the notes of each essay and were instrumental in creating a more complete picture of the history of the School. Marian Jemmott, Secretary of the University, allowed researchers to peruse the Central Files of the University for the documentation which is at the heart of this book; without her

Acknowledgments

gracious and patient assistance, the book could not have been completed in its present form.

The illustrations in the book come from many sources and these are cited. A majority come from the archives of Avery Library, and thus the School and I are grateful for the generous assistance provided by Charling Fagan, the Acting Librarian, and Janet Parks, the Curator of Drawings. In selecting illustrations of projects included in the historical essays and in the portfolio of alumni work, I was joined by a committee of Faculty which included Max Bond, Kenneth Frampton, Alexander Kouzmanoff, Michael Mostoller, and James Stewart Polshek. The illustrations for the thematic essays were selected by the respective authors.

Drafts of all the essays were read by various individuals for tone, completeness, and scholarship. Robert A.M. Stern, Chairman of the Centennial Planning Committee, was especially helpful in this regard. Individuals on the School's office staff played an important role. Sarah McMillan, Karen Krane, and Shirley Driks typed the final drafts of the essays and notes. I am particularly grateful to Sarah McMillan whose careful proofreading and suggestions helped to give a more precise form to the final drafts; I would also like to thank Dean Loes Schiller, Jane Bobbe, David Hinkle, Joseph Smith, and, of course, Dean Arlene Jacobs who helped in numerous important ways at every stage in the production of this book. I also wish to thank the book designer, Abby Goldstein, and the typesetter, Candice Odell, both of whom helped on many occasions to ease the difficulties of a short production schedule.

Finally, the School and I wish to thank Solveig Williams of Rizzoli International Publications for the enthusiasm, care, and patience with which she guided this book through the production process.

Richard Oliver, Editor

Introduction

James Stewart Polshek

For more than two years, scores of alumni, faculty, students, administrators and friends of the Graduate School of Architecture and Planning have been working on the centennial activities that will take place during the 1981–82 academic year. The two principal events that will celebrate one hundred years of educating architects at Columbia are an exhibition at the National Academy of Design and this book — both entitled *The Making of an Architect, 1881–1981: Columbia University in the City of New York*.

In this book, the chronological history of the School has been deliberately interrupted by seven individual essays: while the history of the School shows a strong continuity in architectural education, these seven scholarly and sometimes polemical essays illuminate periods of dramatic change in which the institution reacted with a resiliency that allowed it to endure and grow.

As the century-long panorama unfolds, the picture that emerges out of the variety of curricula, biographies, competitions, projects, buildings and bibliographies is at once complex and orderly. Underlying the intricate and continuous pattern of changing attitudes of new administrators and faculty, of innovations and re-evaluations, is a body of shared beliefs more important than the individual expressions of any one period. Indeed, the two great architectural achievements of the century, the Beaux-Arts (1881–1933) and Modernism (1933–present), were acknowledged in major changes of curricula.

From the order which can be seen in the history of the School, there emerges what I would call a "culture of architecture." By this I refer to a set of prescribed concerns, attitudes, affinities and shared sensibilities that provide the architectural student and practitioner with a unique *esprit de corps*. Those who have studied architecture differ from their professional colleagues in medicine, law, education or the ministry, in the social interaction among themselves and in their relationships to the larger society.

The culture that characterizes the architectural community is comprised of a unique set of behavior patterns and artistic beliefs. In fact, it is not possible to find more highly individualized students, both in their personal style and in their passionate involvement with their environment. In spite of their differences, they are bound together by the principles of architecture that have been defined by the great builders from Alberti to Le Corbusier.

Paradoxically, architectural education has been anything but orderly. Rather, it continues to be highly idiosyncratic — an education that is rigidly orthodox — consistent in its skepticism. In 1939 Dean Leopold Arnaud tried to explain the "tenor of instruction," an aptly vague phrase for architectural education, this way:

We have a fairly clear idea of the subjects recommended for study in the days of Ancient Egypt, as well as of Greece, to say nothing of the accurate record of curriculum proposed by Vitruvius in his first book. We also know with considerable detail the requirements for the various examinations given by the Guilds of the Middle Ages, and furthermore, we know quite exactly the prescribed courses in the schools of architecture established since the Renaissance. It is interesting to notice that in all these periods the tenor of instruction varies but little. In essence, the young professional is expected

to have as broad an education as possible, and more specifically, to develop
as a creative artist and as a conscientious, scientific builder. [1]

Dean Arnaud's point that "the tenor of instruction varies but little" continues to be true. The teaching of design has remained a stable endeavor, absorbing and being enriched by new phenomena: the impact of a new technology and its social implications which became evident in the 1930's, the intensity of the political consciousness of the late 1960's, and even the present interest in historic preservation. *The Education of an Architect 1881–1981* will show that changes of architectural deans, faculties, and students have always been subservient to the larger culture of architecture whose underlying characteristics have remained constant.

It is worthwhile speculating as to why the basic values and attitudes expressed in school have transcended factionalism and fashion. It seems to me that those instincts that lead young men and women to pursue the study of architecture are based on an unshakable belief in the existence of a *better* future. The embryonic architect is both visionary and idealist. Students see themselves as translators of fantasies into realities; as objectifiers of mental images; as creators of new formal languages and as inventors of solutions to human problems. They see the task most central to the architect's mission as one serving a larger purpose, and they sense early on that they are entering a cultural inner sanctum that will prepare them to carry out these responsibilities.

Fundamental to the uniqueness of architectural education is that the student has grown up in a culture whose educational emphasis is on written language and mathematics. Visual communication is de-emphasized starting soon after kindergarten. Drawing and the study of art and architecture take third place. A student studies kings, not castles, and religion, not churches. When a student enters architectural school the introduction to a graphic language can be a catharsis. The requirement to communicate ideas through drawing, rather than through speaking or writing is often confusing and even overwhelming. This radical change is disorienting to new architectural students, particularly those who have been prepared for other disciplines before entering graduate school. This results in a strong dependence on one's peers, as well as on the teacher. It also creates a solidarity amongst students which is impressive. The design studio becomes home and workplace. Openness to criticism — both from fellow students and from teachers — and the necessity to express private fantasies publicly, further cement the "family." This clannishness is one of the more obvious hallmarks of the "culture of architecture."

Almost seventy percent of an architectural curriculum takes place in or is related to the "studio." This part of the student's education is really a series of design "seminars" meeting for sixteen to twenty hours a week with one faculty member serving twelve to fourteen students. It has been axiomatic that architectural knowledge is transmitted most effectively on a one-to-one basis — the teacher sitting with a single student for fifteen minutes to one hour engaged in an often silent dialogue of pencil lines and fragmentary

1. Leopold Arnaud, "The Education of the Architect as We See it at Columbia," *The Bulletin of the Beaux Arts Institute of Design,* 16 (December 1939), p. 2.

sketches. This is then reinforced by small group reviews where peer criticism becomes an important ingredient.

Another circumstance that maintains the culture is the existence of various architectural principles that have been transmitted from one generation of architects to another for thousands of years. Such phenomena as proportion, scale, circulation, surface characteristics and spatial and formal definition are controlled by those principles. Despite the logic inherent in these ordering systems, the manner of their transmission from one generation of architects to another has been more akin to folk art than to the studied and systematic teaching of science. No individual or institution of architecture has succeeded in defining *the* pedagogically correct way of teaching architecture. Architecture had a Vitruvius, not a Vesalius, no single cadaver to dissect, but rather the whole human race to settle and to provide habitat for. All of this has further reinforced the identity of the architectural culture by making it almost immune from the sociological studies which have attempted to rationalize other professional callings.

Even the end product — the built object — is based on a construction process which remains inherently asystematic. The failure to effectively produce buildings by industrial methods and to systemize the process of construction is testimony to the fact that the mentality of the artisan is with us today. Therefore, despite the futurist orientation inherent in the "culture of architecture," the process by which the final product comes to life has remained inherently medieval. This, in turn, has made the effective teaching of technical subject matter extremely difficult and has almost always resulted in an imbalance between the student's interest in technique and design, with design always the winner.

An outgrowth of this education is an antipathy to specialization and a predilection for synthesis. When the word "interdisciplinary" became fashionable during the 1960's, it seemed an appropriate approach to architects, who had been taught that there was no other way to approach architectural problem solving.

Dean Hudnut's pronouncement in 1934 that "before the student takes up the study of design he must have some broad understanding of the nature of the civilization in which he is to practice — its character and its structure, its history, and the intellectual currents which underlie and direct it" has been stated in different ways by all of the deans before and since Hudnut, and is still fundamental to pursuing a professional degree in architecture.[2]

The studio in which the teaching of architecture occurs has further reinforced its unique cultural aspects. From 1881 to 1897 in the *Maison de Punk* on 50th Street and 4th (Park) Avenue, from 1897 to 1912 on the fourth floor of Havemeyer Hall, and since then in the studios of Avery Hall, students have been educated in spaces where learning from peers is almost as important as learning from teachers; where language, dress, ideas and behavior are common to student and faculty; where a special camaraderie has flourished; and where competition defers to creative interdependence. The students' ability to evaluate their own work relative to that of their

2. "Columbia Changes Her Methods," *Architectural Forum,* 60 (February 1935), p. 168.

classmates is basic. Not only are the final products now open to view at the jury, but so is the process of evaluation, which always involves comparative criticism.

The very nature of the studio's space, where ideas and attitudes are shared, has always tended to sustain the culture. With fifty or sixty students in one space, the mass airing of grievances, reactions to rumors and the sharing of perceptions are almost instantaneous. Discussions ranging from national politics and rises in tuition to the quality of faculty and the content of the studio program are commonplace. Fatigue is the common badge of identity — the all-night "charrette" the ultimate test.

Photographs of studios dating from the early part of this century and reminiscences of graduates substantiate the "one-worldness" of the design studio. No other profession requires its students to maintain their individuality while participating in a communal situation where they periodically eat, sleep and work for up to twenty hours a day. The secondhand refrigerator and the foam rubber mattress are part of the "residential" life of the studio. The difficulties that architects sometimes encounter in the world of business and *laissez-faire* competition may stem from the studio atmosphere where individual needs are subordinated to the needs of the group.

In 1915 Abraham Flexner, who revolutionized American medical education, listed the attributes of a profession. I leave the reader to consider them, particularly the last, with the hope that this book will show how architecture remains able to fulfill these requirements.

(1) The occupation must possess and draw upon a store of knowledge that is more than ordinarily complex.

(2) The occupation has to have a theoretical grasp of the phenomena with which it deals.

(3) The occupation must apply its theoretical and complex knowledge to the practical solution of human and social problems.

(4) The occupation must strive to add and improve its stock of knowledge.

(5) The occupation must pass on its wisdom to younger generations in a deliberate and formal manner.

(6) An occupation to qualify as a profession has to be imbued with altruistic spirit.[3]

Ada Louise Huxtable, in an essay entitled "Is Modern Architecture Dead?" reinforced Dr. Flexner's last point when she defined civilization as "the betterment of the human condition at the highest level of shared experience and universal concern."[4] As we turn toward the next century of educating architects, we do so in the belief that they will, through their contributions, continue to strive to achieve such a civilization.

3. As quoted in Walter P. Metzger, "What is a Profession?," *Seminar Reports,* 3 (Fall 1975), pp. 1-3.

4. Ada Louise Huxtable, "Is Modern Architecture Dead?," *The New York Review of Books,* 28 (July 16, 1981), p. 18.

View of the midtown campus of Columbia College, ca. 1880.
Photo: Columbiana Collection.

History I
The Founding of the School

Steven M. Bedford

I n December, 1784, Columbia College undertook its first attempt to establish a course in architecture. On December 14 of that year, the College Regents received a report from their committee appointed to "...digest a plan of education for the College." The report included a proposal to establish a professorship in architecture. Experiencing financial difficulty following the American Revolutionary War, the College was not able to implement the proposal and establish a full architecture course until 1881, a little less than one hundred years later.[1]

In the meantime, however, occasional courses touching on architecture were offered in the College. In 1836, Columbia Professor of Natural and Experimental Philosophy, James Renwick Sr., included in his course "Rational and Practical Mechanics" the study of the "Principles of Civil and Military Architecture,"[2] but this hardly constituted professional architectural training. Throughout the mid-nineteenth century, American architects, with few exceptions, received their training as apprentices in the offices of established architects who were, in turn, often self-taught, or had received only rudimentary training abroad.[3] This lack of formal training was often blamed for what was widely held to be the poor quality of American architecture and for the low professional status of architects. It was hoped that formal education would reverse these trends. The American Institute of Architects (AIA), founded in New York in 1857, frequently served as a forum for the discussion of these matters. In 1867, the AIA Committee on Education suggested that a new school of architecture "be located on the upper part of Manhattan Island or any spot on the Hudson River in Westchester County."[4]

The development of a course in architecture at Columbia College would have been delayed further were it not for the interest,

1. Minutes of the Trustees of Columbia University, vol. 2, p. 64.

2. *Statutes of Columbia College* (Board of Trustees of Columbia College, New York, 1836).

3. A full discussion of architectural education in the first half of the nineteenth century can be found in a number of sources, including: Bannister, T., *et.al., The Architect at Mid-century* (Washington, D.C.: A.I.A., 1954).

4. Upjohn, H., *The American Institute of Architects; the early years* (1931), p. 183. Typescript copy in Avery Library.

determination, and munificence of Columbia Trustee Frederick Augustus Schermerhorn.[5] Schermerhorn single-handedly convinced his fellow Trustees of the need to begin a course in architecture at the College. His motivation was based less upon an interest in improving the aesthetic quality of New York buildings than in a concern for the city's poor housing and sanitary conditions. This concern was fueled by his brother-in-law, Colonel Richard T. Auchmuty, Jr., with whom he shared a house at 101 University Place.[6] Auchmuty, an architect and partner in the firm of James Renwick, Jr., would surely have kept Schermerhorn well informed of the squalid conditions then present in New York, for he was a member of both the Improved Dwelling Association and the Sanitary Reform Society. As a further measure of the timeliness of the subject, "the great dark tenement houses which offend the eye at almost every point" were discussed in an 1877 editorial in *The New York Times*. Schermerhorn would also have been aware of the issue through the 1879 Report of the Board of Health, written by Charles F. Chandler, a Professor of Chemistry at Columbia, as well as through the Tenement House Competition sponsored in the same year by *Plumber and Sanitary Engineer.*[7]

Reacting to these influences, Schermerhorn began to press his fellow Trustees to establish a course in architecture at Columbia. On April 2, 1879, on the motion of Schermerhorn, the Board of Trustees resolved to authorize a report on the subject.[8] On May 5, 1879, Schermerhorn submitted *A Proposal to Establish a Course of Instruction in Architecture in the School of Mines,* of which he was the sole author.[9] "In the first place," he began, "there is a great need in this country of thoroughly educated architects." He continued in a manner similar to the aforementioned editorial, stating, "the need is seen and felt every day whichever way we turn as we look at our buildings, both public and private."[10]

Familiar with the traditional apprenticeship method of architectural education through contact with his brother-in-law, Schermerhorn saw it as the source of many of the problems in American architecture. In 1902, he retrospectively discussed these problems and their relation to architectural education in a letter to President Butler:

There were hardly any such schools and the few existing were of a small feeble kind and such instruction was picked up as well as could be in Architects' offices and the older Architects themselves, with few exceptions were very imperfectly educated and buildings public and private were being everywhere erected of greater or less ugliness and sometimes monstrosities.[11]

Although Schermerhorn felt that American buildings were ugly, his major concern was for their clinically unsafe condition. He consequently advocated for architects special instruction in Sanitary Engineering. As a later justification of such a course, Schermerhorn wrote in a letter to Dr. Cornelius R. Agnew, a fellow Trustee:

From the first inception of the School of Architecture it was always my especial and most important Design to combine with it instruction in

5. Schermerhorn (1844–1919), born in New York, was an 1868 graduate of the School of Mines of Columbia College. He entered with the class of 1865 and subsequently decided to prepare for the United States Military Academy. He withdrew from the College and in 1864, enlisted in the Union Army and was promoted to Captain for his bravery in the Battle of Five Forks. At War's end he returned to Columbia to finish studies for his M.E. (mining engineer) degree. In 1877, he was named a Trustee of Columbia College, a position he held until 1908 (Schermerhorn, R., *Schermerhorn Geneology and Family Chronicle,* New York, Tobias Wright, 1914 – passim).

6. Johnson, A. ed., *Dictionary of American Biography,* vol. 1 (New York: Scribner's, 1943), p. 420.

7. Jackson, A., *A Place Called Home, A History of Low-cost Housing in Manhattan* (Cambridge, Mass.: M.I.T., 1976), pp. 40, 45-55, 59-60.

8. Minutes of the Trustees of Columbia University, vol. 7, p. 418.

9. Ibid., p. 425.

10. Schermerhorn, F.A., *A Proposal to Establish a Course in Architecture in the School of Mines* (Board of Trustees of Columbia College, New York, 1879), p. 1, Columbiana Collection, Columbia University.

11. Schermerhorn to Nicholas Murray Butler, 3 June 1902, Central Files, Columbia University (hereafter Central Files).

Sanitary Engineering...This was my principle reason for wishing to establish the course for I felt at that time owing to the great spread of illness in our city...as I was sensible that the architect's profession was mainly deficient in this particular branch as well as in Engineering knowledge. I dwelt on it every occasion as one of the principle reasons for establishment of the course in order that hereafter architects should be Sanitary Engineers, as they should be, and [I] spoke of it in my very first report.

In the report, Schermerhorn noted that,

drainage and piping are left to the uneducated discretion of a common Irish plumber so that as was shown by the reports of the president of the Board of Health of this city scarcely one in one hundred of even our better class of residence is either fit or safe to dwell in.

He continued, stating, "instruction could be given on the principles of Sanitary Engineering works of Sewerage and Hydraulic Engineering." He also spoke repeatedly of the "great facilities we had for this purpose in already having one of our professors the President of the Board of Health. It [Sanitary Engineering] was one of the main subjects in which I wished to make the education given to our graduates superior to that of other graduates."[12]

Obviously, Schermerhorn's primary goal was to improve the profession's technical expertise to the benefit of the general public. He reinforced this emphasis in his *Proposal*, saying, "with the resources that we have we can supply such instruction that a graduate shall glean enough from the present course in civil engineering to solve all the technical problems."[13] Thus his proposed course was instituted primarily to give the young architect the knowledge to build, at the very least, safe and clean structures.

That expense was a major consideration in the founding of the course becomes clear in later correspondence between President Butler and Schermerhorn:

The finances of the College did not admit of our starting a full-fledged department of Architecture, and were barely sufficient to support the one 'chair' in the School even without assistants or assistance.[14]

Schermerhorn anticipated that the facilities of the School of Mines could readily be pressed into service. As he wrote in his *Proposal:*

To establish a sufficient and even an excellent course in architecture we have now in our hands in the School of Mines facilities that it seems a pity to neglect. With but slight addition we might establish such a school that would become a credit to many young men needing occupation; and to do this will entail upon us not only comparatively, but an actually small expenditure of the funds of the College.[15]

Schermerhorn proposed adding one lecture hall to the Mines building, and from that point it was a foregone conclusion that the course in architecture would begin in the School of Mines.[16]

Using the growth and constant change of New York City as an example, Schermerhorn argued that many more architects would be needed to meet the demands for both new buildings and alterations of existing buildings in the suddenly burgeoning urban areas

12. Schermerhorn to Agnew, 3 April 1883, C.R. Agnew Collection, Rare Books and Manuscripts Library, Columbia University.

13. Schermerhorn, *A Proposal*, p. 3.

14. Schermerhorn to Butler, 3 June 1902, Central Files.

15. See notes 5 and 6. Schermerhorn also served as treasurer and director of the New York Trade School.

16. Schermerhorn, *A Proposal*, p. 4.

of America.[17] To meet this projected need there were only four architecture courses offered in the United States, "and consequently there [were] but few skilled and completely educated architects."[18] In 1880, there were 3,375 architects in the United States, of whom only a very small number had university educations.[19] Three of the university programs were "remote from the great centres of architectural interest" and "were quite unable to supply the growing demand for trained architects and draftsmen."[20] Schermerhorn noted, "new edifices and alterations of old ones are of greater frequency here perhaps, than in any other city of this or other country."[21] In New York there did not exist an institution or course to prepare young professionals to meet the need.

Schermerhorn also forecast a decline in the need for civil engineers because "most of the principal roads and most railway bridges, etc., are already being constructed. Thus, the field of labor for civil engineers, once a great one in this country has now diminished." Schermerhorn saw architecture as the field which would offer the most promise of future employment for those who would otherwise follow the course in Civil Engineering in the School of Mines as well as provide an alternative profession for civil engineers. America's cities, with their seemingly unabated growth would provide jobs for legions of architects.[22]

There is a further influence of Auchmuty on Schermerhorn. In 1880, Auchmuty founded a school to instruct young men in trades that were being taken over by skilled immigrants.[23] Correspondingly, American schools were too few to provide the requisite numbers of architects and European-born or trained architects were rapidly filling the ranks of the profession. In Schermerhorn's founding of a school of architecture there is a parallel to Auchmuty's founding of a trade school. In his *Proposal*, Schermerhorn, while lamenting the general lack of educated architects, refers briefly to "the some few [who] may have been educated abroad in some foreign universities, but even of these few a still smaller number may have taken any but special or partial courses."[24]

Thus, having been convinced of the eminent wisdom of Schermerhorn's argument, on February 7, 1881, the Trustees authorized the offering of a course in "Architecture and Sanitary Engineering"[25] for the coming academic year — 1881–1882. Even before the Trustees agreed to the foundation of the course, they began their search for someone to teach it. It was originally proposed that some recent graduate of the Ecole des Beaux-Arts be hired, but by November 1880, that idea gave way to asking Richard Morris Hunt, the dean of the American architectural profession, to head the course.[26] Hunt, who lived in New York, was a natural choice; he was the first American to have attended the Ecole and since 1857 had been conducting an *atelier* in architecture at his offices.

Of the students of that *atelier*, Charles D. Gambrill, Frank Furness, Henry Van Brunt, George B. Post, Louis Sullivan and William Robert Ware all became influential and successful architects in the United States. In 1876 at the AIA convention, Hunt had been referred to as "the Father of High and Successful architectural

17. Ibid., p. 2. Schermerhorn continued to maintain his home in an area of the city that by 1881 had become a commercial center, and he drew on his personal experiences in writing of the change in American cities.

18. Ibid., p. 1.

19. Noffsinger, J.P., "The Influence of the Ecole des Beaux-Arts on the Architects of the United States," (Ph.d. Diss., Catholic University, 1955), p. 29. Information taken from the U.S. Bureau of the Census Data for 1880.

20. Hamlin, A.D.F., "The School of Architecture," *A History of Columbia University, 1754–1904* (New York: Columbia University, 1904), p. 381.

21. Schermerhorn, *A Proposal*, p. 2.

22. Ibid., p. 3.

23. See note 6.

24. Schermerhorn, *A Proposal*, p. 1.

25. Minutes of the Trustees of Columbia University, vol. 8, p. 45.

26. Hunt, C.C.H., edited by Alan Burnham, *Richard Morris Hunt Papers*, p. 161 (property of the American Architectural Archive). I am grateful to Mr. Paul Baker for this reference.

education in this country."[27] In view of his outstanding qualifications, the Columbia Trustees were anxious to engage Hunt and, as his biographer, Catherine Clinton Howland Hunt, noted, "strenuously urged his acceptance."[28] However, Hunt rejected the offer because he felt it would leave him too little time for private practice. In his stead, Hunt recommended his former pupil, Ware, "who would bring with him experience and scholastic ability."[29] The Trustees took this advice to heart and began their pursuit of Ware.

Schermerhorn had been in touch with Ware since early 1879 and had discussed with him the M.I.T. program and its costs. Schermerhorn believed M.I.T. to be the "one [architectural school] in the United States...in working order." In fact, he believed "the Architectural department [was] taking the lead of the other courses, [due] no doubt, to the excellence of the professor [Ware] and his assistant [Eugene L'Etang]." In light of such high praise, the Trustees began to court Ware aggressively.[30]

Ware did not immediately accept the position, for he visited Hunt on at least one occasion to discuss the terms offered by Columbia.[31] He did, however, finally accept. His decision was perhaps facilitated by the Trustees' offer of an annual salary of five thousand dollars, approximately twice his salary at M.I.T.[32] Despite the generous salary, Ware agreed to join the Columbia faculty only after the Trustees acceded to his demand that he be given complete control of the management of the school in its early years.[33] On April 4, 1881, Ware was elected "Professor of Architecture and Sanitary Engineering, to begin work on October 1, 1881. He to hold office for three years [sic] or at the pleasure of this board."[34]

Following Ware's appointment, the Trustees authorized the expenditure of three hundred dollars to advertise the new program in newspapers throughout the United States.[35] Despite this "media blitz," only two students enrolled in the course in its first year [36] The small enrollment did not perturb Ware, for during the fall of 1881 he wrote to his mentor Hunt:

As to Columbia work, I have very good courage about it. They are in no hurry about organizing the work and I shall begin with one class only, and that for only a few hours a week.

This will give time during the coming winter to prepare for the serious work of the year following, a little time for reading and study... a thing I haven't done since I was with you in Tenth Street. [37]

Ware's debt to Hunt and belief in Hunt's method of education cannot be underestimated. While teaching at Columbia, Ware wrote to his friend Frank Furness that the School of Architecture was "a direct outcome of the 10th Street studio of thirty-nine years ago." As Paul Baker, Hunt's most recent biographer, has noted, "Through Ware the Beaux-Arts tradition which he encountered at second hand in Hunt's *atelier* became an essential component of collegiate architectural education in America."[38]

Once Ware was hired, a curriculum was developed based on his own ideas as well as those of Schermerhorn, who had outlined a

27. Baker, Paul, *Richard Morris Hunt* (Cambridge, Mass.: M.I.T., 1980), p. 102.

28. *Hunt Papers,* p. 161.

29. Ibid.

30. Schermerhorn, *A Proposal,* p. 1, 5.

31. *Hunt Papers,* p. 162.

32. Minutes of the Trustees of Columbia University, vol. 8, p. 45.

33. Ibid., p. 64.

34. Ibid., p. 80.

35. "The New Course in Architecture," *Columbia Spectator,* 2 (1882–1883), p. 64.

36. *Hunt Papers,* p. 162.

37. Ibid., p. 57.

38. Baker, *Hunt,* p. 105.

curriculum in his 1879 *Proposal*. Schermerhorn began his proposed curriculum by describing the way in which he expected the course at Columbia to differ from that at the Ecole des Beaux-Arts:

The full course in Paris is much what is proposed to establish here but... [the course at the Ecole] consists also, perhaps too largely, in a series of projects of different kinds and extent which are given out throughout the course — and as it would seem is usually the case in the French institutions of learning, the students are not brought frequently and constantly in contact with the professors and instructors, but are dependent on each other for assistance or are obliged to employ private tutors. Still, the School of Paris, it is believed, is considered the best in existence.[39]

Following that preamble, Schermerhorn outlined a proposed course of study which drew heavily on the existing course in civil engineering at the School of Mines.[40]

Schermerhorn intended that the new Professor of Architecture teach only those courses directly related to the "artistic" side of architecture, while the technical courses were to be taught by faculty members of the School of Mines.[41] He was also sensitive to the problem of providing the students with practical experience, always considered a necessary component of an architect's training, judiciously leaving "open the question of a student supplementing his education through work in an architect's office."[42]

For his own part, Ware submitted a vague "Memorandum as to the Proposed Course in the School of Mines." In it he noted the general unsuitability of European methods of teaching, saying that "they all...fail to furnish the model we wish to follow. The problem before us in this country is to devise a course of study so carefully adjusted that the practical, scientific and artistic studies may receive equal consideration."[43]

Ware then proposed courses consisting of scientific and technical studies not so rigorous as those normally followed by a civil engineering student. He suggested a course in "artistic and historical studies," to be vaguely modeled on the Ecole program, and a strong emphasis on the study of practical matters (plumbing, painting, masonry). Students would not be required to be expert workmen in each trade, but good judges of the work performed by a skilled tradesman.[44]

Ware resigned himself to the fact that the course would be in an engineering school, but continued to express the sentiment that the course must be separate from the rest of the school just as architecture was a profession distinct from engineering. He wrote:

The question is sometimes raised whether, architecture being counted among the fine arts, it does not belong in a school of science. But if a thorough and comprehensive course of study is to be established, a school of science seems the most convenient place for it. Two out of its three branches are certainly more germane to scientific pursuits than to painting and sculpture, and it is easier and cheaper to add the apparatus needed for the study of elementary design to a school of science than to bring the work-rooms and laboratories of a school of science into a school of art. Still, it needs to be distinctly recognized that the atmosphere of exact science is unfavorable to the growth of the artistic sentiment; and that in temper and

39. Schermerhorn, *A Proposal,* pp. 5-6.

40. Ibid., pp. 6-8 are presented in condensed form below.
First year: Civil Engineering course in School of Mines with substitution of History for German, Botany, Physics of Magnetism and Electricity; a summer drawing course.
Second year: Civil Engineering course except for blowpipe analysis, Zoology and German, with lectures on five orders and detailing.
Third year: Civil Engineering course with testing building materials, Architectural History and Theory, Carving and Modelling in place of Quantitative Analysis.
Fourth year: Architectural History and Theory, Drawing Plans in Carpentry and Masonry; Specifications; Building Laws, Contracts, Quantity Surveys; Sanitary Engineering; Sewerage; Hydraulic Engineering; plus a *"Projet."*

41. Ibid., pp. 5-6.

42. Ibid., p. 6.

43. Ware, W.R., "Memorandum as to the Proposed Course of Architecture in the School of Mines," *School of Mines Quarterly,* 3 (November, 1881), p. 1. See also: Ware, W.R., "Architecture at Columbia College," *American Architect and Building News,* 10 (August 6, 1881), pp. 61-62

44. Ware, "Memorandum," p. 4.

methods a school of architecture must always be, so far as relates to design, at least, not quite at one with the purely practical schools with which it is associated. It must accordingly require special pains to create for it an atmosphere of its own, favorable to the harmonious development of its own students.[45]

Ware's private opposition to the course constituting a component of the School of Mines was even more direct, for Schermerhorn said, "Ware was always in doubt, if not adverse to such a system."[46] Clearly the concept of an architecture course as a subcategory of civil engineering demeaned the profession, relegating it to the position of a specialization within engineering rather than recognizing it as a distinct and separate profession.

When the course opened in October, 1881, the planned curricula of Ware and Schermerhorn had been altered by Ware and Professor Charles P. Trowbridge of the School of Mines. The final curriculum omitted any mention of Sanitary Engineering. Ware "in one of his letters expressed a diffidence in assuming control of a course embracing these studies as he was not versed in them."[47] Schermerhorn, upon reviewing the proposed course which lacked Sanitary Engineering, "feared that the course would be one with little *hard* work in it and that consequently [the course of Architecture] would be burdened with all the dull minds and lazy students." He suggested that "for the present we should add to it certain other studies taught in the School but not particularly appertaining to architecture, to make it a course of equal weight with the other departments."[48] This suggestion was followed as shown in the first public course description, which appeared in the *The Columbia Spectator* in December, 1882.[49] It made clear Schermerhorn's concept that the technical matters of architecture were of paramount importance in the first years of the course, virtually erasing any possibility that architecture could be perceived as a distinct entity from civil engineering. The first official curriculum, leading to the degree of Bachelor of Philosophy, was described in the 1883 *Information Handbook*,[50] and it reflected the same bias toward the technical aspects of architecture that Schermerhorn had stressed in his original proposal.

In 1881, the campus of Columbia College was located on the block bounded by 49th Street, 50th Street, Madison Avenue, and Fourth (Park) Avenue. Initially, the course in architecture was housed in a Greek Revival building which formed part of the campus, and which had once been an asylum for the deaf and dumb. In 1883, partly through a gift from Schermerhorn, a new building was completed at 50th Street and Fourth Avenue to house the School of Mines.[51] The course in architecture occupied the fourth floor, its quarters consisting of a drafting room, lecture hall, and library. The location was not auspicious: the drafting room overlooked the Lion Brewery and the Women's Hospital, across the two narrow roadways which flanked the depressed, open tracks of the New York Central Railroad. The coal-fired, steam-driven engines on those tracks belched smoke into the atmosphere. As a result, the building housing the course in architecture

45. Ibid., p. 4.

46. Schermerhorn to Butler, 2 June 1902, Central Files.

47. Schermerhorn to Agnew, 3 April 1883, C.R. Agnew Collection, Rare Books and Manuscripts Library, Columbia University.

48. Ibid.

49. "The New Course in Architecture," *Columbia Spectator*, 2 (1882–1883), p. 64. The full course is excerpted here: *During the first year the studies are the same as in all the other courses in the School of Mines. In the second year Greek and Roman architectural history, and the elements of Greek and Roman Architecture, take the place of Botany, Zoology, and all of the chemistry of the other courses, except Dr. Chandler's lectures upon the metals. Mechanics, Engineering, Geology and Architectural History, Ornament, Practice, and Design fill the third year. The fourth year is devoted to Civil Engineering, Economic Geology and again to the all embracing subject of Architecture. The professional work is naturally the main feature of the course, and occupies sometimes four hours of the day. It is illustrated by models, photographs and engravings, a valuable collection of which are already on hand. This collection, which is being steadily added to, is the gift of Mr. Schermerhorn.*

50. *Columbia College, Handbook of Information*, 1883, p.113ff. The course listed in the handbook is excerpted here: *First year* (Common to all courses in the School of Mines): Algebra, Geometry, Trigonometry, Physics, Chemistry, French, German and Drawing. *Second year:* Analytical geometry, Descriptive geometry, Calculus, Chemistry, Elements of Architecture, History of Architecture, French, Shades and Shadows, Perspective, Stereotomy, French, German and Drawing. *Third year:* Mechanics and Strength of Materials, Applied Chemistry, Geology, History of Architecture, History of Ornament, Decorative Arts, Specifications and Working Drawings, Architectural Design, Modeling and Drawing. *Fourth year:* Sanitary Engineering, Sewerage, Geology of Materials, Graphics Statics, Bookkeeping, Business Relations, Estimating, History of Architecture, History of Painting and Sculpture, Theory of Architecture, Literature (themes, reports, etc.), Architectural Design.

51. Hamlin, A.D.F., "The School of Architecture," *A History of Columbia University, 1754–1904* (New York: Columbia University, 1904), p. 381.

was known, not so affectionately, as the *Maison de Punk*.[52]

Despite the small enrollment, in 1882 Ware was able to hire an assistant, Alfred Dwight Foster Hamlin, who had been his student at M.I.T. Hamlin's scholarship in the history of ornament complimented Ware's more specifically professional experience, and together the two men set the direction for the School. Because of the College's limited funds, Schermerhorn underwrote the salaries of new faculty members for a period of years, and also supported the School's library.[53]

Thus, the School, although modest in scope and scale, began to evolve a particular character. While the School has subsequently grown in its first century into an independent entity within the University, five themes which have helped to shape the School's later history were present at its inception: the School recognized the unique characteristics of its location in New York City, then, as now, the pre-eminent American city; it defined its obligation to the professional community as a training ground for individuals intending to take up a place in the practice of architecture; it had a sense of its mission to the public, seeking to improve at once the aesthetic, the constructional, and the social aspects of buildings with a degree of responsibility that merited the word professional; it subscribed to the view that architecture is a synthesis of a search for order and responsiveness to pragmatic experience; and it acknowledged that all studies in architecture come together in "design," that simple word that defines the combination of retrospection, analysis, craft, and composition.

In this century, these themes have formed the basis for debate about the essential nature, structure, and content of architectural education as well as that of the profession, a debate which continues. Should the School teach students to be generalists or specialists, to be equipped with broad knowledge or with particular skills, to understand the art and the craft of architecture or the cultural context of which architecture is a part? Although Schermerhorn thought the answer was a balance of these contrasting objectives that leaned toward the technical, the curriculum he proposed underwent changes almost immediately, suggesting that no single approach to architectural education remains valid indefinitely, particularly when a profession is attempting to define its mission in society.

52. In the nineteenth century, the word *punk* referred to a very slow-burning and smoky type of match. The smoke from locomotives moving in and out of Grand Central Terminal blew into the architecture building, creating an atmosphere similar to that of an enclosed space in which a *punk* had been lit. See, "Departmental News," *School of Mines Quarterly*, 11 (1889–1890), p. 94.

53. See note 48. Additionally there is considerable correspondence on this subject in the files on Schermerhorn in Columbia Central Files.

William R. Ware and the Pursuit of Suitability: 1881–1903

David G. De Long

When the program in architecture was organized at Columbia in 1881, various currents of change had begun to reshape American architecture.[1] Henry Hobson Richardson (1838–86) had developed a distinctive mode, as shown by such influential works as his Crane Library, Quincy, Massachusetts, 1880–82.[2] Major examples of "Shingle Style" houses had appeared along the Eastern seaboard by 1881, including the C.J. Morrill house, Mount Desert, Maine, 1879, by William Ralph Emerson (1883–1918).[3] Some of the world's first skyscrapers were standing by 1881; these included the Tribune Building, New York, 1873–75, by Richard Morris Hunt (1827–95); and the first Leiter Building, Chicago, 1879, by William LeBaron Jenney (1832–1907).[4] The poetic expression of this new building type was to be the achievement of Adler and Sullivan, the Chicago firm formally established in 1881. Their Rothschild Store, Chicago, 1880–81, begun before Sullivan was made a full partner, gave early evidence of their later maturity.[5]

Each of these three currents of change has been linked to the eventual development of modernism. Yet it was not these that were initially to affect Columbia's program in architecture, but rather a fourth that had hardly begun by 1881: what Henry-Russell Hitchcock has termed the Academic Reaction. The architects widely regarded as the leaders of the Academic Reaction — Charles Follen McKim (1847–1909), William Rutherford Mead (1846–1928), and Stanford White (1853–1906) — had established their New York firm in 1879, and in April, 1882, work began on the building that largely initiated the movement: the Villard Houses, New York City.[6] This current, too, has been linked with the rise of modernism,[7] and has, in addition, received renewed attention as the major component of what some historians and architects call the American Renaissance.[8]

During the first twenty years of the school's history, the ideals that supported the Academic Reaction came to dominate educational policy. Influential architects considered Richardsonian and Shingled modes as outdated and judged contemporary Midwestern attempts at new expressions of commercial and domestic architecture to be provincial curiosities. It was a period of growing confidence that excluded much good with the bad, and yet still achieved significant results.

The currents of change discernible in 1881 were partly a reaction against the aggressively eclectic work of the immediate post-Civil War years. The dominant modes of that earlier period were Second Empire and High Victorian Gothic, both inspired by examples in France and England, and both characterized by complicated massing, exaggerated silhouettes, and by original combinations of various classically- and medievally-derived details.[9] With a bold inventiveness that typifies American practice, architects soon combined aspects of one or both modes with other sources of inspiration so that conventional stylistic terminology is of limited use in describing their work. The Carson house, Eureka, California, 1885–86, by Samuel Newsom (1853–1903) and his brother, Joseph Cather Newsom (1858–1930), illustrates at a somewhat later date the powerful originality of such work.[10] Like other

1. For background information on the history of Columbia's School of Architecture, I am grateful to Janet Parks, the Avery Archivist; to her assistant, Mary Privo; and to students in my Fall, 1980, colloquium who catalogued collections in the Avery archive and discovered much interesting information. These students were Diane Boas, Gwen Burgee, Gordon Fulton, Robert Guter, Donna Harris, Susan Harris, Steven Hirschberg, Mimi Lines, Diane Lutters, Karen Rosenberg, Faith Schmidt, Henry Taves, Jeanne Teutonico, and Judy Oberlander, who continued to assist me with issues related to the Centennial. I am also grateful for the welcome help of my student assistant, Diane Neff, and to Sarah Bradford Landau, Robert A.M. Stern, and Richard Oliver for their valued suggestions.

2. For information on Richardson, Henry-Russell Hitchcock, *The Architecture of H.H. Richardson and His Times* (New York: 1936, reissued with revisions: 1961).

3. For the evolution of the "Shingle Style," Vincent J. Scully, Jr., *The Shingle Style* (New Haven: 1955; reissued, together with *The Stick Style,* New Haven: 1971).

4. For a discussion of skyscraper history, Carl W. Condit, *The Chicago School of Architecture* (Chicago: 1964), and Winton Weisman, "A New View of Skyscraper History," Edgar Kaufmann, jr., editor, *The Rise of an American Architecture* (New York: 1970), pp. 115-160.

5. Sullivan's work is effectively summarized in Hugh Morrison, *Louis Sullivan; Prophet of Modern Architecture* (New York: 1935; reissued: 1962).

6. The term Academic Reaction is defined in Henry-Russell Hitchcock, *Architecture, Nineteenth and Twentieth Centuries,* 4th edition (Baltimore: 1977), especially Chapter 13. For the work of McKim, Mead and White, Leland M. Roth, *The Architecture of McKim, Mead and White; A Building List* (New York: 1978). For a detailed account of the Villard Houses, Mosette Glaser Broderick and William C. Shopsin, *The Villard Houses; Life Story of a Landmark* (New York: 1980).

7. For instance, Vincent Scully, *American Architecture and Urbanism* (New York: 1969), especially pp. 135-138; and Reyner Banham, *Theory and Design in the First Machine Age,* 2nd edition (New York: 1967), especially Section 1, Chapters 1 and 3.

8. For example, the catalog for the exhibition, *The American Renaissance, 1876–1917* (New York: The Brooklyn Museum, 1979), especially Richard Guy Wilson, Part 1, Chapters 1 through 5, and Part II, Chapter 6. Also, in this volume, Robert A.M. Stern.

9. These modes are defined in Hitchcock, *Architecture,* especially Chapters 8, 9, 10, and 11.

10. For an account of the Newsom brothers, David Gebhard, introduction to Samuel and Joseph C. Newsom, *Picturesque California Homes* (1884; reissued, with the new introduction by Gebhard, Los Angeles, 1978).

buildings that preceded it, it also reflects a personal attitude toward design that, to some in the 1880's, seemed to demand control. One means to such control was a formal system of education. A.D.F. Hamlin (1855–1926), who in 1882 had been the second person to join the faculty of Columbia's school of architecture and who in 1903 became the acting head of the school, alluded to this situation in a 1908 article:

During the Civil War, and the ten years each preceding and following it, our architecture was floundering in the lowest depths of tastelessness and artistic poverty. There were few educated architects; the popular standards were almost grotesquely inartistic, and really fine architecture was nearly as impossible to execute as unlikely to be appreciated. [11]

There were other reasons why American schools of architecture came to be established in the post-Civil War period. These related to the rapid expansion of the country and to the accompanying need for large numbers of new buildings. Significant advances in material fabrication, as well as in structural and mechanical systems, complicated the art of building and provided further impetus for professional training. But underlying these needs — at least in the founding of the school of architecture at Columbia — was a desire for the appropriate artistic expression of certain sorts of buildings. [12] There was a growing sense of nationalism and civic pride in America at this time, and increasing private wealth. Nationalism and civic pride found expression in such events as the Philadelphia Centennial Exhibition of 1876, and in the establishment of such public institutions as the Metropolitan Museum of Art in New York. [13] The architectural character of the structures that contained these various events and institutions was rightly considered as an important means of expression in itself, and the holders of private wealth who often made such structures possible sought a conservative image for these and related private buildings, an image that would reinforce cultural values as they were understood to emanate from European sources. The Ecole des Beaux-Arts in Paris was coming to be viewed by many as the world's most effective school of architecture, and its academic product offered a clearly identifiable model for civic architecture that was highly regarded in Europe and that seemed appropriate for application in America. Dependence upon such authoritatively-generated precedents as those endorsed by the Ecole guaranteed a level of success that a less disciplined sort of innovation did not.

In establishing a program in architecture, Columbia's Trustees understandably sought advice from the person in New York most closely associated with the Ecole des Beaux-Arts: Richard Morris Hunt. He had been the first American to graduate from the Ecole, the first to open an *atelier* in America based on those of the Ecole, and was also one of the nation's most distinguished practitioners. [14] Hunt was evidently offered the opportunity of organizing the school at Columbia, but declined, recommending instead one of his students, William R. Ware (1832–1915). [15]

William Robert Ware.
Photo: Columbiana Collection.

11. A.D.F Hamlin, "The influence of the École des Beaux-Arts on our Architectural Education," *Architectural Record,* 23 (April 1908), pp. 241-247, p. 241. Hamlin, who had studied under W.R. Ware at M.I.T., was originally hired as Ware's assistant at Columbia, as recounted in Theodor K. Rohdenburg, *A History of the School of Architecture, Columbia University* (New York: 1954), p. 10.

12. As expressed in two articles by W.R. Ware: "The Instruction in Architecture at the School of Mines," *School of Mines Quarterly,* 10 (November 1888), pp. 28-43, especially pp. 28-29; and in an earlier article relating to his establishment of a school of architecture at M.I.T.: "On the Condition of Architecture and of Architectural Education in the United States," *Journal of the Royal Institute of British Architects* (January 28, 1867), pp. 81-90. More thorough documentation of the need for architectural schools in America is offered in other essays in this volume.

13. The establishment of several such institutions is discussed in Albert Fein, "The American City: The Ideal and the Real," *The Rise of an American Architecture;* pp. 51-112. Also in Robert A.M. Stern's essay in this volume.

14. For a biography of Hunt, Paul R. Baker, *Richard Morris Hunt* (Cambridge, Mass.: 1980).

15. Baker, p. 105.

Ware, who accepted the offer, was known as both an educator and an architect. He had entered Hunt's New York *atelier* early in 1859 after graduating from Harvard, and left later that same year to open his own office in Boston, where he was joined in 1863 by Henry Van Brunt (1832–1903), a fellow student in Hunt's *atelier*.

Frank Furness (1839–1912) had also been a student in Hunt's *atelier* in 1859, and remained in touch with Ware at least until 1898.[16] As Furness's extraordinarily personal work suggests, Hunt's students were not bound to recognizably academic modes. In the best tradition of the Ecole, Hunt instructed his students in a manner that encouraged an orderly approach to design, yet without strict dependence on French precedents.[17] Hunt's own work reflects the stylistic variety that such an approach allowed. To a certain degree so does the work of Ware and Van Brunt. It is largely in a High Victorian Gothic mode, and tied more to English than French practice, as their First Unitarian Church, Boston, 1865–67; Memorial Hall, Harvard, 1870–78 (but on which designs began in the mid-1860s); and the Boston and Albany Railway Station, Worcester, Massachusetts, 1875–77, all illustrate.[18]

Van Brunt's writings, which include praise for Ruskin and Viollet-le-Duc, reinforce the firm's general preference for medieval architecture. One statement reveals an attitude toward medieval as opposed to classical modes that is of interest in light of Ware's later efforts to maintain a balanced point of view at Columbia:

If Mediaeval architecture was a system based upon the free development of structural forms, that of the Renaissance was based upon authority and discipline.[19]

Such attitudes, and more particularly such work as the firm produced, elicited later apologies, as in Ware's obituary by A.D.F. Hamlin:

Most of Professor Ware's work as a designer, in partnership with the late Henry Van Brunt, was done between 1865 and 1880, before the modern movement in American architecture was fully under way.[20]

In 1864, before their work was so judged and while High Victorian Gothic and related modes were still in fashion, Ware and Van Brunt had opened an *atelier* of their own in Boston. It was successful, and in 1866 officials from the Massachusetts Institute of Technology asked Ware to organize what was to be the country's first real school of architecture.[21] Before students were accepted in September, 1868, Ware traveled to Europe to study methods of architectural education, concentrating particularly on the Ecole des Beaux-Arts, and it was on the Ecole model that Ware's program at M.I.T. was largely based. Among Ware's students at M.I.T. was Louis Henry Sullivan (1856–1924), who attended classes during the 1872–73 academic year. Sullivan later said of Ware:

. . . he was worthy of personal respect and affection. His attainments were moderate in scope and soundly cultural as of the day; his judgments were clear and just. The words amiability and quiet common sense sum up his personality; he was not imaginative enough to be ardent.[22]

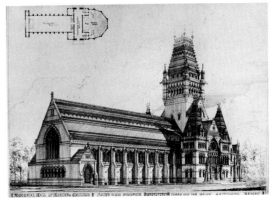

Memorial Hall, Cambridge, Massachusetts 1870–78, Ware and Van Brunt.

16. For an account of Hunt's atelier, Baker, especially pp. 100-107. For Frank Furness, James F. O'Gorman, *The Architecture of Frank Furness* (Philadelphia: 1973); for his connections with Ware, p. 24.

17. Baker, p. 102; O'Gorman, p. 26. For methods of teaching at the Ecole, Richard Chafee, "The Teaching of Architecture at the Ecole des Beaux-Arts," Arthur Drexler, editor, *The Architecture of the Ecole des Beaux-Arts* (New York: 1977), pp. 61-109.

18. For a brief account of the firm's work, Hitchcock, *Architecture*, pp. 192-194.

19. Henry Van Brunt, "The Personal Equation in Renaissance Architecture" (1885), William A. Coles, editor, *Architecture and Society; Essays of Henry Van Brunt* (Cambridge, Mass.: 1969), p. 152.

20. A.D.F. Hamlin, "William Robert Ware, Organizer of First American School of Architecture," *Architect and Engineer*, 42 (July 1915), pp. 100-101. As major architects of the period, Hamlin names Hunt, Richardson, and McKim.

21. Baker, p. 105.

22. Louis H. Sullivan, *The Autobiography of an Idea* (1924; originally published in the *American Institute of Architects Journal*, 1922–23; reissued, New York: 1956), pp. 184-185. The dates are confirmed in Morrison, p. 31.

Ware had the chance to begin again at Columbia, and he revised his approach from what he had initiated at M.I.T., evidently in an effort to create a school of architecture more responsive to American needs. Essentially he modified the Ecole system he had instituted at M.I.T. by incorporating aspects of other European schools together with ideas of his own. As he wrote in 1881:

. . .a school cannot so narrow its range, and although, in fact, the French courses of study are mainly artistic, and the German scientific, and the English practical, they all, from this very fact, fail to furnish the model as we should wish to follow.

The problem before us in this country is to devise a course of study so carefully adjusted that the practical, scientific and artistic studies may receive equal consideration.[23]

Design at Columbia was not stressed to the same degree as it had been at M.I.T. There was less emphasis on the competitive judgment of studio work, and more on the individual development of each student. Discussing the teaching of design, and contrasting its place at Columbia with that at M.I.T., Ware said:

But, though design is the main thing, it is not the only thing, neither can it be taken up to advantage without adequate preparation. The young men we have here are mostly entirely new to the subject, and it is useless to set them to combining and arranging ideas they have never acquired.[24]

Although the tangible results of such attitudes are often difficult to document, an anonymous statement suggests that Ware's modifications had some effect. Identified only as a graduate of Ware's program, one former student recalled the more individualized judgment of design problems:

The most satisfactory thing about them was that we knew they weren't going to be judged. We felt perfectly free to do what we really thought was best, without having to consider what a jury would probably think.[25]

Departing from the precedent of his own work, Ware gave special prominence to classicizing vocabularies of architecture, though not to the exclusion of medievalizing ones.[26] In this he paralleled an approach followed at the Ecole, but with more emphasis on the medieval than his followers would encourage at Columbia. And reflecting a longstanding American trait, Ware expressed doubts about paying too much attention to the purely theoretical aspects of architecture:

. . .there are from week to week more formal discourses under the head of the theory of architecture, upon the received theories of beauty and proportion, in form and color, given, mainly, with a view to show how little value there is in speculations on these subjects. But it is worthwhile to spend a certain amount of time upon them, nevertheless, if only as a prophylactic, *as the doctors say, to prevent these young men from being run away with by such fancies at a later day.*[27]

The problems he dealt with in balancing technical courses with those related to design, and in incorporating liberal arts, remain familiar to those involved today in architectural education, and

23. W.R. Ware, "Architecture at Columbia University," *American Architect and Building News,* 10 (August 6, 1881), pp. 61-62. In 1888 he wrote:

architectural education in France and Germany, like university education in those countries, is so much under government influence, and architects, like the graduates of universities, are so largely dependent upon government patronage for success, that few practical lessons can be drawn by us from their schools. The conditions are too diverse. In England we might expect to find more congenial models, but for reasons easily understood the English architects are rather looking to us for example than we to them. We have, then, not only to run our factory, but to invent our machinery.

Ware, "Instruction in Architecture," p. 31. Ware's departure from strict adherence to the Ecole is noted in Arthur Clason Weatherhead, *The History of Collegiate Education in Architecture in the United States* (Los Angeles: 1941), p. 46; and Rohdenburg, p. 10.

24. Ware, "Instruction in Architecture," p. 38.

25. As quoted in Rohdenburg, p. 11.

26. Ware, "Instruction in Architecture," pp. 36-37, 39-40.

27. Ware, "Instruction in Architecture," p. 37. A similar attitude is expressed in "Architectural Education in the United States, IV: Columbia College, New York," *American Architect and Building News,* 24 (December 1, 1888), pp. 251-252.

show Ware's sensible understanding of major issues. He also realized that some things were better learned in an office, which is the way most schools operate today.[28] By 1891, to extend educational opportunities to those who might not otherwise have them, draftsmen, generally with no prior college education, were allowed to enroll as special students. Ware argued that their presence invigorated the design studios, as they kept the regular students more in touch with the realities of practice and demonstrated a high proficiency in drawing.[29]

The particular components of Ware's program, as discussed elsewhere in this volume, did not always achieve the ideal he sought. Moreover, with the vicissitudes of fashion and with his increasingly cantankerous nature, Ware's objectives were not always viewed sympathetically. Differences between Ware and his colleagues in the profession began to surface in the 1890's, as the Academic Reaction came into full prominence.

The visual impact of the World's Columbian Exposition, which opened in Chicago in 1893, did much to establish the Academic Reaction as the dominant current of America architecture, a position it retained until the First World War.[30] Led by McKim, New York architects largely controlled the design of the fair, and effectively widened their influence over much of the country. Axially-ordered buildings incorporated historic precedents with a degree of authority avoided by Ware in his teaching, and Ware's earlier buildings, loosely massed and with a vocabulary freely adapted from the past, could hardly have seemed more outdated.

The contrast between Ware's approach to design and that coming into prominence in the 1890s was put in sharper focus by the planning of Columbia's Morningside Heights campus. In April, 1892, the Trustees requested schematic designs from three architects: Hunt, McKim, and Charles C. Haight, the architect of the buildings on the former campus at 49th and Madison.[31] These architects submitted schemes in April, 1893, and Ware, together with Frederick Law Olmsted, was asked to combine them into a single scheme. Ware came into conflict with McKim, who criticized Ware's efforts at combining the plans and referred at one point to:

'Uncle William' Ware's block plan.... It seems to me a pudding — and a very indigestible one indeed![32]

McKim, of course, triumphed. He not only secured the Columbia commission for his own office, but also, immediately upon Ware's resignation in 1903, was put in charge of one of the school's newly formed *ateliers*. Officially Ware resigned partly for reasons of health, and partly over a dispute regarding the admission of special students.[33] It seems likely, however, that his reasons for resigning were more deeply rooted, and reflected a general loss of confidence that was partly symbolized by the sort of remarks McKim was making. For there was increasing criticism of Columbia during the last years of Ware's control, with claims that he put too little emphasis on design and had allowed the quality of student work to slip.[34]

28. Ware, "Instruction in Architecture," p. 42.

29. As summarized in Rohdenburg, p. 11.

30. The importance of the Columbian Exposition as a turning point in American architecture is noted in A.D.F. Hamlin, "The Influence of the Ecole," p. 244.

31. For an account of the planning of the Columbia campus, Francesco Passanti, "The Design of Columbia in the 1890s; McKim and His Client," *Journal of the Society of Architectural Historians*, 36 (May 1977), pp. 69-84.

32. As quoted in Charles Moore, *The Life and Times of Charles Follen McKim* (Boston: 1929), pp. 264-265. The founding of the Academy, the arguments between Ware and McKim, and McKim's dominant role is summarized in Baker, pp. 438-441. A few years later, in 1896, when Ware and McKim disagreed on the choice of a director for the newly established American Academy in Rome, McKim wrote that "Ware has tried to make me miserable..."; as quoted in Moore, p. 156.

33. As documented in this volume in *History II: 1881–1912*.

34. Weatherhead, pp. 47-49.

Ware's successors reorganized the school so that it emulated more closely the methods of the Ecole, though with some loss of the latter's flexibility toward architectural modes. Ware's school-run design studios were eliminated in favor of an *atelier* system based upon that in Paris. Design was given greater prominence in the curriculum, special attention was given to techniques of rendering, and problems were judged in a way that promoted competition between students.[35]

According to most contemporary accounts the results were beneficial; one staunch defender of the Ecole and of those schools that followed its example was Paul Cret (1876–1945), who said:

The comparison of architecture today in the United States with that of twenty years ago shows clearly to every fair-minded man the salutary results achieved by French training for American students. [36]

Many regarded the French model as above criticism. According to one writer describing its positive effects at Columbia, "the traditions of the Ecole des Beaux-Arts with its resulting supremacy can not be broken."[37] It was not long before defenders of Columbia regarded its school of architecture as equal to the Ecole.[38] Some even believed it to be superior, for it enforced a stricter attitude towards the past than did the contemporary Ecole, allowed less leeway in manipulating established vocabularies, and even demanded a higher standard of presentation. As A.D.F. Hamlin wrote in 1908:

...we believe that the Ecole draftsmanship is today less thorough, less careful and studied than it once was, and that the pursuit of the new has to some extent diverted the Ecole from the pursuit of the beautiful.... Certainly in all that relates to construction and practice, as well as to the history and theory of the art, the teaching in our leading schools is fully equal if not superior to that of the Ecole. [39]

There were views to the contrary that sometimes supported Ware's modifications of Ecole methods. Ralph Adams Cram (1863–1942), the famous Gothicist whom Ware had helped in 1881,[40] strongly criticized the Ecole in 1896, while Ware was still at Columbia. Cram believed that students coming from schools based too closely on the Paris model were taught how to produce beautiful renderings, but not how to design actual buildings; that they were not encouraged to think for themselves, but rather to accept without question those precedents that were offered; and that the design problems themselves — more often city halls or Italian villas than churches, schools, or houses — did little to prepare the student for actual practice. He felt Ecole-based training effectively limited tendencies towards "...fantastic originality, silly picturesqueness, crazy irregularity," but at too great expense:

If anything can curb the ardor of our untamed American spirit as it expresses itself in architecture, it is the influence of academic training. But just because it may do this, it does not follow that the system is impeccable. For my own part, I still think it is peccable, and I don't know why I shouldn't say so. If, instead of exalting the Ecole and all its works to the skies, its advocates would try to see whether or not the local and contem-

35. Initially three ateliers were established: one on the Columbia campus under W.A. Delano and F.A. Nelson, and the others off campus: one under Thomas Hastings and J.V. Van Pelt, and the other under C.F. McKim and H.W. Corbett. These and other aspects of the reorganization of the school are discussed in A.D.F. Hamlin, "The Atelier System in Architectural Teaching," *Columbia University Quarterly,* 2 (June 1909), pp. 318-325.

36. Paul Cret, "The École des Beaux-Arts: What Its Architectural Teaching Means," *Architectural Record,* 23 (May 1908), pp. 367-371, p. 369.

37. Edward R. Smith, "The Avery Library and Its Building," *Columbia Alumni News,* 4 (September 27, 1912), pp. 60-62, p. 61.

38. For instance, "Architectural Education," *Columbia University Quarterly,* 10 (June 1908), p. 347.

39. A.D.F. Hamlin, "The influence of the Ecole," p. 245. Scully discusses American modifications of Beaux-Arts principles in *American Architecture and Urbanism,* pp. 136-137.

porary conditions in America might not modify it to advantage, we might obtain a system which would be above criticism. [41]

Looking back several years after his retirement, Ware critized the Beaux-Arts approach that emphasized the drawing rather than the design:

The chief danger to which the architect or the student of architecture is exposed, when he employs this art as a help in designing and building, is obvious. He is likely to regard it not as a means, but as an end in itself, and in doing so he is likely to lose interest in the art of building, and in the structures which are to be the remote and intangible results of his pains, and to become fascinated and engrossed by the art which is present and is occupying his immediate interest and attention. [42]

For Ware, such drawings, however beautiful in themselves, failed to present a realistic image of a building. Of coincidental interest in light of Frank Lloyd Wright's early Japanese-influenced renderings, Ware suggested that simpler, less heavily rendered drawings that employed techniques utilized in Japanese drawings would yield better results.

A more critical issue was the type of problem given. Not unusual for the late nineteenth century, Columbia trained architects for a level of practice that reflected little concern for what we today regard as social issues. [43] Design problems tended to be of a rather grand and fanciful sort that dealt with an image of opulence. This fact was admitted, but it was not regarded as something that should be changed. [44] Also more critical was the charge that the Beaux-Arts system supressed individuality. This had been noted at a meeting of the Royal Institute of British Architects held in 1884 for the purpose of evaluating methods of architectural education. Criticizing the possible application of French methods in England, one member replied:

The whole feeling in this country is against centralization, and against depending too much upon authority. We are so anxious and desirous of fostering and giving scope to individual genius that we very much prefer that it should run into individual eccentricity rather than be 'licked into shape'. [45]

Ware had attempted to institute a program that allowed for more personal variation than was ordinarily accepted in a strict Beaux-Arts system, as suggested in an article summarizing his work at Columbia:

He has always endeavored to develop the student's individuality, to bring out his latent powers of original artistic expression in design... [46]

What the record does not show is any real acknowledgement at Columbia of what was going on in and around Chicago in these years. For between 1881 and 1903, roots of what later came to be defined as modernism began to take shape in that part of the world, as evidenced by the work of Louis Sullivan and Frank Lloyd Wright (1867–1959). Yet Ware's approach at Columbia was not totally at odds with that of Sullivan and Wright. Ware shared with those architects an appreciation of certain qualities of medieval

40. As recounted in Robert Muccigrosso, *American Gothic: The Mind and Art of Ralph Adams Cram* (Washington, D.C.: 1979), p. 13. Describing his meeting with Ware, Cram wrote: *that presiding genius of architectural education good old William R. Ware of sanctified memory, then the head of the architectural department of the Massachusetts Institute of Technology.... With that friendliness and sympathetic generosity that marked his whole character, he had listened to the case my father put before him, looked me over with that amused disfavour I am sure my appearance must have engendered in him, examined the quaint 'architectural' drawings I had produced in the attic of the old Hampton Falls house, and then volunteered to intercede for me with his two young friends Arthur Rotch and George Tilden...*
Ralph Adams Cram, *My Life in Architecture* (Boston: 1936; reissued, New York: 1969), pp. 40-41.

41. Ralph Adams Cram, "The Case Against the Ecole des Beaux-Arts," *American Architect and Building News*, 54 (December 26, 1898), pp. 107-109.

42. W.R. Ware, "Drawing, Designing, and Thinking," *Architectural Record*, 26 (September 1909), pp. 159-165, p. 159.

43. According to Baker, p. 107, this was typical of Beaux-Arts schools.

44. Writing in 1906, A.D.F. Hamlin said:
The charge has sometimes been made in the newspapers that the universities — including Columbia University and its school of architecture — are 'aristocratic' in their tendencies and indifferent to the interests of the 'man on the street'...
A.D.F. Hamlin, "The School of Architecture," *Columbia University Quarterly*, 8 (June 1906), pp. 211-222, p. 221. The general attitude of the times was also suggested in a statement by Ware:
When their schooling is over, the young men find a ready welcome, partly because they know something, and partly because the boys who go for two or three years to a professional school are apt to be a better lot, by birth and breeding, as well as in virtue of the schooling itself, than the ordinary run of draughtsmen.
W.R. Ware, "Architectural Education in the United States of America," *Papers of the Royal Institute of British Architects Conference on Education* (London: 1887), pp. 63-68, p. 67.

45. John Slater, remarks on R. Phené Spiers, "The French *Diplôme d'Architecture* and the German System of Architectural Education," *Royal Institute of British Architects Transactions, 1883–84* (London: 1884), pp. 121-132, p. 129.

46. "The Work of Prof. Ware," *Architectural Record*, 13 (January 1903), pp. 91-94, p. 93.

architecture as defined by Ruskin and Viollet-le-Duc. Sullivan regarded Ware as a sympathetic teacher and probably knew of his ties with Furness, for whom Sullivan maintained great respect.

Ware's flexible interpretation of Beaux-Arts principles also seems more sympathetic to Sullivan's and Wright's than does that of his Columbia successors'. Ware found in those principles a means to architectural order that was not tied to strictly applied historic modes. A similar attitude was expressed by Sullivan in acknowledging his debt to the Ecole, where he had studied briefly:

He familiarized himself thoroughly with the theory of the School, which, in his mind, settled down to a theory of plan, *yielding results of extraordinary brilliancy.... Intellectual and aesthetic, it beautifully set forth a sense of order, of function, of highly skilled manipulation.* [47]

Proceeding with tact as he explained his own architecture in the March, 1908, *Architectural Record,* Wright also admitted a tie to the Beaux-Arts:

In laying out the ground plans for even the more insignificant of these buildings a simple axial law and order and the ordered spacing upon a system of certain structural units definitely established for each structure in accord with its scheme of practical construction and aesthetic proportion, is practiced as an expedient to simplify the technical difficulties of execution, and although the symmetry may not be obvious always the balance is usually maintained. The plans are as a rule much more articulate than is the school product of the Beaux-Arts. The individuality of the various functions of the various features is more highly developed; all the forms are complete in themselves and frequently do duty at the same time from within and without as decorative attributes of the whole. [48]

A.D.F. Hamlin appears generally less flexible in his attitudes than Ware, and wrote at a time when mature examples by Sullivan and Wright should have made a greater impression. In the 1923 volume of his *History of Ornament,* Hamlin briefly mentioned Sullivan and Wright as "creating designs of a thoroughly personal and individual aspect" that had properly remained a minor current in American architecture because:

Established traditions were precisely what American art most needed as a foundation upon which to build any healthy progress.... The present dominance of neo-classic taste in public architecture, the revival of the long-forgotten 'Colonial' tradition, and at the same time the new vogue of the Gothic for ecclesiastical and educational buildings, are beginning to provide this foundation. [49]

Wright may not have noticed this, but he probably read what Hamlin had written in 1908:

It seems to me high time to break these leading-strings [of foreign influence], and to develop our architecture, as our engineers have developed their engineering, independently of any foreign practice or foreign fashions.

I believe if all our young graduates would follow such a program [of university study and foreign travel] our national architecture would rapidly develop a freshness, a freedom, a self-reliance and boldness of style

47. Sullivan, *Autobiography,* p. 240.

48. Frank Lloyd Wright, "In the Cause of Architecture," *Architectural Record,* 23 (March 1908), pp. 155-221, p. 160. Wright later saw merit in the 1893 Columbian Exposition: *At the Columbian Fair the provincials of the United States saw, for the first time, architecture as coordination on the grand scale.... There was much to be said for the eclecticism of 1893 as a picture, especially for the United States.* Frank Lloyd Wright, "The Chicago World's Fair," *Architect's Journal,* 78 (July 13, 1933), pp. 45-47. Parallels between Wright's work and that of the Ecole des Beaux-Arts are discussed in Henry-Russell Hitchcock, "Frank Lloyd Wright and the Academic Tradition of the Early Eighteen-Nineties," *The Journal of the Warburg and Courtauldt Institutes,* 7 (1944), pp. 46-63.

49. A.D.F. Hamlin, *A History of Ornament,* 2 vols. (New York: 1916, 1923), Vol. II, pp. 474, 485-486. In his *A Textbook of the History of Architecture* (New York: 1896), neither Ware, nor Sullivan, nor Wright are mentioned. They are still unmentioned in the Fifth Edition, 1904. In the Eighth Edition, 1911, Ware is praised as an educator, and Sullivan's work is mentioned as an example of a "personal style" developing in Chicago: *Certain Chicago architects have developed an original treatment of architectural forms by exaggerating some of the structural lines, by supressing the mouldings and more familiar historic forms, and by the free use of flat surface ornament* (pp. 409-410). Wright is mentioned in a concluding chapter by Talbot Faulkner Hamlin in the New Revised Edition, 1928: *In Tokio the great Imperial Hotel, by the American, Frank Lloyd Wright, is an excellent example of the romantic beauty attainable by purely modernist methods* (p. 455).

and expression which it now greatly lacks, and which dependence on Parisian models and training can never give it.[50]

This appeared in the April issue of the *Architectural Record,* one month after Wright's eloquent description of just such an achievement. When Ware wrote such statements in the 1880's, such work hardly existed. When A.D.F. Hamlin wrote them in the first decade of the twentieth century, he displayed the sort of academic blinders that Wright came to despise. In 1930, Wright referred to academically trained architects when he said:

Instead of being arbiters of principle as a blessed privilege, they became arbiters or victims of the taste that is usually a matter of ignorance. When leisure and money came these progenitors of yours became connoisseurs of the antique, patrons and peddlers of the imitation.

. . . you may be interested to know that the Beaux-Arts that made most of your American progenitors is itself confused, now likely to re-interpret its precepts, disown its previous progeny and disinherit its favorite sons or be itself dethroned. . . . Yes, it is becoming day by day more evident to the mind that is a mind how shamefully the product of this culture betrayed America.[51]

If Ware's successors had emulated his gentle authority, the whole tired, cliché-ridden argument over academic versus indigenous architecture in this country might have been far less pronounced, and Wright might even have softened his later indictments and been more supportive of what was, after all, a worthy approach to design. For in a very real way, as Wright himself intimated, the sense of order and civic responsibility encouraged by Ware and his successors contributed significantly to a cohesive urban environment, and Columbia graduates produced assured buildings that dignify American cities. Moreover, it seems unlikely that genuine creative talent can ever be destroyed by strict schooling, and that such schooling can provide an acceptable and urbanistically sensitive manner of expression for those designers who lack the imagination to develop their own.

Regardless of Ware's ultimate fate, he established a program that was a model of its kind and that had great influence throughout the country. Perhaps more poignantly, no subsequent program at Columbia has escaped comparison with Ware's, for each has been viewed in the light of his achievement and characterized partly by the degree to which it has supported or rejected his ideals.

50. A.D.F. Hamlin, "Influence of the Ecole," pp. 246-247.

51. Frank Lloyd Wright, "To the Young Man in Architecture," *Two Lectures on Architecture* (Chicago: 1931), pp. 33-63, p. 41-42. Wright also cautions, "beware of the architectural school except as the exponent of engineering," p. 61. These two lectures were originally given at the Art Institute, Chicago, on October 1 and 2, 1930; Robert L. Sweeney, *Frank Lloyd Wright; An Annotated Bibliography* (Los Angeles: 1978), p. 44.

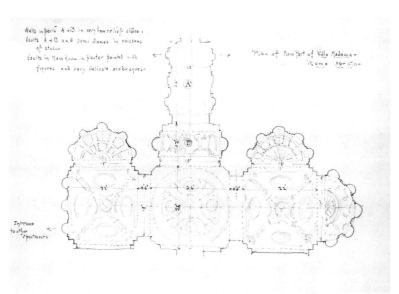

Top: Travel Sketch of Sard, 1883, A.D.F. Hamlin, Avery Archive.

Above: Travel Sketch of the Villa Madama, William F. Lamb *(1906)*, Avery Archive.

Right: Travel Sketch of Chateau Langeais, Ely Jacques Kahn *(1907)*, Avery Archive.

The faculty of the school, 1894. *Left to right:* Maximilian K. Kress, Charles P. Warren, Frank Dempster Sherman, William R. Ware, Grenville Temple Snelling, Alfred Dwight Foster Hamlin. Photo: GSAP Archives.

History II
1881–1912

Steven M. Bedford
and Susan M. Strauss

Although Ware had originally acquiesced to the course in architecture being a part of the School of Mines, he continued to hold the belief that architects should pursue a distinct course of study. It was not until the fall of 1888 that architecture students began to study drawing in their first year of the program, while actual instruction in architectural design in the first year began in 1891.[1] A.D.F. Hamlin observed triumphantly, "We got our hands on the young men from the first day of the first year."[2]

Replacing scientific courses with architectural ones continued in the upper years as well, so that "little by little the chemistry and physics, the botany and hygiene, the sanitary engineering and the economic geology...were crowded out or dropped,"[3] each replaced by courses in drawing, design, specifications, and building materials. This effort to remove irrelevant courses from the upper years continued until 1893 when the Handbook of Information noted that "in the third and fourth years most of the time [was] given over to strictly professional work."[4] As this trend continued, the requirements for entry also changed, so that by 1897 the equivalent of two years of undergraduate education were recommended for entry into the first year of the architecture program.[5]

As Ware gradually freed his curriculum from that of the School of Mines, additional staff were hired. In 1887, Frank Dempster Sherman *(Columbia, 1884)* was appointed to teach "analytics, calculus, analytical mechanics, descriptive geometry, and shades and shadows as well as the more practical courses of stereotomy,"[6] and in 1889, Grenville Snelling began a course in graphic statics.[7] These courses were eventually woven into a single group of courses entitled Architectural Engineering, in which the theoretical discussion of the subject was reduced to a minimum and the application of the

1. *Columbia College Handbook of Information, 1888–1889,* p. 109; *1891–1892,* p. 31.

2. Hamlin, A.D.F., "The School of Architecture," *History of Columbia University, 1754–1904* (New York: Columbia University Press, 1904) p. 385.

3. Ibid.

4. *Columbia University Handbook of Information, 1893–1894,* p. 68.

5. *Columbia University Bulletin of Information, 1897–1898,* p. 30.

6. Hamlin, "The School of Architecture," p. 388.

7. Ibid., p. 389.

information to architecture was specifically explicated through a series of problems covering all aspects of engineering design.[8]

The practical aspects of architecture proved to be the most difficult for Ware to teach effectively. Even an experiment that entailed sending students to R.T. Auchmuty's New York Trade School failed.[9] There seemed to be no efficient means of teaching architects how to recognize good masonry, plumbing, or steel construction except through long experience. Ware then decided merely to familiarize his students with proper construction techniques through a series of courses taught by Charles P. Warren.[10] In them Warren discussed architectural engineering, building materials and construction.

Along with a firm grounding in professional practice, Ware considered a knowledge of the history of architecture and ornament to be of fundamental importance, and courses covering the Ancient, Medieval, and Renaissance periods were taught in the upper three years. Ware attempted to involve his students in their work by requiring them to produce illustrated reports on a historical subject once a week for six weeks of the spring term in the second and third years.[11] This type of study not only improved their writing, research skills, and draftsmanship, but compelled the student to "resort to books and to learn the aspect of the great monuments of the various styles."[12]

Ware thought that all of this work — mathematical, practical, and historical — was preliminary to the work in drawing and design. This area, despite its emphasis, was the weakest aspect of the Columbia curriculum during the School's early years. The School of Mines kept the program in architecture under the domination of "the scientific ideas and ideals which rightly controlled the Departments of Chemistry, Mining and Engineering."[13] Consequently, "the artistic side of the architects' training was wholly overshadowed by this scientific environment."[14] Nevertheless, using his unique method of teaching drawing and design, Ware managed to produce some very fine designers.

In teaching drawing, Ware stressed the development of skills without the need for instruments.[15] He divided the teaching of freehand drawing into six progressive steps. First, the students traced from prints and photographs so that they could develop their line-drawing and coloring techniques without worrying about the form of the object being portrayed. Since the objects being copied were historically significant buildings, the student accumulated "valuable memoranda for future reference."[16] After tracing had been mastered, the student learned to draw forms and render shapes, shades, and shadows.[17] The third step was the freehand construction of various forms such as the *fleur de lys* and the *guilloche,* which were then drawn foreshortened as if applied to an architectural element.[18] The fourth step required freehand plans, sections, elevations, and perspectives of simple objects such as a barn, a stable, or a dog kennel.[19] Brush work with India ink was the fifth step in the sequence, followed by outdoor sketching.[20] Once students had mastered drawing, they moved on to learning such tectonic matters as the orders of architecture,

8. Ibid., p. 387. See also: Ware to Seth Low, 12 September 1892, Central Files, Columbia University (hereafter Central Files).

9. Hamlin, "The School of Architecture," p. 387. See also: "Departmental News," *School of Mines Quarterly,* 10 (1888–1889), p. viii.

10. Warren, C.P., "The Course in Architectural Practice," *School of Mines Quarterly,* 21 (July 1900), pp. 18-20.
Charles Peck Warren (1869–1919), born in Brooklyn, entered the School in 1886 and graduated in 1890. In 1892 he was awarded an A.M. In 1893 he began to teach at the School and did so until his death. He was described as having a clear and logical mind and a gift for illustration and concise exposition which enabled him to compress large amounts of information on building construction and professional practice into the relatively small time allotted to it in the course.
While he taught, he also actively practiced architecture with, among others, Grenville Snelling. For a few years he was also associated with A.D.F. Hamlin on the design and construction of several buildings for Roberts College in Constantinople.
Grenville Snelling came to the School in 1889 as an Assistant in Architecture. In 1891 he became an Instructor in Architectural Engineering and in 1895 he began to teach Architectural Design, which he continued to do until 1907. He was also a partner in the firm of Potter and Snelling. This firm designed the Stapleton, S.I. Ferry Terminal as well as country houses in Westchester County, N.Y. and churches and clubs in Jacksonville, Florida.

11. Hamlin, "The School of Architecture," p. 388.

12. Ibid. See also: *American Architect and Building News,* 94 (1908), pp. 173-4. Not only was Ware interested in history, but his assistant A.D.F. Hamlin was also an historian who contributed frequently to *American Architect and Building News.* See "The So-called Colonial Architecture of the United States," *American Architect and Building News,* 48 (1895), pp. 63-65, 75-77, 87-88, 97-99, 107-108, 115-118, 130-131.

13. Hamlin, "The School of Architecture," p. 388.

14. Hamlin, "The School of Architecture," p. 381.

15. Ware, W.R. "The Study of Architectural Drawing in the School of Architecture," *School of Mines Quarterly,* 17 (July 1897), p. 61. I quote him at length:
We begin, to be sure, with the use of mathematical instruments, so as to establish at once a certain standard of exactness. But we discontinue their use as soon as possible and find every advantage in doing everything free-hand until most things are done. For the draftsman who has been trained only with the dividers and ruling-pen, however skillful he may become, is as helpless when they are not at hand as he was before he began to learn their use, while the man who can do whatever needs to be done without them has no difficulty in doing it with them. They come to him as helps and auxiliaries, which is what they should be, not as necessaries. He is thus saved the early experience of anxiety and caution in their use which produces a hard and timid drawing at the hands of a hard-fisted and merely mechanical draftsman.

16. Ware, "The Study of Drawing," p. 7.

17. Ibid., p. 9.

18. Ibid., p. 15.

19. Ibid., p. 19.

20. Ibid., pp. 20-24.

Design for a Memorial Chapel, 1889, William S. Post *(1890)*, Avery Archive.

2 DAY PROBLEM
SEA SIDE COTTAGE
W.E. PARSONS
1897

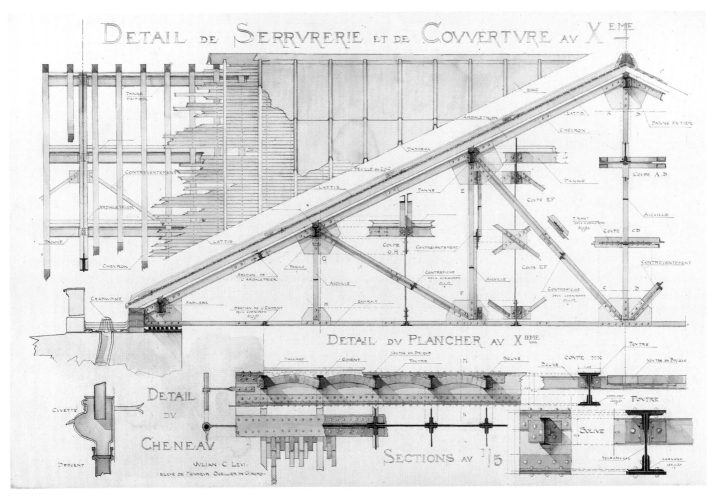

Above: Constructional Analysis Drawing (completed at the Ecole des Beaux-Arts), Julian C. Levi *(1897)*, Avery Archive.

Right: Shades and Shadows, Anonymous, Avery Archive.

Opposite page.
Above: Seaside Cottage, 1897, William E. Parsons *(1898)*, Avery Archive.

Below: Section of a Casino, 1894, Benjamin Wistar Morris *(1894)*, Avery Archive.

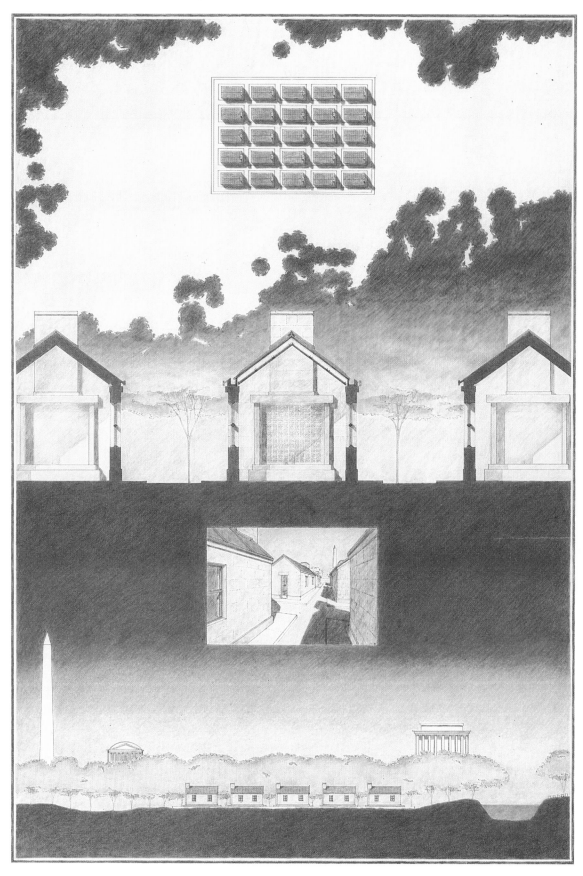

Vietnam War Memorial, Washington, D.C. 1980, Elaine Felhandler *(1982)*.

Opposite page.
Above: Restoration drawing of the Capitolium at Ostia, Italy (project completed at the American Academy in Rome), 1927, C. Dale Badgeley *(1925)*.

Below: Greenhouse at the Bronx Botanical Gardens, 1978, Tyler Donaldson *(1978)*.

ELEVATION

CAPITOLIVM AT OSTIA

RESTORATION BY C·D·BADGELEY · AMERICAN ACADEMY IN ROME · MAY 1928

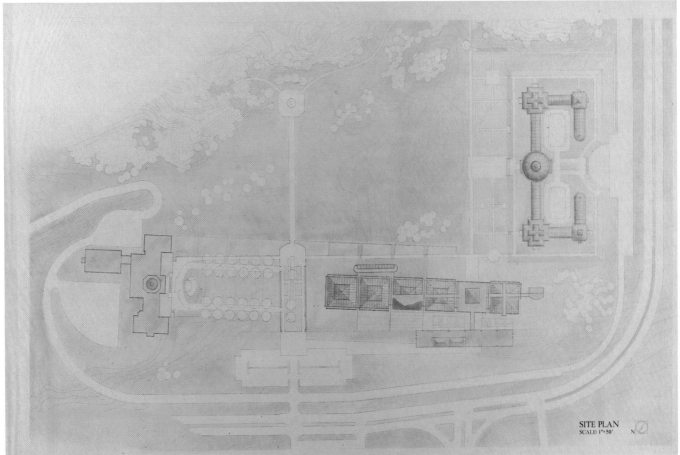

SITE PLAN
SCALE 1"=50'

N

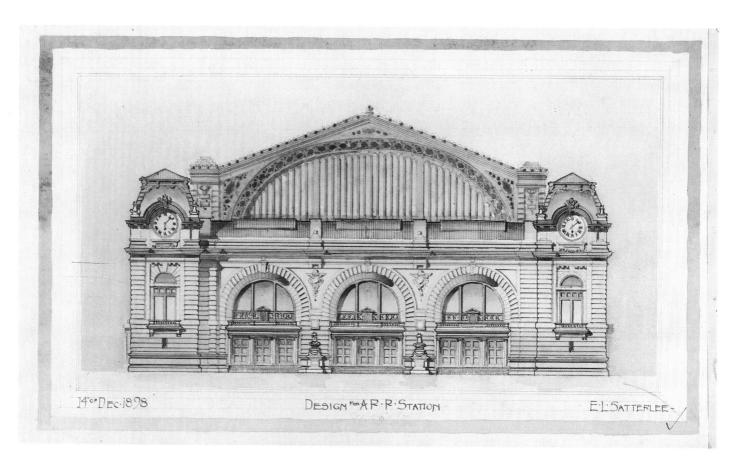

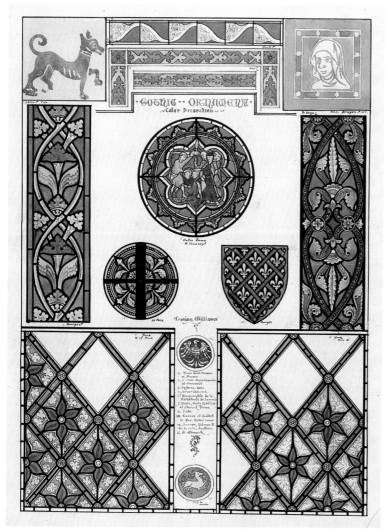

Above: Design for a Railroad Station, 1898, Edward L. Satterlee *(1900),* Avery Archive.

Left: Gothic Ornament, 1918, Lessing W. Williams *(1919),* Avery Archive.

INSTITUTE AND VILLAGE, LOOKING NORTH

SITE PLAN 1":200'0" (CONTOURS AT 12.5')   1. INSTITUTE   2. VILLAGE   3. EXCAVATION   4. EXISTING SERVICE ROAD   5. FOOT PATH

Center for Minoan Studies, Santorini, 1979, Ronald Rose *(1979)*.

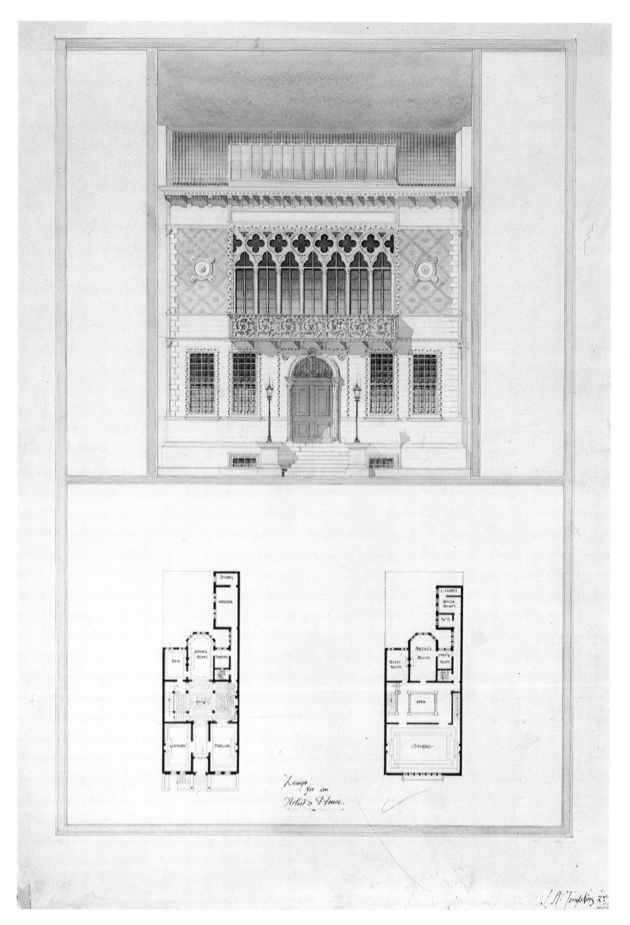

Design for an Artist's House, ca. 1894, John A. Tompkins *(1894)*, Avery Archive.

staircases, vaults, domes, and spires, and the use of these elements in an architectural composition.[21] Having completed the six steps, the student finally was equipped to begin work in design.

From 1882 until 1894, instruction in design was given by A.D.F. Hamlin, and it was taught much as it is today.[22] Students were assigned progressively more difficult building programs and their efforts were criticized by their professors. Projects included *A Hall for Antique Sculpture*, *A Mausoleum*, *A Public School*, *A College Library*, and *A City House*. From the first, in contrast to the method of teaching design at the Ecole, the stimuli of awards, prizes, and advancement through competition were absent. Although the absence of competition was a source of criticism, Ware was sure of his methodology, noting,

We have done what we have without any aid from juries, awards, mentions or any external stimulus whatever. The men miss, of course, the experience of the high pressure and white heat of the charrette. But experience for experience, is not the experience of having produced a notable success and substantial achievement, at low pressure, so to speak, an equally useful one if less exciting?[23]

In addition to these courses, historically significant structures and elements were drawn by the student, following a pedagogic process known as Design by Dictation, in which the student would draw a building that had been described verbally. The benefits of this process were two-fold: first, it formed a bridge between the courses that taught the orders and elements of architecture and the courses in design, and it demonstrated to the student the historical solutions to various building problems; second, by presenting important buildings of the past as a series of solutions to the problems that their builders faced, insight into the cultural context of the period was gained. At the same time, the exercise served as a lesson in the application of design motifs and instilled the student with "the same good taste and good sense, the same readiness of invention and happy ingenuity to which the masterpieces were due."[24]

In the design courses, draftsmanship was considered secondary to composition, for Ware showed little interest in the production of highly finished drawings. This bias caused critics to downgrade the work of Columbia students in comparison with the more polished work produced by students of other schools. To improve this situation, three graduates of the Ecole were hired starting in 1894, to bring to Columbia students the drawing skills acquired in Paris: Grenville Snelling, William Partridge, and Henry Hornbostel *(Columbia, 1891)*.[25]

In addition to training architects, Ware felt the School had a duty to the architectural community to meet its needs for educated draftsmen. He proposed to do this by allowing men with at least three years experience or those students with college degrees in some other field to enter the Department as non-matriculated special students. Although this was contrary to School of Mines policy, Ware finally gained permission to begin the program in 1891.[26]

21. Ibid., pp. 24-27.

22. Ibid., p. 29. Reviews of student work as well as student theses were frequently published in *American Architect and Building News*, as well as *Architecture and Building*. Theses even included an historical survey of plazas and squares in Europe; see *American Architect and Building News*, 43 (1894), pp. 52-54, 64-67, 87-89, 101-104, 137-138. Other student work appeared in the following issues of *Architecture and Building*: 12 (1890), p. 284; 27 (1897), pp. 42 ff.; 28 (1898), p. 206; and 30 (1899), p. 200.

23. Ware to Laird, 17 June 1894, Avery Archives, Avery Library, Columbia University (hereafter Avery Archives). Ware not only opposed competitions as components of an architectural program, but also opposed the awarding of large commissions by this means. See "Competitions," a paper delivered by Ware at the Thirty-third Annual Convention of the American Institute of Architects at Pittsburgh, 16 November 1899, and printed in *American Architect and Building News*, 66 (1899), pp. 107-112.

24. Ware, W.R., "The Study of Architectural History," *School of Mines Quarterly*, 17 (July 1897), p. 61. Ware's zealous emphasis on the study of history, which he justified as being essential for the liberally educated architect, proved to be a source of criticism. In this approach to architectural education Ware failed to recognize the profession's need for more technically proficient, rather than historically enlightened, architects. This will be discussed further below. See also: "Study of History of Architecture," *American Architect and Building News*, 50 (1895), pp. 100-101.

25. Hamlin, "The School of Architecture," p. 390.

Henry Fred Hornbostel (1867-1961), born in Brooklyn, N.Y., attended Brooklyn High School before entering Columbia. In 1891 he graduated at the head of his class. He then worked in the office of Palmer and Wood for two years before leaving for Paris to study in the *Atelier Ginain* at the Ecole des Beaux-Arts. There his brilliant drawing skills were brought out and he became known as "l'homme perspectif." While a student at the Ecole, he worked for such architects as Girault and Blavette. In 1897 Hornbostel returned to the United States where he found work as a freelance delineator, working for several well-known firms, including McKim Mead & White, and Carrere and Hastings. His abilities attracted the attention of Ware who employed him to teach Architectural Design, a position which he held until 1903. In 1907 Hornbostel and his friend Lloyd Warren traveled to the Yucatan, bringing back the first photographs of sites that have since been frequently visited and published.

Possessing an ability to distill the essential components of building programs and to render them in a forceful style, Hornbostel was extremely successful in open competitions. Associated with Howells and Stokes, he won second prize in the Hearst competition for the University of California (1899). In 1904, associated with William Palmer, he won the Competition for Carnegie Institute of Technology. In 1905 the firm moved to Pittsburgh for the construction of the Institute and while there Hornbostel founded the School of Architecture at Carnegie Institute. From then on he continued to practice from Pittsburgh, designing city halls in Oakland, Cal. (1910), Pittsburgh, Pa. (1910), Wilmington, Del. (1910) and Hartford, Conn. (1911), and the Soldiers and Sailors Memorial in Pittsburgh, Pa. (1907).

Hornbostel was best known for his designs of New York City bridges and their approaches. His first was the Manhattan side of the Brooklyn Bridge (1903) followed by the Williamsburg Bridge (1905), the Queensboro Bridge (1905), and the Hell Gate Bridge (1917).

In World War I Hornbostel served as a gas officer for the 36th Division of the United States Army. After the War, Hornbostel returned to Pittsburgh where he continued his successful practice, designing Oakland Technical High school, Oakland, Ca. (1917), the Oakland Auditorium (1920), Emory University, Atlanta, Ga. (1920), the Harding

Even before Columbia established a course in architecture, travel, especially to Europe, was considered an essential component of the education of the young American architect. This in part stemmed from a prevailing sense of inferiority Americans felt about their own buildings, and the corresponding sentiment that the best works of art of any kind were to be found in Europe. Charles McKim observed that "the value of constant and long-continued study in proximity with the best examples of architecture cannot be over-estimated and is of incalculable advantage to the student before entering upon his professional career."[27] Furthermore, McKim thought that the lack of training in design fundamentals could be remedied by exposing the graduate to the architectural patrimony of Europe. In 1889, McKim met with Ware to donate $20,000 to establish a travelling fellowship, the recipient to be chosen through competition in design.[28]

These competitions were judged by McKim, Thomas Hastings, and Richard Morris Hunt.[29] McKim was disappointed by the abilities of the students entering the travelling fellowship competitions, and this further reinforced his feelings that the program at Columbia was inadequate. In a letter he sharply criticized Ware: "The thing that has struck me most forcibly in these prize competitions of the Columbia students is the evidence of defective grounding in the elementary principles."[30] Ware realized the School suffered from these deficiencies, as he observed in a memorandum in 1892:

Our best men leave school with only just about skill enough to pass with credit the entrance examinations of the Ecole des Beaux-Arts in Paris. This is the utmost that we have been able to accomplish. But it is fair to say that, once admitted, our best men have greatly distinguished themselves there.

It does not seem to me that this is fulfilling the purpose for which the School was founded. It does not meet the necessities of the community, nor the requirements of the profession nor the intentions of the Trustees, for us to stop where other schools begin.[31]

Furthermore, a non-competitive curriculum in design such as the one supported by Ware relied heavily on the abilities of the teachers, not all of whom, Ware and Hamlin in particular, were brilliant designers. Ware had been criticized for not having someone equivalent to Eugene L'Etang, an Ecole graduate whom Ware had hired at M.I.T. and who was the driving force behind the ability of M.I.T. students to produce beautiful drawings on a par with those of the Ecole graduates, on the Columbia staff. Ware was able to temper this criticism by hiring successful fellowship competitors such as Partridge and Hornbostel. Hornbostel, especially, was known for his skill in drawing, as well as his ability to compose quickly the essential elements of a competitive program into a scheme and to render it in a striking manner.[32]

In addition to establishing a travelling fellowship in his name at Columbia, McKim founded the American Academy in Rome in 1894 to remedy the lack of training of American architects. He envisioned the Academy as an advanced training ground, modeled

Memorial Tomb, Warren, Ohio (1924) and the Seward Monument, Seward, Alaska (1929).

William T. Partridge (1866–?) attended the School of Mines at Columbia from 1885 to 1887. He worked in Boston for three years before winning the Rotch Travelling Fellowship in 1890. On his return from Europe he worked for the St. Louis firm of Eames and Young before coming to Columbia in 1897 as a lecturer in Architectural Design. He became secretary to the McKim and Schermerhorn Fellowship program at Columbia, but left in 1903 for Washington, D.C. There he worked on the "McMillan Plan" for Washington, D.C., staying on, as consulting architect, after its completion, a position which he held until 1951. He also ran a one-man *atelier* in his office in Washington. In 1951 he retired to Red Bank, New Jersey.

26. Ware, W.R. "Professional Draughtsmen as Special Students in the School of Architecture," *School of Mines Quarterly,* 17 (July, 1897), pp. 423-429. In the first six years, eighty-four students, eighteen of whom were graduates of other colleges, took advantage of this program. They attended courses for periods varying from two months to three years, most spending at least a year, and almost half spending two years. Some even joined the fourth year class and received their degrees from Columbia. Many of these special students used their time at Columbia to "tune up" for the Ecole des Beaux-Arts entrance exams before leaving for Paris. Others used special student status as a kind of post-graduate education, which allowed them to take advanced courses as they pleased. Special students included several men who would later become prominent in their field including Donn Barber, I.N. Phelps Stokes, William A. Delano, Phillip Sawyer, and William A. Boring. See also: typescript copy of "Report on Special Students in the School of Architecture," (Feb. 15, 1898) pp. 1-5, Central Files; Hamlin, A.D.F. "Some Alumni of the School of Architecture," *Columbia Alumni News,* 9 (Mar. 22, 1918), p. 778.

27. Moore, C.B., *The Life and Times of Charles Follen McKim* (New York: Houghton, 1929), p. 128.

28. Ibid.

29. Baker, P., *Richard Morris Hunt,* (Cambridge: M.I.T. Press, 1980), p. 440.

30. Moore, *McKim,* p. 129.

31. Typed report "Memorandum on the School" given by Ware to Butler, 1892, np., Central Files.

32. Swales, F.S., "Master Draftsmen: XVII, Henry Hornbostel," *Pencil Points,* 7 (1926), pp. 72-92.

on the French Academy in Rome, to which students chosen through competition would be sent to follow a supervised course of study and travel. McKim felt that the Ecole des Beaux-Arts in Paris was a modern institution that merely interpreted classical tradition, and he preferred that Americans go directly to the original source for inspiration, that is, to Rome. Ware was chosen as chairman of the managing committee of the American Academy, but soon resigned in a dispute over the supervision of the students abroad as well as the extravagant nature of the project. He felt students should be allowed to roam the continent at will, seeking out their own examples of fine architecture, rather than studying only those dictated by the Academy.[33] At the same time the Society of Beaux-Arts Architects withdrew support for the Academy, claiming Paris, not Rome, was the center of modern architectural activity.[34] Hunt replaced Ware as chairman of the managing committee and in May, 1895, the first competition to select a student to go to Rome was held.[35] John Russell Pope, (*Columbia, 1894*) was the first Rome Prize winner.[36] Soon after the prize was awarded, Ware aggravated his architectural peers by suggesting to Pope that he postpone his trip a year so that he might better prepare himself.[37] This was not an altogether altruistic suggestion, for Pope had been working as Ware's personal assistant since his graduation.[38] Hunt prevailed over Ware, and Pope sailed for Europe in September, 1895.[39]

McKim was not alone in his concern for the quality of Columbia graduates. The Society of Beaux-Arts Architects, founded in 1894, was composed of Ecole graduates who, upon starting their offices in New York, "found a dearth of good designers and draftsmen." The Society thus instituted an *atelier* system that was so successful that "the men trained in these *ateliers* proved so superior to the graduates of our schools that the latter clamored for the introduction of the *atelier* and competitive system in their schools."[40] Out of this grew the Beaux Arts Institute of Design (B.A.I.D.), a national organization that judged student design competitions in New York. In 1903, Samuel B.T. (Breck) Trowbridge, President of the Society, proposed that a foreign scholarship be created for study at the Ecole, and the first Paris Prize was awarded in 1904.[41]

By 1897, many of the major buildings designed by McKim, Mead & White for the North Campus on Morningside Heights were complete. The School moved from the cramped quarters of the *Maison de Punk* downtown to the top two floors of Havemeyer Hall, a building it shared with the Chemistry Department.[42] Drafting rooms were located at the east and west ends of the floor, separated by the library, lecture rooms, and offices.[43] The library, an important working resource, at that time contained more than 600 books and 15,000 photographs, and was supplemented by the Avery collection housed in the Low Memorial Library. The hall connecting all these rooms was the heart of the School, where current work was pinned up for display and criticism. In this hall, in the stairway, and in the drafting rooms, the walls were covered with prints of great architecture and with plaster casts of building

33. Moore, *McKim*, pp. 128-139, as well as Ware to Laird correspondence, Avery Library, Ware Collection.

34. Baker, *Hunt*, p. 440.

35. Ibid. Several subsequent Columbia graduates have won the Rome Prize, including Richard Smythe in 1911, Walter L. Ward in 1913, Phillip T. Shutze in 1915, Henry Marceau in 1922, Arthur Deam in 1923, C. Dale Badgeley in 1926, Cecil Briggs in 1928, Olindo Grossi in 1933, and Amy Anderson in 1980. This information was obtained from the American Academy in Rome. See also *American Architect*, 104 (1913), p. 69.

36. Baker, *Hunt*, p. 440. See also *American Architect & Building News*, 48 (1895), pp. 53-54.

37. Baker, *Hunt*, p. 440.

38. Ware to Low, 10 August 1894, Central Files.

39. Baker, *Hunt*, p. 440.

40. Noffsinger, J.P., "The Influence of the Ecole des Beaux-Arts on the Architects of the United States," p. 38.

41. Through the efforts of Lloyd Warren, the prize continues to be awarded and is now known as the Lloyd Warren Fellowship, Paris Prize in Architecture. Columbia graduates have not been frequent winners: Max Abramovitz won in 1932, and J.B. Bell, Jr. in 1962.

The School has continued to support the idea of travel as an integral part of architectural education. In addition to the McKim prize, there is the Columbia Travelling Fellowship, donated by Schermerhorn in 1913, as well as the Perkins Fellowship given in 1896, Boring Fellowships given in 1925, and the William Kinne Fellows Memorial Fellowships in Architecture, first given in 1953. See N.I.A.E., *Winning Designs 1904–1963; Paris Prize in Architecture* (New York: 1964). Rohdenburg, Theodor, *A History of the School of Architecture, Columbia University* (New York: Columbia University Press, 1954), pp. 99-101.

42. Stuart, P.C., "Architectural Schools in the United States. Columbia University," *Architectural Record*, 10 (July, 1900), p. 1. Stuart described the view from the drafting rooms thus:
To the south and east the city throbs and smokes for countless miles and is lost in the horizon mist. To the north and west, over the roofs of Barnard College, across the vacant lots and straggling shanties that still punctuate the city's growth, beyond the great white tomb that marks the end of the world's finest driveway, lies the Hudson River.

43. Rohdenburg, *A History of the School*, pp. 13-15. Also *American Architect & Building News*, 26 (1889), p. 214.

ornament, many of the latter donated by McKim. In a small departmental museum on the next floor, a student could study models of the Parthenon and a full bay of Rheims Cathedral.[44]

In realizing his goal of a fully independent School of Architecture, Ware had formed one of the most influential schools in the country. Despite early criticism, the influence of the School extended beyond the small numbers of its graduates. A large percentage of the School's alumni became successful and prolific architects, affecting the environment of every major city in the United States.[45] Those who played an influential role in New York are reviewed in another essay in this book. Outside of New York, early Columbia graduates earned equal respect in their field. George Cary *(1885)* became a prominent architect in Buffalo; Edward P. Casey *(1888)* became Supervising Architect of the Library of Congress; Seth I. Temple *(1892)* was the leading architect in Davenport, Iowa; John Russell Pope *(1894)*, although based in New York, achieved great success in Washington, D.C.; Kenneth Murchison *(1894)* designed railroad stations throughout the Northeast; W.E. Parsons *(1898)* became the government's architect in the Philippines; C.S. Kaiser *(1901)* and A.E. Curlett *(1905)* were successful in San Francisco, as was S.S. Labuoisse *(1903)* in New Orleans.

As conspicuous as the success of the School's practicing architects was, those who went into teaching became as distinguished and indeed virtually monopolized the field of architectural education. Three of the first five graduates became teachers: Frank Dempster Sherman *(1884)* taught at Columbia; Alvan Nye *(1884)* became the first professor of architecture at Pratt Institute; Thomas Nolan *(1884)* became Professor of Architectural Engineering at the University of Pennsylvania; A.A. Stoughton *(1888)* founded the School of Architecture at the University of Manitoba in Winnipeg; and Charles P. Warren *(1890)*, Henry Hornbostel *(1891)* and Lucian Smith *(1901)* all taught at Columbia. Hornbostel went on to become the first director of the School of Architecture at Carnegie Institute of Technology; Lloyd Warren *(1891)* was instrumental in the founding of the B.A.I.D.; E. Raymond Bossange *(1893)* was professor of design at Cornell and New York University; L.F. Pilcher *(1895)* taught fine arts at Vassa: College; Goldwin Goldsmith *(1896)* was the first Professor of Architecture at the University of Kansas; Huger Elliot *(1900)* became the Director of the Rhode Island School of Design; R.H. Dana *(1904)* was for eight years Professor of Architecture at Yale University; John Wynkoop *(1904)* taught at the University of Pennsylvania; and Nathanael Curtis *(1904)* and Samuel Labouisse *(1903)* taught at Tulane.[46] Thus, Ware's principles of teaching men to think as well as to draw were carried about the country. In the process, of course, he had not pleased everyone nor had his conception of architectural education always coincided with that thought to be most appropriate by influential members of the profession.

As early as 1898, Ware had discussed his impending retirement with Schermerhorn, indicating that in four years he would be

Study for a Corinthian Capital, 1889, Henry Hornbostel *(1891)*, Avery Archive.

44. Ware, W.R., "The School of Architecture in its New Quarters," *Columbia University Quarterly*, 19 (1898), pp. 289-296. See also: "Alumni and University News," *Columbia University Quarterly*, 19 (1898), p. 104; *School of Mines Quarterly*, 21 (1899–1900), p. 88.

45. It should be noted that many of these graduates had also attended the Ecole des Beaux-Arts and had not developed successful practices until after Ware's retirement — too late to stem criticism of the program and stay Ware's departure.
  In 1889 *American Architect and Building News* referred to the Columbia College course as the best in architecture in the country, an opinion no doubt influenced by the fact that the magazine's editor, William Rotch Ware, was a cousin of William Robert Ware. See *American Architect and Building News*, 25 (1889), p. 95.

46. Hamlin, A.D.F., "Some Alumni of the School of Architecture," *Columbia Alumni News*, 9 (March 22, 1918), pp. 775-782.

finished with his experiments in architectural education. In addition, by 1902 he would be 70 years old.[47] In pursuing the development of a liberal academic curriculum, as opposed to the professional program favored by other school directors, Ware had disturbed many of his colleagues, particularly since his program had not immediately produced astounding results. Ware had had strained relations with such powerful members of the profession as Charles F. McKim, George B. Post and Richard Morris Hunt. Furthermore, Ware continued to offer unwelcome criticism of McKim's designs for buildings on the Columbia campus.[48]

In addition to these difficulties, by 1902 Ware had suffered two severe strokes; one in 1890, from which he had recovered, and a second in 1902, which had severely reduced his abilities to lead the School. Furthermore, he suffered from painful bouts of erysipelas, which often kept him from his duties. These illnesses, coupled with a lack of leadership among Ware's subordinates, left the School in a disorganized and demoralized state.[49] Consequently, President Butler formed a special committee to look into the problems besetting the School. The Committee's primary recommendation was the removal of Ware, who was informed of his retirement and appointment as Professor Emeritus on June 1, 1903, effective June 30, 1903. He resisted this move on the Trustees' part to no avail.[50] Hamlin, worried that such action would enrage Ware's loyal following, consisting primarily of alumni of the School, cautioned Butler:

Professor Ware has endeared himself to a rather large and enthusiastically loyal following of former students, and to many others whom he has befriended, or known for years. Many of these are men of influence in the community in their various circles. I imagine that comparatively few of these appreciate the extent to which Professor Ware's powers have been failing the past year or two, and his dismissal from active service would seem to them a flagrant injustice to one of the most distinguished and faithful servants of the University. They would resent it and make their resentment publicly known. There would be a public turmoil which would inevitably involve the School of Architecture and bring it into disfavor at the outset of the new regime. The University could not protect itself from misjudgment by spreading forth the facts to public gaze.[51]

As a measure of Ware's support, Henry Hornbostel *(Columbia, 1891)* organized a testimonial dinner; J. Monroe Hewlett *(Columbia, 1890)* presided over the dinner, which was held on November 3, 1902. At that time Ware was presented with a bound volume containing the signatures of almost four hundred former students, inscribed with an English version of the Latin inscription upon his diploma of Doctor of Laws conferred by Harvard University in 1900:

The Creator of two serviceable schools of architecture, the first at the Massachusetts Institute of Technology, the second at Columbia University in the City of New York; the Friend, Exemplar, and Instructor of a generation of American architects.[52]

In the end, Ware acceded to the Trustees' demands and retired to his home in Milton, Massachusetts.

47. Ware to Schermerhorn, 1898, Ware Collection, M.I.T. Archives, Cambridge, Mass. The authors are indebted to Ms. D. Cozort for this reference.

48. Further evidence of this animosity may be found in the Central Files of Columbia University. As Dennis McFadden has observed in his "Research Notes on the History of the School of Architecture" (unpublished ms., GSAP Archives), Ware's emphasis on historical scholarship rather than on technical skills created a program that failed to meet the needs of the New York profession, whose commissions for complex projects created a need only for those architects with developed technical and drafting skills (p. 13). See also *The Record and Guide,* 39 (April 10, 1887), p. 511.

49. The School's condition was described as follows in a memorandum sent by Hamlin to Butler, October, 1902, Central Files:

(1) Pervading sense of discouragement and demoralization, among both students and staff.

(2) Lack of well-defined authority and strong control in the carrying out of any positive policy.

(3) The architectural essays are magnified to a matter of predominant importance to the prejudice of the more strictly professional subjects. "Down town" sneers at the School as a literary instead of a professional institution. Students, instructors and most of the alumni unite in disparaging the essay.

(4) There has been a gradual drifting away from the active profession, a loss of the enthusiastic sympathy and support the School ought to have from its alumni, the Society of Beaux-Arts Architects, and the profession at large.

(5) The administration is diffused and lacking in coherence, both as to personnel and functions. Design is taught by four persons with no controlling head to this department. Drawing is taught by four persons. History of architecture is taught by three persons, mathematical subjects are divided among three and practical engineering and practice, which could very well be taken care of by one, is divided between two. Four persons, with salaries aggregating $7000, give only partial service. Four of the staff as now organized, perform each wholly diverse and unrelated duties. Thus, Professor Ware teaches Theory, a little History, a little Design, the Perspective and the Essays, Professor Hamlin teaches all the Ornament, some History, a little Design and some Drawing. Mr. Kress is Curator, and teaches some History, the French and German (archeology), and a little Drawing.

(6) The School has been practically stationary, if it has not retrograded, since 1895, in numbers. For the past 8 years the enrollment (as taken from the catalogues) has been 93, 97, 87, 96, 95, 68, 80, 81. Omitting special students whose numbers depend largely on conditions in the business world, these figures become: 71, 79, 73, 78, 58, 72, 71.

(7) Impracticable to secure practising architects of long-established reputation as professors of Design. They cannot spare the time. Must take the younger men.

(8) Board of Visitors, representing alumni, Society Beaux Arts Architects and profession at large, to visit, criticise and suggest.

50. The move to retire Ware actually began in early 1902 but he was able to resist it. The Special Committee on Education was particularly disturbed by Ware's proposal to prepare students for the School of Architecture through a correspondence course. See McFadden, "Research Notes," pp. 13-14.

51. Hamlin to Butler, 17 May 1902, Central Files.

52. *Columbia University Quarterly,* 5 (December, 1902), pp. 71-73.

The keys to understanding the course of development upon which the School was to embark following the realization of complete independence from the Faculty of Applied Science in 1902 and the forced retirement of William R. Ware, are to be found in a letter dated June 2, 1903 from President Butler to Professor Hamlin. In addition to informing Hamlin that on June 1 the Trustees had voted to retire Ware effective June 30, 1903, Butler advised that the following resolutions had been adopted:

Resolved, *That Professor Hamlin be assigned temporarily to the headship of the Department of Architecture, and requested to prepare for the Trustees a special report upon the reorganization of the Department.*

Resolved, *That the President be authorized by the Trustees to designate a visiting committee of practicing architects, the committee to contain representatives of (1) the alumni of the School of Architecture; (2) members of the Society of former students of the Ecole des Beaux-Arts; and (3) of members of the profession not associated with either of the foregoing, with the request to visit and inspect the School of Architecture as at present organized and conducted, and to prepare such recommendations to the Trustees as may seem to them proper.*[53]

Hamlin's appointment seems to be indicative of a certain conservatism or a desire to maintain the status quo in the newly formed School of Architecture. The intended impermanence of the position is central, however. Hamlin had studied under Ware at M.I.T., and, in 1882, had been invited by Ware to teach at Columbia.[54] Needless to say, Hamlin was a central figure in the establishment of the School even in the early years prior to his appointment as its Acting Director. While Hamlin taught architectural history and shades and shadows, as well as design, his strengths were along academic lines. His philosophy of architectural education was consistent with that of Ware in that he rejected a merely technical approach and emphasized instead the academic and the historical — the necessity for grounding in the liberal arts. Another characteristic that he shared with Ware and that would become exceedingly significant in the search for a permanent head of the department was his not being an active practitioner.[55]

While it may be somewhat of an oversimplification, it is fair to say that the essential difference between the two men centered around Ware's being an idealist and Hamlin's being a realist. Ware had been unwilling or unable to assimilate the changed nature of the architectural profession and to accept the concomitant need for architectural education to respond thereto. He clung firmly to an ideal of education which, by its very nature, he believed to be universal; his inflexibility eventually necessitated his losing control of the architecture school. Hamlin, on the other hand, although not without a philosophy of architectural education, was alert to the changed nature of things. His greater awareness was due in part to his having been employed in the offices of McKim, Mead & White from 1881 to 1883 — a time when the firm was beginning its move to the forefront of the profession.[56]

If Hamlin's appointment followed logically, the resolution that a visiting committee of practitioners be formed to prepare

Alfred Dwight Foster Hamlin.
Photo: Columbiana Collection.

53. Butler to Hamlin, 2 June 1903, Central Files.

54. Rohdenburg, *A History of the School*, pp. 30-31.

55. Despite his academic preference, Hamlin had designed and executed a number of buildings, the most important of which were the academic buildings at Roberts College (founded by Hamlin's father Cyrus Hamlin) on the Hisar Campus near Bebek, Turkey. Hamlin built Albert Long Hall in 1891, Washburn Hall in 1906, and Anderson Hall in 1913. His designs, although personally interpreted, were strongly influenced by those of H.H. Richardson and C.F. McKim.

56. Rohdenburg, *A History of the School*, p. 30.

recommendations for the Trustees respecting reorganization was unprecedented. It indicated the University's unwillingness to entrust Hamlin with full responsibility for the reorganization of the new School as an independent unit in the university system.

Nonetheless, Hamlin's appointment was, in a sense, imperative if the President, the Committee on Education and the Trustees were to be able to effect the transition to a new regime without complete upheaval. Hamlin was well aware that all sorts of recriminations would be voiced following the announcement of Ware's retirement.[57] It was hoped that the appointment of Hamlin would stem the negative criticism, and that he would serve as a stopgap until the Committee on Education had been able to assimilate the results of the advisory committee and had decided in which direction the reorganization would proceed. Until such time, it would have been pointless to designate a permanent director.[58] Aside from the fact that the establishment of the School as an independent entity necessarily pointed to reorganization, a decline in reputation beginning in the 1890's indicated the need for revamping.[59] Regarding the publication of a yearbook that would serve as a complete illustrated *resumé* of graphic work and as a means of advertising the School, Hamlin wrote:

The School of Architecture is the only School and Faculty that has not grown notably in the past few years. It has increased during the past two years barely enough to recover the ground it lost from 1896 to 1900. Yet its work has been increasingly efficient and its reputation high. I think that with the help of the proposed book it would rapidly recover its relative position among the Schools.[60]

In response to a request from Butler that Hamlin confer with his colleagues respecting the proposed reorganization and submit suggestions thereon, Hamlin delivered a list of nominations for the Visiting Committee, on June 10, 1903, and suggested changes in the curriculum and in the faculty. He begged more time, however, for consideration of larger policy matters. The faculty agreed that the pedagogical thrust of the School must be to orient the student toward the practice of architecture, or, in other words, toward design by means of a logical sequence of courses focused on the practical demands of the profession, rather than on the liberal ideals of Professor Ware. The staff of the School was unanimous in its opinion that "especially in view of Professor Ware's resignation, the Architectural Essays be omitted from all four years of the course" and that it was "unwise to devote to writing time needed for professional work."[61] It was suggested that more time be accorded to Graphics and Freehand Drawing and less time to Historical Drawing, and that the series of classes on Theory of Architecture be replaced in the final year of study by a series of lectures given by Hamlin and outside practitioners, including Cass Gilbert, Thomas Hastings, and George Post. As to appointments, Hamlin advised that Harriman, Snelling and Warren be reappointed, and that A.F. Gumaer replace Partridge.[62] It is significant that Hamlin desired that the appointment of Lecturer in Design, held by Hornbostel, be held in abeyance. Hamlin clearly

57. Hamlin to Butler, 17 May 1902, Central Files.

58. Moreover, in light of Ware's stubborn insistence on a liberal academic approach proven incapable of keeping pace with that of architectural education (the focus of which increasingly had turned toward design), there was a reluctance on the part of the Administration to concentrate sole responsibility in the hands of one man. To initiate a search for a new Director immediately and to designate one with strong ideas of his own respecting the organization of the School would negate the purpose of the visiting committee. On the other hand, to designate a "lame duck" from outside the School would have been unwise in light of the recognized need to upgrade the quality of the School in part by instating a strong Director with a professional orientation. In this respect, Hamlin could not have been a more appropriate or more convenient choice to be "temporarily placed...in charge of the administrative work..." (Butler to Ware, 2 June 1903, Central Files).

59. Hamlin, A.D.F., "The School of Architecture," pp. 381 ff.

60. Hamlin to Butler, 2 April 1902, Central Files.

61. Hamlin to Butler, 10 June 1903, Central Files.

62. Ibid.

recognized the importance of the position, especially in light of the proposed reorientation of the department, and much as he disliked Hornbostel as an instructor, he considered him "one of the most brilliant designers in the country."[63]

That the reorganization of the School would proceed along lines similar to those established by the Ecole des Beaux-Arts was certain even before the actual guidelines had been formulated. The construction of the Visiting Committee was indicative:[64] not only was Ecole training represented by the Society of Beaux-Arts Architects, but the remaining nominees had been trained in *ateliers* in the United States modelled after those in Paris. Furthermore, during the summer of 1903, Hamlin had made overtures to a number of designers affiliated with the Ecole, notably Messrs. Duray and Hébrard, in the hope of persuading them to teach design at Columbia. In Paris, he had conferred with approximately twenty former Columbia students studying at the Ecole, soliciting from them suggestions and criticisms regarding Ware's retirement and the reorganization of the department.[65]

While in Paris, Hamlin was to have met with Charles F. McKim.[66] Apparently there was some confusion as to the terms of the meeting for the two did not meet, and McKim expressed his irritation in a letter to Hamlin.[67] Hamlin attempted to exonerate himself in a letter to Butler, painting McKim as "heady, indignant and immovable" and warning that although McKim could make trouble for the School as well as be of great service, the logic of the situation demanded that he serve on the Visiting Committee.[68] Fearful that the Committee would not understand the proper scope of its function and perhaps would attempt to legislate rather than to advise, Hamlin requested that he have a hand in drafting the notifications to those appointed to serve.[69] Hamlin's counsel notwithstanding, in September, 1903, President Butler invited McKim to chair the visiting committee of practicing architects, assuring him that the staff of the School had concurred on the subject of his appointment.[70]

Hamlin subsequently submitted a memorandum outlining the functions of the proposed Visiting Committee. The primary purpose was to establish a close bond between the School and the profession at large and to communicate to the administration with respect to strengthening and broadening the work of the School. Hamlin recommended that the Committee hold meetings during the year, but charged the members with visiting the School individually in order to acquaint themselves with its methods, resources and needs. The Committee was expected to help enlist not only the interest and support of members of the profession for the work of the School but of "men of means." Hamlin hoped that Committee members would influence their colleagues to participate in third and fourth year design reviews. In order to ensure his own role in its function, Hamlin advised that "the professor in charge should be a member, ex-officio, of the Committee."[71] Additionally, he insisted that "it should be made very clear to the Committee that their duties are of an advisory character and intended to cooperate and strengthen the administra-

63. Hamlin to Butler, 12 June 1903, Central Files. Integral to Hamlin's attitude toward Hornbostel is the separation of theories of design and theories of education. Although Hornbostel had benefited from his experience at the Ecole des Beaux-Arts, he was known to oppose the French method of architectural education.

Hamlin's political acuity must not be underestimated: he suggested that Hornbostel be invited to contribute to a competition for the design of the Milbank Quadrangle at Barnard College: "if he were to be invited, there would be an incidental advantage in making up to him for the probable loss of his Columbia appointment and making him less disposed to 'blab' to the injury of the School" (Hamlin to Butler, 12 June 1903, Central Files). Shortly thereafter, Hornbostel was replaced as Lecturer in Architecture by W.A. Delano, a Yale graduate who had been a special student at Columbia and was Diplômé from the Ecole des Beaux-Arts (Hamlin to Butler, 22 September 1903, Central Files).

64. Nominations for the constitution of the visiting committee were as follows: from the Alumni — B.W. Morris, H.M. Hewlett, A.A. Stoughton, M.J. O'Connor, A.M. Welch, R. Warren, L.F. Pilcher, E.P. Casey, R.D. Kohn; from the practitioners — G.B. Post, C.F. McKim, Cass Gilbert, P. Sawyer, H.R. Marshall, W.R. Mead, J.M. Carrere, Walter Cook; and from the Society of Beaux-Arts Architects — W.A. Boring, A.M. Howells, W.A. Delano, E.L. Tilton. In a postscript, Hamlin warned respecting the scope of responsibilities of the visiting committee:

They ought to be very carefully defined to prevent misunderstanding and possible officious meddling with what they are not really concerned with. In other words, this Committee may be either a very useful or a very officious and embarrasing institution. I would leave the appointment of Chairman to election by the Committee. I have reasons for thinking that the appointment of one certain person I have in mind as chairman is undesirable (Hamlin to Butler, 10 June 1903, Central Files).

Later, in a letter to President Butler (29 October 1903), Hamlin expanded his original list of nominees. To the Alumni he added: S.B. Colt, V.C. Griffith, S.W. Andrews, C.H. Aldrich, J.A. Tompkins and V.E. Macy. To the practitioners he added W.H. Russell. To the Society of Beaux-Arts Architects he added Whitney Warren, A.S.G. Taylor and Donn Barber.

65. Hamlin to Butler, 5 August 1903, Central Files.

66. Hamlin to Butler, 26 August 1903, Central Files. McKim had been at the American Academy in Rome during the summer.

67. Ibid.

68. Ibid.

69. Ibid.

70. Butler to McKim, 16 September 1903, Central Files.

71. Memorandum: Hamlin to Butler, 10 October 1903, Central Files.

tion; so that they may not fall into the mistake of imagining that their function is to interfere and find fault."[72] Later, responding to what were objections apparently raised by McKim to the effect that a committee of nine members representing three different groups would never agree upon any important or controversial subject, Hamlin asserted that

we are not looking to this committee for legislation but for the view of the profession. . . . such a committee would afford the means of keeping the profession informed as to what we are doing — of which they are still ignorant — and through them many of the offhand criticisms made by members of the profession would be discounted and made ineffective because this body, representing the practicing architects, would really be acquainted with what we are doing; while on the other hand, we should learn as it is hardly possible for us otherwise to do, what is being said and thought in the profession about the problems of education, and what are the needs and demands of the profession which we do not supply or which we meet imperfectly.[73]

Most importantly, the Visiting Committee was to bridge the gap between academics and practice. To this end, Hamlin suggested that if the Committee on Education were to deem it unwise to authorize such a Committee,[74] at least the Alumni Association of the School ought to be revived. Its Executive Committee then would be expected to furnish the desired means of contact with the active profession.[75]

Another aspect of the reorganization concerned the formation of a School and a Faculty of Fine Arts. Following its separation from the Faculty of Applied Science, the School of Architecture was brought under the direct administrative authority of the President as it had no Faculty of its own in the technical sense of the term. The School remained under the administrative rules of the Faculty of Applied Science but not under its authority: the head of the department performed the duties of a Dean and reported only to the President who represented the School in the University Council. In the *Columbia University Quarterly* for September, 1901, Hamlin had

presented a scheme and a plea for the formal recognition of the fine arts as a department of the university instruction and had suggested that the academic and theoretic branches of a complete course of art instruction could well be given in the university while leaving the studio work to be done in the existing schools of the city.[76]

It is fair to say that while the creation of the Visiting Committee cannot be viewed as having been a mere formality, the requirements of the department with respect to reorganization were manifestly clear all along. Furthermore, in light of the character of the Committee, the final restructuring was predictable in general outline. It is not inconsistent, therefore, that at least five months prior to the approval by the Committee on Education of a plan for reorganization, Butler suggested to John B. Pine, who was then clerk to the Trustees, that:

We might just as well go ahead and fill the Professorship of Architecture, if

72. Ibid. As if his insistence that the visiting committee "know its place" and act merely in an advisory capacity while the Administration of the School proceeded virtually independently, were not completely clear, Hamlin added a postscript:
In inviting the chosen architects to serve, I should much like to have it made known to them that this Committee has been constituted by the Trustees upon my suggestion: lest it be thought that the Trustees have constituted it on account of lack of confidence in the new acting head of the department. This would be a very unfortunate result of the realization of an idea which I have cherished for years but been unable to bring into being until now (Ibid.).

73. Hamlin to Butler, 29 October 1903, Central Files.

74. On November 4, 1903, the Committee on Education voted to constitute the visiting committee of: Grosvenor Atterbury, William A. Boring, John M. Carrere, Edward P. Casey, Walter Cook, Charles C. Haight, J. Monroe Hewlett, Charles F. McKim, Henry R. Marshall, Russell Sturgis and Lloyd Warren. Butler advised that the committee would have no formal organization and that the members should not feel obliged to confer with one another in groups or as a body, but that each should feel free to tender his personal opinion concerning the present status and future development of the School. The architects were charged with considering: the adequacy of the present organization and equipment of the department; the sufficiency and scope of the course of instruction, both theoretical and practical; and the best ways and means of relating the School and its work more closely to the architectural profession as represented in the City of New York and vicinity (Butler to members of the Visiting Committee of Architects, 4 November 1903, Central Files).

75. Hamlin to the Graduates and Former Students of the School of Architecture, 4 November 1903, Ware Collection, Avery Archives.

76. A.D.F. Hamlin, "For a Columbia School of Art," *Columbia University Quarterly*, 3 (September 1901), pp. 366-370.

the Committee is ready to act. I think we are all agreed that the first step must be the appointment as Professor and head of the School of a practicing architect of undoubted position and strong personality, leaving Hamlin, as chief of staff, to run the details of the Department.[77]

Butler's first choice for the head of the department was McKim, whom he believed he could secure only if he were to go about it "wisely and carefully," and his second choice was Carrère, of whose acceptance he was more certain.[78] While Pine agreed that action should be taken in the spring of 1904, "as longer delay must inevitably injure the School,"[79] he was not particularly enthusiastic about McKim, although he was willing to accept the opinion of the profession:

While I am not at all convinced that Mr. McKim will make a success, if appointed head of the school, the opinion of the profession is so unanimous in his favor, that I think we ought to make every effort to get him, and I have no doubt that our committee and the Board will concur in his appointment.[80]

That Butler was set on McKim is certain. After McKim had declined the position on the grounds that he was too busy and not necessarily the most appropriate candidate, Butler decided that the Professorship should be held in abeyance, "for if we cannot find just the man who suits us, we can at least start such a new system as is proposed very satisfactorily with our existing staff."[81] Subsequently, Hamlin was appointed Executive Head of the Department and, in 1911, Director. Guidelines for organizing the new School were extracted from individual directives contained in a confidential report to the President dated February, 1904.[82] Proceeding from the premise that the aim of a school of architecture must be to best train students for professional practice, a number of revisions were introduced.[83]

The first was the elimination of the strict four-year curriculum upon which Ware had insisted throughout his tenure. This was replaced by a program of indefinite duration according to which the requirements for the degree were stated in terms of points, enabling the student to proceed at his own pace and eliminating the problem of "back work." The degree was awarded upon successful completion of the requisite number of points in given categories, that is, when the student had reached a certain standard of excellence. The point system was intended to liberate the fourth year for intensive design work.[84]

Secondly, courses were modified to shift the emphasis of the curriculum to design, drawing, and office practice. In summers, the student was required to work in an office, to render one design program, and to write an essay or prepare a set of measured drawings. The study of history, which was to be couched in terms of its application to creative work in design, was considered a danger if undertaken for its own sake. It was feared that such study would lead to applying conventional solutions to particular problems rather than to exercising one's creativity.

Third, to help bridge the acknowledged gulf between the School and the profession at large, three new actions were taken:

Sixth Floor Studio, Avery Hall, ca. 1912.
Photo: GSAP Archive.

77. Butler to John B. Pine, 10 May 1904, Central Files.

78. Ibid.

79. Pine to Butler, 11 May 1904, Central Files.

80. Ibid.

81. Butler to Pine, 26 May 1904, Central Files.

82. Letters had been solicited and received from Atterbury, Warren, Marshall, Hewlett, Hastings, Haight, Cook, Casey, Carrere and Boring respecting reorganization. McKim presented his recommendations orally to Butler, and Post and Sturgis had not responded as of the publication. While the letters varied in their degree of detail, the thrust of the recommendations was much the same. *Confidential Report to the President* (February 1904).

83. Ibid. Also note that the following points are extracted from the *Confidential Report.*

84. "The School of Architecture, Columbia University," *American Architect and Building News,* 88 (December 30, 1905), pp. 212-213.

one, an alumni association was established with A.A. Stoughton *(Columbia, 1888)* the first president and J.M. Hewlett *(Columbia, 1890)* the first secretary; two, leading architects and decorative artists were invited to speak at the School, including Edwin Blashfield on "Tone and Color in the Masterpieces of Decorative Painting," Arnold Brunner on "Hospital Design," Henry Hornbostel on "The Influences of Modern Steel Framed Construction on Architectural Design," William Boring on "The Country House," J. Monroe Hewlett on "Fundamental Principles of Professional Ethics," and Grosvenor Atterbury on "The Administration of the Office;"[85] and three, the practice was introduced of having fourth-year design work judged by a jury of three, consisting of the instructor and two members of the profession.

Fourth, as a means of approximating actual office conditions[86] and of introducing healthy competition, which had been conspicuously absent during Ware's tenure, the *atelier* system of instruction in design, modeled after that of the Ecole, was introduced in 1905.[87] While instruction in elementary design and the history of architecture was given at the University, two *ateliers* downtown and a third in Havemeyer Hall were maintained by the University for instruction in advanced design. Charles McKim and Thomas Hastings were asked to direct the downtown *ateliers,* with the status of Professors in the University, with John Russell Pope and John V. Van Pelt as their respective associates. The drafting room on campus was directed by W.A. Delano *(Columbia, 1899),* assisted by A.H. Gumaer. In addition, advanced students had the option to enroll in the private *ateliers* headed by Hornbostel, Barber, Perkins, Warren, and Atterbury.[88]

Following the example of the Ecole, each student was permitted to elect the *atelier* in which he wished to complete his advanced design work. Representatives of the three *ateliers* were responsible for constituting the details of the design curriculum, and students' designs were judged competitively by a jury composed of professional architects and of instructors from each of the three *ateliers.* That practicing architects would sit on juries was intended to place the profession at large in a position of responsibility for determining the development of architectural education.

In broad outline, the organization of the design studios followed Ecole principles. However, the belief was widespread that Ecole methods were not entirely appropriate to American objectives in architectural education. Most significantly, the centralized, absolute control of the Ecole over taste and standards of design was rejected as a limitation on creativity.[89] Although Hamlin, like Ware before him, balked at the idea of a centralized school for the study of architecture and the fine arts as being absolutely anathema to the American democratic ideal, he endorsed the idea of collaborative work among various schools. Hamlin supported interschool competitions in which each school would be free to participate as it saw fit, but reiterated that "it would be a great misfortune if our art education, the whole country over, were ever subjected to the domination of any one body or institution —

85. *Columbia University Quarterly,* 6 (March 1904), pp. 196-198; 6 (June 1904), pp. 359-361; 7 (June 1905), pp. 375-377.

86. The nature of the rift between academic study and professional practice was one that constantly necessitated rearticulation, but the nature of the relation also required redefinition.

87. *American Architect and Building News,* 86 (November 12, 1904), p. 49. While the article announces that the *atelier* system had been adopted formally, in fact this did not occur until 1905.
Respecting the relative advantages to the *atelier* system, Hamlin commented:
I suppose the purpose of our new arrangement is to bring our men under the instruction of men who are practicing architects, and not mere theorists, and that it is expected that the new atelier *instructors will stand to their work and profession respectively...in carrying on actively a successful business practice, while giving to the drafting room a part of their time, not necessarily defined by an iron clad schedule of hours* (Hamlin to Butler, 6 May 1905, Central Files).

88. Butler to Hamlin, 9 December 1904, Central Files.

89. Hamlin, A.D.F., "The Influence of the Ecole des Beaux-Arts on our Architectural Education," *Architectural Record,* 23 (April 1908), pp. 241-247.

national, central or anything else." He believed that the Society of Beaux-Arts Architects and "Columbia cultivate different fields though they are side by side and sometimes overlap."[90]

In 1907, the Committee on Education of the American Institute of Architects put forth the possibility of holding interscholastic competitions among Harvard, M.I.T., Cornell, Columbia and Penn. The Directors of the five schools in collaboration with architects of the AIA would organize the competitions and act as juries.[91] In 1909, Columbia and Penn engaged in an interscholastic competition. Programs for a museum facade and a maritime customs house, prepared by Paul Cret of Penn, were completed by second and third year students respectively. The best designs of each school were judged by a jury composed of John Mead Howells, Austin Lord, Henry Hornbostel, and a representative of each school. Later the designs were exhibited at each school.[92]

Even by the first decade of the twentieth century, the study of architecture was considered to be a highly specialized pursuit requiring firm grounding in the liberal arts. For this reason, Ware and Hamlin had insisted on the integration of liberal arts courses within the architecture curriculum. However, the new concentration on design and the concomitant de-emphasis on history and on allied subjects not immediately related to professional practice necessitated that the candidate for admission have acquired background knowledge elsewhere. This requirement was intended in part to raise the intellectual calibre of the School. To this end, in 1906, the standards for admission to the program for the Bachelor of Architecture degree were stiffened. Students were required to present two years of college or scientific school work or the equivalent, including languages, ancient and medieval history, and allied subjects.[93]

Beginning with the academic year 1905–06, the School recognized two categories of students besides those pursuing the Bachelor of Architecture. Students who were unable to meet the two-year college prerequisite for the Bachelor of Architecture degree but who had had secondary school education and additional training in drawing and the elements of architecture were accommodated by a program leading to a professional Certificate of Proficiency. For this, the curriculum for the Bachelor's degree was modified only with respect to mathematics and engineering, for which a course in structural design based upon graphical statics and elementary mathematics was offered.[94] The second group was composed of non-matriculated students, who were admitted to any courses for which they could present satisfactory evidence of adequate previous training and experience (usually three years employment). Additionally, the University Council determined that work done by students in Paris under programs organized by the School of Architecture could be submitted as work toward a degree. The liberal nature of these provisions must not be underestimated:[95] the certificate program and the provision for special students ultimately made a degree accessible to those who otherwise would have been prevented from achieving it. Should they ever want to earn a professional degree, previously non-matricu-

Travel Sketch of the Church of St. Ours, August 11, 1908, William F. Lamb *(1906)*, Avery Archive.

90. Hamlin to Lloyd Warren, 11 December 1905, Central Files. Whereas Hamlin ardently endorsed decentralization, his was by no means the only view. Architects such as Austin Lord, who eventually would become the Director of the School, supported the contrary position. Indeed, the platform of the Society of Beaux-Arts Architects included the development of a national school.

91. *Columbia University Quarterly,* 11 (June 1909), p. 369.

92. *American Architect and Building News,* 87 (January 14, 1905), p. 9.

93. Ibid.

94. Hamlin to Butler, 3 November 1904, Central Files.

95. *American Architect and Building News,* 88 (November 18, 1905), p. 162.

lated students could present their work as qualifying for advanced standing in the degree program.[96]

Despite advances in the quality and scope of professional training at Columbia and at the other American schools, the reputation of the Ecole remained constant in American architectural circles. Indeed, both the number of Paris-bound students and the length of their stays dramatically increased even over the days when the dearth of American schools of architecture made study abroad imperative. Ruefully, the *Columbia Quarterly* observed that "the services rendered by the Ecole to American architecture have been so great, the fascination of the Parisian art atmosphere and student cafés is so engaging that it will be long, no doubt, before the tide turns, as someday it surely must." Nonetheless, Columbia began to enjoy a national reputation, and the *Columbia Quarterly* observed "the widening field from which the School is drawing its students, and into which it is carrying the name and reputation of the University."[97]

The School of Architecture was considered to be the nucleus for a future School of Fine Arts to be established with the National Academy of Design and the Metropolitan Museum of Art.[98] An arrangement with the National Academy of Design to provide instruction in drawing for fourth year students of architecture was the first step toward that goal. Intending to take up the matter with the Committee on Education during the summer, Butler asked Hamlin, in February of 1903, to prepare a prospectus for a School of Fine Arts.[99]

After approximately three years of consideration and deliberation respecting the appropriate means to improve instruction in architecture and the fine arts generally, in June of 1905, the Trustees formally resolved to establish a School of Fine Arts in cooperation with the National Academy of Design.[100] The plan for joint action by the University and the Academy had been approved by the Council of the National Academy.[101] While the proposal entailed the integration of the School of Architecture, the Department of Music (which had recently been separated from the Faculty of Philosophy), and the Academy of Design into a Faculty of Fine Arts, the University and the Academy were to retain their autonomy.[102] Nonetheless, the University was extremely anxious to be identified with the venture and therefore proposed that a building be erected on the Morningside campus to accommodate the several departments of the Faculty of Fine Arts, and possibly the administrative apparatus of the Academy. The scheme had idealistic underpinnings: its purpose was to offer the historical and critical study of art as a means to culture.[103] However, those who questioned the wisdom of introducing the fine arts into a university curriculum voiced major objections. To counter these objections, Hamlin maintained that: "not only has art education itself suffered by long exclusion from the universities, but the universities and their educational ideals have suffered through the exclusion of the art element, itself one of the most important factors in the history of culture."[104]

The period until 1912 can be described as a time of confusion

Travel Sketch of a dormer at Blois, Ely Jacques Kahn *(1907)*, Avery Archive.

96. *Columbia University Quarterly,* 8 (December 1905), pp. 80-82.

97. Ibid. See also, *American Architect and Building News,* 87 (April 28, 1905), p. 129.

98. Hamlin to Butler, 29 September 1903, Central Files.

99. Butler to Hamlin, 24 February 1903, Central Files. See also *American Architect and Building News,* 87 (April 22, 1905), p. 125 and 87 (April 28, 1905).

100. A.D.F. Hamlin Notes on Trustees Meeting of 5 June 1905, dated 7 June 1905, Central Files.

101. Clark, Eliot Candee, *History of the National Academy of Design 1825–1953* (New York: Columbia University Press, 1954), p. 153.

102. Ibid.

103. Pine to F.D. Millet, 17 January 1911, Central Files. In light of his historical bent, it is no wonder that Hamlin was so enthusiastic about the consolidation. Although design was fast becoming the focus of the architecture program, a School of Fine Arts, concentrating on history and theory rather than on technique would guarantee that the architecture school would not become merely a trade school. Hamlin's concern with scholarly study remained an issue, and indeed would become a central issue under the Directorship of Austin Lord.

104. A.D.F. Hamlin, Notes on Trustees Meeting of 5 June 1905, dated 7 June 1905, Central Files.

resulting from the demands of a new regime. Pressure from the profession at large and from the students to respond to changed views respecting the nature of architectural practice and education exacerbated the situation. Despite the fact that the School collaborated with other schools of architecture, expanded its scope and its degree program,[105] and proceeded rather determinedly with the overhaul of the curriculum in order that courses immediately related to design and professional practice would predominate, by 1911, rumblings of discontent focusing on the need to broaden work in design and to bring the School more closely in touch with the profession were evident. Cooperation with the National Academy of Design had proceeded unsatisfactorily as well. As a corollary, Hamlin's overly academic orientation met with sharp criticism.

Doubtful that the consolidation of the School of Fine Arts ever would occur given the diverse nature of the constituents, in November, 1911, Butler suggested the possibility of abrogating the agreement with the National Academy by mutual consent, of discontinuing the Faculty of Fine Arts as constituted, and of reinstating the School of Architecture under a director and an administrative board instead of under a full-fledged faculty. Acknowledging the failure of the venture, Butler stated that dissolving the institution would serve to "retrace the steps that we took hopefully but which events have not justified."[106] Although clearly aware of the problems, John Pine counselled that Butler's condemnation was somewhat misplaced. Pine insisted that the premise upon which the School of Fine Arts had been constituted — the contention that the fine arts have a place in a university — remained relevant. The failure of the proposition had more to do with there not having been a strong individual to head the Faculty than with the scheme's being inherently unworkable. Pine wrote:

If we could now appoint such a professor and also a competent man at the head of the Department of Architecture, the situation would be materially changed. As to the latter, it seems to me that the demand is imperative. We cannot afford to let architecture go from bad to worse as it must do under Hamlin, and I think we should go to work seriously at once to find the man we need.[107]

In 1914 the agreement between Columbia and the National Academy was dissolved by mutual consent, but in 1916 Columbia constituted its own School of Fine Arts with Hamlin as its Chairman.

Within the first ten years of this century, both the School of Architecture and Avery Library had outgrown their quarters. In 1912, the Library and the School moved into a new building donated by Samuel Putnam Avery, Jr., in honor of his parents and his brother, accordingly named Avery Hall.[108]

On June 23, 1890, Samuel Putnam Avery, public-spirited art collector and gallery owner, and his wife, Mary Ogden Avery, donated the library of their son Henry Ogden Avery to Columbia College. This bequest included a sizeable endowment to round out

Design for an Office Building, ca. 1896, George Tremaine Morse *(1896)*, Avery Archive.

105. In the fall of 1911, a course leading to the Bachelor's degree in Landscape Design and in 1912 a course in City Planning were offered.

106. Butler to Pine, 13 November 1911, Central Files.

107. Pine to Butler, 20 November 1911, Central Files.

108. An editorial in *American Architect and Building News*, 87 (April 8, 1905), p. 109, commented on the need for a building to accommodate the School of Architecture.

and maintain the collection, and to purchase more books. The conditions of the gift were as follows: first, the books should be kept in the same room; second, the Library must be non-circulating; third, there should be a tablet to state that the Library had been founded by the parents of Henry Ogden Avery in his memory; and fourth, a catalogue should be published and distributed free of charge from time to time. The Trustees accepted the conditions of the gift on October 6, 1890.[109]

The Library that Henry Avery had amassed consisted of approximately 2,000 volumes, some of which were quite notable, although as J.A. Schweinfurth observed:

It is not a collection of books every architect ought, or need have. It is a collection from which historical questions can be studied by the student, the architect, the critic, or the general public. The development of any building movement in any definite region can here be traced, its growth followed, its decadence and decay noted. It is an historical library. . . it is not a collection of scarce books to delight a bibliophile or of scarce and unique prints, but rather a library for the investigator and the student as well as the professional man.[110]

An advisory committee, consisting of Edward Robinson Smith, William Ware, and Russell Sturgis supervised the acquisition of books in the early years. Even at this time there was an expressed concern to build up a large collection of contemporary city planning materials. According to James Grote Van Derpool, the sixth Avery Librarian, Smith was the driving force behind "the scholarly development of Avery Library, and he directed the Library's influence throughout the architectural profession and academic circles in this country."[111]

A major purpose of the new building was to accommodate the Avery Collection, then housed in the Low Memorial Library. Additionally, on an upper floor in the new building, space was reserved for an exhibition gallery:

The building will be a library temporarily, but with many of the features of a museum. It will contain books; not only books to be read, but books to be seen; casts, models, photographs, engravings and other illustrations. An important feature might well be a collection of autograph drawings by architects and artists, similar to that which is a chief attraction of the library of the Ecole des Beaux-Arts in Paris, and which would serve as a monument to the men who have produced works of American architecture hardly less beautiful than those of the classic schools.[112]

Although the latter feature never was formally instituted, a collection of original 'autograph' drawings began to grow nonetheless. The importance of the consolidation of the School and the Library into one building is clear:

The greater part of the building will be used to give much needed relief to the Department of Architecture. This Department with its interesting record, its fine body of students, and its still finer body of alumni, is now inadequately and inconveniently housed, and the provision of ample and well-lighted space, in immediate proximity to the great sources of supply, will be of inestimable advantage to our students of architecture.[113]

109. *Catalogue of the Avery Architectural Library* (New York: Columbia College, 1895), pp. vi-vii. Admittance to the collection was to be governed by the general library rules.

110. Schweinfurth, J.A., "The Avery Memorial Library," *American Architect and Building News*, 51 (1896), pp. 15-16.

111. Edward Robinson Smith was the first Avery librarian. Van Derpool, J.G. "The Avery Memorial Architectural Library" in Rohdenburg, *The History of the School*, pp. 76-77.

112. "The New Building of the Avery Library," *Columbia University Quarterly*, 13 (June 1911), p. 286.

113. Ibid., pp. 286-287.

The completion and occupation of Avery Hall provided a new impetus to restructure the School, including the appointment of a new Director. In early 1912, a number of practicing architects were considered for the position, including Henry Rutgers Marshall, Austin Willard Lord, George Cary *(Columbia, 1885),* Lloyd Warren *(Columbia, 1891),* Samuel B.T. Trowbridge *(Columbia, 1886),* J. Monroe Hewlett *(Columbia, 1890),* and William Delano *(Columbia, 1899).* Most important, however, was John Galen Howard, then at the University of California at Berkeley and considered to be "preeminently the man to take charge of the direction of the school."[114]

Butler had solicited Howard's advice respecting the reorganization of the School. After careful study of the problems plaguing the School over the years, Howard thought that the primary need was not for sweeping reorganization but for proper coordination of its present elements, revitalization of its functions, and expansion of its field of activities. And, "above all, it should come into closer touch with active practice."[115] Howard proposed that the first and essential step was to secure not merely a Professor of Architecture but a Director who was a practicing architect. The Director's role "should be rather that of vital link between the School and the outer professional world, in touch with one as with the other, and stimulating both."[116] To accomplish this bridging of what seemed after ten years to be an unbridgeable gap between the profession and the School, Howard recommended that the Director be given free reign to carry out a broad program of development.[117]

Howard called attention to the unique position Columbia occupied with respect to its location in New York City, and the unique position it would occupy with respect to architectural education in general. Although he resisted becoming intimately involved with the situation at Columbia, preferring to remain at Berkeley, Howard freely gave advice on restructuring the School.[118]

Several factors made it imperative that the search for a strong director be intensified: Howard's decision to decline the Directorship; pressure from the students and the architectural community to replace Hamlin's theoretical approach with a more professionally oriented training; Hamlin's desire to give up the administrative operation of the School; and the pending dissolution of the Faculty of Fine Arts. When Austin Willard Lord was appointed Director, the search for a prominent architect to head the School of Architecture was brought to a close, at least for the moment. The Trustees believed they had completed the work begun in 1905 upon McKim's decision to decline the directorship.

114. Pine to Butler, 11 April 1912, Central Files.

115. John Galen Howard to Butler, 15 February 1912, Central Files.

116. Ibid.

117. Ibid. Howard stated:

The curriculum as outlined in the 'Bulletin of Information' seems excellent so far as it goes; but undoubtedly the atelier system, already recognized in principle, should be much expanded and strengthened. With extension come dangers and uncertainties which must be met by a strong administration of the school buttressed perhaps by an advisory board of representative architects. I have found on all sides the most cordial desire to cooperate on the part of the prominent architects of the city; but effectual cooperation on their part can be brought about and made to build up the Columbia school, only by the opening out of the school's heart to them, by taking them into its counsels, by identifying them with it.

118. Ibid. Howard further advised:

The position and opportunities of your School of Architecture are (and must become more so) materially different from those of any other. It should aim to become the dominant factor in architectural education in this country, extending its influence in every direction, and making for a distinctive American character. It has ready to its hand one of the most vital forces in the Beaux-Arts Society work whose headquarters are at its doors. It is, of course, desireable, and it is not necessary for the University to yield anything essential to its identity or its authority in order to take advantage of this great force. Both the School and the Society have everything to gain by closer intimacy. The School needs the vital out-of-door enthusiasm of the Society, just as the Society needs the mature staying power, sanity and thoroughness of the University.

Apropos 1900: New York and the Metropolitan Ideal

Robert A. M. Stern and
Gregory Gilmartin

No other city in the world is improving itself at the rate which New York is doing. We have under way tunnels, bridges, reservoirs, public buildings, new driveways and new parks, the total cost of which is literally stupendous.

It is all improving the metropolis on a scale and at a rapid pace not equalled anywhere else in the world. Ten years hence New York will be transformed. Ours is a wonderful city to advance.

From the *New York Sun* quoted in *The American Architect and Building News,* July 6, 1901, pp. 5-7.

Architects, historians and the general public share an admiration for the period at the turn of the nineteenth into the twentieth century, a period which has been described in French alternatively as the "fin de siecle," and "La Belle Epoque," and in English as the "Mauve Decades" and the "Banquet Years."[1] The admiration for the aura and artifacts of the two decades that begin in 1890 began almost as they ended; the horrors of the First World War so completely transformed the West's perception of itself and its values that the era immediately preceding that War — though heavily intertwined with its origins — has much more frequently been seen at least by literary and art critics as the last golden age of civilization, the like of which we shall never see again.

Although some of the interest in La Belle Epoque is rooted in nostalgia, such is not necessarily bad: it is surely an appropriate sentiment for the era of Proust, James, and Wharton. Such nostalgia reflects as well an understanding of the city's symbolic role as cultural artifact. As Nathan Silver *(Columbia, 1958)* has noted in his book *Lost New York,* a pioneering examination of the City's architectural heritage which began as an exhibit at Columbia's School of Architecture,

The Past is important because a sense of continuity is necessary to people — the knowledge that some things have a longer than mortal existence. Cities, as the greatest works of man, provide the deepest assurance that this is so... by revealing and asserting the sometimes hidden mysteries of their being. Cities are places where different styles converge and mix. As a cultural manifestation, this may be a city's greatest function — its ability to present the full record of the past. Lewis Mumford put it most succinctly of all: 'In the city, time becomes visible.'[2]

But the nostalgia for the particular spirit of 1900 goes beyond what Andrew Saint has recently characterized as the search for "cultural coherence that has led people to idolize Periclean Athens or Florence under the Medici." More to the point, Saint goes on to observe, "are plain, perceptible facts of completeness and variety" which foster our admiration for the great cities of 1900.[3] In short, architects and urbanists look to the architecture and urbanism of fin de siecle London, Paris and New York in order to better understand the origins of the twentieth century's characteristic urban form, a form best described by the term "metropolitanism," a form wherein city and suburb are combined in one complex, collective, governmental and social system supplying in microcosm all the services and benefits of the nation as a whole. While the term is somewhat loose, it bespeaks an architecture and a society that take its cities seriously, that honors its responsibilities to the public

1. See Thomas Beer, *The Mauve Decade: American Life at the End of the Nineteenth Century* (New York: 1926); also Roger Shattuck, *The Banquet Years* (Garden City, New York: Doubleday, 1961).

2. Nathan Silver, *Lost New York* (New York: Weathervane Books, 1967), p. 9.

3. Andrew Saint, review of Alastair Service, *London 1900,* in *Journal of the Society of Architectural Historians,* 39 (December 1980), pp. 327-382.

realm.[4] Herbert Croly best defined the metropolitan ideal when he wrote in 1903 that

In order to be actually metropolitan, a city must not only reflect large national tendencies, but it must sum them up and transform them. It must not only mirror typical American ways of thought and action, but it must anticipate, define and realize national ideals. A genuine metropolis must be, that is, both a concentrated and selected expression of the national life.[5]

Despite dramatic changes since the turn of the century — largely as a result of the automobile — the fact remains that the spirit of metropolitanism as Croly outlined it once again exerts its magic on a considerable section of the population. Many of the most generally admired and characteristic elements of such major cities as New York are those built around 1900, when the destiny of cities was seen as inextricably linked to that of an optimistic and progressive civilization. The metropolitan ideal fostered the interaction between the prevailing modes of architectural thought — the classical, technological and vernacular — to produce an appropriately complex expression of the modern condition, a condition born of diversity, of special interests, of energy, vitality, and a passion for excellence.[6]

It is the intention of this essay to begin fleshing out an account of the evolution of New York's architecture and urbanism in the age of metropolitanism, the fifty or so year period between the nation's Centennial in 1876 and the collapse of its economic activity in the early 1930's.[7] Clearly, such a task is daunting in scope, and anything approaching a full account would extend well beyond the boundaries of this essay. Nonetheless, given the general lack of available material devoted to an overall discussion of the entire period, to focus on one moment or phase of metropolitanism cannot suffice. Thus the essay is divided into two unequal parts: the first, shockingly brief, undertakes to paint with broad brush strokes the general character of New York in the Age of Metropolitanism and covers the entire period between 1876 and 1933. The second part, "New York: 1890–1915," concentrates on the character of the new buildings and public places built in New York during these years and emphasizes where appropriate the role played by Columbia in shaping the city.[8]

PART I: NEW YORK IN THE AGE OF METROPOLITANISM: 1876 – 1933

New York City is such a central force in American thought that we tend to think it has always been a major American metropolis. In fact, New York was not even a major city in colonial days or the early years of the Republic. It did not achieve its prominence until well into the nineteenth century when, largely as the result of its ideal situation with respect to national and international commerce — its great all-year-round port and splendid water and rail connections to the interior of the continent — it underwent a period of staggering economic and physical growth. In the fifty years following 1825, the city's population increased eightfold. At the end of the century, in 1898, when New York City achieved its ultimate physical size by annexing the Bronx, Brooklyn, Queens,

4. Alastair Service, *London 1900* (New York: Rizzoli, 1980); Franco Borsi and Ezio Godoli, *Paris 1900* (Brussels: M. Vokaer, 1976). Grace M. Mayer, *Once Upon a City* (New York: MacMillan, 1958), is a pioneering study of New York at the turn of the century, but primarily a social rather than architectural history.

5. Herbert Croly, "New York as the American Metropolis," *Architectural Record,* 13 (March 1903), pp. 193–206.

6. These themes or "Modes" are discussed in my articles, "Notes on American Architecture in the Waning of the Petroleum Era," *G.A. Document 1980,* pp. 6–11; "Post-Profligate Architecture," *A + U American Architecture: After Modernism,* 1981, pp. 12–17; "Modernism and Postmodernism" in Helmuth Gesollpointer, Angela Hareiter, Laurids Ortiner, editors, *Design ist Unsichtbar* (Osterreiches Institut Für Visuelle Gestaltung, Locker Verlag, 1981), pp. 259–272.

7. There are a few recent discussions of New York's urbanism in addition to those cited above: Harvey Kantor, *Modern Urban Planning in New York City: Origins and Evolution, 1890–1933* (PhD. diss. New York University, 1971), and "The City Beautiful in New York," *New York Historical Society Quarterly Bulletin,* 57 (April 1975), pp. 148–171; Christopher Tunnard and Henry Hope Reed, "The Vision Spurned: Classical New York," *Classical America,* 1 (1971), pp. 31–41 and 1 (1972), pp. 10–19; Henry Hope Reed, *The Golden City* (Garden City, N.Y.: Doubleday, 1959); Mel Scott (*American City Planning Since 1890* (Berkeley: University of California Press, 1971).

8. No work of scholarship can be truly objective — even should one want it to be. An author's biases always affect the final synthesis of his material into a cohesive and compelling text. So it must be stated that this account is intended as an homage to my city, the only city I have ever lived in, and the only one I know well. New York continually gives me more than I can ever repay. I am pleased to be writing this essay at a time when New York's "fortunes," as measured in terms of its self-esteem and that of others, are higher than at any time I can remember, perhaps as high as they were in its Metropolitan age. Yet I do not think we love our city today as much as those who put it together from scattered villages and open land eighty years ago. Perhaps we love our city less because it seems so complete that we take it for granted; perhaps, because it seems to be falling apart physically and socially, we feel helpless before the forces of its destruction. On the other hand, because we have lost the capacity to imagine on the grand scale commensurate with its problems, we may be hastening the city's demise. For many reading this, the past may seem brighter and more optimistic than the present. Perhaps it was.

A further note. Though this essay is the product of an unimaginably intense ninety-day blitz, it has its origins in two earlier and very modest efforts which I would not mention did they not somehow illuminate the relationship between city and university which is so much at the heart of the School's Centennial efforts. The first was a seminar report and paper prepared in 1960 for Professor Dwight C. Miner's senior seminar in American History in Columbia College, in which I attempted to establish a relationship between the evolution of Manhattan's plan and the architectural character that emerged from it. The second was a course on the evolution of New York's architecture and urbanism which I taught at Professor Romaldo Giurgola's invitation during my first year on the GSAP faculty in 1970–71.

and Staten Island, it had a population of 3,100,000, half of whom were foreign born.[1]

The story of New York as a modern metropolis begins around 1876, when the city, enriched by the Civil War and Reconstruction, and in the thrall of what John Dewitt Warner termed "the capital tendency of wealth and art, the flow of each toward the point where the greatest amount of it is already gathered,"[2] began to assume its position as a national center of commerce and culture. By 1903, Herbert Croly could write that New York

is undoubtedly on the road to becoming the most national and the least suburban of American cities, the city to which men will be attracted in proportion as their enterprises, intellectual or practical, are far-reaching and important... In the making of a metropolis, every part of the country must contribute a portion of its energies and talent..."[3]

Caught up in the burst of activity that followed America's Centennial, acutely sensitive to the era's paradoxical process of expansion through consolidation and the need for a "national" cultural expression, New York's artists and architects developed almost at once a sense of both a lost past and a new, almost unimaginably bountiful future. The artifacts of pre-industrial America were suddenly rediscovered, as artists and architects struggled to accomodate their heritage to the pressures of tremendous growth, to transform the cultural and commercial programs of the day into glorious monuments commensurate with the already archetypal stature of those of the past.[4]

While the pre-industrial past was seen as a stable icon, the political democracy, economic capitalism and social heterogeneity of the present were viewed as continually changing. Not surprisingly, in such a period of social and cultural flux, the traditions of the past and their expression in art and architecture were seen as stabilizing influences on current production.

The pattern of growth and consolidation that affected the nation as a whole affected its principal cities, particularly New York, and the host of new institutions then founded; principal among them the Metropolitan Museum, The American Museum of Natural History, and The Metropolitan Opera Company. The city's principal college, Columbia, consolidated by affiliating with the College of Physicians and Surgeons while expanding into a major university with the establishment of professional schools and affiliated colleges.

Most importantly, the city itself expanded its borders as it consolidated its role as cultural, economic and communications capital of the nation. In the late 1870's and early 1880's a number of major technological developments were introduced in New York that would help ensure the city's leading position as the nation's commercial center: in March 1876, the Bell Telephone Company opened its first exchange; in 1882 Edison began to supply the city with electricity. In 1878 the steam elevated railroad transformed the city's sense of its own geography, while the completion of the Brooklyn Bridge in 1883 announced a new era of growth for the twin cities of New York and Brooklyn, an event comparable in

I am indebted to early discussions with John Massengale for the overall character of this investigation; Massengale and I propose to collaborate on its further development into a book with Gregory Gilmartin (*Columbia College, 1981*), whose diligent research and mastery over the written word have permitted this essay to come to fruition so quickly; Gilmartin began as my assistant but quickly revealed himself more than my equal. Ours has been a genuine and stimulating collaboration. Invaluable though the contributions of my colleagues have been, I alone bear the full responsibilities for the final effort, scholarly warts, interpretative *faux pas* and all.

R.A.M.S.

1. John A. Krout, "Framing the Charter," in Allen Nevins and John Krout, editors, *The Greater City: New York, 1898– 1948* (New York: Columbia University Press, 1948).

2. John Dewitt Warner, "Matters that Suggest Themselves," *Municipal Affairs*, 2 (March 1898), p. 123.

3. Croly, "New York as the American Metropolis," *Architectural Record*, 13 (March 1903), pp. 193-206.

4. See Vincent Scully, *The Shingle Style and the Stick Style* (New Haven and London: Yale University Press, revised edition, 1971); Richard Guy Wilson, *Charles F. McKim and the Development of the American Renaissance: A Study of Architecture and Culture* (Ph.D Diss., University of Michigan, 1972).

importance to that of the trans-continental railroad's completion in 1869 for the nation as a whole.

The magnitude of New York's technological advances was equalled by a tremendous growth in human resources as a result of the wave of immigration which touched its shores between 1880 and the First World War. Very many of the immigrants chose to remain in the city. Their presence, in combination with the native stock, gave New York the distinctly cosmopolitan character that was, and remains, its most obvious distinction. John F. Sprague, describing *New York the Metropolis* in 1893, observed that the diversity of the city's architecture may be attributable to the diversity of the nationalities who come to New York and

stay long enough to leave some impression of their manners and customs. Hence, with a great, throbbing, ever increasing, cosmopolitan population and a conglomeration of races and ideas, a diversity in the architecture is a natural result.[5]

The architectural spirit of the 1880's in New York was itself cosmopolitan; individual buildings represented an eclectic design process usually informed by an associational interpretation of the program and of the building's desired character.[6]

It is precisely this diversity of culture and architecture in the 1870's and 1880's that triggers the reaction of the 1890's and after; that is to say, the call for a uniform classicism must be seen at least in part, Richard Wilson has pointed out,

as a response to new wealth and to new building material and methods, but also a response to the need for order and discipline in American architecture. The American Renaissance embodied the principles of greatness and timelessness; it gave a national architectural style to America that could be the background for a great civilization.[7]

The eclecticism of the 1870's and 1880's, comingling and synthesizing a variety of historical styles in a given work and romantically tending to equate novelty with genius, gave way to a greater emphasis on historical prototypes and stylistic purity; a transformation which reflected the twin beliefs that America was the heir to Western civilization, and that the spiritual life of the nation could be elevated by an art and architecture which itself incorporated elements of the ideal.[8]

Just as the diversity of the culture of the 1880's triggered the urge to seek a more singular or "composite" expression in the 1890's, so too did the technological innovations of the 1870's and 1880's lead to the partial undoing of the city in the 1920's and 1930's, as the automobile and telecommunications each diminished the necessity for the massive, centralized concentrations of population that gave New York its particular energy.

The architectural and urban history of New York in its metropolitan age extends through a cycle of three phases, each emphasizing an aspect of the urban condition present to a lesser degree in the other two: cultural cosmopolitanism, political and economic consolidation, and functional pragmatism. The three phases of New York's metropolitan era also correspond to the

5. John F. Sprague, *New York the Metropolis* (New York: 1893), p. 36.

6. See Carroll L.V. Meeks, "Wright's Eastern Seaboard Contemporaries; Creative Eclecticism in the United States Around 1900," in *Acts of the Twentieth International Congress of the History of Art* (Princeton: 1963), pp. 64-77; also, Harvey Kantor, *Modern Urban Planning in New York City, Origins and Evolution, 1890–1933* (Ph.D. diss., New York University, 1971), pp. 21-26.

7. Wilson, *Charles F. McKim and the Development of the American Renaissance*, p. 339.

8. Richard Guy Wilson, "The Great Civilization," *American Renaissance, 1876–1917*, catalog of an exhibit at the Brooklyn Museum (New York: Pantheon, 1979), pp. 28-30, 57-58.

general cycle of metropolitan development advanced by Henry Isham Hazelton, who wrote in 1924 that

a metropolis grows first by its natural expansion, then leaps forward by adding large areas to itself, taking into the city overnight many villages and settlements; and thereupon, proceeds to consolidate its position by filling up the intervening area with rows of houses, stores and factories.[9]

The first or "cosmopolitan" era of New York's metropolitanism extends from 1876 to 1890; the second period, the "composite" era extends from 1890 to 1915; the third, the era of "convenience" from 1915 to 1933.

The first stage of New York's Metropolitan Age is one in which the cosmopolitanism of the population is mirrored in the outlook of its leading artists and architects as well as its influential citizenry, the newly rich corporate barons who saw the New York of the 1870's and before as little more than a provincial backwater and proceeded to catapult the city into a position of prominence through the establishment of cultural institutions deemed fundamental to a city which might be described today as "world-class."

In 1876 the city was only beginning to expand beyond its historic core (portions of the Bronx alone having been annexed in 1876). This expansion was made possible by the opening of elevated railroads along Sixth and Third Avenues in 1878, for the first time providing easy access to the upper island and thereby providing the low-income worker with a reasonable alternative to the hopelessly overcrowded conditions of the tenement districts on the lower East Side. The rowhouses of the upper West Side, the district between 72nd and 106th Streets known as the West End, characterized by a dialogue between the unity of the row and the individual house, provide the fullest expression of cosmopolitanism on a domestic scale.[10]

The era of cosmopolitanism was preeminently, however, an age of independent monuments, best exemplified by the Brooklyn Bridge, completed in 1883. The bridge provided the city with its first direct connection to a major land mass (although Brooklyn was itself a city on an island, albeit a much larger one). Like the elevated railroad, it supplied a major avenue for the city's expansion, opening up a vast land area for residential development in close proximity to what was still the city's business and governmental center in Lower Manhattan. Though the bridge tied the two cities together, its very poetry resides in its ability to soar free of its context and to be seen as an independent object apart, a freedom reinforced at the symbolic level by the aspirational Gothic gateways of its piers. At the practical level the bridge's functional aloofness was only too obvious to the commuters forced to cope daily with its absolutely unconsidered connections to the cities at either end.[11]

The age of cosmopolitanism coincides also with the development of Columbia College's midtown campus at Madison Avenue and 49th Street and its emergence from the status of a local college for commuting students to a university with a national outreach. Here too the ideals of the era were clearly to be seen: the College

9. Henry Isham Hazelton, *The Boroughs of Brooklyn and Queens, Counties of Nassau and Suffolk* (New York: Lewis Historical Publishing Co., 1925), p. 380.

10. See Montgomery Schuyler, "The Small City House in New York," *Architectural Record*, 8 (April–June 1899), pp. 357-388.

11. Alan Trachenberg, *Brooklyn Bridge: Fact and Symbol* (New York: 1965).

campus was a loose cluster of buildings around a garden, most of them designed by Charles C. Haight in the Ruskinian Gothic manner *(fig. 1, 2)*. Although the Gothic style related vaguely to the adjoining St. Patrick's Cathedral and perhaps to the Oxbridge tradition, in all likelihood it was merely the expression of a romantic view of scholarship divorced from the public life of the city, and of the widely held admiration for contemporary English ideas. Unlike the Gothic of Oxbridge, the campus had no sense of collective expression; no grand open court and no particularly strong attitude toward the block pattern of the city.[12]

By 1890, the cosmopolitan city reached its fullest and conclusive expression with the new Croton Water System, capping the series of technological innovations that made the vast scale of the city's expansion possible, Stanford White's Madison Square Garden, and the selection of Heins and La Farge to build the Cathedral of St. John The Divine. Madison Square Garden was perhaps the ultimate expression of cosmopolitanism — a wildly eclectic pleasure palace on an unprecedented scale, combining restaurants, theaters, and a hall for horse shows.[13] Its financial difficulties reflected the anachronism of an enterprise built almost solely for the elite; the ambitions of the very rich had exceeded their grasp, and White was soon called upon to devise spectacles for less exclusive audiences. The competition for St. John The Divine and the scheme selected exemplify the cosmopolitan era, even as the building's subsequent history reflects the new ideals of the consolidated city. The decision to follow standard ecclesiastical orientation, thereby facing the building west rather than south, made only after the 1889 competition,[14] deprived the cathedral of a forecourt and of any dialogue with the city at large, while its exotic and associationally evocative synthesis of forms failed as an expression of faith. The adoption of Ralph Adams Cram's more explicitly Gothic design in 1911 reflects the new era's predilections for greater stylistic purity and more legible form; the chapels of the chevet, dedicated to the patron saints of the city's immigrants, honor the composite city's ideal of the homogenizing melting-pot.

By the 1890's, the stage was set for the new era, whose city planning ideals were perhaps most clearly and publicly expressed by Edward Bellamy in his book *Looking Backward 2000 – 1887* (1888) which described a new kind of city with

broad streets, shaded by trees, and lined with fine buildings, . . . large open squares filled with trees, among which statues glistened and fountains splashed. . . and Public buildings of a colossal size and an architectural grandeur unparalleled.[15]

We will defer discussion of New York's second Metropolitan phase, its era of consolidation, until part two of this essay, and go on in this introduction to survey the third phase of the city's development, its era of convenience, which extends from about 1915 until the early 1930's. It is an era in which the consolidated city, growing at an unprecedented pace, begins to confront its massive scale and the massive improvements needed to remedy its shortcomings in the areas of housing, transportation and such public

Top: fig. 1 Hamilton Hall, Columbia College Midtown Campus, 1880, Charles Coolidge Haight. Photo: Columbiana Collection.

Above: fig. 2 Library Reading Room, Columbia College Midtown Campus, 1884, Charles Coolidge Haight.
Photo: Columbiana Collection.

12. Haight may have owed his commission in part to his father, the Rev. Benjamin I. Haight, a prominent member of the Episcopal Clergy and a trustee of Columbia College from 1843 to 1847. See Sarah B. Landau, *Edward T. and William A. Potter: American High Victorian Architects, 1855 – 1901* (Ph.D. diss., New York University, 1978), p. 15.

13. See Mariana Griswold Van Rensselaer, "The Madison Square Garden," *The Century,* 47 (March, 1894), pp. 732-747.

14. "The Cathedral Plans," *Architecture and Building,* 15 (Dec. 26, 1891), p. 324.

15. Quoted in Wilson, *American Renaissance,* p. 88.

places as parks. It is a time when concern for the city as a monumental artifact gives way to concern for its very survival as a workplace and a habitable environment, when the emphasis shifts from civic improvements to city planning, when declining immigration results in a reduced pool of cheap labor and forces a reconsideration of the scale of public and private accomodation and the problems of physical maintenance of buildings and public places. It is an era in which labor-saving devices are introduced to the domestic realm and the office, devices which, together with the automobile, transform the character of urban life by enabling vast numbers of city dwellers to take full advantage of what is meant by the term "metropolitan scale" for the first time, and causing the undoing of the city's metropolitan scale as a vastly larger land mass, a region, is made accessible for urban and suburban development. Most importantly, it is an era in which innovations in electronic communication reduce the role of cities themselves: radio, the talking movie, and later television replace the live theatre as a principal entertainment form, while improvements in telecommunications appear to lessen the need for people to concentrate themselves in a small area. Thus the very nature of the technological advances that made the metropolis what it was at its peak ultimately caused its decline. With the inauguration of a new, far more physically diffuse concept of urbanism — the concept of the region — the metropolitan city is reduced to a mere participant in a wider political and economic realm.

The era of convenience is quite appropriately an era of city planning: it opens with the enaction of laws to control the height and bulk of buildings as well as the uses land may be put to;[16] it closes with a sweeping reform of the laws that control multiple dwellings for the rich and poor alike and with the first formulation of a comprehensive physical plan for the region, one in which the skills of "scientific" planning are combined with the "City Beautiful" movement's last burst of artistic passion.[17]

The important buildings of the age of convenience often combine commercial and institutional or cultural uses; they are "working monuments." The skyscraper is the preeminent exemplar of the age, a building type whose greatest flowering begins with the Woolworth Building of 1913 — a cathedral of commerce — and concludes with a veritable cannonade of corporate towers in the late 1920's, these memorializing the Daily News, McGraw-Hill, the Chrysler Corporation, the Bank of Manhattan Company, cities Service, and the Radio Corporation of America.[18] The skyscrapers of the 1920's embody the remarkable synthesis between the rationalism of technique, the romance of symbolic aspiration, and the need to provide decent, efficient working environments that gives this era its particular character. Never since the completion of the original Rockefeller Center have concerns for natural light and ventilation been taken so carefully into account in the design of tall buildings, never since has the concept of the metropolitan city, the city at once cosmopolitan, monumental and convenient, been so perfectly realized.[19] Other achievements of the era, such as Robert Moses' parkways system to Jones Beach[20]

16. Commission on Building Districts and Restrictions, *Final Report* (New York: 1916); Kantor, *Modern Urban Planning in New York City*, pp. 165-229; Mel Scott, *American City Planning Since 1890* (Berkeley: University of California Press, 1971), pp. 153-161.

17. Committee on the Regional Plan of New York and its Environs, *The Graphic Regional Plan*, I (New York: 1929); Thomas Adams, Assisted by Harold M. Lewis and Lawrence M. Orton, *The Building of the City*, II (New York: 1931); Kantor, *Modern Urban Planning in New York City*, pp. 230-327; Mel Scott, *American City Planning Since 1890*, pp. 261-265, 287-294.

18. See Winston Weisman, "New York and the Problem of the First Skyscraper," *Journal of the Society of Architectural Historians*, 12 (March 1953), pp. 13-21, and "A New View of Skyscraper History," in Edgar Kaufman, ed. *The Rise of an American Architecture* (New York: Praeger, 1970), pp. 115-160; Arnold L. Lehman, *The New York Skyscraper: A History of its Development, 1870–1939* (Ph.D. diss., Yale University, 1974); Rosemarie Haag Bletter and Cervin Robinson, *Skyscraper Style: Art Deco New York* (New York: Oxford University Press, 1975); Carl W. Condit, *American Building* (Chicago: University of Chicago Press, 1968) Chapter IX, "The New York Skyscraper," pp. 114-119; Manfredo Tafuri, "New-Babylon: Das New York Der Zwanzigerjahre und die Suche nach dem Amerikanismus," *Metropolis 3: Amerikanismus, Skyscraper und Ikonografie* (whole issue of Architese. No. 20, 1976), pp. 12-24; Vincent Scully, *American Architecture and Urbanism* (New York: Praeger, 1969); Manfredo Tafuri, Francesco Dal Co, *Modern Architecture* (New York: Harry N. Abrams, 1979), Chapter IV, "Architecture and City in the United States, 1870–1910," pp. 50-82, Chapter XIII, "Architecture and City in the United States: The Progressive Era and the New Deal, 1910–1940," pp. 221-245.

19. Carol Herselle Krinsky, *Rockefeller Center* (New York: Oxford University Press, 1978).

20. Robert A. Caro, *The Power Broker* (New York: Knopf, 1974).

and the large scale housing proposals of Andrew Jackson Thomas, as well as the Waldorf Astoria Hotel, and the River House apartments[21] — also combine these characteristics; a sense of workable, manageable grandeur and self-confidence that looks back to the apogee of the metropolitan era and forward to the more democratic if less imaginative functionalism of the post-World War II era. This synthesis is perhaps most succinctly stated on the cornerstone of Hampshire House on Central Park South, which proclaims the hostelry to be dedicated to "yesterday's charm and tomorrow's convenience."

The completion of the George Washington Bridge in 1931, the first Hudson River crossing on a scale commensurate with the River's, can be seen not only as an appropriate culmination of the entire metropolitan age, whose opening is best symbolized by the Brooklyn Bridge of 1883, but as the opening chord of its antithesis, the Regional Era of 1930–1975.[22] While poetry triumphed over logical planning at the Brooklyn Bridge, the opposite is true of the George Washington; the decision to abandon Cass Gilbert's design of a romantic and expressive masonry skin encasing the towers and to leave their steel structure exposed marks the end of an era of rhetorical poetics and the inauguration of one of matter-of-fact realism; the synthesis between rationalism and romanticism gives way to one of structural and social engineering. Fifty years later, as the city looks back on its age of idealized materialism with less and less affection and more and more dismay, the utopistic pragmatism of the era of suburbanizing regionalism seems increasingly the embodiment — both the symptom and cause — of the collapse of our urban environment.

PART II: AT THE APOGEE OF METROPOLITANISM:
NEW YORK 1890–1915

"Architecture, like government, is about as good as a community deserves." Lewis Mumford, *Sticks and Stones,* 1924, pp. 150-151.

The second phase of New York's cycle of metropolitanism begins about 1890, at a time when, as Charles Lockwood has observed, "New Yorkers…had to face, not avoid, the very nearly uncontrolled growth that had been altering the area of the city that had long been built up."[1]

For the nation as a whole, the period 1890–1915, which might be described as its Imperial Age, was one of intense geographical consolidation at home (the growth of cities, the closing of the frontier), and physical expansion abroad (the acquisition of the "protectorates" in the Caribbean and South Pacific). It was also an era of economic expansion and consolidation, though those might seem mutually exclusive. With major natural resources beginning to be tapped, the monopolist corporations solidified their control over them and fueled a burgeoning production-based economy on a scale hitherto unimagined. "Suffice it to say," Herbert Croly wrote in 1903,

that the 'skyscrapers' of New York are as much filled with the offices of

21. Robert Stern, "With Rhetoric: The New York Apartment House," *VIA,* 4 (1980), pp. 78-111.

22. For Gilbert's project, see *American Architect,* 131 (February 6, 1927), p. 169.

1. Charles Lockwood, *Manhattan Moves Uptown* (Boston: Houghton Mifflin, 1976), p. 289.

corporations, which conduct a business in other parts of the country, as Fifth Avenue is filled with the residences of capitalists who made their money in the West. New York is steadily attracting a large proportion of the best business ability in the country, not only as a matter of business convenience, but just as much because of the exceptional opportunity it offers to its favored inhabitants of making and spending money. [2]

For New York the two and one half decades between 1890 and 1915 were a period of intense physical and political consolidation, culminating locally in the creation of greater New York in 1898, an event which Croly observed, "touched public pride..." and resulted in an "awakening of municipal vanity. Thus neither is it fanciful," Croly further mused,

to trace some connection between the aroused public spirit of the citizens of New York and the outburst of national feeling which accompanied and followed the Spanish War. For...New York is national or nothing, and whatever intensifies and consolidates national life also quickens and consolidates the growth of public spirit in New York. [3]

It was a period of corporate, mercantile and institutional consolidation as well, a time when the city was beginning to have a sense of itself as a metropolis on the scale of London or Paris, a "cosmopolis" or world capital, to use Moses King's term. [4] It was in this period that New York began to believe itself the representative American city, by 1903, according to Croly, "the most highly organized and the most distinguished collective expression of American social life." [5] It was a time when the city began to develop a sense of its own history [6] and to become concerned for its past as pockets of its own antiquity began to fall in the path of progress. [7]

The threat to these neighborhoods and monuments not only gave birth to movements for their preservation but also encouraged some old line New Yorkers to oppose the so-called path of progress so vehemently that it actually bypassed certain districts in its otherwise seemingly inexorable march north. Such was the case for the neighborhood north of Washington Square where, as Mariana Griswold Van Rensselaer, the critic, historian, and poet observed in 1893 the

desecrated dwellings [were] being restored within and without, and a belief [was] gaining ground that, whatever may happen a little further up the avenue, this quarter-mile stretch will remain a good residence neighborhood.

The residents of the neighborhood, of which she was one,

are proud of the aroma of fifty years antiquity which we breathe, and we delight to maintain that this is the only part of New York, outside of the tenement districts, where a 'neighborhood feeling' exists. [8]

Not only were old neighborhoods disappearing, but stretches of the natural landscape that had defined the limits of the city were threatened with development. Most notable among these was the Palisades, [9] across the river in New Jersey, sections of which were ultimately preserved by the Rockefeller family from the ravages of

2. Herbert Croly, "New York as the American Metropolis," *Architectural Record*, 13 (March 1903), pp. 193-206.

3. Ibid., p. 194.

4. Moses King, *New York: The American Cosmopolis, The Foremost City of the World* (Boston: M. King, 1894).

5. Croly, "New York as the American Metropolis," p. 199.

6. A partial list of books and articles written on New York history during the period includes: Moses King, *King's Handbook of New York City: An Outline History and Description of the American Metropolis* (Boston: M. King, 1892); Thomas A. Janvier, "The Evolution of New York," *Harper's New Monthly Magazine*, 86 (May 1893), pp. 813-829, (June 1893), pp. 15-19; also *In Old New York* (New York: Harper & Bros., 1894); Benson J. Lossing, *History of the City of New York*, engravings by George E. Perine (New York: Perine, 1894); Alice Morse Earle, *Colonial Days in Old New York* (New York: Scribners, 1896); Mariana Griswold Van Rensselaer, "The Mother City of Greater New York," *The Century*, 54 (May 1898), pp. 138-146; Maude M. Goodwin, Alice C. Royce, Ruth Putnam, editors, *Historic New York* (New York and London: G.P. Putnam's Sons, 1898–99); Thomas E.V. Smith, *The City of New York in the Year of Washington's Inauguration, 1789* (New York: A.D.F. Randolph, 1899); Frank Bergen Kelley, Ed., *Historical Guide to the City of New York* (City Historical Club of New York, F.A. Stokes Co., 1909); Mariana Griswold Van Rensselaer, *History of the City of New York in the Seventeenth Century* (New York: MacMillan, 1909); Isaac Newton Phelps Stokes, *The Iconography of Manhattan Island, 1848 – 1909* (New York: R.H. Dodd, 1915 – 1928).

7. Montgomery Schuyler, "The Small City House in New York," *Architectural Record*, 8 (April–June 1899), p. 359; "New City Hall," *Architecture and Building*, 14 (March 21, 1891), p. 138.

8. Mariana Griswold Van Rensselaer, "Fifth Avenue," *The Century*, 47 (November 1893), pp. 5-18.

9. Frederick Stymetz Lamb, "Planning of Cities, Paper No. 5: On The Embellishment of New York City Waterfronts," *Public Improvements*, 2 (December 15, 1899), pp. 75-77.

stone quarrying. Other areas, particularly in the Bronx, were reserved by the City for parkland.

By the mid 1890's the ideal of a cosmopolitan city had given way to one that strove for a homogeneous character. In 1894 James W. and Daniel B. Shepp described this new conception of the city as "composite" — "a city made up of men and women from the uttermost ends of the earth, with their own peculiar habits and customs, all blending together into a more or less homogeneous whole."[10] But as Croly remarked,

the homogeneity so characteristic of American democracy at its best tends to disappear in the complicated hurly burly of the life of a great city, and the underlying separation of interest and point of view in its make-up comes plainly to the surface.[11]

It was the interaction between an ideal of homogeneity and an insistently pluralist reality that determined much of the character of the "composite" city; for example, the tension between the aspirations of the City Beautiful movement and the rampant exploitation of economic forces, whose most spectacular product was the maturation of the skyscraper as a building type and whose gravest consequence was the tenement. The term "composite" city is meant, therefore, to suggest an urbanism "composed," like the columnar order, of diverse elements, yet despite the heterogeneity of its parts, an urbanism characterized by an overall vision of unity and public responsibility.

The ideal of the City Beautiful did not spring up with the World's Columbian Exposition held in Chicago in 1892, though that event, and New York's failure to capture it for its own,[12] did set in motion a vast outpouring of energy, wealth, and talent in an effort, very successful in many ways, to give New York a physical expression commensurate with that of the older world capitals. An early, isolated example of the Fair's influence is Charles F. McKim's design for the new campus of Columbia University, with its rigorous plan of courtyards defined by buildings of uniform elevation, all grouped around a domed library set atop broad stepped terraces.[13]

In 1893, the artist Edwin H. Blashfield issued a "Plea for Municipal Art" in which he urged New Yorkers to regard the Chicago Fair as a "colossal object lesson." New York, Blashfield argued,

must wish that some grand buildings should be translated into enduring stone...the good time is coming. May not we...stand at the beginning of a movement in which architecture, sculpture, painting crystallized together as one immense factor, may be enlisted in the city's service to outlast the great exhibition.[14]

The ideals and strategies first tested in plaster in Chicago were the logical tools with which to effect the consolidation of New York's diffuse urbanism. The forms of the classical past were the most generally accessible physical expression of the national self-image; they connected contemporary experience with the high political ideals of the early Republic while also stirring archetypal memories of Greece and Rome. Moreover, they seemed the only forms to have behind them a grammar and syntax that suggested

10. *Shepp's New York City Illustrated. Scene and Story in the Metropolis of the Western World* (Philadelphia and Chicago: Globe Bible Pub. Co., 1893).

11. Croly, "New York as the American Metropolis," pp. 199-200.

12. In 1889 New York's press actively lobbied for the city's selection as host to the Fair, generally favoring its location in Pelham Bay Park. See "Exposition of 1892," *Building*, 11 (July 13, 1889), p. 9; also "The Site for the Exposition of 1892," *Building*, 11 (August 31, 1889), p. 67. The Chicago site was chosen by an Act of Congress, however, presumably because of that city's central location. The occasion was celebrated in New York by a competition for the design of an arch which was won by a student, Henry B. Herts (*Columbia 1897*). A temporary version of Herts's design was built at Fifth Avenue and 58th Street and G. Russo's rostral column at Columbus Circle (see Henry Hope Reed, "The Vision Spurned: Classical New York. The Story of City Planning in New York," *Classical America*, 1 (1972), pp. 10-19. The proposal for Herts's Arch is described in *Architecture and Building*, 17 (October 8, 1892), p. 178.

It should be noted however that Morningside Heights was also considered as a possible site by New York's Fair Committee in 1889. The suggestion was abandoned when the Bloomingdale Insane Asylum refused to sell its property. The construction of Columbia's new campus on the same site in 1893 can thus be pictured as New York's ironic revenge upon Chicago, rendering lithic the aesthetic ideal Chicago had only briefly achieved in plaster. See John Murray, "The Topic of the Hour — The Exposition," *Real Estate Record and Guide*, 44 (August 24, 1889), pp. 1155-56; also *Real Estate Record and Guide*, 44 (November 2, 1889), p. 1466.

13. See H.H. Reed, "The Vision Spurned," who claims that the Trustees freely admitted that the vision in Chicago had influenced their choice; and also Francesco Passanti, "The Design of Columbia in the 1890s, McKim and His Client," *Journal of the Society of Architectural Historians*, 36 (May 1977), pp. 69-84.

14. "A Plea for Municipal Art," paper read at the first meeting of the Municipal Art Society 1893, reprinted in *Yearbook of the Art Societies of New York, 1898–1899* (New York: 1899), pp. 94-98.

strategies sophisticated and developed enough to implement the kinds of planning reforms that had been discussed since the 1880's and were only now about to be realized.

The impact of the Chicago Fair took a number of distinct forms in New York: it legitimized the classical approach to individual building design; it encouraged those involved with important institutional buildings to see their responsibilities at a larger scale than that of the individual building; and it fostered a gradual move toward comprehensive urban planning.

Initially, Blashfield's aestheticized view was symptomatic of the expressed purpose of the newly founded Municipal Arts Society, which under its founding President, Richard Morris Hunt, sought "to provide adequate sculptural and pictorial decorations for the public buildings and parks of the City of New York."[15] Its original intention was to donate one work of art to the City each year. Quickly, however, a broader comprehension of the problem began to emerge.[16]

In 1898, the year of the city's consolidation, Julius Harder, the architect, wrote in the newly founded magazine, *Municipal Affairs*, that "civic pride and interest in municipal affairs will in time evolve a logical city plan." The growing spirit of civic consciousness was summed up by Charles Rollinson Lamb:

There is a competition of cities...of capitals as personifying countries... It behooves us to realize that our representative city, New York, is under surveillance.[17]

A growing tide of public opinion in behalf of the formulation of a comprehensive plan that would serve as a framework for private and public efforts at beautification was reflected in the New York Reform Club's founding of two magazines, *Municipal Affairs* in 1897 and *Public Improvements* in 1901, as well as in countless editorials in newspapers, especially in the *Times, Herald* and *Tribune.* The *Herald,* for example, asked a number of experts to comment on how New York could be made beautiful.[18]

The example of the McMillan Commission's plan for Washington, D.C. of 1902 crystallized the move toward the formulation of a similar document for New York. In 1902, the *Times* proposed that a commission be initiated to draw up a city plan, suggesting that Charles F. McKim and Augustus Saint-Gaudens, each a New York resident who had served in Washington, act in similar capacities in New York.[19] The ideals and strategies of the City Beautiful, as they were being promulgated by such polemicists as Charles Mulford Robinson, were the logical tools with which to effect this transformation.

Seth Low's election as mayor in 1901 provided the movement with governmental recognition. Low was himself a member of the Municipal Art Society, and was instrumental in establishing the Municipal Art Commission with a provision in the 1898 charter.[20] Furthermore, his role in commissioning McKim to design the new Columbia campus on Morningside Heights and its Low Memorial library had already demonstrated his commitment to realizing the ideals of the City Beautiful on a large scale. At the Mayor's request, a broad planning agenda was drawn up in January, 1903 by a

15. "Public Art in American Cities," *Municipal Affairs,* 2 (March 1898), pp. 1-13. See also Lamb, "New York City of the Future," *House and Garden,* 2 (June 1903), pp. 195-319.

16. Illustrated in Kantor "The City Beautiful in New York," *New York Historical Society Quarterly Bulletin,* 57 (April 1975), pp. 148-171.

17. Charles Rollinson Lamb, "Civic Architecture from its Constructive Side," *Municipal Affairs,* 2 (March 1898), pp. 67-86. Julius Harder, "The City's Plan," *Municipal Affairs,* 2 (March 1898), pp. 24-45. As Greater New York was created in 1898, the Municipal Art Society was itself incorporated with an expanding membership and program, now attempting to sponsor works to be executed at the city's expense, and also lobbied successfully for the new charter's provision for a Municipal Arts Commission, with veto power over all public art and, at the mayor's discretion city buildings and bridges. The Society now numbered among its members Andrew Carnegie, Robert W. De Forest, Seth Low, George B. Post, John La Farge, Charles R. Lamb, Charles Follen McKim, and Frederick Stymetz Lamb. See John M. Carrere, "The Art Commission of the City of New York and its Origins," *New York Architect,* 2 (March 1908), no pagination. See also Kantor, *Modern Urban Planning in New York City,* p. 40.

18. *New York Herald,* "How Can New York Be Made the City Beautiful," April 29, 1900, cited in Kantor, "The City Beautiful in New York," p. 152.

19. See Mel Scott, *American City Planning Since 1890,* p. 157.

20. John M. Carrere, "The Art Commission of the City of New York and its Origins."

temporary conference organized by the Municipal Arts Society; among the Conference's members was A.D.F. Hamlin, of Columbia's School of Architecture. Its report constituted what has been characterized as "the first comprehensive survey of New York City's present and long-range improvement needs."[21]

From the first it was recognized that Manhattan's gridiron plan worked against any conventional concept of monumentality. In 1898, Harder had proposed a plan for a new civic center located on an expanded Union Square, linked to major arteries by diagonal vistas.[22] This plan made it apparent that the introduction of any new radial street would be extremely disruptive to the city's fabric. In addition, as Harder had already suggested and as the *Times* was quick to reiterate, the commercial nature of the city was at odds with the prevailing conception of a city as a monumental place. Neils Gron, a foreign sociologist travelling in the United States had put the matter succinctly in the *Herald*:

Before I came to this country, and in all the time I have been here, it has never occurred to me to think of New York as being beautiful. Therefore, all this talk of beautifying New York seems strange to me...We expect of her power and magnificence, but not beauty. If a European came over here and found that New York was beautiful in the same way as the European cities he knew, he would be very much disappointed. I do not see how you can make New York beautiful in that way, with the laws and democratic spirit you have here. The kind of beauty that makes Paris charming can only exist where private rights and personal liberty are or have been trampled on.[23]

Despite these drawbacks — many of which would be overcome in a democratic manner in the next fifteen years, the idea of any grand plan at all was generally viewed as positive in that it would focus attention on the problems of traffic, transportation and housing which plagued the newly consolidated city. The Commission presented a preliminary report in 1904 which enumerated a list of topics such a plan must necessarily address "if New York is to take its place as one of the great Metropolitan Cities of the World." Principal among these were the "laying out of parks, streets and highways, the location of city buildings, improvement of water fronts..." These features were intended to fit together in such a manner "that all its parts shall be consistent, the one with the other, and form a homogeneous whole."[24]

While the plan and its successor in 1907 have frequently been compared unfavorably with Chicago's of 1909, it was not without some audacious proposals, including an elevated highway along the Hudson River waterfront (not realized until 1931) as well as coordinated pier development in Chelsea which could combine the usual commercial facilities and the new elevated roadway with roof-top recreational parks. The acquisition of parkland was advocated, particularly in the rapidly developing sections of upper Manhattan and the Bronx; there were also proposals for parks in the other boroughs where the development pressures were far less intense.

While no comprehensive, coordinated transportation plan was included in the report, a number of ingenious solutions to specific

21. Kantor, "The City Beautiful in New York," p. 158.

22. Julius F. Harder, "The Planning of Cities: Paper No. 1," *Public Improvements*, 1 (October 15, 1899), pp. 297-300.

23. Quoted in Kantor, "The City Beautiful in New York," p. 152.

24. *Report of the New York City Improvement Commission to the Honorable George B. McClellan* (New York, 1904), p. 2.

25. Ibid., p. 16.

problems of congestion were proposed, among them a rather naive suggestion by Carrere and Hastings for a grade separation at the intersection of 42nd Street and Fifth Avenue. More impressive were the proposals for various bridge terminii: a subway loop terminal for the Queensboro Bridge and a transformation of Delancey Street at the foot of the Williamsburg Bridge into a landscaped parkway were each complexly conceived responses to the problems brought about by traffic concentration at the bridge.

The Commissioners also struggled to evolve a coherent plan for the civic center, the area around City Hall, which the report emphatically described as "one of the few good monuments possessed by the City..."[25] This observation in itself was important, for only fifteen years earlier the city fathers had proposed its demolition and replacement with a more commodious building in order to meet the needs of an expanding bureaucracy.[26]

In 1904, John R. Thomas's Hall of Records was completed on Chambers Street, its program of decorative murals and sculpture the fullest representation of the Municipal Art Society's early goals. Though lauded as "New York's Most Beautiful Building,"[27] its haphazard relationship to City Hall acutely illustrated the need for a broader plan for the civic center. Croly alleged that the city had

degraded one of the most spacious and delightful squares with which any City Hall in America was surrounded into an insignificant little park, over-run with buildings with no approaches, no vistas, very little atmosphere, and no disposition of any kind to give space, distinction and dignity.[28]

While the 1904 report offered no specific suggestions for the civic center, its focus on the value of the historic City Hall and the appropriateness of its location, the need for a coordinated development plan, as well as attention to problems of congestion at the bridge terminii (the traffic on the Brooklyn Bridge debouched virtually on the doorstep of City Hall), combined to trigger a sequence of events that led to the construction of the Municipal Building (1907–1913) as well as a series of unrealized attempts to deal with the transportation problem, the most ambitious of which was the plan devised in 1904 by George Post and Henry Hornbostel *(Columbia, 1891)* who were commissioned by Gustav Lindenthal, the Commissioner of the City's Department of Bridges, to design a new terminal and restructured trolley loop at the bridge while providing a comprehensive scheme for City Hall Park.[29] Post and Hornbostel proposed that save for City Hall, the park be cleared of buildings (A.B. Mullett's post office, erected in 1875, stood at the southern tip of the park, the Tweed Courthouse lay to the north), with new City offices provided on the north side of Chambers Street, again in a tripartite building incorporating the Hall of Records *(fig. 3).* Pedestrian bridges and a clocktower would connect this new building with the bridge, the park, and a proposed 650 foot municipal office tower. In contrast to the earlier schemes to replace City Hall, Post and Hornbostel treated it as a cherished cultural artifact, its now anachronistically small scale enhanced by the proposed architectural backdrop, while the

Fig. 3 Project for the Brooklyn Bridge Terminal and Civic Center, City Hall Park, 1904, Henry Hornbostel *(1891)* and George B. Post.

26. In 1888, 1893 and 1894, competitions were held for a new city hall to replace the notorious Tweed Courthouse and to envelop the original building in a U-shaped court. Recognizing the inevitable northward expansion of the city's business center, the new building was to face uptown. The winning schemes of 1888 and 1893 by Charles B. Atwood and John R. Thomas respectively, were never realized, but Thomas was compensated with the commission of the Hall of Records. The 1894 competition was marred by the scandalous manipulations of Tammany Hall, and the thoroughly undistinguished entries. Excepting Cram, Wentworth and Goodhue's scheme, the designs failed to achieve an appropriate civic expression of monumental scale. The eventual winners, Gordon, Bragdon and Orchard, had to sue the City for payment of their prize. "The New York City Hall Competition," *Architecture and Building,* 20 (January 27, 1894), pp. 37-38. Atwood's scheme is illustrated in *Building* 9 (December 29, 1888). See also *American Architect and Building News,* 52 (May 9, 1896), and 55 (January 30, 1897).

The replacement of the City Hall had in fact been proposed in 1893 by Richard Morris Hunt, Napoleon LeBrun, and William Robert Ware, serving as advisors to the Municipal Building Commission. See *American Architect and Building News,* 39 (March 18, 1893), pp. 161-162. City Hall's interiors were eventually restored by Grosvenor Atterbury *(Columbia, 1892)* from 1902-1920.

27. "The New Hall of Records," *Architects' and Builders' Magazine,* 8 (January 1907), pp. 142-155.

28. Herbert Croly, "New York as the American Metropolis," p. 198.

29. "Proposed Brooklyn Bridge Terminal and City Offices," *Architects' and Builders' Magazine,* 4 (August 1903), pp. 483-489. For a comparison of the Post and Hornbostel project with a Carrere & Hastings scheme for the bridge terminal, see "The Extension of the Manhattan Terminal of the New York and Brooklyn Bridge," *Architects' and Builders' Magazine,* 6 (September 1905), pp. 521-530.

pyramid-topped skyscraper appropriated the symbolism of commercial towers to achieve a big scale, expressive of the new metropolitan conception of government. The project's cost defeated it, but the skyscraper and bridge across Chambers Street were reflected in the program of the 1907 Municipal Building Competition, which was won by McKim, Mead & White.[30]

The Commission's life was extended for three years to 1907 at which time it submitted its final report,[31] which has ever since enjoyed a certain notoriety for what was perceived as its overemphasis on aesthetic issues and its failure to address such specific planning issues as zoning and housing standards that directly affect the everyday lives of the bulk of the citizenry. Perhaps because the plan was so singleminded in its emphasis on the physical beautification of the city, it was not forgotten; its failings seemed glaring enough to merit Lewis Mumford's attention in his book of 1924, *Sticks and Stones,* where it was castigated for its "pages and pages" devoted "to showing the improvement that would follow the demolition of the wall around Central Park — and the importance of clipped trees on the design of grand avenues!"[32]

George B. Ford, the city planner, offered a somewhat more measured assessment of it, and the City Beautiful movement in general, in a lecture delivered at Columbia in 1911 that is a milestone in the shift from the second to the third stage of metropolitanism: "America," Ford stated ironically,

is the only country that has devoted its attention in planning its centers of population almost exclusively to the aesthetic side. In America the cry has been 'The City Beautiful.' Abroad it has been 'The City Logical, Convenient!'[33]

Fig. 4 General Map of Proposed Improvements, New York City Improvement Commission, 1907 City Plan.

Though the 1907 plan was not nearly so sweeping as Chicago's was to be two years later, nor as comprehensive as its early formulation, and though its final publication was something of an anticlimax, it does bear some scrutiny; many of its proposals were in fact sound and some prefigured later improvements actually realized. The Brooklyn approaches to the Manhattan and Brooklyn Bridges, united in a circular "Bridge Plaza," and the boulevard intended to link Prospect Park and the Brooklyn Municipal Center, were all worthwhile proposals, as was the plan's boldest stroke — the widening of 59th Street into a topiaried boulevard, connecting Central Park with the Queensboro or Blackwell's Island Bridge, the conversion of the island itself into a park, and the conclusion of the axis with another "etoile" in Queens *(fig. 4, 5, 6)*. The parkways — connecting the parklands of the outer boroughs with the inner city areas in Brooklyn and Manhattan, one of the plan's chief glories, were based on ideas initially proposed by Olmsted in the 1870's, here enlarged to an appropriately metropolitan scale. While the overall intention was to foster the unity of the newly consolidated city, the individuality of each Borough was expressed by symbolic gateways that were also functional, facilitating the flow of traffic at critical points of congestion.

The 1907 plan represents New York's most comprehensive effort to establish for itself a civic identity akin to that of Paris, or

30. See *American Architect and Building News,* 63 (May 27, 1908). Other entrants included Carrere and Hastings, Howells and Stokes, and Clinton and Russell. McKim had been reluctant to enter the competition, not finding the skyscraper form congenial, and the building was in fact designed by William Kendall, who was to become the firm's principal designer after McKim's death in 1909. Although it draws heavily on the firm's earlier work — the layered stages of the tower from White's Madison Square Garden and Grand Central projects, the three-part organization from the Gorham Company Building — Kendall's design provided an early example of the skyscraper's potential to shape urban space. Seen from the southwest, the U-shaped plan defers to City Hall by apparently embracing it, and the tower seems an elaboration of, and homage to, the older building's cupola. It also combined a skyscraper with the Imperial Roman overtones which McKim had proposed as appropriate to the city's metropolitan character. Leland Roth, *Urban Architecture of McKim, Mead and White, 1870–1910* (Ph.D. diss., Yale University, 1973), pp.730-742 includes a discussion of McKim's reluctance to enter the competition.

31. *The Report of the New York City Improvement Commission to the Honorable George B. McClellan, Mayor of the City of New York and to the Honorable Board of Aldermen of the City of New York* (New York, 1907).

32. Lewis Mumford, *Sticks and Stones* (Dover, ed., 1955), p. 18.

33. "City Beautiful," *New York Architect,* 5 (March 1911), pp. 95-96.

Vienna. Given the complexity of the problem, it is arguable that the 1907 plan failed because it was at once too early and too late. Too late, because by 1907 the great urban set pieces were in place or well underway: the Public Library, the two railroad stations, the development of an acropolis of learning at Morningside. Too early, because the grandness of scale of the park, parkway and boulevard plan would not happen until the automobile became an everyday thing ten years later. One can say, however, that the plan represented a public affirmation of the need for an artistic response to a complex urban condition.

As a result of the 1907 plan and the agitation of a number of citizens, including Robert W. De Forest (former Tenement House Commissioner) and Frederick Stymetz Lamb, a Committee on Congestion of Population in New York was founded in 1907 by such reformers as Lillian Wald, Mary Simkhovitch and such prominent citizens as Dr. Herman C. Bumpus, the Director of the American Museum of Natural History. Benjamin C. Marsh, who was appointed its secretary, can be credited with shifting attention away from issues of beautification to "more important" issues such as

the securing of decent home conditions for the countless thousands who otherwise can only occasionally escape from their confining surroundings to view the architectural perfection and to experience the aesthetic delights of the remote improvements. [34]

In March 1908, the Committee organized an exhibition on city planning at the American Museum of Natural History which came to be called the "Congestion Show," filled as it was with charts, maps, models that made all too vivid the enormous growth of cities in the previous twenty-five years. [35] The very selection of the Natural History Museum as opposed to the Metropolitan Museum of Art for the exhibition was surely symptomatic of the changing values of the city planning movement. The "Congestion Show," under Marsh's guidance, strongly advocated legislated town planning along the German model and the introduction of zoning. Recognizing that the developing subway system was not relieving but rather fostering congestion, and that it was allowing tenements to sprout in undeveloped areas of the city, the exhibit proposed a variety of solutions: among them the distribution of

Above left: fig. 5 Bird's eye view of Lower Manhattan, showing proposed 59th Street boulevard, 1907 City Plan.

Above right: fig. 6 Proposed Manhattan entrance to Queensboro (Blackwell's Island) Bridge, 1907 City Plan.

34. Quoted in Scott, *American City Planning,* p. 82.

35. The exhibition is described in great detail in *Charities and the Commons,* 20 (April 4, 1888), pp. 26-53. See also Kantor, *Modern Urban Planning in New York City,* pp. 116-177.

factories throughout the city in zones surrounded by working-class housing created in tandem with parks and recreational facilities (a concept of city planning which reflects the writings of Ebenezer Howard); and the creation of model villages, new and logically planned communities created on unsettled land within the city limits. The exhibition can thus be said to have brought before the public the shift from the City Beautiful ideals of the previous decade to a new, more socially responsible, more scientific and pragmatic approach which we would label the "City Convenient."[36]

In a similar vein, the Russell Sage Foundation was founded in 1907 with Robert De Forest as its first president; its generous endowment was committed to the improvement of the physical environment of the masses. The Foundation's creation was hailed by the journalist-reformer Jacob A. Riis as an opportunity to document the social and economic conditions of the city, and by Professor Edwin Seligman of Columbia as a possible "laboratory of social experimentation."[37] Its first project, the planned suburb of Forest Hills Gardens, was designed by Frederick Law Olmsted, Jr. and Grosvenor Atterbury *(Columbia, 1892),* and may be seen in part as a realization of the model village concept forwarded at the Congestion Show, while the Foundation's eventual role in the creation of the Regional Plan Association in the 1920's hastened the demise of the Metropolitanism it had once nurtured.[38]

The era of the composite city was brought to a close in New York, when, in 1911, the city turned its attention from issues of beautification to problems brought about by the enormous height and bulk of the new skyscrapers and by the incursions of manufacturing activities into prime residential and commercial neighborhoods, particularly in the vicinity of Fifth Avenue above Union and Madison Squares.[39] The concerns of the new era had in fact been foreshadowed by Croly, whose comments on the failure of the 1907 plan touched on the contradictory values of the times:

The interest of the real estate speculator demands congestion and concentration of business and population, which enormously increases real estate values along particular lines and at particular points, while the interest of the whole people in a beautiful and convenient city demands the distribution of population and business in the most liberal manner and according to an organic plan.[40]

In 1913, the Merchants Association, a coalition of commercial and civic groups brought together by the Fifth Avenue Association, organized the City Planning Exhibition held at the New York Public Library. The exhibit, including material from two hundred cities, demonstrated the wide public support for city planning, and later toured America and France.[41] The completion of the Equitable Building in 1915 brought the early period of the skyscraper's evolution to a reprehensible climax; by filling its site thirty times over it provided graphic evidence of the effects of unrestricted development on air, light, and congestion.[42]

Despite the inadequacies of the 1907 plan, the ideals and strategies of beautification informed the public and private sectors

36. Scott has labeled it the "City Efficient," *American City Planning,* p. 1.

37. *Charities and the Commons,* 18 (1907), pp. 77-78, p. 191.

38. Kantor, *Modern Urban Planning in New York City,* pp. 132-135; also David P. Handlin, *The American Home: Architecture and Society, 1890–1915* (Boston and Toronto: Little, Brown and Co., 1979), pp. 141-158; Jacques Greber, *L'Architecture Aux Etats-Unis* (Paris: Payot & Cie, 1920), Vol. I, pp. 101-110; Charles C. May, "Forest Hills Gardens from the Town Planning Viewpoint," *Architecture,* 34 (August 1916), pp. 161-172, Pl. CXXX-CXXVII.

39. *New York Architect,* 4 (December 1910), Editorial, p. 3. A report on the first annual dinner of the Fifth Avenue Association held in November, at which Borough President McAneny spoke. According to Donn Barber *(Columbia, 1894),* the editor, "It is plainly evident that gradually the idea that the great City of New York can be made to meet the tremendous new demands upon it, in an artistic as well as practical way has now come to full maturity and that presently something real will be done. The formation of the Fifth Avenue Association just entering upon its fifth year was the first step in the right direction...Many of its members who are largely property owners...consider the architectural future of New York largely in the hands of its prominent architects." See also Henry Collins Brown, *Fifth Avenue Old and New, 1824–1924* (New York: Fifth Avenue Association, Wynkoop Hallenbeck Crawford Co., 1924).

40. Herbert Croly, "Civic Improvements: The Case of New York," *Architectural Record,* 21 (May 1907), pp. 347-352. Otto Wagner, invited by A.D.F Hamlin in 1910 to address the proposed International Conference on Civic Art in New York, responded with an "Ideal Design for XXIInd Viennese District," a new quarter of the city, a project used to illustrate his book *Die Grosstadt* (Vienna: Schroll, 1911). Wagner wrote of the conflict of public and private realms in his explanatory essay: "Art and the artist must be governing factors, in order that the beauty-destroying influence of the engine may be forever destroyed, and the power of the vampire, speculation, which now makes the autonomy of the city almost an illusion, may be reduced to a minimum." But Wagner's comments on the inner city core suggest the pragmatism that would characterize the 1916 zoning resolution: "The characteristic impression produced by a city results from its existing or inherent beauty and its potential beauty. The City's general 'physiognomy' is the most important consideration in its plan. Upon it depends the success of the effort to make the first impression as pleasing as possible. This impression is furthermore dependent on the pulsating life of the city as a whole." See "The Development of a Great City, by Otto Wagner, Together with an Appreciation of the author by A.D.F. Hamlin," *Architectural Record,* 31 (1912), pp. 487-500.

41. "New York City's Planning Exhibition," *American City,* 9 (December 1913), pp. 504-512; Kantor, *Modern Urban Planning in New York City,* pp. 152-154.

42. By 1916, a zoning resolution was adopted by the Board of Estimate which for the first time regulated the city's density. Through the establishment of use districts, the character of neighborhoods was established. The 1916 document typifies the very nature of New York in that it provides regulation of planning in the form of zoning without any overall plan of its own, save for the gridiron of the Commissioners and the character of the city as it had pragmatically evolved.

alike in the era of the composite city; even without a planning framework, the sheer quantity and quality of buildings built between 1890 and 1915 transformed the city's identity. The imposing aspect of the public buildings, the diversity of the individual houses within the classical framework, the exuberance of the commercial structures, and the Arcadian idyll of its suburbs defined a golden age in city development. Yet, as the full panoply of building types and urban conditions which characterize the Metropolitan age is so vast, it seems appropriate to concentrate in this essay on the public realm, the monuments of transportation, government, culture and education which constitute the city's identifying set pieces. Other expressions of the age — the skyscrapers, clubs, hotels, apartment buildings, residences, suburbs — must await treatment in a more generous format. Furthermore, a sense of occasion requires that the city be viewed through the lens of Columbia, both the institution's architectural expression, and the work of some of its distinguished alumni. Hence, the seemingly parochial shift in emphasis in the concluding pages of the essay.

While the authors of the 1907 plan were to some extent remiss in failing to prepare a coordinated transportation plan, there may well be a simple explanation in that such a plan was already being implemented at the time. The plan, in effect, had two aspects, one providing for regional rail transportation, the other an intra-city system connecting Manhattan to the outer boroughs. It resulted in the electrification of the New York Central and New Haven Railroads, the construction of a new Grand Central Station, (the third on the site), the unification of the Pennsylvania and Long Island Railroads and their entrance to Manhattan via tunnels under the Hudson and East Rivers, the construction of the McAdoo tunnels under the Hudson (the so-called "Hudson Tubes" now known as PATH), and the construction of the New York Connecting Railway's bridge across Hell Gate, which for the first time provided a land connection between the railroads serving New England, Long Island, Manhattan and the West.[43]

The plan for an intra-city system, then under construction by the Interborough Rapid Transit Company, would by 1917 link the East and West sides of Manhattan with the Bronx and Brooklyn. While the subsequent construction of subway lines by another company (the Brooklyn and Manhattan Transit Company, which consolidated many existing surface and elevated lines in Brooklyn), and the city itself (the Independent System), would make a mockery of the idea of coordinated intra-city subway transportation, such an incongruous turn of events could not have been anticipated in 1904–1907.[44]

Grand Central and Pennsylvania Stations represent the translation of programs of unprecedented complexity into working monuments, achieving an appropriate sense of public place through a remarkable reconciliation of traditional form with the techniques of modern production. Together, as Carl Condit observed, the two terminals

from their conspicuous architectural features to their hidden operating ele-

43. For a general discussion, see Carl Condit, *Port of New York* (Chicago: University of Chicago, 1980).

44. See *Interborough Rapid Transit: The New York Subway, Its Construction and Equipment* (New York: Interborough Rapid Transit Company, 1904; Arno Press, 1969); Stan Fischler, *Uptown, Downtown: A Trip Through Time on New York's Subways* (New York: Hawthorn Books, 1976).

Left: fig. 7 Concourse, Pennsylvania Station, 1906–10, McKim, Mead & White. Photo by Bernice Abbott, courtesy of The Museum of the City of New York.

Top: fig. 8 Grand Central Terminal, 1906–13, Warren & Wetmore and Reed & Stem: Whitney Warren *(1889)*.

Above: fig. 9 St. George Ferry Terminal, Staten Island, 1904–07, Carrere & Hastings.

ments, possessed a grandeur and a power that placed them in the front rank of modern technical-artistic achievements. They are…the greatest architectural engineering works ever undertaken in the United States. They are the centerpieces of a rail and waterway network of magnitude and complexity…[45]

In McKim's Pennsylvania Station the main Waiting Room is a reintrepretation of the Baths of Caracalla; in the Concourse next to it the same basilical forms are molded in glass and steel, establishing a remarkable association and continuity of forms over time *(fig. 7)*.

Pennsylvania Station, which was shamelessly demolished in 1963, was admired by critics from the first. Even Lewis Mumford, who derided its machine-produced ornament, valued its carefully modulated system of arcades and corridors which provided a sequence of spaces varying from low to high, narrow to wide, as circulation patterns required swift movement or allowed relaxation.[46] Yet that circulation system, so clear on paper, and so articulate to those familiar with it, seemed not a little confusing, not to mention daunting, to weary travellers such as Arnold Bennett, the English novelist who is said to have remarked that "everything could be found there except the trains."[47]

Grand Central Station, planned by Reed and Stem in association

45. Condit, *The Port of New York*, p. XVI. See also Carroll L.V. Meeks, *The Railroad Station: An Architectural History* (New Haven: Yale University Press, 1956).

46. Montgomery Schuyler, "The New Pennsylvania Station in New York," *The International Studio*, 41 (October 1919), p. LXXXIX. Mumford's "The Disappearance of Pennsylvania Station," *Journal of the American Institute of Architects*, 30 (October 1958), pp. 40-43 (reprinted from *The New Yorker* June 7, 1958) represents a favorable reassessment of his caustic appraisal in *Sticks and Stones*, pp. 137-140.

47. Quoted in Margaret Clapp, "The Social and Cultural Scene" in Allen Nevins and John Krout, eds., *The Greater City: New York 1898–1948* (New York: Columbia, 1948), p. 221. Perhaps Pennsylvania Station's splendor was best captured by Thomas Wolfe, in his novel *You Can't Go Home Again:*

The station, as he entered it, was murmurous with the immense and distant sound of time. Great, slant beams of moted light fell ponderously athwart the station's floor and the calm voice of time hovered along the walls and ceiling of that mighty room distilled out of the voices and movements of the people who swarmed beneath. It had the murmur of a distant sea, the langorous lapse and flow of waters on a beach. It was elemental, detached, indifferent to the lives of men. They contributed to it as drops of rain contribute to a river that draws its flood and movement majestically from great depths, out of purple hills at evening.

with Warren & Wetmore, is in some respects more thoughtful on the level of urban planning. Its underground concourses, connecting the neighboring hotels and office buildings with arcades of restaurants and shops, established the entire complex as itself a city in microcosm, a *tour-de-force* of urban connections and mixed use which foreshadows the age of the City Convenient. But in contrast to such later developments as the present Madison Square Garden, the above-ground isolation of the terminal itself and the monumental character of its public spaces retain its rhetorical impact as a symbolic gateway to the city. That rhetoric is sustained in Whitney Warren's "Modern French" (Beaux-Arts Baroque) facades, elevated on a hodium which allows the continuation of Park Avenue, and concentrated in the dynamic sculpture of Mercury by Jules Alexis Coutan at its center *(fig. 8)*.[48]

The pier development was an aspect of transportation that received considerable attention in both reports of the Municipal Improvement Commission. Although most of their proposals were not specifically carried out in any single new facility, the Whitehall Ferry Terminal by Walker and Morris was built as a direct result of the plan. Recalling its plea for recreational facilities incorporated into pier design, Walker and Morris provided a roof garden, its pergolas overlooking the bay. Like Kenneth Murchison's *(Columbia, 1894)* Erie Ferry House at the foot of West 23rd Street, also built in 1907, and Snelling and Potter's Stapleton Ferry Terminal of 1908, it employed a loosely classical Modern French vocabulary reinterpreted in steelwork and copper, with even the joints and rivet patterns worked into the decorative design. The most beautiful of New York's ferry terminals, however, was by Carrere and Hastings at St. George, Staten Island (1907), its tapered stone pylons supporting graceful metal keel-shaped arches, the concourse behind a metal shed supported on unadorned transverse arches, with thermal windows at either end and metal walls panelled with etiolated pilasters *(fig. 9)*.[49]

The new ferry terminals celebrated the connection of the Boroughs, as did the new bridges that spanned the East River to connect Manhattan with Brooklyn and Queens. The visual impact on the city's riverscapes of the sudden flurry of new bridges required to link the new Boroughs, demanded some sort of aesthetic control; the original engineer's designs for the Blackwell's Island (Queensboro) Bridge was characterized by John De Witt Warner in 1899 as a "surrender of the City Beautiful to the City Vulgar."[50] The issue of the new city bridges led George Post to demand that the city engineers be required to collaborate with architects, a practice begun when Seth Low appointed the eminent engineer Gustav Lindenthal as Commissioner of the Department of Bridges and regularly referred new bridge designs to the Municipal Art Commission for approval.[51]

Perhaps the most notable of these collaborations was between Lindenthal and Carrere and Hastings on the Manhattan Bridge, where the architects were able to embellish the Manhattan entrance with an elliptical plaza surrounded by Doric colonnades and a triumphal arch modelled on the Porte St. Denis in Paris. The juxtaposition of masonry and barely adorned steel, of the direct

Few buildings are vast enough to hold the sound of time, and . . . there was a superb fitness in the fact that the one which held it better than all others should be a railroad station. For here, as nowhere else on earth, men were brought together for a moment at the beginning or end of their innumerable journeys, here one saw their greetings and farewells, here, in a single instant, one got the entire picture of human destiny. Men came and went, they passed and vanished, all were moving through the moments of their lives to death, all made small tickings in the sound of time — but the voice of time remained aloof and unperturbed, a drowsy and eternal murmur below the immense and distant roof (Quoted in Nathan Silver, *Lost New York*, pp. 8-9).

48. For an earlier, "Modern French" scheme for the terminal, see "The New Grand Central Station, New York," *Architects' and Builders' Magazine*, 6 (March 1905), pp. 267-271. See Leland Roth, *Urban Architecture of McKim, Mead & White*, pp. 693-698, for a discussion of the competition, and of Stanford White's entry; also William D. Middleton, *Grand Central: The World's Greatest Railway Terminal* (San Marino, California: Golden West Books, 1977).

49. See "The New Stapleton Ferry Terminal: Snelling & Potter, Architects," *American Architect and Building News*, 94 (August 1908), p. 98; for Walker and Morris, Edward W. Hudson, "Architectural Design in Steel Work," *RIBA Journal* (3rd Ser.) 19 (1912), pp. 330-339; for Kenneth Murchison, see Charles C. Hurlbut, "Modern Architectural Copper Work," *Architects' and Builders' Magazine*, 10 (November 1908), pp. 99-106; "The Ferry Terminals at the Foot of West Twenty-Third Street, N.Y. City," *Architects' and Builders' Magazine*, 8 (May 1907), p. 374. For Carrere & Hastings, see "The Municipal Ferry Terminals," *Architects' and Builders' Magazine*, 8 (May 1907), pp. 396-399.

50. John De Witt Warner, "Bridges and Art," an address delivered before the National Sculpture Society on December 19, 1899, published in *Public Improvements*, 2 (January 1, 1900), pp. 97-99.

51. See George Post, "The Planning of Cities," *Public Improvements*, 2 (November 15, 1899), pp. 26-27; also Montgomery Schuyler, "Bridges and the Art Commission," *Architectural Record*, 22 (December 1907), pp. 469-475.

classicism of the approach and its transformation in the steel towers, is symbolic of the era's attempts to synthesize aesthetic and utilitarian ambitions.[52]

The Manhattan Bridge was only the most elaborate of the bridge improvements. Henry Hornbostel *(Columbia, 1891)* who had produced earlier schemes for the Manhattan Bridge before being replaced by Carrere and Hastings, was called in at an advanced stage to redesign the Blackwell's Island (Queensboro) Bridge (1903).[53] Hornbostel included reinterpreted rostral columns as the finials on the towers. While the finials are now sadly removed, the detailed design and execution of Hornbostel's design is still more or less intact, surely one of the virtuoso displays of the riveter's art.[54] Hornbostel's achievement with the East River Bridges was summed up by A.D.F. Hamlin, who described him in the general interest magazine, *Forum,* as

a talented young architect... who has not only given to the design of piers, abutments, approaches, and decorative detail of these bridges a touch of elegance sadly wanting in most of our public engineering works; he has also succeeded in bringing into the work of the engineers themselves new conceptions, and in suggesting to them practical modifications of original plans which have resulted in greater convenience, beauty and economy.[55]

Hornbostel's masterpiece, however, the Hell Gate Bridge, on which he again collaborated with Lindenthal *(fig. 10)*, was not realized until 1914. Its austere towers buttress and counterpoint Lindenthal's flowing arch without disrupting its visual continuity, the simple masses of stone only slightly cut back to reveal emergent pilasters.

A variety of other government buildings were constructed during the period. Carrere and Hastings provided Staten Island with a government center beginning with the Richmond Borough Hall in 1907.[56] Planned in concert with the firm's St. George Ferry Terminal, and located on the steep hill directly above it, the Borough Hall's "U" shaped plan receptively acknowledges the arriving passenger, while the clock tower behind functions as a symbolic beacon. Its legible massing, unarticulated base, and engaged Doric order reflect the scale of the harbor and achieve a monumental civic expression, while the vernacular mixture of brick and stone and the typology evoked — that of the French Mairie — enhance the Borough's suburban ambiance. Carrere and Hastings later built the neighboring courthouse, its hexastyle Corinthian portico again overlooking the bay, as well as the Carnegie Branch Library on the ridge of the hill.[57] While these buildings reflect the 1907 plan's plea for the concentration of municipal buildings as architectural ensembles in each Borough, the deliberate informality of their grouping reinforces Staten Island's individual character.

In Manhattan, the United States Custom House Competition had been won by Cass Gilbert in 1900.[58] Though only six stories tall, its location, terminating the vista down Broadway, and the bold scale of its high, rusticated base, colossal order, and cascading steps dwarf the neighboring skyscrapers. Figures of the port cities of Europe circle the attic, and Daniel Chester French's sculptural

Fig. 10 Original proposal for the Hell Gate Bridge, 1907, Palmer & Hornbostel and Gustav Lindenthal: Henry Hornbostel *(1891)*.

52. "The Borough of Manhattan Approach to Brooklyn Bridge," *American Architect* 102 (August 14, 1912), pp. 61-63; also Blake, *Architecture of Carrere & Hastings* (Ph.D. diss., Columbia University, 1976), pp. 310-312.

53. Henry F. Hornbostel, "The New East River Bridges," *Architecture*, 8 (August 1903), pp. 103-105.

54. Aymar Embury, II, "The Decorative use of Steel," *Architecture*, 24 (December 15, 1911), pp. 179-181, p. 191.

55. Quoted by Barr Ferree, "In Street and Papers," *Architecture and Building*, 5 (February 1904), p. 299.

56. *Brickbuilder*, 16 (January 1907), pp. 1-3.

57. Blake, *Architecture of Carrere & Hastings*, pp. 266-280.

58. For a description by Cass Gilbert and competition entries by Carrere & Hastings, Shepley, Rutan & Coolidge, Robert Gibson, and Trowbridge & Livingston, see "Cass Gilbert's New York Custom House Design," *Inland Architect and News Record*, 35 (February 1900), pp. 6-7.

representations of the Four Continents express the era's sense of world leadership in what would later be less sympathetically characterized as America's first Imperial Age. New York's status as the magnet of immigration found architectural expression in the New Ellis Island Immigrant Station, designed by Boring and Tilton (William A. Boring, *Columbia 1887*), and opened in 1901. The island itself was enlarged to accomodate buildings "of a character and dignity in keeping with the magnitude of the nation to which these structures were to be the entrance."[59] The main building's towers provide a skyline that established the complex in the bay; on a closer scale, its monumental portals are enriched with symbolically apt American eagles and a profusion of Modern French ornament. In both plan and elevation, the ensemble constitutes one of the most dramatic examples in New York of the influence of the Ecole des Beaux-Arts.[60]

The 1907 plan assumed that public monuments and memorials would be erected in the city, but generally avoided the subject of their specific locations. It did recommend that a $50,000 bequest of the late Joseph Pulitzer be expended at 59th Street and Fifth Avenue.[61] Pulitzer's will called for a memorial fountain based on the fountains in the Place de la Concorde. His executors expanded the program, however, suggesting that competition entrants be conscious that the site was a gateway to Central Park, and requiring the inclusion of a park shelter and subway entrance. What was originally conceived of as a hermetic memorial developed into a major urban space with positive linkages to the new infrastructure made possible by the mechanical progress of the age.[62]

The plaza site had once been intended for the Soldiers' and Sailors' Monument. Stoughton, Stoughton and Duboy (Arthur A. Stoughton, *Columbia 1888*) had won the 1894 competition with a design for a memorial column topped by a Victory and surrounded by equestrian groups. The project was opposed by the Municipal Art Society, however, for failing to provide a comprehensive scheme for the entire plaza,[63] and its site was eventually shifted to Riverside Park and 89th Street where the monument was redesigned in response to the park's romantic landscape. Carefully positioned to lie on the axis of the stretch of Drive to its South, from the North it crowns a promontory. The final design of 1902 evokes the Choragic Monument of Lysicrates, but with greater mass and chiaroscuro. The vista down 89th Street is terminated by a flagpole on a transverse axis, allowing the view from the East to continue across the Hudson.

Farther up Riverside Drive, the view is dominated by Grant's Tomb. The Tomb's unconventional proportions are calculated to its position on the bluff. John Duncan's 1890 design was revised before its execution, becoming more classically correct. The interior, however, is a theatrical effect inspired by Napoleon's tomb in Les Invalides, the sarcophagal chamber being viewed from the floor above.[64]

The Dewey Arch of 1900 was perhaps the most complex of those proposed since White's Washington Arch of 1889. Appropriately enough it was built — if only in lath and plaster — at the height of American imperialism and at the peak of the American

59. "The Ellis Island Immigrant Station," *Architects' and Builders' Magazine,* 2 (July 1901), pp. 345-352; *Architecture and Building,* 30 (April 1, 1899).

60. Boring spent three years at the Ecole after studying at Columbia as a special student. Ellis Island received the Gold Medal Award of the Paris Exposition of 1900.

61. *Report of the New York City Improvement Commission* (1907), p. 32.

62. *American Competitions,* 3 (1913), p. XXXIII-XXXIV, pp. 132-149 (also includes entries by McKim, Mead & White, H. Van Buren Magonigle, and John Russell Pope).

63. "Public Art in American Cities," *Municipal Affairs,* 2 (March 1898), p. 10. The original scheme is illustrated in *American Architect and Building News,* 70 (November 17, 1900), p. 55, pl. 1299. See also "The Soldiers and Sailors Memorial Monument," *Architects' and Builders' Magazine,* 5 (October 1903), pp. 1-8.

64. The competition entry is illustrated in *American Architect and Building News,* 30 (October 18, 1890). See also General Horace Potter, "The Tomb of General Grant," *The Century,* 3 (April 1897), pp. 839-847.

Renaissance *(fig. 11)*. Located in one of the city's most prominent intersections, where Broadway, Fifth Avenue, and West 24th Street meet at Madison Square, the monument was a collaborative effort of the National Sculpture Society (whose second Vice-President, Charles R. Lamb, modelled the arch on that of Titus in Rome) and the American Society of Mural Painters, and served as a showcase of New York's artists as much as a celebration of Dewey's exploits. According to one anonymous writer in *Scribner's* it "gave certain persons fresh ground for belief that the plastic expression was the most natural expression of the art impulse of Americans."[65] *Architects' and Builders' Magazine* reflected,

New York has come to be recognized as the Great Art Center of America. Its schools of Art...have made a vast growth in the last decade, until there is no world center save Paris which takes a higher stand in Art matters, and has before it a future of great promise. The Dewey Arch will evidence to the world the ability and fertility of sculptural and decorative talent in our New York Art Colony.[66]

Fig 11:   The Dewey Arch, Madison Square at Broadway, New York City, 1899, Charles Rollinson Lamb and the members of the National Sculpture Society.

The period 1890–1915 also saw a dramatic expansion of cultural institutions in New York City. Every major museum in the city including the American Museum of Natural History, the Museum of the City of New York, The Metropolitan and the Brooklyn Institute of Arts and Sciences (the Brooklyn Museum) assumed their present form in these years.

The enormous expansion and consolidation of institutions at the *fin de siecle* can be understood in many ways; from an architectural point of view, it can be argued that institutions supported by the established, largely Anglo-Saxon citizenry set out to build in a monumental way in order to reinforce the sense of American traditions in the face of the enormous wave of immigration from non-Northern European countries.[67]

While the palatial headquarters created for these institutions were surely intended to impress the new arrivals with the substance of established American traditions, and have been criticized in some quarters as examples of conspicuous consumption, they must at the same time be seen as appropriate expressions of the mood of the new immigrants, who, realizing that they would never be able to fully assimilate their manners to those of native Americans, saw these institutions as places their children could not only enjoy at a distance but more importantly *use* in their efforts to share in the benefactions of the American way. So the situation is laden with irony; and these new complexes must be seen, at least in part, as expressions of a pessimistic establishment and of an optimistic proletariat.

When McKim's firm replaced Hunt at the Metropolitan it was already at work on the Brooklyn Institute of Arts and Sciences, which it had won in a competition in 1893, proposing a building larger than the specifications but suited to construction in segments.[68] The masterplan for the Brooklyn Institute called for a square building with terminal pavilions at each corner and domed pavilions at the center of each facade linked to a central rotunda with a taller dome. Based on McKim's Agriculture Building at the World's Columbia Exposition of 1893, the facades were mod-

65. "Point of View: American 'Style,'" *Scribner's,* 28 (July–December, 1900), p. 123.

66. "The Dewey Arch," *Architects' and Builders' Magazine,* 1 (October 1899), pp. 1-8.

67. More than half of New York's population was foreign born in 1898. Margaret Clapp, "The Social and Cultural Scene" in Nevins & Krout, *The Greater City,* p. 196. This situation is once again the case: see "Immigrants Revitalize City, but Strain its Resources," *New York Times,* May 6, 1981, p. 1.

68. Competition entries are illustrated in *American Architect and Building News,* 41 (August 12, 1893).

ulated with a pilastered order and a broken entablature supporting sculptures by Daniel Chester French.

Although never finished, and compromised since by the additions and remodellings of William Lescaze and others, the Institute of Arts and Sciences (now known as The Brooklyn Museum) catalyzed the development of the Prospect Park area. McKim, Mead and White also undertook a series of shelters and entrance gates at Prospect Park itself. Executed in stone and terracotta, these classical pavilions contrasted with the romantic naturalism of the elder Olmsted's landscaping.

Also inspired by the new Institute was a project for the Brooklyn Central Library and the buildings around Grand Army Plaza. The great arch in the center of the Plaza had first been proposed by Seth Low while he was mayor of Brooklyn (1882–1885), but it was only in 1889 that the competition was held, won by John Duncan. While McKim, Mead and White had collaborated on several sculptural monuments, the perimeter buildings, many of which such as Francis H. Kimball's Montauk Club and the Guido Plessner House by Frank Freeman, exemplified the more individualistic spirit of the cosmopolitan era and were not scaled to the plaza's vastness.

The City Improvement Commission Plan had designated Grand Army Plaza as an ideal location for public buildings, and in 1908 Raymond Almiral suggested a comprehensive treatment of the Plaza in conjunction with the proposed Brooklyn Central Library. A.D.F. Hamlin, of Columbia, served as consulting architect for the library. The perimeter would have received a uniform facade, with the Plaza's central section developed as a public promenade. The entrance to Prospect Park received a colonnaded gateway, echoing the ellipse but not concentric to it, and to either side were the proposed Library and Zoological Museum.[69]

Hamlin appears to have done what is so often the case, that is he assigned the Library Project as a studio project. In this case he assigned it as the program for the post-graduate McKim Fellowship Competition in 1905; and quite interestingly the winning scheme of Lucien E. Smith *(Columbia, 1901)* prefigures Almiral's proposal in very many significant ways. Smith's scheme arranged offices and stacks along the perimeter of the trapezoidal site, with a vast domed reading room set within the interior courtyard.[70]

Almiral's design is essentially a developed version of Smith's, retaining the basic part but improving on its somewhat awkward connection between parts. The elevations are correspondingly similar, but Almiral's dome, greatly heightened, is better calculated to be seen in perspective *(fig. 12).*

The growth of the library system in New York was largely fostered by private philanthropy. The New York Public Library was formed by the merger of the Astor and Tilden Trusts, the consolidation resulting in one of the most important collections in the country. To house the collection a competition was held in 1897. This was structured along Beaux-Arts lines with an open *esquisse* held from which twelve finalists were chosen to develop their sketches.[71]

Carrere and Hastings defeated McKim in the final stage of the

Fig. 12 Proposed Brooklyn Central Library, Grand Army Plaza, 1908, Raymond F. Almiral.

69. H.W. Frohne, "The Brooklyn Plaza and the Projected Brooklyn Central Library," *Architectural Record,* 23 (February 1908), p. 97-110. Hamlin's role as consulting architect to the library presents an interesting, if unusual, intersection between the School and the city as a whole. Hamlin's selection for the job is easily understood; he could bring to the situation, otherwise immured in local squabbling over the site selection, the impartiality and respect that his position at Columbia commanded. Moreover, he was an outspoken proponent of the beneficial impact of environment on work and of the values of civic beautification. In 1900 he had castigated the citizenry for the absence of any "single work of decorative architecture erected at the public expense." That same year, he addressed the Woman's Club of Brooklyn on "How to Make Brooklyn Beautiful" and in 1902 he acted as advisor to the Committee for Erecting Carnegie Libraries in Brooklyn. See "Architecture and Citizenship," *Public Improvements,* 2 (April 16, 1900), pp. 265-68; "School of Architecture," *Columbia University Quarterly,* 4 (March 1902), pp. 209-210. Ware also served frequently as a professional advisor in competitions. *American Architect and Building News,* 36 (May 14, 1892), p. 93, observed that:

It is notorious that respectable architects, feeling sure of being hampered by ridiculous amateur stipulations in regard to arrangement of design, and not feeling by any means sure that their works or themselves will be fairly judged or treated, have long left public competitions alone. With the appearance of Professor Ware as advisor in such matters, their attitude has, however, altered.

70. *Architecture,* 12 (August 15, 1905).

71. *Architectural Review,* 4 (December 1, 1897), p. 68 includes a description of the competition and entries from its second round. Entries from the preliminary stage are illustrated in *American Architect and Building News,* 45 (October 2, 1897 and November 20, 1897). See also Blake, *The Architecture of Carrere & Hastings,* pp. 203-250.

competition, and a comparison of their elevations reveals Hastings' Modern-French stylistic predelictions versus McKim's more archaeological Classicism.[72] Carrere and Hastings' building is perhaps New York's finest example of Modern-French design, that is the combination of academic principles and styles formed at the Ecole des Beaux-Arts between about 1880 and 1910 *(fig. 13)*. Monumental in character, the elevations express the functions of the plan within. Pediments mark the main reading rooms, the attic over the cornice indicates the picture galleries, the large scale windows on the Fifth Avenue facade correspond to the special reading rooms, the simpler side facades house administrative and utilitarian functions, while the vertical arrangement of narrow windows indicates the location of the book stacks. The circulation expresses the hierarchy of functions; the main reading room lies at the rear and top of the building, culminating the vertical and horizontal procession. An extensive use of metal and glass ceilings is typical of the acceptance of technological innovation by advanced architects of the day in a manner that established a dialogue between traditional form and technological innovation.

The Public Library was the first important building to provide its own monumental setting; not only was the pediment placed on the axis of 41st Street to provide a monumental vista from the east, albeit down a minor residential side street, but the building was set back from the streets to provide for landscaped terraces and broad steps that to this day are one of midtown's few public amenities.

The New York Library Building was not intended to supply the outlying wards of the city where the demand for library services was rapidly escalating. From 1898 to 1903 the central branch experienced a thirty percent increase in withdrawals for home reading. The goal of building a series of branch libraries throughout the City went unrealized until 1901, when Andrew Carnegie offered the city $5,200,000 for the construction of sixty-one branch libraries. Three firms designed most of the branches in Manhattan: McKim, Mead & White, Carrere & Hastings, and Babb, Cook and Willard.[73] A.D.F. Hamlin's position as advisor to the Brooklyn Building Committee led, however, to commissions for J.M. Hewlett, and J.T. Tubby (*Columbia 1890* and *1896* respectively), a typical instance of Hamlin's support of Columbia graduates.

The building committee's instructions to the architects called for a standardized plan type and uniformity of character, materials and design. Maximum accessibility to the stacks was demanded, but also their easy surveillance from the circulation desk. The reading room was to be at street level so that the library would advertise itself as such, the readers being visible as through a showroom window.

These instructions were easily carried out in suburban Brooklyn where large sites usually prevailed. But in Manhattan, where most of the branches were built, constricted urban lots forced the plan type to be rearranged vertically, with reading rooms frequently placed on the top floor, away from street noise, and roofed terraces provided in several branches.

The consolidation of public institutions seen in the history of

Fig. 13 New York Public Library, 5th Avenue between 40th and 42nd Streets, 1903–10, Carrere & Hastings.

72. For McKim's project, see Leland Roth, *Urban Architecture of McKim, Mead & White*, p. 478-479.

73. See Theodore W. Koch, *A Book of Carnegie Libraries* (White Plains, N.Y.: Wilson, 1917).

New York's museum and library systems is paralleled in the development of its institutions of higher learning. Their architectural character is determined by a fundamental choice of imagery — whether the campus is expressed as a cloistral haven from the city devoted to education, or as an active force in the city's life, its education a preparation for entry into public life.[74]

Columbia's previous campus on 49th Street, by Charles Coolidge Haight, was an intimate complex of sober Victorian Gothic buildings focused inward on a small garden. Since the 1860's the College had been adding affiliated professional and pre-professional schools functioning increasingly like a university. With no room for further expansion, Columbia's Trustees decided in 1890 to move to Morningside Heights, and in 1896, as the new campus was about to be occupied, Columbia formally transformed itself into a University.[75]

Columbia's removal to Morningside Heights (first called University Heights) confirmed the popular characterization of the area as the cultural acropolis of the city, an image earlier suggested by the location of Grant's Tomb and the Cathedral of St. John the Divine, which were still under construction.

As the Columbia Committee on Buildings and Grounds noted, the new campus was to be "appropriate to the municipal character of the situation."[76] McKim's master plan of 1893 addressed the Trustees' desire for a public profile for the college and exploited the site's terrain with a terrace at the highest point. In contrast to Hunt's and Haight's proposals for the campus, McKim's plan tied the campus to the street grid along the avenues. In keeping with the municipal character of the problem, the central quadrangle and library opened to the south, towards the city, and the classical style employed signified the campus as a complex of public buildings. While the grandness of vision in the campus plan reflects the aesthetic impact of the Chicago Fair, the decision to address the public realm also reflects the character of education offered at Columbia. As Montgomery Schuyler wrote in 1910, it was "decidedly characterized as a preparatory school for learned professions."[77]

McKim's design is, in fact, a complex typological and iconographic representation of the prevailing sense of what constituted the public realm *(fig. 14)*. Although Schuyler viewed the new campus as "the complete obliteration of the architectural traditions of Columbia" as represented by the English-inspired Gothic of the former campus, whose "Anglicism supplied precisely what had for generations been recognized as the most appropriate and attractive architecture for a place of education for English-speaking mankind,"[78] McKim's design must also be seen as an evocation and glorification of Columbia's more distant heritage, the hybrid vernacular and classicism of King's College and other artifacts of pre-industrial America. Through the evocation of the classical ideal, one compromised in the classroom buildings, less so in the library, McKim responded to both contemporary conditions and a historical continuity. Albert Winslow Cobb noted in 1899, "On the heights of Morningside the genius of architect, artisan, and artist,

74. See Montgomery Schuyler, "Architecture of American Colleges: Part Four, New York City Colleges," *Architectural Record,* 27 (June 1910), pp. 443-469.

75. "Columbia University and its New Buildings," *Architects' and Builders' Magazine,* 33 (October 1900), pp. 11-19.

76. Montgomery Schuyler, "New York City Colleges," p. 445.

77. Ibid., p. 447.

78. Ibid.

Fig. 14 Low Library, Columbia University, Morningside Heights Campus, 1897, McKim, Mead & White. Photo: Columbiana Collection.

endowed by munificent public patronage, is evolving glories, new now, but in the future days to be classic as are the glories of Greece and Italy today."[79]

If Morningside Heights has lost some of its aura as the city's acropolis, the reason lies in part in the rapid residential growth around the area's monuments, and in the fact that many of those institutions are located at the center, rather than the edge of the plateau. Charles Rich, however, who designed Millbank Hall at Barnard College in 1899, developed a master plan for Barnard in 1904 which sought to establish a connection with the river, by extending Riverside Park across the Drive to Claremont Avenue. The campus itself was to be raised on a terrace, grouped around three sides of a quadrangle overlooking the Hudson, with smaller courtyards to the North and South. The building themselves would have been linked with intimately scaled arcaded cloisters, the quadrangle treated as a romantic garden populated with antique statuary and architectural fragments, thereby establishing a relationship with the park, its romanticism an intensification of the park's studied naturalism.[80]

In 1893, construction began on St. Luke's Hospital, Ernest Flagg's first major commission and one which he had won in competition. Like Columbia, St. Luke's had previously been located in midtown, on West 54th Street and Fifth Avenue, but its 1858 building had become technologically outmoded. Flagg's design concentrated a plan of ten pavilions on a constricted urban site. The pavilions ensured the wards adequate light and ventilation, and the open arcades between served as "fresh air cut-offs" preventing the spread of infection.[81]

With the construction of Columbia, St. Luke's, and St. John the Divine, Morningside Heights' institutional character was firmly established, but the area's development climaxed with the construction of The Union Theological Seminary, the Institute of Music by Donn Barber,[82] and the Robert Fulton Memorial competition. The Seminary, by Allen & Collens, reflects the transformation of the generally accepted urban ideal in the twenty years since the close of the cosmopolitan era. Restricted to the perimeter of the site, the complex at once reinforces the urban fabric created

79. Albert Winslow Cobb, "New York's Architectural Problems," *Architecture and Building*, 30 (April 1, 1899), pp. 99-100. Low Plaza evokes Olmstead's terraces before the U.S. Capitol. Francesco Passanti detects references in Low Memorial Library to the reading room of Smithmeyer & Pel's Library of Congress, Hunt's Administration Building at the World's Columbia Exposition, and Grant's Tomb, thus expressing its combined functions of library, administration, and memorial. All were highly public buildings prominent in the popular mind, and their evocation at Columbia placed the University in that public context. The individual references are entirely synthesized in the new building, however, and the entire ensemble — Low Library's chaste classicism, its timeless correctness and play of large masses contrasted with the unarticulated, stolidly rectangular brick and stone classroom buildings and their debased, Italo-French details — is without any direct parallel. In part the Library's special character reflects its role as a memorial to Seth Low's father, and its function as a public gesture of philanthropy by the polished democratic aristocrat and political reformer who was soon to be the City's mayor. See Francesco Passanti, "The Design of Columbia in the 1890's, McKim and His Client," *Journal of the Society of Architectural Historians*, 36 (May 1977), pp. 69-84.

The era was also marked by the construction of Stanford White's New York University Campus on University Heights designed in 1893 and by George B. Post's Campus for the City College of New York, on Amsterdam Avenue and 157th Street, competition 1897. Columbia's relocation on Morningside Heights coincided with that of Teachers College, chartered 1889. The campus was designed by William A. Potter in 1892, who had served on the Teachers College Board of Trustees. Columbia and Teachers College affiliated in 1893. See Sarah B. Landau, *Edward T. and William A. Potter*, pp. 338-345.

80. "Barnard College," *Architecture*, 10 (November 1904), pp. 172-173.

81. H.W. Desmond, "Description of the Works of Ernest Flagg," *Architectural Record*, 11 (April 1902), pp. 8-22. Among other hospitals built in the period were Bellevue, constructed incrementally by McKim, Mead and White between 1903 and 1913, and Mount Sinai, by Arnold W. Brunner, built in 1912.

82. "The Institute of Musical Art," *American Architect*, 97 (May 25, 1910), p. 208.

Fig. 15 Accepted design for the Robert Fulton Memorial, Riverside Drive between 116th and 114th Streets, 1910, H. Van Buren Magonigle.

by the street grid and establishes a communal expression within the courtyard. Schuyler found that, "our street architecture has nothing better to show in this kind, and very few things so good."[83] Even though the language of the Seminary is Gothic, its composition and its attitude to the urban context is securely rooted in the academic traditions of the Beaux-Arts and the American Renaissance.[84]

The competition for the Robert Fulton Memorial was won by H. Van Buren Magonigle in 1910 *(fig. 15)*. Conceived to provide the reception point for distinguished visitors — the visitor was to have entered the city at the foot of 116th Street, on Columbia's transverse axis. As Magonigle put it, "to the foreign visitor... the Memorial has to be not merely the gateway of the city but of a new world."[85] Like the Pulitzer Fountain, the Fulton Memorial was designed as a "useful" monument, providing recreation piers, a museum, and screening the railroad tracks, (not covered over until the mid 1930's when Robert Moses built the Henry Hudson Parkway) through Riverside Park. The long horizontal of the peristyle was intended as a visual base for the varying skyline of the apartment houses on Riverside Drive. Just as Columbia's Morningside Campus provides one of the earliest examples of the City Beautiful Movement in New York, the Fulton Memorial is one of the last. The *American Architect* noted that the competition demonstrated the success of

the comparatively small number of individuals, who, through their persistent efforts, have guided the weaker to higher ideals and a broader outlook for the future of art in America. We are not ripe for the indigenous art of which a few forerunners have given us many remarkable and few really meritorious examples. There are still too many incongruous elements in our national system that need adjusting before assimilation is possible, and without a thorough assimilation of important material and intellectual factors there can be no real progress in art. The development of art involves the establishment of a tradition founded on such settled state of mind as cannot [yet] exist in this country...[86]

The high standard of design apparent to those who viewed the Fulton Memorial Competition and the uniformity and decorum evident in the monuments of the composite city had developed in the context of the city's expansion and economic growth. C.H. Reilly remarked in 1901 that

the immense material prosperity which is not inseparable from our idea of

83. Montgomery Schuyler, "New York City Colleges," p. 460.

84. Beaux Arts Principles of Gothic Design were discussed by David Van Zanten in the Mathews Lectures at Columbia in the Fall of 1980.

85. H. Van Buren Magonigle, "The Robert Fulton Memorial," *American Architect*, 97 (June 15, 1900), pp. 225-226. For earlier attempts to address the Hudson River waterfront, see Milton See's project, "The Planning of Cities: Paper No. 4," *Public Improvements*, 2 (December 1st, 1899), p. 51; also Palmer and Hornbostel's visionary scheme for a Columbia Stadium, Naval Reserve, Public Recreation Pier and Water Gate, stretching from 112th St. to 120th St. on the Hudson, published in *Architecture*, 16 (August 1907), pp. 140-141.

86. "Some Aspects of the Robert Fulton Memorial Competition," *American Architect*, 97 (June 15, 1900), pp. 226-227. *Architecture* found that Magonigle had "rid himself of the French influence which... has marred many of his previous efforts, and has raised himself to a height of simplicity and pure beauty which McKim, Mead & White alone have hitherto attained." *Architecture*, 21 (June 1910), p. 82-83, 90.

America is a matter of the last twenty years or so. Curiously enough —for art and wealth but rarely walk hand in hand —architecture has during the same period shown its most distinctive products and achieved its finest results...And this cannot be solely accounted for by plentiful opportunity...To find the reason we must go further back and trace the system under which both American Architecture and American Architects have grown up. [87]

Reilly goes on to suggest that it was the system of education in American architectural schools which was

the secret of the Renaissance of American Architecture: the influence of a definite system by which all the young architects are trained along the same lines should obviously show itself in greater uniformity of character and greater consistency of detail, and these are exactly the points most noticeable in modern American building. For by their system of teaching design the schools have narrowed but deepened the channel, and thereby strengthened the current of architectural thought, so that instead of spreading itself out in a vast variety of styles...it has for the last ten years been spending its force, as it did in Grecian days, in perfecting and refining a few definite and allied types. [88]

In view of the role played by the American system of architectural education in fostering the values of the American Renaissance, and in transforming the city into a metropolis, it seems appropriate, and far less partial than one might originally suspect, in the concluding section of this essay to turn to a consideration of Columbia's School of Architecture during the period, and to focus in particular on the role played by a number of its alumni in rendering lithic the metropolitan ideal. In so doing, because of limitations of space, we have selected only a handful of the quite considerable number of graduates of Ware's program who went on to solid achievements in the profession, but it does seem clear the first twenty years of architecture at Columbia, as measured by the achievements of its alumni, surely were a golden age.

While the interaction between the University and the city was only occasionally acknowledged, and while in fact, as in the case of the design of the campus itself, it seems more likely that the relationship between the two was one of personalities as much as ideals, as when the leading architect in the community, Charles F. McKim, was able not only to influence the physical character of the university but also to remodel its architectural curriculum to suit his own conception of practice.

Just as the physical growth of Columbia between 1890 and 1915 to a considerable extent mirrors the architectural development of the city, its architectural program not only mirrored the values of the professional community but also to a considerable extent shaped them as it did the very fabric of the city, so numerous and so influential were its graduates. At another level, the connection between the University and the spirit of consolidation was surely reinforced through Seth Low, the University's President, who was a principal advocate of the union of New York and Brooklyn, and was the guiding spirit behind the university's move to Mor-

87. C.H. Reilly, "The Modern Renaissance in American Architecture," *Journal of the Royal Institute of British Architects*, (3rd ser.) 17 (June 25, 1910), p. 630.

88. Ibid., p. 632.

ningside Heights, resulting in New York's single most coherent expression of the American Renaissance.

Though the architectural faculty in the 1880's and 1890's was small, it was certainly not invisible. Both Ware and in particular his chief assistant, A.D.F. Hamlin, frequented the lecture platform at a time when such appearances were a principal forum for the communication of ideas to the general public. Hamlin and Ware not only lectured frequently before professional groups, such as the Architectural League, and lay audiences, such as those of the Brooklyn Institute of Arts and Sciences, but also helped write programs and organize competitions.

After the retirement of Ware, that is, in the flood tide of metropolitanism between 1900 and 1915, when the faculty was relatively large, the university exercised considerable influence through them. Henry Hornbostel, for example, was with his partner, Palmer, the consultant to Gustav Lindenthal on the design of the Queensboro Bridge; Austin Lord was a prominent practitioner, and his successor, William A. Boring, whose career pretty much coincides with the declining years of metropolitanism, had earlier been a partner of a very influential firm, Boring and Tilton. Nonetheless, because the general attitude of the day separated academic architects from practitioners, one cannot look too closely to the professional offices of the School's faculty for signs of its influence.

A rather more accurate barometer can be found in the careers of the various students of the late 1880's and early 1890's who began to exercise their talents as independent practitioners almost immediately upon their graduation (or more usually, their return from post graduate study at the Ecole des Beaux-Arts in Paris or at the newly founded American Academy in Rome).

The University's program in architecture exercised a strong influence over the city's architectural profession as well as its physical growth from its inception in 1881, but increasingly so after the late 1890's, when a remarkable group of former students including John Russell Pope, Henry Hornbostel, William Adams Delano, Chester B. Aldrich, Henry Herts, Robert D. Kohn and Harry Allan Jacobs, all of whom went on to the Ecole des Beaux-Arts in Paris, returned to rise almost meteorically to professional prominence.

Though the quality of the program at Columbia in this period — the years of Ware's hegemony — was fine, training is surely not enough to ensure success. Columbia's talented graduates succeeded because New York's economy was booming and there was enough work for all. The vast size of a number of New York's architectural practices assured employment to talented graduates, and allowed them greater design responsibility than was common elsewhere. As C.H. Reilly points out, this "American system is only possible with a highly trained staff, and, more than that, with a staff trained in a definite tradition."[89] In this essay we have focused mostly on the new major institutional buildings and on the evolution of the city's sense of its physical self, but a host of other building types, including department stores, apartment buildings,   89. Ibid.

townhouses, even whole residential suburbs, as well as public baths and small parks offered opportunities for architects to make significant contributions. (One graduate, Louis Korn *(Columbia, 1891),* combined the services of architect with those of developer).

It goes without saying that the mere prosperity of the time cannot alone explain the meteoric rise to prominence of some of the young Columbia graduates, else the names of others from Columbia, not to mention those trained at other major schools of architecture such as Syracuse, Illinois, and M.I.T. would also figure importantly in this account. Two factors at least can be cited in explanation of the phenomenal showing of some of the graduates: because Columbia in the 1890's was still an elite college for established New York families, including those of German-Jewish descent who were only beginning to gain a foothold at other universities such as Harvard and Yale, it is safe to say that the gates were already open to many of these men of talent. In addition, because Columbia not only served the families of the New York establishment but was in fact located in New York, it offered its graduates those immediate professional and business contacts so useful to a fledgling architect, contacts that such isolated schools as those at Syracuse or Champaign could not, and that M.I.T., somewhat overshadowed by Harvard (which was just beginning its own program), for sociological and geographical reasons could not.

The first graduate of Ware's fledgling program to attain distinction was Edward Pearce Casey *(Columbia, 1888),* who was responsible for the completion of the Library of Congress after the dismissal of the original architects, Smithmeyer and Pelz.[90] But Casey's career is slightly off the subject, since his field of action was Washington and not New York; thus it is Samuel B.P. Trowbridge, Class of 1886, and his partner, Goodhue Livingston, Class of 1892, who represent the first significant expression of Columbia's architectural impact on the city. Trowbridge and Livingston also represent the heritage of New York's and the nation's past, each descended from established families of an older social order whose influence the new monies and new immigration patterns were quickly supplanting.

After graduating from Columbia, Trowbridge supervised the construction of the American School of Classical Studies in Athens, went on to the Ecole, and returned in 1890 to work for George B. Post. His partnership with Livingston began in 1894. The firm's first large commission, won in a competition, was Col. John Jacob Astor's St. Regis Hotel (1904).[91] Arthur C. David claimed it was "The Best Type of Metropolitan Hotel", adding that the standards of quality and luxury expressed in the homes of the wealthy had been "transferred to a hotel, and in some respects even transcended."[92] Like the St. Regis, the store for B. Altman & Co. (1906) reflected the beginning of a transformation in Fifth Avenue's still residential character. Perhaps in deference, the department store — itself a relatively new building type — was designed with "all the appearance of a fashionable store without any suggestion of mere ostentation."[93] In 1906, Trowbridge and

Fig. 16 Bankers Trust Company Building, 1911, Trowbridge & Livingston: Samuel B.T. Trowbridge *(1886)* and Goodhue Livingston *(1892).*

90. Wilson, *American Renaissance,* p. 106. Note that Wilson, claiming Casey was an engineer graduated from Columbia in 1886, incorrectly interprets the nature of the College program in the 1880's. Casey later attended the Ecole for three years.

91. Previous commissions included the House of Mrs. Richard A. Gambrill on Park Avenue (*American Architect and Building News,* 64 June 3, 1899), also an artist's studio and stable, 121-123 East 63rd Street (*Architectural Record,* 2, October 1901, p. 721). In 1898 Trowbridge and Livingston built the St. Luke's Nursing Home, now Columbia's Hogan Hall, on Broadway and West 114th Street.

92. Arthur C. David, "The St. Regis — The Best Type of Metropolitan Hotel," *Architectural Record,* 15 (June 1904), pp. 552-623.

93. Arthur C. David, "The New Fifth Avenue," *Architectural Record,* 30 (July 1907), pp. 1-14.

Livingston also built the Hotel Knickerbocker on Broadway and 42nd Street,[94] and their career climaxed with a series of corporate office buildings in the financial district of which the Bankers Trust[95] (1912) with its wonderfully evocative stepped pyramidal top — is surely the most memorable *(fig. 16).*

The Class of 1890 was a particularly notable one; its talented members included J. Monroe Hewlett, Henry C. Pelton and Robert D. Kohn. Hewlett later entered into partnership with Austin W. Lord, who became dean of Columbia's School of Architecture in 1912. Kohn was the first graduate to represent the newly established German-Jewish population of the city, a group which constituted much of his clientele. Kohn was perhaps the most experimental architect of his generation in New York. His first significant work, the Ethical Culture Society School,[96] was executed in collaboration with Carrere and Hastings. Later independent works, including the adjacent Hall of the Ethical Culture Society, the New York Evening Post Building, and the extension to Macy's in the 1920's, are each too little appreciated essays in a "progressive" kind of Classicism very much akin in spirit to the work of Otto Wagner and Josef Plecnik in Vienna. The Society's adjacent hall in 1911, was praised by the *Architectural Record for the austerity of the treatment in general, the leaving of square arises in so many cases where one would expect a moulding of transition, the point at which the development of the corbels has been arrested, insomuch that one may also be inclined to say that the fronts are 'en bloc' instead of being finished.*[97]

This abstraction of the temple form was held to be appropriate to a religion which "not only deprives itself of spiritual sanction, but denies itself those ritual observances which constitute the data and the material of the ecclesiastical architect."

Kohn's now largely forgotten Evening Post building (1907) *(fig.17)* was praised by Montgomery Schuyler as "the thing itself," the "skeleton" — inverted commas are Schuyler's —

hardly draped, but articulated, developed and decorated in accordance with the facts of the case. Instead of being concealed and confused, the essential structure is emphasized that the spectator understands it better than he would have understood the mere steel frame before the architectural treatment of it was begun.

Schuyler found the composition not merely explanatory, but "highly artistic and effective...one of the best things in our recent street architecture, one of the most exemplary and interesting of the skyscrapers."[98]

Kohn later formed a partnership with Clarence Stein and Charles Butler, specializing in hospitals. The firm was responsible in New York for the Goldwater Memorial Hospital on Welfare Island, completed in 1939,[99] as well as additions to Mount Sinai and Montefiore Hospitals. Their most monumental contribution to New York was, however, the new Temple Emanu-El on Fifth Avenue and East 65th Street, designed with Goodhue Associates as consultants. Faced with expressing a religion which did possess ritual, but without an identifiable architectural tradition, a prob-

Fig. 17 New York Evening Post Building, 20 Vesey St., 1907, Robert D. Kohn *(1890).*

94. Herbert Wynham-Gittens, "The Hotel Knickerbocker," *Architects' and Builders' Magazine,* 8 (December 1906), pp. 89-102.

95. "The Banker's Trust Company Building," *The Architect,* 6 (May 1912), pp. 241-247.

96. The Ethical Culture Society's school at Central Park West and West 63rd Street, intended as a model for educational reform, was designed by Kohn and Carrere & Hastings in 1902. Its facades are marked by their sophisticated expression of a nonstructural skin, the subtle panelling of the brick abstracting the forms of pilasters and rustication while the steel and glass infill of windows and the openwork metal cornice exploit the potential of new technology without sacrifice of traditional composition. See *Architecture,* 10 (September 1904), Pl. LXXXI; also Blake, who neglects Kohn's collaboration: *The Architecture of Carrere & Hastings,* pp. 78-79; Carrere & Hastings probably received the commission through the influence of Hendon Chubb, a prominent Ethical Culturalist for whom they had already built the Chubb Building on South William Street in 1899–1900.

97. "Architectural Appreciations: Hall of the Society of Ethical Culture, New York City," *Architectural Record,* 30 (August 1911), pp. 175-180.

lem that had earlier brought from Leopold Eidlitz his finest and most cosmopolitan building, Kohn was led to an eclectic synthesis of Romanesque and Islamic motifs, rendered with a massiveness requisite to give the synagogue an authoritative, "classical" scale.[100]

John Russell Pope came from an affluent and distinguished background; his family had settled in Massachusetts in 1630 and his father, John Pope, was a noted portraitist. Before studying architecture formally Pope had already worked for several years in McKim's office.[101] His strong talent as a designer was immediately recognized at Columbia; in his second and third years of school he was unofficially functioning as an assistant to Ware.[102]

In 1895 Pope won both the Schermerhorn travelling fellowship and the McKim Scholarship, the latter with a design for a savings bank.[103] As the first architectural fellow of the American Academy in Rome, Pope was encouraged by its Director, Austin Lord, to undertake a serious study of Italy's ancient and Renaissance monuments. According to Royal Cortissoz, McKim later "put forward Pope as an example of what he was driving at" in establishing the Academy. "Pope's work was to him ample proof of his contention that Rome was the place to bring out the talents of the picked men of the rising generation."[104] After continuing on to the Ecole des Beaux-Arts and completing his courses there in an astonishing two years, Pope returned to America to work for Bruce Price, and later served as assistant in the *atelier* McKim conducted at Columbia after Ware's retirement.

Pope began independent practice in 1903, but his *oeuvre* lies largely outside the bounds of this essay, flowering instead in the field of country estates (many, however, for New York families) and in the residences and monuments of official Washington. Yet Pope was responsible for the last significant artifact of the City Beautiful movement in New York City, the Theodore Roosevelt Memorial at the Museum of Natural History *(fig. 18)*.[105] Built in 1931–1935, the distilled purity of its then seemingly anachronistic classicism reflects Pope's early exposure to the unadulterated sources of classical Rome, and marks Pope as the heir to what C. H. Reilly termed McKim's "great, impersonal" architecture.[106]

The evolution of Delano and Aldrich's practice progressed slowly from domestic commissions for wealthy clients to buildings for the social and commercial institutions of the same clientele; typical of many, Delano augmented his fledgling practice with other positions, most notably as a Professor at Columbia from 1903–1910.

Aldrich graduated from Columbia in 1893. Delano, after graduating from Yale, attended as a special student in 1899. The two had first met in 1895 while working in the office of Carrere & Hastings,[107] and both later continued their education at the Ecole des Beaux-Arts. After forming their partnership in 1903, Delano and Aldrich first established themselves through competitions, winning such commissions as the Walters Art Gallery in Baltimore (1904) and the Philadelphia Orphanage at Wallingford, Pennsylvania (1908).[108] Domestic architecture was a mainstay of their

98. Montgomery Schuyler, "Some Recent Skyscrapers," *Architectural Record*, 22 (September 1907), pp. 161-176. See also "The New Evening Post Building," *Architects' and Builders' Magazine*, 8 (September 1907), pp. 569-573, and Schuyler's appraisal of Kohn's Hermitage Hotel: "An Interesting Skyscraper," *Architectural Record*, 22 (November 1907), pp. 365-368.

99. *Architectural Forum*, 71 (November 1939), pp. 379-398.

100. Charles Butler, "The Temple Emanu-El, New York," and Clarence S. Stein, "The Problem of the Temple and its Solution," *Architectural Forum*, 52 (February 1930), pp. 150-168. For Leopold Eidlitz's synagogue of 1868 for the same congregation (at 5th Avenue and 42nd Street) see Montgomery Schuyler, "A Great American Architect: Leopold Eidlitz, Part I, Ecclesiastical and Domestic Work," *Architectural Record*, 24 (September 1980), pp. 164-179.

In his later career, Kohn devoted himself to professional and public service. He was president of the American Institute of Architects from 1930–1932, director of the housing division of the Public Works Administration from 1933–1934, vice-president and chairman of the theme committee of the 1939–1940 New York World's Fair. In 1910, lecturing at Columbia, Kohn expressed his view of the proper function of the architectural profession ("The Architect as Reformer," *Real Estate Record and Guide* 85, p. 976):

The environment in which our modern life is to find itself will have a great effect on the development of that life. The architect must be a reformer, must see further than those for whom he works, going beyond what they ask, giving them not only more beautiful structures, but nobler structures, ... The architect will only take his proper position in a community, a position worthy of the art which he practices, when he realizes his position is that of leader not only in his art but also in his relations with the great civic movements of his time.... The new view... must require of the architect that through his knowledge of the world, his imagination, his idealism, he transforms the envelope of all our varied human activities in such a way that he helps to transform and ennoble the activities themselves.

101. Herbert Croly, "Recent Works of John Russell Pope," *Architectural Record*, 29 (June 1911), pp. 441-511.

102. *The Architecture of John Russell Pope* (New York: William Helburn, 1925), Vol. 1, introduction by Royal Cortissoz, no pagination. Pope's thesis in 1894, prophetic for his later work, was for a group of college buildings. The editors of *Architecture and Building* were lavish in their praise for its "imposing" character, "with the domed chapel as the central point and the library and museum to the right and left connected by an arcade which encloses the grounds in front of the chapel." See *Architecture and Building*, 20 (June 16, 1894), p. 289.

103. Francis S. Swales, "Master Draftsmen, VIII: John Russell Pope," *Pencil Points*, 5 (December 1924), pp. 64-80.

104. *The Architecture of John Russell Pope*, vol. 1, Introduction by Royal Cortissoz, no pagination.

105. *The Architecture of John Russell Pope*, Vol. II, pl. 37-44. The competition had been held in 1925, the other participants being H. Van Buren Magonigle, Edward Green & Sons, Helmle & Corbett, Gordon & Kaelber, Trowbridge & Livingston, York and Sawyer, and J.H. Freedlander. See *American Architect*, 128 (July 1, 1925), p. 14, pl. 168-178. It was originally intended that a tree-lined concourse extend axially from Pope's facade through Central Park to the Metropolitan Museum of Art (the reservoir was soon to be reclaimed as parkland). See *History Plan and Design of the New York State Roosevelt Memorial*, prepared under the direction of the Board of Trustees by Henry Fairfield Osborn, chairman (1928); also *The New York State Roosevelt Memorial, Dedicated January 19, 1936*, prepared under the direction of the Board of Trustees by George N. Pindar, secretary (1936). Pope's Memorial supplanted Trowbridge & Livingston's 1911 master plan,

Fig. 18 Accepted design for the New York State Theodore Roosevelt Memorial, Central Park West between 77th and 81st Streets, 1925, John Russell Pope *(1894)*.

practice from the very beginning, with city residences and country houses for such affluent New York families as the Sloans, Astors and Vanderbilts.[109] The recently demolished townhouse built for Robert S. Brewster at 100 East 70th Street, corner Park Avenue in 1906[110] is typical of the restraint and refinement which would characterize their later work, and of the sense of architectural decorum which characterized much of the work of the generation of academic architects, more influenced by the example of McKim than by the Ecole.

Delano and Aldrich achieved their greatest distinction in their club buildings. In the age of the city convenient (1915–1930) they succeeded McKim, Mead & White as the city's preferred club architects, typically providing new quarters for established clubs as they relocated uptown. The Union Club, for example, marked its centennial in 1936 with a new building on Park Avenue and 69th Street; two of its previous homes, on 5th Avenue and 21st Street by Griffith Thomas (1852), and on 5th Avenue and 51st Street by Cass Gilbert (1903), had both been caught up in the city's encroaching commercialism *(fig. 19).*[111] Delano and Aldrich had already built a new home for the Colony Club in 1916 on Park Avenue and 62nd Street,[112] replacing Stanford White's building of ten years earlier on Madison Avenue.

Their partnership concluded with the Main Building and Marine Terminal of La Guardia Airport, built for the New York World's Fair of 1939–1940, an evocative essay in Art Deco which is at once unexpected from the firm yet somehow in its tradition of sophisticated, elegant yet lighthearted formalism.[113]

Henry B. Herts was from a family of decorators. After briefly attending City College, he worked for Bruce Price, who encouraged him to study architecture at Columbia.[114] While still an undergraduate, Herts won a competition for the design of an arch dedicated to the memory of Christopher Columbus, intended for a site at the Fifth Avenue entrance to Central Park. A temporary wooden one was erected according to Herts' design in 1892.[115]

By 1898 Herts and his partner Hugh Tallant were established practitioners.[116] In 1904 they inaugurated the mature phase of their career with the opening of two theatres, the New Amsterdam (41st to 42nd Streets, West of 7th Avenue) and the Lyceum (44th Street, east of 7th Avenue).[117] The interior decoration of the New Amsterdam was immediately characterized as a restrained, thoughtful expression of the "L'Art Nouveau," its character "fixes

illustrated in "The Conference on City Planning," *Real Estate Record and Guide,* 86 (May 20, 1911), p. 1076.

106. C.H. Reilly, *McKim, Mead & White* (London: 1924; reissued Blom: 1972), p. 24.

107. Obituary, C.H. Aldrich, *New York Herald Tribune,* December 26, 1940.

108. *New York Architect,* 2 (June 1908), no pagination.

109. For country houses, see *Portraits of Ten Country Houses Designed by Delano & Aldrich,* Introduction by Royal Cortissoz, drawings by Chester Price (New York: Doubleday, 1924).

110. *New York Architect,* 2 (June 1908), no pagination.

111. *American Architect,* 148 (April 1936), pp. 27-28. For a discussion of the club house as building type in America see Anne W.D. Henry, *The Building of a Club: Social Institution and Architectural Type, 1870–1905,* Introduction by Anthony Vidler (School of Architecture and Urban Planning, Princeton University, 1976).

112. *Architecture,* 33 (1916), Pl. 59-62.

113. *Architect's Journal,* 93 (March 20, 1941), pp. 195-199.

114. Abbott Halstead Moore, "Individualism in Architecture: The Works of Herts and Tallant," *Architectural Record,* 15 (January 1904), pp. 55-91.

115. *Architecture and Building,* 17 (October 8, 1892), p. 178.

116. "Harmonie Club House, 42nd Street," *Architecture and Building,* 29 (December 10, 1898).

117. *Architects' and Builders' Magazine,* 5 (February 1904), pp. 185-98.

more or less the purpose of the house," which was intended for light comedy. The Lyceum, though a very small theatre, has a grandly conceived elevation with a bold, glass marquee.

The firm's residence of 1903 for Philip Henry at 1053 Fifth Avenue is equally inventive; a low-key, almost informal townhouse for a narrow 20 foot lot, combining inventively turned limestone and wrought iron trim with a brick and tile facade.[118] This facade, and even more the interior design, no matter how jarring they probably were to the consistent whiteness of the neoclassical city then emerging, are nonetheless interesting examples of a modernist sensibility, revealing strong influences from Paris and Germany. The Art Nouveau influence can also be seen in the "wavy line" abstractions of their Joel Goldenberg mausoleum at Salem Fields Cemetery.[119]

The Folies Bergère Theatre (since remodelled as the Helen Hayes) was the firm's most flamboyant design,[120] and a building type new to America, a dinner theatre: "The impression conveyed, when the house is lighted and occupied, is that of a modern restaurant, with all the charm and handsome appointment that is the attribute of the cosmopolitan restaurant of the first order."[121] The facade was richly patterned with ivory, turquoise, and gold glazed terracotta, with an allegorical painting by William De L. Dodge of the characters of Vaudeville *(fig. 20)*.

The culmination of the firm's career was the design of the Academy of Music in Brooklyn (1906–08),[122] a vastly more complex cultural center than any tried in New York since Madison Square Garden. The Academy of Music includes a large hall for over 2,000 people, a smaller 1500-seat theatre as well as small lecture and banquet halls and the usual offices and back-up spaces.[123] The Academy was a replacement for an earlier facility that burned in November, 1903. It was regarded as a very important civic monument, particularly in the light of the recent consolidation with Manhattan, which was quickly overshadowing Brooklyn and threatening its sense of independence.

In terms of architectural education at Columbia the apogee of the era of consolidation was marked by McKim's campaign to retire Ware and by the subsequent changes that McKim imposed on the curriculum. Ware's curriculum was intended as a preparation for professional education: concentrating on aesthetic ideals, it was meant to be succeeded by apprenticeship in an architect's office or more formal study abroad at the Ecole des Beaux-Arts. While it was never explicitly so stated, it appears to have been the slave to two conceptions of professional training, the more elitist ideal of the 1880's in which college-educated men became architects, while others merely became draftsmen, and the newer, more democratic ideal in which a man or woman could qualify as an architect by a variety of means including that of strict apprenticeship or university training or a combination of both. It would appear that Ware, in trying to accommodate both groups (he admitted students as non-degree candidates) compromised the rigor of the program in the eyes of McKim, who viewed its proper function as one of strict professional preparation for practice, rigorous enough so as to

Fig. 19 Union Club, Park Avenue and 69th Street, 1936, Delano & Aldrich: William A. Delano *(1899)* and Chester H. Aldrich *(1893)*. Photo by Samuel Gottscho, courtesy of The Museum of the City of New York.

118. *Architecture and Building,* 5 (May 1904), pp. 354-63.

119. *Architects' and Builders' Magazine,* 5 (August 1904), p. 538. See also their mausolea for other families at Salem Fields Cemetery, pp. 537-541.

120. *Architectural Yearbook,* 1 (1912), pp. 379-381, 383.

121. "The Folies Bergere, New York," *New York Architect,* 5 (June 1911).

122. *American Architecture,* 90 (1906), pp. 150-152.

123. "The New Academy of Music," *Architecture,* 18.

omit the need for students to attend the Ecole des Beaux-Arts, which he distrusted.

Ware was of course hampered by the undergraduate nature of his program; and by the fact that many students, such as Samuel Bloomingdale, chose not to pursue careers in architecture at all (Bloomingdale continued the family tradition in merchandising). Moreover, Ware and Hamlin shared a view that, as Hamlin put it, "there is no line of professional study I know of so liberalizing and widely valuable as that of the architect; and there is no line of professional study of which so large a proportion is practicable, valuable and fascinating for the unprofessional student."[124]

McKim's course of study was meant to replace that of the Ecole with a program that provided in America its type of strict professionalism but adapted its techniques to a wholly different set of professional and cultural conditions. This shift in emphasis seems at first to reflect idealism succumbing to pragmatism, but McKim's strategy was in fact a reaction to what many Americans came to regard as the Ecole's increasing rigidity and the debased classicism of the "Modern French" or "Beaux Arts Baroque" style. These stylistic proclivities had been less well established during McKim's own time at the Ecole, and the Ecole's influence on him lay in its strict professionalism and its more fundamental theories of composition.[125] Similarly, McKim's founding of the American Academy in Rome in 1894 (with the help of Richard Morris Hunt) was intended to expose American students to the primary, unadulterated sources of classicism and to bypass France. As John La Farge noted, "Such study would free us from the subserviency of other European training, for the extremely sensitive mind of the artist is especially impressed by authority and it is evidently desirable that that authority, however various, should be the highest that we know."[126] An editorial in *New York Architect* of 1909, probably by editor Donn Barber (who attended Columbia as a special student in 1893–94 before spending four years at the Ecole) observed:

Although (McKim) and the several members of his firm all received more or less training in Paris, they have in their practice constantly refused to sanction the spread of the so-called Beaux-Arts influence in this country. The fact that the followers of the Beaux-Arts had coupled with their organization a system of training and education for draughtsmen, thereby exerting on these young men a powerful influence, and they in turn disregarding American conditions, were producing designs and buildings which outrivaled even their French examples, made Mr. McKim feel that the Americans in Paris had gone to extremes. He realized that his best means of improving all of American Architecture was to take a stand diametrically opposed to the French School. . . . through the founding of the American Academy at Rome and the endowing of certain scholarships at Columbia University for Italian study. His idea most strongly impressed was that American students in Europe should study faithfully the great classical and Renaissance monuments.[127]

As such, the establishment of the American Academy was opposed by the American Society of Beaux-Arts Architects, who

Fig. 20 Folies Bergere, 46th St. west of Broadway, 1911, Herts & Tallant: Henry B. Herts *(1897).*

124. A.D.F. Hamlin, "Architecture and Citizenship," *Public Improvements,* 2 (April 16, 1900), pp. 265-268.

125. C.H. Reilly wrote of McKim, "Although he appreciated the great worth of the Paris system of training, he never liked the Modern French taste, and was always, according to Robert Peabody, the architect, a Paris colleague of those days, nearer to Rome than to Paris." See Reilly, *McKim, Mead & White,* p. 10.

126. Quoted in Alfred Hoyt Granger, *Charles Follen McKim: A Study of His Life and Work* (Boston and New York: Houghton Mifflin, 1913), pp. 92-93.

127. "Charles Follen McKim," Editorial, *New York Architect,* 3 (September 1909), pp. 1-5.

argued that the center of modern architectural activity was Paris, not Rome.[128]

McKim's antagonism to Ware should also be seen in the light of Ware's increasing emphasis on historical studies in the mid-1890's. For McKim, the emphasis on historical problems frequently based on American examples would have involved not simply a drain on the time available for design, but a threat as well of stylistic corruption.[129]

The continuation of the research approach into the 1890's was an anachronistic vestige of the synthetic eclecticism of the 1880's, of the romantic individualism and casual attitude toward prototypes which characterized the architecture of the cosmopolitan city. McKim personally practiced a less capricious sort of historical research. Not a great draftsman himself, he frequently travelled to Italy with a draftsman to make measured drawings of the unadulterated archetypes of classicism, employing a "scholarly" rather than personal approach to the study of prototypical monuments.[130] McKim's antagonism towards Ware must be seen as a reflection of the idealism of the American Renaissance. As Reilly wrote of those ideals:

the architectural world is too wide, it knows too much of the past to be content today with merely eccentric or purely personal solutions to great problems. McKim felt this very strongly. He and his firm have always stood...for the same solution to every problem — the solution, that is to say, which has its roots in the general history of civilization.[131]

The era of composite metropolitanism drew to a close as the world plunged into the most devastating war in history. The high ideals of a balanced metropolitan order that motivated Andrew H. Green, Seth Low and others in their efforts to consolidate the scattered cities and villages into a metropolis comparable to London or Paris, seemed quite naive and certainly far less attainable fifteen years later, as the city of three million grew to one of five million, with every municipal service overtaxed and significant segments of the population ill-housed.

The generation of political and architectural idealists who had formulated the structure and the image of the composite city was no longer alive to see its ideals shattered. Green, the "father of Greater New York," died in 1903; Charles Follen McKim in 1909; Seth Low in 1916. A new and more pragmatic generation was now taking command. Not without ideals of its own, to be sure, this generation tempered its idealism with more "realism" than its immediate predecessor, applying the architectural techniques of the composite era to the economic, political and social constraints of a far more typically democratic set of problems. Their task was to make New York more convenient and efficient for all those who used its commercial and public facilities, and in particular for those who had too little means and too little education to benefit from the grand plans of the *fin de siecle*. Convenience and efficiency now jostled for recognition with beauty and grandeur in the boardrooms and drafting rooms.

128. Ware himself also objected to the establishment of a formal course of a study at the Academy, and resigned as chairman of the Managing Committee in protest. See Paul R. Baker, *Richard Morris Hunt* (Cambridge, Massachusetts and London: MIT Press, 1980), pp. 438-439.

129. Beginning in 1894–95, measured drawings of existing buildings were required of third and fourth year students. *Architecture and Building* noted in 1897:

It is, perhaps, the special characteristic of this school that the students devote themselves largely to historical studies, sacrificing to them time which would otherwise be given to the practice of original design. Indeed of the twenty-six working weeks which comprise the academic year, we understand that the second and third year men this year gave up the afternoons of four or five to the making of sketches and measured drawings from buildings in the city, and eight to historical research, sketching and drawing our buildings and parts of buildings from books and photographs. This left barely thirteen weeks for the problems in design, which is hardly enough for what is really the main object of the endeavor.

See "Thesis Drawings of the Columbia School of Architecture," *Architecture and Building*, 27 (July 31, 1897), p. 42. Ten years earlier, in 1888, a looser time, *Building* first described the Columbia program, and the value of sketching from books and existing buildings was enthusiastically endorsed:

This will create an interest among the students while reading the various histories of architecture, and when they come across some building which appeals to their taste, or a plan or detail which strikes their fancy, if they make a drawing or sketch it will remain more firmly impressed on their memory. As Professor Ware said: 'The students are allowed to do anything with books and photographs except put them away.'

See "Architectural Exhibition — Columbia School of Mines," *Building*, 8 (June 23, 1888), pp. 202-203.

130. Reilly, *McKim, Mead & White*, p. 15.

131. Ibid., p. 17.

Despite the new emphasis on utility and on the problems of everyday life — housing, transportation, the office, and the school — the values of the American Renaissance had become so deeply ingrained in the general value system that, especially after World War I, a remarkably vital and uniquely American (some might even argue uniquely New York-ian) synthesis emerged between the pragmatic and poetic ideals. This synthesis has its vulgar side certainly, resulting in forms which have been accurately characterized as "beautilitarian" by Arnold Lehman.[132] The Deco skyscraper is perhaps the most noticeable example of this synthesis.

Ware and to a much lesser extent McKim in different but related ways, each sowed the seeds of beautilitarianism, perhaps by overemphasizing scientific or technical training, and by seeking to render the aesthetic ideals of French academicism useful to the hurly-burly of American practice. So it is fitting that Columbia's graduates of the *fin de siecle* should play a leading role not only in holding on to the ideals of the American Renaissance, as did Pope, but in adapting them to the less idealistic temper of the 1920's: Ely Jacques Kahn, Arthur Loomis Harmon, Robert Kohn, William Adams Delano and Chester B. Aldrich each contributed significantly to the evolution of the "beautilitarian" ideal, and the image of the city of the 1920's is very much the product of their work. But that takes us ahead of the story. . . .

Perhaps the last word to be had on the problems and possibilities of New York as a metropolis was to be written by an anonymous editorial writer for the *Evening Mail* who observed in the waning of the composite era that

Ours is the city beautiful by virtue of its crystal skies, its bays and harbors, and islands, its ocean airs, the Babel-splendor of its skyscrapers, and the disjointed but imposing fact of its parks, its palace-like public schools and three or four of its municipal buildings. In other things it is too often, like most American cities, the city dreadful.[133]

The achievements were splendid to be sure; but the essential challenge of the twentieth-century city, the challenge of mass democracy lay before all, only to be taken up in earnest after world economic collapse twenty years later.

132. Arnold L. Lehman, *The New York Skyscraper: A History of Its Development, 1870–1939* (Ph.D. Diss., Yale University, 1970).

133. Quoted in *New York Architect*, 3 (August 1909), pp. 1-2.

A Large Hotel, 1926, plan and elevation, John C. Byers *(1926)*. Photo: Avery Archive.

Avery Hall, Columbia University, 1912. Photo: Columbia University.

History III
1912–1933

Susan M. Strauss

1. Born in Rolling Stone, Minnesota on August 27, 1860, Lord was graduated from M.I.T. with a degree in architecture in 1888. A Rotch Traveling Scholarship permitted travel in Europe, and upon his return in 1890, Lord accepted a position in the office of McKim, Mead & White. In 1894, he and James Monroe Hewlett *(Columbia, 1890)* formed a partnership, which continued until Lord's death in 1922.

The circumstances surrounding Austin Lord's appointment as Director are somewhat mysterious. Although a number of candidates were suggested, all of whom were practicing architects, there appear to have been no overtures made to any of them, nor is there any explicit indication of why their names were eliminated. It is fair to say that Butler and the Trustees had been set on John Galen Howard. When he rejected their offer, they decided not to let the matter slide as it had in 1905 (in 1905, McKim had declined the directorship, and Hamlin was installed as Acting Director). However, despite his excellent credentials, Lord was not endorsed unreservedly (John B. Pine to Nicholas Murray Butler, 11 April 1912, Central Files). Pine recommended that action on Lord's appointment not be taken until William Rutherford Mead, who appears to have assumed the position once occupied by McKim as informal advisor to Butler, had spoken on it. Yet, when Mead finally addressed himself to the question of Lord's appointment, his comments appear to have been indefinite. This is rather strange in that Lord, who had worked in the office of McKim, Mead & White and had directed the American Academy in Rome with which McKim had been so intimately involved, surely must have been familiar to Mead. Hamlin, on the other hand, seems to have endorsed the designation, albeit indirectly:

Hamlin's letter seems to show that he is alive to the needs of the situation, but do you not think that such promiscuous inquiry has its dangers? Of the men whom he suggests, I think that Hastings and Cram are about as impossible as any two who could be mentioned. What he writes of Austin Lord is more to the point, and I am glad to learn that Lord is willing to consider the appointment. I have talked to Mead about him, but have been unable to get any very definite opinion. Mead thinks well of him and likes him personally, but thinks he is rather "dead and alive" and seems to be doubtful as to whether he is in good health (Pine to Butler, 29 April 1912, Central Files).

In the end, Lord's having been the first Director of the American Academy in Rome (1894–1896) and his friendship with McKim must be considered the determining factors in his appointment.

2. Austin Lord to Butler, 8 May 1912, Central Files, Columbia University (hereafter Central Files).

3. Lord to Butler, 24 May 1912, Central Files.

4. Ibid.

5. Butler to Lord, 27 May 1912, Central Files.

6. Lord to Frank Fackenthal, Secretary of the University, 14 August 1912, and Richard Bach to Fackenthal, 19 August 1912, Central Files.

Van Pelt remained at Columbia until his contract had expired, in spite of Lord's resistance and strong criticism with respect to his teaching ability.

The Trustees appointed Austin Willard Lord Professor of Architecture and Director of the School on May 6, 1912, effective July 1.[1] Lord's first action as Director, heralding the reorganization of the School, was to demand the resignations of the entire staff.[2] While the call for resignations represented merely a formality with respect to most of the senior staff members such as Professors Hamlin, Sherman and Warren, Lord's intention to replace existing personnel demanded the *actual* resignations of some of the junior faculty, a point that met with resistance.[3] Nonetheless, Lord was convinced that the methods of teaching design at Columbia required change and for this, a staff of his own choosing was imperative.[4] Sympathetic to the absolute necessity for reorganization and mindful of John Galen Howard's insistence that the Director be given free reign, Butler assured Lord that he would support him completely, even to the point of securing additional funds so that Lord might hire his own design instructors.[5] In the end, Lord prevailed and all of the junior instructors with the exception of John V. Van Pelt, who was asked to resign three times, tendered their resignations.[6]

Focusing on the inadequacy of instruction in design and the overwhelming emphasis on history, Lord proposed to eliminate as required all courses that bore no direct relation to professional practice. In order not to hamper the new Director's activity and as a vote of confidence, the staff approved the reduction of the number of required history courses and the abolition of research altogether. By the following year, however, research was restored as collateral to the lecture courses.[7]

Lord was anxious to introduce town planning as a pivotal course in the program beginning in the third year; landscape architecture, previously a distinct division in the School, was incorporated into a fourth year advanced town planning course.[8] George Burdette Ford was enlisted to teach a course in town planning and to assist in the *ateliers* when projects related to his subject were assigned,[9] and Lord supported Hornbostel's desire to teach a course on the history of planning.[10] By 1914, Hamlin was clamoring for augmentation of history courses, and Lord was recommending institution of special projects in construction. In an apparent aboutface though, Lord suggested that certain requirements in the curriculum be abolished in order to liberate time for more work in the humanities and the fine arts including painting, sculpture and drawing.

A major revision in the teaching of design entailed Lord's insistence, despite the protests of students and faculty alike, that the three university-affiliated *ateliers* that had been in operation since 1905 be consolidated in Avery Hall. Paradoxically, Lord had stated in his inaugural address as Director that:

I do not believe that the best results can be obtained where an architectural department is an adjunct to a university, for the simple reason that the methods which must necessarily be applied in the teaching of an art are so absolutely different from the methods employed in teaching any other subject.[11]

Lord's reasons for proposing consolidation were manifold. Students of the downtown *ateliers* maintained that due to their more immediate association with professionals, they were more serious than their "schoolboy" classmates on Morningside Heights. Lord, however, would not tolerate the elitism of the *ateliers,* contending that the "fraternity" constituted an impediment to the effective and economical operation of the Department. As a corollary, Lord insisted that all university students should be at the University. Although he believed that the number of students in architecture was too small to emulate successfully the exact structure of the Ecole des Beaux-Arts, he argued that combining the younger and the older men, the weaker and the stronger would result in a situation approximating that of the French *atelier*[12] "which permits of instruction being given by the older men to the younger and offering the younger men the opportunity to assist in the more advanced work."[13] All of these reasons were subordinate to Lord's ardent preoccupation with a central school of the fine arts:

We are only beginning in this country — we cannot do everything in a hundred years. Time is the solution of the problem, and I believe we are on the right track. When our present schools are organized into one central school of art we shall then have an organization calculated to develop the student under the most favorable conditions.[14]

In 1912, Avery Hall was completed, offering the School more classroom space than ever before. Thus, Lord's desire to consolidate all

Austin Willard Lord.
Photo: Columbiana Collection.

Later, the opinion prevailed that many of Lord's decisions should be reversed. Upon reassessing John Van Pelt's dismissal in light of Lord's unsatisfactory performance, Butler recommended that Van Pelt be rehired as Associate in Design [Butler to William Henry Carpenter, 8 June 1915, Carpenter Papers, Butler Library, Columbia University (hereafter Carpenter Papers)].

7. *School of Architecture Bulletin of Information, 1913–1914.*

8. Lord to Butler, 3 June 1912, Central Files. Effective 26 June 1912, the degree program in Landscape Architecture was eliminated from the curriculum (Lord to Barrett, Chief Clerk of the University, 26 June 1912, Central Files).

9. Lord to Butler, 13 June 1912, Central Files.

10. Lord to Butler, 26 June 1912, Central Files. Hornbostel and Lord were known to be good friends, and although Hornbostel no longer was associated with the University, it is likely that he would have taught a course if asked.

11. *Columbia Alumni News,* 4 (November 15, 1912), p. 145.

12. Lord to Butler, 26 June 1912, Central Files.

13. Lord to Butler, 12 November 1912, Central Files.

14. *Columbia Alumni News,* 4 (November 15, 1912), pp. 145-146.

the *ateliers* under one roof was a real possibility for the first time.[15]

Despite Lord's initial success at consolidation and reorganization, the President and the Trustees were not satisfied with the performance of the new Director. A first indication was Butler's reminding Lord that it was customary in the University for the head of a department to initiate conferences with his staff respecting the organization, scope, and character of the work. Quite the opposite of his almost monomaniacal interest in controlling the reorganization of the School, it was Lord's subordinating his day-to-day duties as Director to those of his professional practice that precipitated his eventual dismissal. Although the University could be expected to assume partial responsibility for Lord's having focused his attention on his practice and especially on a project in Panama,[16] Pine insisted that the School could no longer tolerate the complete inattention of its leader. Observing that the interest and energy Lord had shown so willingly at the outset had evaporated, and reiterating the point that the School required a dynamic and dedicated Director, Pine warned Butler that if marked improvement were not in evidence shortly, the Trustees would have no choice but to request Lord's resignation.[17] Despite Professor Sherman's reporting that Lord had begun to show greater interest in the administration of the School following the loss of the Panama commission,[18] the situation went steadily downhill. The lingering and major fear about Lord was "that he is so out of sympathy with university instruction in architecture, that he may never be able to do what we had hoped."[19]

Without formally requesting that he tender his resignation, the Committee on Education made its dissatisfaction with Lord's performance exceedingly clear. The Committee cited the "new stimulus Lord had given to the School of Architecture particularly in design and in bringing the work of students into competition with others and under the scrutiny of architects not related to the University" as exemplary and admirable; nonetheless, the University could no longer afford to pay the Director's $5000 salary given the inordinate amount of time that Lord spent in active professional practice. The Committee instead offered to relieve Lord of the administrative responsibilities of the Directorship and to make him Professor of Design. His salary would be reduced to $2000 to cover his spending one or two days per week in the studio teaching design.[20] The academic year 1914–1915 would be a probationary year.

Despite Lord's promises to devote more time to the School, in November of 1914 students presented Butler with a list of criticisms respecting its organization.[21] In brief, the students claimed that: strong, consistent and definite administration of the work was lacking; an obvious lack of harmony between different members of the teaching staff was manifested openly; and there was neither adequate instruction in theory of design nor proper training and criticism of advanced design. They cautioned that the School was losing prestige and that within a few years, it would be unable to attract the best students. Essentially, censure of Lord turned on two points:[22] he did not devote sufficient time to

Monumental Approach to the Hudson River Bridge, 1929, designer unknown.
Photo: Avery Archive.

15. Notwithstanding Lord's insistence that the downtown *ateliers* be disbanded, he spoke in defense of the students' demand for access to the studios in Avery Hall through the night and on Sundays. Lord defended the demand on the grounds that the concept of the *charrette* was integral to the Ecole des Beaux-Arts system. In addition, projects of the Society of Beaux-Arts Architects (the calendar of which the School followed as closely as possible in these years), were usually due on Monday requiring Sunday work (Lord to Goetze, Treasurer of the University, 28 August 1912, and Butler to Lord, 31 October 1912, Central Files). Lord was unable to persuade the central administration, which insisted that it was the responsibility of the University to inculcate sound physical, moral and mental habits in its students. To allow the students to work in the studios during the night and on Sunday would directly contradict this purpose (Butler to Lord, 29 May 1914, Central Files). In addition, the administration maintained that Columbia University should not "propogate foreign traditions" inapplicable to American circumstances (Bach to William Henry Carpenter, 22 June 1914, Central Files).

16. The University had been instrumental in Lord's having received the commission in Panama (Pine to Butler, 30 September 1913, Central Files).

17. Ibid.

18. According to Butler, Lord lost the Panama appointment for reasons similar to those that aroused dissatisfaction at Columbia, i.e. Lord was devoting insufficient time to the project (Butler to Pine, 2 October 1913, Central Files).

19. Ibid.

20. Butler to Lord, 12 January 1914, Central Files.

21. Ibid.

22. Lord to Butler, 1 March 1915, Central Files.

academic affairs,[23] and he either did not understand or was not in sympathy with the ideals of a university school of architecture as distinct from a practical school of architectural design. Lord contended that neither accusation was accurate. He reiterated his commitment to promote the efficiency and prosperity of the School, but he conceded that "if these great ends [efficiency and prosperity] can best be promoted by my retiring from the Directorate, I am ready to retire."[24]

Meanwhile, in February 1915, Hamlin and Sherman suggested that the dissolution of the Faculty of Fine Arts afforded a convenient opportunity to reorganize the Department[25] and made recommendations to Butler concerning the organization and conduct of the School.[26] Hamlin and Sherman argued that the duties of the Director could be

at least as well performed by a member of the staff, who should be more familiar with the traditions, ideas and methods of the School and University than any Director can be who devotes and can devote but a small part of his time to the work.[27]

The major thrust of their argument concerned the advantages of diffusing the power of the School rather than concentrating it in one man. To this end, the Committee on Education recommended that the position of Director be abolished, that Lord be appointed Professor of Design, and that the Provost be designated executive head of the School until such time as a permanent arrangement was deemed feasible and prudent. Not without resistance,[28] on May 26, 1915, Lord declined the position. At issue was the contention that the policy adopted by the Trustees would reduce the Professor of Design to a mere instructor, and although the Professor would retain responsibility for the success of the School, he would have no controlling voice over the other professional courses. In parting, Lord stressed that because the success or failure of an architecture school must be measured on the basis of students' performance in design — design being the culmination of all departmental effort — anyone occupying the position of Professor of Design should have supervision over the other courses in the curriculum. He believed that his policy for reorganization had not been allowed adequate time for development, and he rejected the reduced remuneration as inadequate.[29]

Pursuant to their order of 1915, the Trustees designated William Henry Carpenter Acting Director of the School of Architecture.[30] Carpenter, as Associate Dean of the Graduate Faculty, had assumed that he would succeed Dean Burgess upon the latter's retirement in 1912. The appointment was not forthcoming, and the position of Provost was created. Notwithstanding his competence as an administrator, which he had demonstrated as Acting Dean of the Faculty of Philosophy in 1908–09 and as Provost of the University, Carpenter was not particularly knowledgable about architecture. Therefore, the task of advising him on architectural matters fell to members of the faculty — especially to William A. Boring, who was appointed Associate Professor of Design in 1915, and to Richard Bach.[31] In fact, although Carpenter served as Act-

23. A.D.F. Hamlin, F.D. Sherman and R.F. Bach accomplished most of the administrative work, while M. Prevot and Arthur Ware carried out much of Lord's responsibility in the studios.

24. Lord to Butler, 1 March 1915, Central Files.

25. Hamlin and Sherman to Butler, 13 February 1915, Central Files. In 1914, the Faculty of Fine Arts was dissolved at the concurrence of the Dean, the Faculty itself and the University Council. The attempt to create a school of fine arts through the cooperation of the National Academy, the University, and the Metropolitan Museum had failed due largely to the intrinsically different organizations and orientations of the three constituents (Fackenthal to Carpenter, 9 January 1914, Carpenter Papers).

26. Recommendations respecting reorganization were as follows: one, to authorize the administrative board to elect anually one of its own to act as executive head or professor in charge until such time as the Trustees should choose to appoint a permanent administrative head; two, to create an office of Professor of Design; three, to assign the difference between the salary formerly tendered to the Director and that of the new Professor of Design to increasing the staff of instruction in design or drawing or both; and four, to constitute an advisory board or visiting committee of representatives of the organized profession in New York and to charge it with periodic visitation of and report upon the School. Initially, it was proposed that the Committee be constituted of the Presidents of the New York chapter of the American Institute of Architects and of the Architectural league, the Chairmen of the Educational Committee of the Society of Beaux-Arts Architects and of the Alumni Association of the School and five or seven other architects. A majority of the members of the Visiting Committee were to be alumni of the School. The Committee would be charged with an advisory rather than a legislative function. The positive attitude toward the Committee recalls the optimism of 1905:
Its reports would be of great value in pointing out defects, suggesting improvements, commending excellences, and making known the needs of the School, its equipment, methods and personnel and establishing close relations between it and the profession generally (Hamlin and Sherman to Butler, 23 February 1915, Central Files).

27. Hamlin and Sherman to Butler, 23 February 1915, Central Files.

28. Lord attempted to negotiate on the grounds that until he was apprised of the extent and the character of the duties he would be expected to perform, he would be unable to consider the proposal (Lord to Butler, 21 May 1915, Central Files).

29. Lord to Butler, 26 May 1915, Central Files.

30. Carpenter was not an architect, but he was a competent administrator. He had come to Columbia in 1883 as a language instructor and by 1908–09 was Acting Dean of the Faculty of Philosophy. By 1912 he was Associate Dean of the Graduate Faculties and assumed he would be appointed Dean upon the retirement of Dean Burgess, but was named Provost of the University instead. In 1915, following the resignation of Lord, the Trustees appointed Carpenter Acting Director of the School. After Boring had been appointed Dean, Carpenter returned to the position of Provost, which he held until his retirement in 1926 [Gordon William Fulton, Notes on Henry William Carpenter, Graduate School of Architecture and Planning Archives (hereafter GSAP Archives)].

31. Bach was the Curator of the School of Architecture.

ing Director until 1919, he relied more and more upon Boring's guidance.

Finding itself once again in a transition period following Lord's inability to bring the School into line with the demands of the students and of the profession and with current ideals concerning architectural education, the School struggled to find a proper direction and to stem the tide of decreasing enrollment and general dissatisfaction.[32] A number of important changes occurred during Carpenter's tenure, most of which were initiated by members of the architecture faculty or of the administration of the University itself. Among them, the hiring of new instructors and the reinstatement of courses abolished under Lord, the removal of the Certificate of Proficiency in Architecture program from the curriculum of the School to the Department of Extension Teaching in 1917,[33] and the establishment of a visiting committee of practitioners were the most important.[34]

Because courses in the history and theory of architecture and in research were reinstated,[35] new faculty members were required to teach. Mindful of the need to proceed cautiously with the reorganization especially with respect to hiring practicing architects who were not accustomed to university conditions, in 1915, Hamlin and Sherman transmitted three names as possible associates or professors in the theory of architecture: William A. Boring, John Mead Howells and Frederick L. Ackerman.[36] Rather than speculate about their relative merits, Hamlin and Sherman suggested that "in view of our rather trying experiences, having now an open field, it might not be a bad plan to try all three men next year as lecturers in Theory."[37] In June, on behalf of the Administrative Board, Carpenter nominated Frederick L. Ackerman as Lecturer in the Principles of Architecture, Francis A. Nelson as Associate in Architecture assisting Hamlin and Arthur Ware, and William A. Boring as Associate in Charge of Design with a seat on the Administrative Board.[38] Carpenter's premonition about the central role Boring would play in the future was intimated:

I am very much pleased with this outcome of the matter, which seems to me to mark what I most devoutly hope it will prove to be — the beginning of a new era in the School of Architecture. The three new men: Boring, Ackerman and Nelson, will greatly strengthen our hands and will presently bring about new conditions. I am particularly pleased with Boring's personality and with the cautious spirit with which he has approached the problem, of whose importance he is deeply impressed and which he will, I am confident, do his best to solve.[39]

By the end of 1915, the design curriculum of the School had become more closely aligned with that of the educational arm of the Society of Beaux-Arts Architects. While the course remained of indefinite duration (continuing the point system), it would be completed in four years under normal circumstances. The valuations in Elements, Applied Elements and the thesis were fixed, but the judgments for design proper were competitive. Insofar as possible, design problems were intended to be coordinated with work in other subjects, such as Principles and Theory of Architecture, in

William Henry Carpenter.
Photo: Columbiana Collection.

32. Carpenter to Butler, 15 October 1915, Carpenter Papers.

33. Data submitted to the Secretary of the Association of Collegiate Schools of Architecture, November 1915, Central Files.

34. The most important move toward reorganization was the establishment by the Trustees of the Visiting Committee composed of three representatives of each of the three organizations: the Alumni Association, the New York Chapter of the American Institute of Architects, and the Society of Beaux-Arts Architects. The major purpose of the Visiting Committee was to inaugurate a new mode of cooperation between the profession and the School (Data submitted to the Secretary of the Association of Collegiate Schools of Architecture, 19 November 1915). The Committee was to visit the School, make recommendations, and sit on juries.
   The original Committee of nine included: I.N. Phelps Stokes, John Russell Pope and Goodhue Livingston for the Alumni Association; Egerton Swartwout, Charles A. Platt, and Bertram G. Goodhue for the New York Chapter of the American Institute of Architects; and Henry F. Hornbostel, Lloyd Warren and Thomas Hastings for the Society of Beaux-Arts Architects. (Memorandum: Carpenter to Butler, 6 October 1915, Carpenter Papers). Responding to the more humanistic and less technical orientation of the architecture program, in 1918, the Asministrative Board proposed and the Trustees affirmed the addition of representatives of the Society of Mural Painters and of the National Sculpture Society to the Visiting Committee (Carpenter to Augustus Lukenan, 7 May 1918, and Carpenter to Butler, 30 April 1918, Carpenter Papers).

35. These courses had been eliminated in favor of design and design related courses.

36. It is not clear why John Mead Howells was not appointed and why Francis A. Nelson was appointed as Associate in Architecture.

37. Hamlin to Butler, 21 May 1915, Carpenter Papers.

38. Carpenter to Butler, 3 June 1914 and 4 June 1915, Central Files.

39. Carpenter to Butler, 3 June 1915, Central Files.

order to "broaden the vision of the student so that he will then have an intelligent conception of the humanistic qualities in the architectural problems he must solve."[40]

The emphasis on design and professional practice is clear: design was considered to be the application of studies in history, graphics, mathematics, construction and drawing to actual architectural problems. Boring's performance with respect to revamping instruction in design was considered exemplary:

Professor Boring has completely reorganized the mode of criticism in Design.... Certain developments in the way of sound pedagogic methods have also been applied in this department, which unfortunately has never been considered in most schools. The chief characteristic of the School's present system is that of coordination with all departments and interior coordination of the various grades of design with one another.[41]

Boring broadened the design course, upgraded the performance of Columbia students on Society of Beaux-Arts Architects competitions, and stressed sound design and planning over rendering, thereby defusing the charge that Columbia's graduates were "paper architects." History courses were restored to their former importance, and more time was assigned to drawing from life, which had been by far the weakest part of the program.[42] The development of a revised system of government involving the final control of the Administrative Board, the internal control of the staff, and the direct operating management of the Committee on Instruction occurred in 1916. The day-to-day administration of the School remained in the hands of the Curator in consultation with the Acting Director.[43]

In the interest of administrative unity and as a step toward the reduction of the many and heterogeneous Bachelor's degrees offered in American universities, in June 1916, the Trustees proposed the substitution of the degree of Bachelor of Science in Architecture for the degree of Bachelor of Architecture.[44] The Administrative Board of the School unanimously opposed the change, citing the necessity for distinguishing between a four year curriculum (Bachelor of Science) and one of six years duration (Bachelor of Architecture). In fact, in 1918, the Administrative Board resolved that it would be unwise for the School to enter into affiliation with any Society that would not recognize the distinction between the four and six year course leading to the degree in architecture.[45]

Beginning in 1917, the School admitted only students interested in pursuing a Bachelor of Architecture degree. One important ramification of the change was the elimination of the Certificate of Proficiency program from the School. However, the reasons for its having been created — the belief that individuals who were employed on a full-time basis should be able to benefit from the university course in architecture and the recognition that individuals lacking two years preparatory liberal arts work in an accredited institution should not be prevented from undertaking systematic architectural study — did not disappear. Therefore, beginning with the academic year 1917–18, a professional

William Alciphron Boring.
Photo: The Architectural League of New York.

40. Memorandum on Architecture, William Alciphron Boring, 16 December 1915, Central Files.

41. Bach to Carpenter, 22 June 1916, Carpenter Papers.

42. Indeed, Boring recommended to Carpenter that life classes be held in Avery Hall (Boring to Carpenter, 23 June 1916, Central Files). Although classes at the National Academy of Design had been satisfactory, Boring contended that the architecture students would benefit from the stimulus of artists close at hand. Beginning in 1917, an arrangement with Teachers College enabled Columbia architecture students to enroll in life classes there (Carpenter to M.A. Bigelow, 23 March 1916, Carpenter Papers).

43. Bach to Carpenter, 22 June 1916, Carpenter Papers.

44. Carpenter to Butler, 13 December 1916, Carpenter Papers.

45. Carpenter to Underwood and Gilbert, 1 May 1918, Carpenter Papers. At the May 1921 meeting of the Association of Collegiate Schools of Architecture, a decision was taken binding delegates to promote at their respective institutions, the extension of the four year course in architecture to five years. (H. Vandervoort Walsh to Carpenter, 11 May 1921, Carpenter Papers).

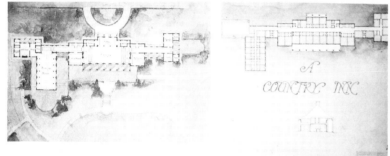

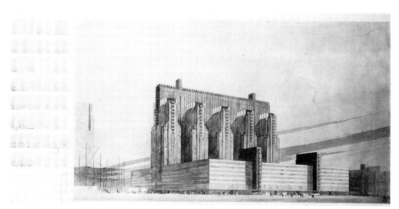

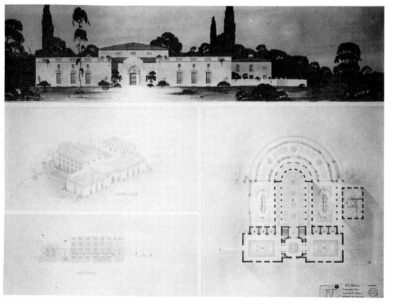

Above: A Synagogue, 1925, Joseph J. Black *(1926)*. Photo: Avery Archive.

Above left: A Country Inn, 1926, Charles E. O'Hara *(1927)*. Photo: Avery Archive.

Middle: An Urban Building, ca. 1930, designer unknown. Photo: Avery Archive.

Below: A Library for a Collector, ca. 1927, designer unknown. Photo: Avery Archive.

curriculum leading to a Certificate of Proficiency in Architecture was established in the Department of Extension Teaching.[46]

Despite the reduction by about fifty percent in the number of students during the war years, the quality of the work steadily increased and the School became *de facto* a graduate school since nearly all candidates for the Bachelor of Architecture degree had graduated from undergraduate institutions. The intensive instruction in design, made possible due to fewer matriculants, resulted in the students' taking greater responsibility for their design work, the final projects reflecting less and less the work of the instructor.

Cooperation among the University, the National Academy and the Metropolitan Museum with regard to the School of Fine Arts had not succeeded. Nevertheless, optimism respecting such coordination had not diminished. In 1918, the Architectural League, the Art Alliance of America, the Beaux Arts Institute of Design and the Metropolitan Museum considered the establishment of a school of industrial design and craftsmanship; Columbia's affiliation with the Beaux Arts Institute of Design would provide the connection. Although the Institute would be established as an autonomous entity, Columbia would endeavor to provide facilities through its Department of Extension Teaching.[47] Bach expressed a desire, as yet unsatisfied, to establish a center for the Fine Arts in part to enhance Columbia's position and prestige:

It is my humble hope that whatever meager efforts I may be able to command will be of avail in achieving ultimately a more direct affiliation between Columbia and the Metropolitan Museum so that the Museum eventually will feel that in any of its major undertakings the advice of Columbia is indispensable.[48]

Since his appointment to the faculty in 1915, William Alciphron Boring[49] had demonstrated an unflagging commitment to the improvement of architectural education at Columbia University.[50] Not only had he instituted an improved method of teaching design, laid particular stress as a practicing architect on the practical application of architectural theory, and been instrumental in coordinating the program of the School with that of the Society of Beaux-Arts Architects, but he was well liked and highly respected among the staff. Butler was especially enamored with Boring's expressed concern to participate, if only in an advisory capacity, in University decisions respecting architecture and planning.[51]

In contrast to Lord, who had shirked his responsibilities in the studios in order to devote more time to his practice, Boring, who was encouraged by the overwhelmingly positive response to his methods, determined to spend more time at the University. Boring's decoration of Avery Hall and of the campus for a special convocation honoring representatives of France and England was indicative of this. Furthermore, feasibility studies for the erection of an annex to St. Luke's Hospital, completed as student projects, were so well received that the School itself was designated architect for the project.[52] In addition, representative practitioners seemed to endorse Boring's methods.[53]

46. Carpenter to James C. Egbert (Extension Teaching), 8 February 1918, Carpenter Papers. Admission would be granted on the basis of a high school diploma and one year's office work. Design work continued to be conducted as in a Parisian *atelier*, and the programs and schedule of the Beaux-Arts Institute of Design were employed. The Institute had been formed to encourage architectural competitions of the kind at the Ecole des Beaux-Arts in Paris (Frederick A. Godley to Carpenter, 17 February 1917, Carpenter Papers). Courses in Extension could be credited toward the Bachelor's degree as preparatory work. The program was to be administered by the Curator of the School of Architecture; thus, Richard Bach was its first advisor. The program leading to the certificate continued until 1936; at that time, the New York State Board of Examiners of Architects amended its statutes to provide that only individuals with professional degrees in architecture would be eligible for licensing.

47. Bach to Carpenter, 5 August 1918, Carpenter Papers.

48. Bach to Carpenter, 13 August 1918, Carpenter Papers.

49. On paper, Boring represented the ideal choice for Director. He was born on 9 September 1859 in Carlinville, Illinois. His introduction to architecture had been rather practical: his father had been a building contractor, and Boring had held summer jobs with architects and carpenters. Following a brief period of study at the University of Illinois, Boring opened a practice in California, which he gave up in 1886 in order to study with Professor William Ware at Columbia. Finding the design course "rather puerile," he accepted employment with McKim, Mead & White. Shortly thereafter, he and a colleague, Edward Tilton (with whom he eventually would form a partnership), embarked for the Ecole des Beaux-Arts. Boring's commitment to Beaux-Arts ideals is evident most clearly in his having been one of the founding members of the Society of Beaux-Arts Architects in 1893 and in having co-founded and served as Trustee of the American School of Architecture in Rome. With respect to his philosophy of architectural education, Boring maintained: *The aim is to give a well-rounded education, the Art of Architectural design being the objective. The Associate in design is to be the controlling spirit in moulding instruction to that end* (Boring to Carpenter, 3 June 1915, Central Files).

50. Boring to Carpenter, 23 May 1918, Central Files.

51. Carpenter to Butler, 21 May 1919, Carpenter Papers. Boring maintained that entrusting the Director with practical as well as administrative work would enhance the prestige of the School. Moreover, Boring had insisted that services rendered should be regarded as part of his academic work rather than as professional service requiring the payment of a commission.

52. The St. Luke's Hospital feasibility studies were completed by the School on the basis of an assignment to the students over an eight day period. Boring was appointed supervising architect with C.P. Warren responsible for structure and Arthur Ware for construction. An architectural office was established on the sixth floor of Avery Hall (Annual Report of the School of Architecture, William Henry Carpenter, 30 June 1917, Carpenter Papers).

53. Hornbostel, who was then a member of the Visiting Committee, wrote in 1917:
I could not be at the Columbia judgment because I was away, and I have seen the problems as judged the other night. I want to congratulate you and your school for the projects so excellently studied and presented at our last judgment. It seems as if a real renaissance has started at the architectural school at Columbia, and that my growlings for years have now become less and less, and lately have turned into songs in praise of what has been done. Someday the School of Architecture at Columbia is going to rank as the first, and then I will be willing to help from the outside (as quoted in Boring to Butler, 21 February 1917, Central Files).

Butler had thought of appointing Boring Director of the School in the spring of 1917, while allowing Carpenter to retain his position on the Administrative Board. Butler reconsidered the appointment in the spring of 1918, but Boring was not asked to assume the Directorship until the spring of 1919.[54] Boring's performance and his reputation were exemplary; therefore, the delay in his designation represents neither dissatisfaction nor doubt as to his ability to lead. In view of the decreased enrollment due to World War I, the financial difficulties faced by the School as a result of this and general war-time conditions, and the fact that Butler had encouraged junior members of the faculty to accept other positions for the duration, it is likely that the President felt the significance of the appointment would not have been appreciated were it to occur during such an unstable period. It was unlikely that sweeping changes would have been instituted, or if instituted, would have been effective with the student body so small. Furthermore, it was no secret that Carpenter had relied heavily on Boring throughout the years; the administration of the School could proceed in like manner for a few more years. Since Boring was already in large part responsible for the direction of the School, it was not expected that he would institute major changes in any event. Then too, he was no stranger to the problems. If they were not clear to him, an insider, how much less clear would they be to an outside appointee?

For a number of reasons, Boring's eventual designation as Director in 1919 came as no surprise. He had been appointed Professor in Charge of Design with a seat on the Administrative Board in 1915; Carpenter, as temporary head of the School, had not aspired to run the School and had no long range plans for its development; and most importantly, Boring's philosophy of architecture and of architectural education coincided for the most part with that of mainstream professional opinion at the time. It is conceivable that the years intervening between Boring's initial appointment to the School and his becoming Director were intended as a trial period. Boring was able to crystallize his ideas respecting architectural education in the absence of administrative pressures. In addition, because he answered to the Provost of the University, the likelihood of the University's making another mistake with respect to the Directorship was slight. The appointment of a practicing architect as Professor of Design and later as Director following a period of uncertainty under a caretaker director was a familiar refrain. Even more familiar was the hope for improvement under this individual. Shortly after Boring's appointment, Butler wrote: "I feel quite sure that your coming to the School will, in connection with other arrangements that have been made, strengthen it and put new life into this work."[55]

Boring proceeded to administer the curriculum largely as it had stood under Carpenter's tenure. All teaching in the School was intended to strengthen the students' design faculties, and Boring, who continued in professional practice, considered design:

the tap root into which flow the other rootlets of learning, and from this

A Museum and a Memorial Monument, ca. 1932, designer unknown. Photo: Avery Archive.

54. Carpenter to Butler, 21 May 1919, Carpenter Papers.

55. Butler to Boring, 7 June 1915, Central Files.

central stem grows and flowers the culmination of all effort, Architectural Design. And in design we recognize not alone beautiful drawings, we value the knowledge behind the drawings, which discerns architecture in the round, architecture constructed as represented by the drawings, a knowledge of those constructive elements and the aesthetic values which must govern every work of art.[56]

Despite his rather conventional stance with regard to architectural education, Boring's theory of design was, although conservative, certainly not retrogressive. Of architecture, he taught:

it embraces the other arts and it is pure invention. You can't go to nature and get the basic idea of architecture, you are going to nature for details for elaboration, but the main thing of architecture is like music. It is the pure creation.[57]

Boring's idea of architecture as essentially an abstraction was further articulated in his directives to his design students. In reference to a project for a hotel in the city, Boring advised:

Some of you may want to show your hotel by making a perspective of it, but you don't need to put in any details.... You have to show where the windows go, but the biggest way of attempting to solve a problem is to solve it in masses, study the main things first and then afterwards the details.[58]

Between 1915 and 1932, Boring's Principles of Planning and Principles of Composition were recommended courses for every student. Boring also taught the four courses in the basic design sequence, assisted in teaching architectural rendering, advanced construction, and graduate design.[59]

The principles of the Ecole respecting cooperation in the studio were followed at Columbia, and the method of teaching design was much the same. To this end, problems in design were assigned at intervals of three to six weeks to be solved in much the same way as they would have been in a professional office. A jury of practicing architects would assist in judging, and the majority were sent to the Beaux Arts Institute of Design for judgment in competition with other schools. Underlying the use of Ecole methods was the belief that experimentation within a prescribed outline would teach self-motivation and orderly study and would inspire creativity.[60]

Throughout Boring's tenure, the School was affiliated with the Beaux Arts Institute of Design. In 1918–1919, typical Beaux Arts Institute of Design programs used at Columbia were *A Theatre, A Community Building to be used as a War Memorial,* and *A Yacht Club;* sketch assignments included *A Battle Monument, A Life Saving Station,* and *A Decorative Treatment of a Public Square;* and archeology programs included *A Monument to a Greek Athlete* and *A Roman Triumphal Arch.* By the late 1920's a majority of the Beaux Arts Institute of Design programs were used at Columbia, and completed designs were returned to the Institute for judgment in competition with those from other architectural schools and *ateliers.* In 1926–1927, of six Class A-1 programs, only one, *A Park on an Island,* was not used for a Columbia assignment. Typical programs for that year were *An Exterior Stairway, An Embassy, A*

Stevens Institute, Hoboken, New Jersey, 1929, designer unknown. Photo: Avery Archive.

56. Boring to Carpenter, 27 April 1922, Central Files.

57. Lecture notes for second term course A52 & A54, Lecture 5, 14 February 1933, on mass composition, GSAP Archives.

58. Lecture notes for first term course A51 and A53, on the City Hotel, GSAP Archives.

59. Fulton, Gordon William, "Notes on William Alciphron Boring," GSAP Archives.

60. The Beaux-Arts requirements were considered essential to proper instruction in design. To this end, a preliminary small scale sketch was expected after several hours study of the program, followed by a carefully rendered drawing at small scale but without the aid of criticism, the free criticism and dev3lopment of the design with the help of the critic until a determined solution had been reached, one half scale rendered studies of the solution, and finally, full-size renderings.

Summer School of Fine Arts, A Municipal Observatory, and *A Town Hall;* sketch assignments included *A Summer Resort, A Display Sign for a Theatre,* and *A Catafalque for a President;* and archeology programs included *An Egyptian Barge, A Mayan Temple, A Romanesque Church,* and *An English Banquet Hall.*[61]

Boring encouraged students' input with respect to the curriculum, and in 1923 the Committee on Instruction met with a committee of students (created and elected by the student body on Boring's advice) to discuss prevailing feelings of dissatisfaction. The students presented six suggestions, all of which focused on the need to strengthen instruction in design.[62]

An incident illustrative of the sympathetic relationship between students and the Dean was the Reed Harris affair of April, 1932. In a series of articles in the student newspaper, *The Columbia Spectator,* Editor Reed Harris had lashed out against the poor quality of food in the University dining halls and the high cost and danger of university athletic programs. When Harris was expelled by President Butler as a result of these criticisms, the issue became one of free speech, which precipitated a student strike. While the original organizers had intended a peaceful demonstration of support, "instead...a war between the sympathizers and the athletes" (so-called administration men) ensued. "The former perhaps made the better speeches, but the aim of the latter with apples and eggs made up for that."[63] Administration men laid seige to the upper floors of Avery Hall from which architecture students had hung a banner reading "No Gagging Free Speech." The athletes wrested the sign from the architecture students, carried it down the stairs and burned it while the students emptied a tub of water from the window. A similar incident occurred later in the day, although that time, Harold Vandervoort Walsh, Professor of Architecture removed the signs and threw them to the athletes below, who again burned them. Apparently, during the riot, "Dean Boring stood like Horatius, keeping the rioters at bay and dodging tomatoes and other missiles which were pitched at him."[64]

Although a course in town planning had been given by Ford in 1912, that interest appears to have remained dormant until revived by Boring, who believed that the scholarly study of city planning should be accomplished under the auspices of a school of architecture. In view of this emphasis on architectural practice, it is interesting that Boring would stress academic subjects with respect to city planning.

While the training of men for the actual field work is important, the study of the subject in a scholarly way and under conditions which would insure continuance of the effort and high quality of attainment, seem to be as much or more important than the training of men.[65]

As a means of implementing such study, Boring suggested cooperation between the University and the Regional Plan Committee of New York. Accordingly, on May 3, 1928, the Committee and the University sponsored a conference at Columbia attended by representatives of the New York State Regional Plan Committee, Amherst College, Columbia Univer-

A House by the Sea, 1928, David B. Clark *(1928).* Photo: Avery Archive.

61. Students' grievances were articulated as follows:

(1) More time needed for design work; to secure this time: (a) condense history of ancient ornament; (b) eliminate the requirement for ornamental plates; (c) eliminate the requirement for plates in the decorative arts; (d) eliminate historical research as a course and make it an elective; (e) drop stereotomy; (f) condense work covered in shades and shadows, descriptive geometry, and stereotomy into one course; (g) condense graphics;

(2) Rendering as formally given in Applied Elements should be reinstated;

(3) Twenty-four hour sketches in Intermediate and Advanced Design covering large plan problems should be introduced;

(4) There should be stricter judgments;

(5) The best students in the Extension Design Class should work in the daytime studios in order to inspire the other students;

(6) Better teaching is required in the life drawing classes and drawing from the antique (Carpenter to Butler, 13 February 1923, Carpenter Papers).

62. *The New York Times,* "Columbia Students Riot in the Strike Over Harris; Eggs hurled, Many Fights, 1500 Cut Classes," 7 April 1932, p. 14.

63. Rohdenburg, Theodor K. *A History of the School of Architecture, Columbia University* (New York: Columbia University Press, 1954), p. 90.

64. Boring to Butler, 26 April 1927, Central Files.

65. Henry James to the Invitees of the Conference, New York, 12 April 1928, Central Files.

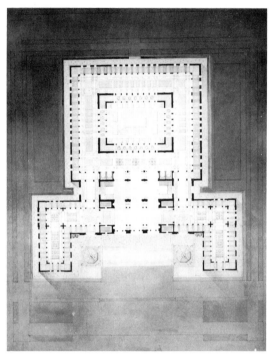

Above: A Museum of the Peaceful Arts,
1927, Newell C. Granger *(1927)*.
Photo: Avery Archive.

Top left: A Highway Restaurant, ca. 1932,
Logan S. Chappell *(1936)*.
Photo: Avery Archive.

Middle left: A Hotel, designer unknown.
PhotoAvery Achive.

Below left: A Court Room, 1931, Olindo
Grossi *(1932)*. Photo: Avery Archive.

sity, the Russell Sage Foundation, the architectural profession at large, and the city planning profession.[66] Speakers addressed the issue of city planning, stressing the changed character of the modern city, the unprecedented amount of city building and the resultant problems, the need for trained professionals and the general development of the profession. On the basis of a series of propositions, primary among them being that city planning is not a field unto itself but draws upon all of the arts and sciences, the participants agreed that the existence of an institute of city planning was a necessity.[67]

The results of the conference struck a note to which Boring was sensitive.[68] Following the conference, Boring held informal meetings with members of the staff of the School in order to gauge their willingness to participate in the venture. He reported to Butler:

It is considered in the School of Architecture that the interlocking of the proposed Institute with this School can be made without difficulty and that for the present at least, proper space can be provided in Avery Hall... If we desire to locate this School at Columbia, where I think it should be, we will have to make the presentation convincing.[69]

Boring then submitted a proposal for an institute of research and city planning, the objectives of which would be: to guide research in city planning, to cooperate with other agencies in the field, to disseminate knowledge in the subject by conferences and publications, to assist in solutions of problems in the subject, to train professional practitioners, and to organize a working office that would keep these activities in motion at all times for the purpose of developing, stimulating and teaching the art of city planning. Boring went so far as to formulate detailed plans for the staff, the curriculum, and the administration of the school. Consistently he stressed the necessity for its being part of the Columbia University system. Accordingly, President Butler urged that Boring "leave no stone unturned to find the funds necessary to put this institute into operation at Columbia University."[70] Although there was much discussion back and forth on details of the scheme, including whether the proposed city planning institute should be a School of Civic Design or a Department of Town Planning in the School of Architecture (which was favored), no real action was taken witt respect to the actual formation of a program.[71]

Recalling the premise of a previous experiment, Boring believed that the School of Architecture should become the nucleus of a larger School of Fine Arts that would teach painting, sculpture, architecture, music and drama. In 1929, Boring suggested that the first steps toward organizing such a school could be made by establishing courses in elementary art subjects under University Extension; such courses could be continued under Extension Teaching until advanced courses were demanded, at which time the School of Fine Arts would come into its own. Boring maintained that:

if the idea should find a large response from the public, Columbia would be taking on a responsibility which must be faced when the School grows.

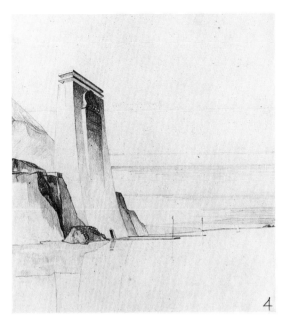

A Monument to an Aviator, 1930, G. Manson *(1932)*. Photo: Avery Archive.

66. Eight points emerged from discussions at the conference:

(1) City planning is not merely a special field for the application of the skill of any single profession;

(2) City planning must draw upon the several arts and sciences;

(3) It would be expedient to organize a unit for teaching and research not as a part of an existing department in a university but as a separate and independent unit;

(4) The institute or school of research and instruction should be affiliated with some large university where most or all of the allied disciplines are already developed;

(5) As the course of work would be in some degree experimental, the granting of degrees should be postponed;

(6) A large proportion of the energy and time of the institute would be devoted to research and publication as distinguished from instruction;

(7) The staff should be expected to give part of its time to outside consulting work; and

(8) The school(s) should be located in a large city where suitable 'clinical' material would be readily available and where there are numerous academic institutions and social agencies whose cooperation could be enlisted (Report and Recommendations, Conference, 3 May 1928, Central Files).

67. Boring's Annual Reports had suggested the idea of an institute expressly for city planning, and his original idea, formulated with Major George Herbert Gray, had been to institute a course in Extension Teaching (Boring to Butler, 13 December 1928, Central Files). Unfortunately, not enough students responded favorably to justify the course.

68. Boring to Butler, 1 December 1928, Central Files.

69. Fackenthal to Boring, 31 May 1929, Central Files.

70. Butler to Boring, 19 August 1929, Central Files.

71. Boring to Butler, 12 December 1929, Central Files.

The City of New York, which is the artistic center of the United States, needs such a great School of Art and Columbia should take the lead in this work. [72]

In 1930, having reached the age for retirement, Boring asked to remain at the University in order to continue his work concerning the School of Fine Arts. [73] In conjunction with the School of Fine Arts, he advocated establishing a museum on Morningside Heights to contain objects of artistic merit for the use of students in architecture, art, decoration, and the fine arts; he suggested Fayerweather Hall as a possible location. Boring also submitted a scheme whereby the area between Fayerweather and Avery Halls would become an architectural museum court with objects that reproduced standard and historically significant artistic objects in cement, and therefore could withstand the rigors of the climate. He even proposed including some original pieces. [74]

In 1931, perhaps to commemorate the fiftieth anniversary of the founding of a course in architecture, the administrative structure of the School was nominally changed. Boring's title was changed from Director to Dean and the Faculty of Architecture was substituted for the Administrative Board. [75] Attendance at the School had increased twenty-nine percent over that of the preceding year, and the quality of the students was thought to be considerably better. Due to the increased enrollment, Boring suggested that three new assistants in design be hired. Because many new students were transfers from other schools of architecture and thus were beginning at an advanced level, instructors in advanced design were especially necessary. [76]

Public competitions were more generously awarded than at any other time during the life of the School. By and large, design problems were those articulated by the Beaux Arts Institute of Design. Boring was extremely concerned with Columbia's status among other schools of architecture and its ability to attract good students. He relied on a simple argument to substantiate his conservative approach to instruction in design:

We have done this [used Beaux Arts Institute of Design programs] for the reason that the world measures the success of a school of architecture by the awards obtained in the competitions of the Institute. The best students go to the school which has the best record at the Institute. [77]

In 1929, the 175th anniversary year of the founding of Columbia College, Boring became the first incumbent of the newly created Ware Professorship of Architecture. [78] The anniversary in part was commemorated with a series of lectures respecting the University's development and growth. Boring had reported on the School and had recommended that Joseph Hudnut, Professor of History of Architecture, be selected to give the " pendant lecture." The pendant lecture entailed an evaluation both of the achievements of Columbia University in teaching the art of architecture and of the influence of Columbia's ideals and methods of instruction on the architecture of America. [79] Boring's confidence in Hudnut did not wane, for Boring had wanted to turn over the teaching of theory to Hudnut for the academic year 1931–32 before budget require-

A Door Study, ca. 1930, designer unknown. Photo: Avery Archive.

72. Boring to Butler, 11 January 1930, Central Files.

73. Boring to Butler, 27 April 1925, Central Files.

74. Beaux-Arts Institute of Design programs for the academic years 1918–1919 and 1926–1927 with indications of which projects were used in Columbia design studios (GSAP Archives).

75. Fackenthal to Boring, 6 April 1931, Central Files.

76. Boring to Butler, 18 March, 1931, Central Files.

77. Ibid.

78. Butler to Boring, 4 November 1929, Central Files.

79. Boring to Butler, 11 June 1929, Central Files.

ments made that impractical. Boring's ultimate recommendation came in 1933 when he requested that the Trustees designate Hudnut Acting Dean for the duration of Boring's leave of absence.[80]

Boring did not resist the idea of retirement, but he believed it advantageous that he remain with the University at least through the academic year 1930–1931:

My special interest in the School and in the new School of Fine Arts seems to me to indicate that my duty is to stay at the University for the present, but of course my resignation will be handed in at any time you call for it. For next year, however, I am convinced that I should stay with the University.[81]

It was Boring's hope that the School of Fine Arts would "enlist the sympathies of the highest authorities on art, such as the American Academy in Rome, and have an advisory council in sympathy with the movement."[82]

Evidently Butler was supportive of the request to remain on the Faculty, for Boring did not in fact retire until 1934, following a leave of absence during the academic year 1933–1934.

A model in clay. Photo: Avery Archive.

80. Boring to Butler, 13 January 1933, Central Files.
81. Boring to Butler, 11 January 1930, Central Files.
82. Boring to Butler, 12 December 1929, Central Files.

A Presidential Dining Room (An Analytic Drawing), 1931, Max Abramovitz *(1931)*. Photo: Avery Archive.

An Exterior Stairway, ca. 1930, designer unknown. Photo: Avery Archive.

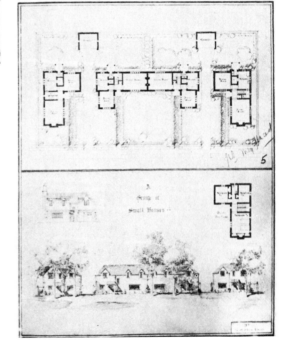

Above: Bureaux Francais Office building, 1929, Howard A.
Van Vleck *(1929).* Photo: Avery Archive.

Above right: A Street Clock, ca. 1932, Elmer S. Tuthill *(1935).*
Photo: Avery Archive.

Right: A Group of Small Houses, 1929, John D. Evans
(1930). Photo: Avery Archive.

As I was completing my architectural studies in 1927...we had at Columbia a sort of insulated academic background — so much so that none of the instructors or professors would even talk about the International Style, the Bauhaus, and what was going on in Europe...It was only in one lecture that we were told about it... We were almost taken in, as if we were going to be told some dirty stories. 'We'll tell you about it, but forget it...'[1]

These are the words of Morris Lapidus about a lecture given by William Alciphron Boring, a man in his sixties and the Dean of the Columbia School of Architecture. Seven years later matters had not changed perceptibly. Ronald Bradbury, a foreign student from England who graduated in 1934, recalls his educational experience in the early thirties in this way: "The years 1931 to 1934 were still in the Beaux-Arts period at Columbia and on antiquarian boards we all wrestled with monumental schemes of a type never seen, or likely to be seen, on land and sea."[2]

The Beaux-Arts system of education did indeed hold sway during this time. Many of the professors who were teaching at Columbia had either themselves spent some time at the Ecole des Beaux-Arts in Paris, or had attended American schools where this teaching method was quite common in the late nineteenth and early twentieth centuries. Though the American schools which had adopted the Beaux-Arts curriculum tried to stay close to the French prototype, it is important to point out a number of crucial differences.[3] Architectural education in France could not have been more centralized; from its inception in 1819 until 1968 there was only one official school of architecture, the Ecole des Beaux-Arts (in this it was the spiritual successor of the Académie Royale d'Architecture, founded in 1671, one of the academies established under Louis XIV in order to centralize the power of the king). This total lack of any competition must be in large part responsible for the school's extraordinary slowness in adapting its teaching to modern requirements. Furthermore, anyone in France could become an architect simply by buying a patent;[4] but only those who chose to go through the onerous program of the Ecole could expect to join the elite group that was used to fill official posts. For this reason the school's curriculum tended to be geared primarily to a grand and imposing program, the kind of important public buildings the Ecole student would be expected to carry out later in his government job.

By contrast, the institutional underpinnings of the Beaux-Arts method as applied in this country were much more relaxed. This method ended up being taught in a number of private and state schools, making for a high degree of competition and diversification, a heterogeneity that would never have been possible at the monopolistic Ecole. The centralized stranglehold and hierarchic schooling of the Ecole were further loosened by the introduction here in 1921 of what amounted to a correspondence course in Beaux-Arts education. This was the year when John F. Harbeson started a series of articles in *Pencil Points,* later published in book form, that was intended to impart to its readers Beaux-Arts ren-

Modernism Rears Its Head — The Twenties and Thirties

Rosemarie Haag Bletter

Fig. 1 "Temple of Castor and Pollux," 1931, Caesar de Sina *(1935)*. Photo: Avery Archive.

1. John W. Cook and Heinrich Klotz, *Conversations with Architects,* (New York: 1973) p.148. For their assistance with the research for this article, I wish to thank Steven Bedford, Sophie Gobran, Judith Oberlander, and Alfred Willis.

2. Theodor K. Rohdenburg, *A History of the School of Architecture — Columbia University* (New York: 1954) p. 89.

3. In Arthur Drexler's *The Architecture of the Ecole des Beaux-Arts,* (Cambridge: 1977), American examples of the Beaux-Arts style are shown simply as an extension of the French method.

4. Richard Chafee, "The Teaching of Architecture at the Ecole des Beaux-Arts," Ibid., p. 85. Though neither author pinpoints the differences between French and American Beaux-Arts education, the following two works provide helpful background information: James Phillip Noffsinger, *The Influence of the Ecole des Beaux-Arts on the Architects of the United States,* (Washington, D.C.: 1955) and Joan Draper, "The Ecole des Beaux-Arts and the Architectural Profession in the United States: The Case of John Galen Howard," in Spiro Kostof, ed., *The Architect — Chapters in the History of the Profession,* (New York: 1977) p. 209-237.

dering and design.[5] Even students who were not associated with the American centers of Beaux-Arts education could thus imbibe some of this training at long range. This greater accessibility was also reinforced by the architectural competitions sponsored by the Beaux Arts Institute of Design. The B.A.I.D. had been set up in 1916 in New York by the Society of Beaux-Arts Architects (of which William Boring had been a founding member)[6] to encourage the kind of architectural competitions that were an integral part of French Beaux-Arts training. But unlike the Ecole competitions, which were open only to students of that institution (in fact, its most prestigious competition, the *Prix de Rome,* was open only to Ecole students of French citizenship), the B.A.I.D. competitions could be entered by anyone who belonged to an architectural club or *atelier,* and the B.A.I.D.'s Paris prize competition was open to all U.S. citizens under the age of 27. Many architectural schools also used the B.A.I.D. to judge their students' work. The peak of this activity occurred in 1929–1930 when forty-four schools sent in almost 10,000 drawings.[7] Though the style and content of the American Beaux-Arts program never strayed too far from its French model, because of the institutional diversity in this country it did not attain the force of law to quite the same degree as it had in France. This accounts for the fact that it lost some of its most hierarchic, stultifying, and petrified features. This may also explain why Beaux-Arts inspired architecture in America became considerably more lively and inventive than that which was being built in France by former Ecole students. There are the examples of Louis Sullivan, who had studied at the Ecole but also at M.I.T., of Frank Furness and Frank Lloyd Wright, both of whom got to know the Beaux-Arts style indirectly, Furness through his work in Richard Morris Hunt's *atelier* and Wright through his apprenticeship with Sullivan.[8]

The best and worst aspects of the Beaux-Arts approach are in evidence in Columbia student work from the twenties and early thirties. There are wonderfully precise archaeological first-year studies of classical details *(fig. 1, 2).* Premiated student projects that were also submitted to the B.A.I.D. for competition show the same conjunction of outstanding draftsmanship and Roman Imperial planning that had characterized most Ecole projects. The Ecole had not rejected medieval styles outright, but since its most coveted prize was the *Prix de Rome,* the winner of which was sent to Rome to draw and measure ruins, the general stylistic emphasis of most designs understandably looked to Rome. And, because the Ecole had been set up to produce architects of the state, the tendency was to adopt the more imposing and controlling central axes of Imperial Roman planning, rather than the more loosely organized schemes of Greek or Republican Roman architecture. Occasionally the same highly controlled sequence of spaces was done in a Baroque palace style with a series of forecourts and flanking pavilions or wings that lead up to the always centralized main building. Such plans, which would require a great deal of land for their ceremonial approaches, showed little regard for specific sites. They follow the same ritualized pattern whether the

Fig. 2 "Greek Capital, Parthenon,"
1933, Theodore Rohdenburg *(1937).*
Photo: Avery Archive.

5. Starting with vol. II, January, 1921, p. 19-21 close to forty articles appeared in *Pencil Points* between 1921 and 1924. The book was published two years later (*The Study of Architectural Design,* New York, 1926).

6. Everett Victor Meeks, "Foreign Influences on Architectural Education in America," *The Octagon,* 9 (July 1937), p. 37.

7. Noffsinger, *The Influence of the Ecole,* pp. 70-71. "The Paris Prize," *Pencil Points,* 4 (February 1923), p. 29.

8. Although H.H. Richardson's late work became freer and more expressive than the normative Beaux-Arts style, his architectural education was exclusively French.

Left: fig. 3 A Campo Santo, ca. 1929, Morris Ketcham *(1931)*. Photo: Avery Archive.

Below: fig. 4 A Museum of the Peaceful Arts, 1926–27, Warren A. Draper *(1927)*. Photo: Avery Archive.

building is meant to be in the Alps or in Alaska.[9] They are particularly unrealistic for a dense, urban setting. To be sure, they were the most appropriate expression of the power of a centralized state, but not nearly such good teaching tools for private or commercial commissions for a restricted site. It was this programmatic unreality of the projects, exacerbated by an overemphasis on draftsmanship, that eventually led to a critical reaction against the Beaux-Arts system.

The Columbia student drawings from this period, like most Beaux-Arts drawings, are a delight to look at, and as with the latter, the plans seem more like elaborate embroideries than rational designs *(fig. 3, 4)*. Some of the schemes, especially those in the "archaeological" category, displayed the same anachronistic abandon as the Ecole projects. Where the Ecole had favored "Casinos" or a "Staircase for a Palace", the Columbia designs included, along with more sensible projects for libraries and museums, designs for "An Egyptian Barge" or "A State Bedchamber in the Empire Style". The contexts to which these styles were applied were flagrantly out of touch with contemporary social needs. One of the few exceptions was an archaeological prob-

9. See Drexler, *The Architecture of the Ecole des Beaux-Arts,* "A Hospice in the Alps" by Julien Guadet, 1864 (p. 255-257) and "A Large Trading Post in Alaska" by Alphonse Gougeon, 1896 (p. 304-305).

lem for a Gothic tower done by Morris Lapidus *(fig. 5),* a historical exercise that could conceivably be of use in the design of churches. Among over fifty drawings published in *Illustrations of Student Work in the Regular Exercises in the School 1924 – 1929*[10] only two were for office skyscrapers *(fig. 6),* a building type that was one of the most important American contributions to architecture, and a building type that by the late twenties was radically changing the Manhattan skyline with the construction of the Chrysler Building, the Empire State Building, the Chanin Building, the Daily News and the McGraw-Hill Buildings, the RCA Building, and many others.[11] William Ward Watkin, a fairly conservative critic, in an estimate of modern architecture both here and in Europe wrote in 1931: "It is only when we come to the skyscraper that we can feel a newness, a modernism in American work…"[12]

The Crash of 1929 did not affect the architectural profession immediately — projects with already committed budgets and buildings already under construction generally went on to completion. But by the early thirties few new projects were started. During this period of increasing hardship Columbia reacted to the changing times with more practical proposals. In 1932 Dean Boring suggested to President Butler the erection of a skyscraper tower on top of McKim, Mead and White's incomplete University

Left: fig. 5 A Gothic Tower, 1926, Morris Lapidus *(1927).* Photo: Avery Archive.

Right: fig. 6 An Office Building, ca. 1929, Morris Ketcham *(1931).* Photo: Avery Archives.

10. *Columbia University School of Architecture — Illustrations of Student Work in the Regular Exercises in the School 1924 – 1929,* (New York: 1929).

11. For architects' names and dates of buildings, as well as other skyscrapers under construction at this time see Cervin Robinson and Rosemarie Haag Bletter, *Skyscraper Style — Art Deco New York,* (New York: 1975).

12. William Ward Watkin, "Impressions of Modern Architecture," *Pencil Points,* 12 (May – July 1931), p. 525 (this is No. III of a three-part series).

Hall.[13] A competition was held with a jury consisting of architects Everett V. Meeks, Arthur Loomis Harmon, Harvey Wiley Corbett, Ely Jacques Kahn, and William A. Delano. Howard Bahr received the Charles Follen McKim fellowship for his design of a thirty-story skyscraper done in a pared-down classical style *(fig. 7)*. The tower, which was intended for a variety of functions, would have equaled all currently available teaching space on the campus. In Boring's opinion the scheme would have effectively solved Columbia's space problem.[14] Boring pointed out that other universities were adapting the skyscraper, originally a commercial building type, to this new use. He surely must have had in mind the University of Pittsburgh's 52-story Cathedral of Learning (1924–1928) by Charles Z. Klauder. Though the Columbia project for a campus tower would have been eminently practical, it was projected to cost seven million dollars, money the university probably did not have at a time when the Depression was really beginning to be felt.[15] Had it been built, it would not only have solved Columbia's later problems in expanding beyond the original campus, but it also would have created a more appropriate crowning element behind the dome of Low Library than the School of Business which was eventually erected on this site.

The Beaux-Arts training Columbia students still received at this time nevertheless stood them in good stead, at least for certain kinds of jobs. Morris Lapidus, for instance, before he established his own firm, worked for Warren and Wetmore:

I worked on the ornamentation of the New York Central Building because I could draw acanthus leaves with my eyes closed... All they had to do was give me a surface and I would cover it with acanthus leaves, volutes, egg and darts, and dentils. Just call it out; I had my alphabet...[16]

It was an alphabet of classical details that the Beaux-Arts education had imparted so well, but it was not an alphabet that guaranteed a coherent style. Lapidus believed that the professors at Columbia had been so reticent about Le Corbusier, De Stijl, and the Bauhaus because they were all fighting for their professional lives.[17] They probably realized full well that the new European style would upset everything that they had learned and stood for. Understandably, they did not spend time to proselytize it.

But the Chicago Tribune Tower competition of 1922 and the Exposition Internationale des Arts Décoratifs et Industriels Modernes in Paris of 1925 had made Lapidus and his fellow students realize that new things were in the offing. They were particularly impressed with Eliel Saarinen's entry for a stripped-down Gothic skyscraper rather than by Raymond Hood's winning entry, which was more fussily detailed, and in theory should have appealed more to students who had worked on problems in Gothic archaeology. If the teachers were in no mood to discuss European modernism, the students, at least, kept asking questions. Harvey Wiley Corbett, design critic at Columbia from the teens through the thirties, was queried by the students about the comparative merits of the Neogothic Woolworth Building by Cass Gilbert and what they regarded as a "modern" skyscraper, Saarinen's Tribune

Fig. 7 Columbia University Skyscraper, Charles Follen McKim Fellowship, 1932, Howard Bahr *(1932)*. Photo: *Pencil Points,* 13 (1932), p. 498.

13. "His Design wins $2,500 Award," *The New York Sun,* May 31, 1932, p. 22.

14. "Wins Prize for Plan of Columbia Tower," *The New York Times,* May 31, 1932, p. 19.

15. "Columbia Studies Skyscraper Plan," *The New York Evening Post,* May 31, 1932, p. 6.

16. Cook and Klotz, *Conversations,* p. 150.

17. Ibid., p. 148.

Tower design. Corbett told them confidently that "dress is unimportant." In his opinion, the Woolworth Building was modern, too, because its structure was modern: "If you took a Chinese man and dressed him in Caucasian clothing, he would still be Chinese."[18] It is a curious analogy, to say the least, in which the structure is not just compared to the human skeleton, as had been done in the nineteenth century, but to the whole man. The building's envelope, instead of being compared with the skin that covers the skeleton, represents here a more dispensable cover, i.e. dress. Of course, Corbett was probably influenced in his response by the fact that he had worked at one time for Cass Gilbert and that he himself had a Neogothic entry in the Tribune Competition. But Corbett's attitude is really rather typical of the Beaux-Arts-trained architect of this period (Corbett had received his diploma from the Ecole in 1900). The exterior of the building was commonly treated as a ceremonial dress, rather than an integral expression of the structure. The exteriors were treated as the curtain walls they were, but the curtains remained drawn, so to speak, whereas buildings in the Chicago engineering tradition tended to have envelopes which were treated as "open" curtains.

The Art Deco exhibition in Paris of 1925 produced an even stronger reaction than Saarinen's Tribune Tower design. This time Columbia students as well as the profession at large took note. The exhibition had originally been conceived in 1912 as a patriotic and economic reaction to the popular success of an exhibition of German crafts at the *Salon d'Automne* in 1910 (crowds had to be controlled by the police). This had made French designers aware of a "design gap" in an area in which they had traditionally regarded themselves as preeminent. To regain for France the competitive advantage they felt they had once possessed, an exhibition highlighting current French design was planned for 1915, an exhibition that was to be an answer to Germany's dominance in the design field. World War I intervened, however, and plans did not get under way again until 1922 for the show that finally took place in 1925. Other nations were invited to give it the cachet of earlier international expositions. What was at the outset planned as an artistic/economic contest took on more political overtones. Germany was now a conquered nation. It was invited to participate, but apparently too late for proper organization and it therefore declined. Thus Germany, the original stimulus for the whole enterprise, had been conveniently placed *hors de concours*. To insure the novelty of what was to be on display, the exposition committee required that any work submitted must possess new inspiration and real originality. Any imitation of historical styles was "strictly prohibited".[19] If France had not been producing modern design so far, the organizers might have reasoned, perhaps it could be jolted into doing so by such an official decree. America was also invited to the exhibition. However, when Herbert Hoover, then Secretary of Commerce, read the requirement for originality and prohibition against eclecticism, he answered that the United States could not take part since no new design of that sort was being

Top: fig. 8 Tony Garnier, "Pavilion for Lyons-St. Etiènne," Paris, 1925. Photo: M. Roux-Spitz, *Exposition des Arts Décoratifs Paris 1925.* 1928, plate 33.

Above: fig. 9 J. Hiriard, Tribout & Beau, "Pavilion of the Galéries Lafayette," Paris, 1925. Photo: M. Roux-Spitz, Exposition des Arts Décoratifs Paris 1925, 1928, plate 54.

18. Ibid., p. 149.

19. For references and a fuller discussion of issues concerning the Art Deco exhibition see Robinson and Bletter, *Skyscraper Style,* p. 44-48.

produced here. Hoover did, nevertheless, seem to be aware of the economic importance such an exhibition could have. Before the opening of the show he appointed a commission to visit Paris and write a report for the benefit of American manufacturers. The commission in turn invited various trade associations to pick delegates who would visit the exhibition once it had opened to the public. Thus, in the summer of 1925 eighty-seven delegates from such organizations as the American Institute of Architects, the Architectural League of New York, the Furniture Designers' Association, the Association of National Advertisers, the Society of Arts and Crafts, United Women's Wear, the Metropolitan Museum, and *The New York Times* visited the exposition.

The Art Deco show did in fact have a few radically modern buildings: Konstantin Melnikov's pavilion for the Soviet Union and Le Corbusier's *Pavillon de l'Esprit Nouveau*. The commissioners of the exhibition, after an unsuccessful attempt to keep Le Corbusier's pavilion from being built altogether, had a six-foot palisade fence erected around its site, effectively separating it from the rest of the exposition. Revolutionary forms apparently were not wanted, despite the prohibition against eclecticism — only a generally acceptable image of "modernism."

Nearly all the regional buildings, such as Tony Garnier's pavilion for Lyons-St. Etiènne and those for Parisian department stores *(fig. 8, 9)* used a stripped-down classicism with little nods to modernity in the flat decorative panels or spandrels which contained touches of Cubist, Futurist, and Expressionist ornament. This was a sharply modified modernity that could be safely accommodated within the Beaux-Arts tradition. Though it came to be seen as a French style, Art Deco was in truth a pastiche of many old and some new elements. Its simplified classicism with stylized ornament or stylized vestiges of a classical order had actually been pioneered by Joseph Hoffmann and the Wiener Werkstätte in their Berlin exhibition of 1904 and in the design of Hoffmann's Palais Stoclet in Brussels of 1905–1911 *(fig. 10)*. Just as the International Style was not created at Weissenhof, so Art Deco was not created in Paris. Both shows merely focused and synthesized earlier developments. But while the Weissenhof Exhibition of 1927 passed almost unnoticed in this country, the Art Deco show of 1925 made quite a stir.

Thousands of visitors, among them Ely Jacques Kahn, came from the United States. More importantly, when the delegates appointed by Hoover's commission returned to this country, they not only made reports to their respective trade associations and institutions, but also published articles in trade publications about the new "French style". By all accounts, the Art Deco show was a tremendous popular success, taking advantage of most of the new public relations channels. The exhibition was an imperfect marriage between art and commerce, a marriage made on earth, not in heaven. Out of this union was born a species that might be called mass modern. Art Deco was a style that pointed to its modernity with arrows and exclamation marks, but without ever giving up

Fig. 10 Josef Hoffmann and Koloman Moser, "Entrance, Wiener Werkstätte Exhibition," Hohenzollern-Kunstgewerbehaus, Berlin, Fall 1904. Photo: Deutsche Kunst and Dekoration, 15 (1904–5), p. 203.

the past. It was the kind of modernism that American architects, steeped in the Beaux-Arts tradition, could feel quite comfortable with.

The Columbia teacher, who, according to Lapidus, introduced him and his fellow students to Art Deco was Frederick C. Hirons.[20] Lapidus also reports that Hirons, who taught at Columbia from 1922–1926 and who had been a classicist, was doing then "...what he thought was contemporary architecture uninfluenced by anything that was taking place in the International Style... Instead of a Corinthian capital, he would use foliage, influenced partly by Art Nouveau, partly by De Stijl, and partly by his own innovative approach."[21] This kind of reduction of classicism, where classical proportions and pilasters might be kept, but where a capital might be replaced by some stylized new invention became the preferred way that the Beaux-Arts trained architectural establishment in this country adapted to modernism. The International Style, because of its apparently complete rupture with the past, was easier to accept by those who had attended either European or American polytechnic institutes, where architectural education had stressed construction rather than composition, history, and archaeology. Hirons, who had attended the Ecole, applied Art Deco modernism together with his partner, Ethan Allen Dennison, quite explicitly in the Manufacturer's Trust Bank of 1927–1928 *(fig. 11)*. It is essentially a traditional, neoclassic bank design turned into a banker's modern by colorful terracotta plaques that are used in place of capitals. The same is true of the new building Dennison & Hirons designed for the Beaux-Arts Institute in 1928. Inspired by Hirons, Lapidus bought the catalogue of the Art Deco show and later in the thirties, when he began to practice architecture on his own, he used it frequently, almost as if it were a pattern book: "I kept referring to my book."[22]

Dean Boring, who had been at Columbia since 1915, retired from the School of Architecture on June 30, 1933, and Joseph Hudnut, Professor of the History of Architecture since 1926, was appointed Acting Dean. At the same time President Butler appointed a committee with, among others, Wallace K. Harrison, William F. Lamb (of Shreve, Lamb & Harmon), and Ralph Walker (of Voorhees, Gmelin & Walker) to study possible changes for the school's curriculum. Hudnut's own annual report of July 1934 coincided with many of the revisions recommended by the commission. Most importantly, design courses were to be more realistic and down-to-earth than the highly idealized and occasionally far-fetched design problems assigned under the Beaux-Arts method. Projects were now to be considered in relation to a specific site, something that had not been done under the older method. Design was no longer to be geared as closely as in the past to the competitions of the Beaux Arts Institute of Design, and both beginners and advanced students were to work together in groups with specific "Studio Masters." The Studio Masters were not to be responsible to each other, thereby, presumably, allowing for the development of a much greater variety of approaches within the school.[23] The new program was instituted in the fall of

Fig. 11 Manufacturer's Trust Bank, New York City, 1927–28, Dennison & Hirons. Photo by Cervin Robinson.

20. Interview: Morris Lapidus by Richard Oliver, February 5, 1981, typescript, p. 37, Graduate School of Architecture and Planning Archive (hereafter GSAP Archive).

21. Cook and Klotz, *Conversations*, p. 148.

22. Interview: Lapidus by Oliver, p. 6 and 10.

23. "Columbia Reorganizes Teaching of Architecture," *The Architectural Record*, 76 (July 1934), verso of frontispiece. "Columbia Adopts New System of Teaching Architecture," *The Architectural Record*, 76 (November 1934), p. 320. "Columbia Changes Her Methods," *The Architectural Forum*, 62 (February 1935), p. 168. Rohdenburg, *A History*, p. 35–36.

1934, the same date that Hudnut was officially appointed Dean of the School. Theodore Rohdenburg, who started at Columbia in 1933, the year before the changes were made, remembers the shift as something of a shock: "For one who had toiled over the niceties of a problem in superimposed classic orders just before the summer recess to pledge allegiance in the autumn to the harsh discipline of the new 'functionalism' required considerable mental agility."[24]

Though Hudnut had received a master's degree from the Columbia School of Architecture in 1917, he did not quite fit the Columbia mold. Before coming to Columbia, he had received a bachelor's degree in architecture from the University of Michigan's Engineering School in 1912.[25] But he never made the pilgrimage to the Ecole des Beaux-Arts, and for this reason he was not entirely indoctrinated into Beaux-Arts teaching. Because he had gone through both a polytechnic and Beaux-Arts education, he was quite familiar with the advantages and disadvantages of both methods. *The Architectural Forum* in discussing the changes at Columbia stated that the proposed curriculum was not really so new, but was basically that used in the "German technical high schools [sic] where the emphasis is placed upon the technical development of the student rather than upon graphic presentation."[26] The "new" curriculum in some ways also instituted the modifications of the Beaux-Arts method that William Ware had sought half a century earlier.[27] In a meeting of the Associated Collegiate Schools of Architecture in 1934 Hudnut clarified his pedagogical beliefs further. He advised against the teaching of archaeology as it had been taught under the Beaux-Arts system. He felt that the study of "archaeology as now taught encouraged a romantic attitude toward architecture, and it gave too great an emphasis toward a pictorial method and that it divorced the history of architecture from the social and economic facts which underlie it."[28]

Hudnut had voiced similar sentiments as early as 1931, in an essay on "The Education of an Architect" published in the *Architectural Record,* an article that makes it quite clear that his ideal program was no simple utilitarian functionalism or a straight polytechnic course. He cited three responsibilities that a school of architecture has: one, to teach the science of construction; two, to explain the economic and intellectual currents in which the student lives; and three, to encourage the creation of beauty. He thought the last — aesthetic education — would be the most difficult to carry out properly. Open aesthetic discussion, he wrote, was until recently hampered "...by the hocus-pocus of Vignola. The Five Orders were invaluable for that conspiracy of bewilderment that is essential to every profession — especially to the profession of teaching — and even big business men were willing to abdicate their right to pass judgment in the presence of a professor who could clearly distinguish a Corinthian capital from a cauliflower."[29] But he found the doctrine of functionalism equally obfuscating in the teaching of aesthetics: "Since Le Corbusier provided the necessary mystifications the dogma of functionalism has

24. Rohdenburg, *A History,* p. 37.

25. Ibid., p. 45-46.

26. "Columbia Changes Her Methods," op. cit. The German "Technische Hochschule" is not a "technical high school," but a college-level polytechnic institute.

27. Rohdenburg, *A History,* p. 35.

28. Associated Collegiate Schools of Architecture, minutes, 21 (1934), p. 6.

29. Joseph Hudnut, "The Education of an Architect," *Architectural Record,* 69 (May 1931), p. 412.

taken on an almost religious character."[30] He regarded as naive the belief that beauty is automatically created by building logically, the shibboleth of "form follows function." If this were correct, he wrote, no school of architecture would have to concern itself with beauty; it would be enough to teach only economics, business, and the cost of materials, and beauty would arise automatically. It is obvious from this that Hudnut was no "functionalist." He merely wanted to impart a degree of reality into the more abstract features of Beaux-Arts design, without, however, becoming a technocrat in the process:

It was a fault of the Renaissance tradition, from which our system of architectural education is sprung, that it ignored too often the practical common sense that must necessarily be the basis of a useful art like architecture. But that fault does not discredit the ardent and ennobling search for form that is the important fact about Renaissance architecture. Indeed, the effort to reconcile the needs of contemporary life with abstract conceptions of form is the very heart of the Renaissance. The Renaissance committed many absurdities, but never the supreme absurdity of mistaking a condition of beauty for its source. It never supposed beauty to be a by-product of science.[31]

Hudnut's balanced point of view was to be repeated in numerous essays on architectural education written during the thirties even after he had become the Dean of the Harvard Graduate School of Design in 1935, where he was responsible for hiring Walter Gropius, an association that clouded the later understanding of Hudnut's own attitudes. As late as 1942 Hudnut wrote that a design program should be within the range of a student's experience: "*A Palace for the Governor of Algiers, a Nymphaeum in the Argentine,* may be excellent subjects for the application of abstract principles of plan and composition; and yet, in the end, they deaden rather than vivify the imagination." In his opinion a fateful step toward excessive romance is taken when students are asked to "...interpret in a pattern of architectural forms a pattern of social conduct unknown to them."[32] While today critics of the International Style believe that its forms were too abstract, Hudnut had reacted against Beaux-Arts design because he felt that its *programs* were too abstract.

Hudnut was by no means alone in his criticism. A climate of dissatisfaction with Beaux-Arts design began to develop at other schools as well, though in the thirties there were few professors or deans of architecture who were willing to change established programs as Hudnut had done. For example, Joseph Esherick, who began his architectural studies at the University of Pennsylvania in 1932, in his reminiscences of that period complained about the projects assigned through the Beaux Arts Institute of Design in New York. They included such bread-and-butter building types as *A Building to Enshrine the Chalice of Antioch, An Amusement Park, A Ski Club, A Pyrotechnic Display,* and *The Decoration of a Gymnasium for a Celebration.* He recalled "...we were never given problems with real sites. The nature of the site, its physical characteristics and general appearance might be described, but it was never a real

30. Ibid., p. 413.

31. Ibid. See also Joseph Hudnut, "The Post-Modern House," *Architectural Record,* 97 (May 1945), p. 70-75. Although Hudnut criticizes functionalism and structural invention for its own sake, he exempts Le Corbusier, Gropius, and Mies from this attack.

32. Joseph Hudnut, "Education and Architecture," *Architectural Record,* 92 (October 1942), p. 38.

site one could go to and look at and stomp around on."[33] This was true of the nationally distributed programs of the B.A.I.D., but more objectionably, it was also true of programs generated from within the schools.

An indication that the new curriculum at Columbia had made somewhat of a difference was the announcement in *The New York Times* in 1936 of a student project for a new Museum of Modern Art. It was to replace the inadequate building at 11 West 53rd Street. The students' designs were to be exhibited at the Architectural League. This project, based on an actual site, according to Professor Leopold Arnaud "...closely approximated the conditions under which architects work."[34] One of the factors for a change in attitude toward Beaux-Arts education may well have been the Museum of Modern Art's show "Modern Architecture: International Exhibition" of 1932 as well as the publication in the same year of *The International Style* by Henry-Russell Hitchcock and Philip Johnson. The highly influential book featured European modernism with relatively few American works included. It had now become more difficult for professors of architecture to tell their students to forget all about Le Corbusier, Mies van der Rohe, or the Bauhaus. Columbia did in fact get a sampling of more avant-garde education when, coinciding with Hudnut's changes in 1934, Jan Ruhtenberg was hired to teach architectural design. Ruhtenberg had received his education in Germany. In 1931 he briefly worked for Mies van der Rohe at the Berlin Building Exposition. Ruhtenberg left Germany in 1932 and practiced architecture in Stockholm until he came to the United States in 1933.[35] At the school he introduced the use of transparent models made of celluloid, something that, after so much emphasis on drafting, the students were not quite ready for.[36] At a meeting of the Associated Collegiate Schools of Architecture in 1936 Ruhtenberg read a paper on architectural education which was discussed by the participants afterwards. Stressing the need for more practical education, Ruhtenberg stated that in Germany students were required to work as carpenters or bricklayers for at least six weeks, in Sweden this course was recommended but not required. A number of questions were asked about Bauhaus education. Some of those in the audience were not aware that the Bauhaus had closed in 1933. Ruhtenberg answered that, as far as he knew, only the Royal University in Stockholm had taken an active interest in continuing the Bauhaus method.[37]

In 1930 Henry-Russell Hitchcock complained in the pages of *The Architectural Record* that few schools of architecture had come to terms with a contemporary style. He wrote that if it was used at all, it was "admitted on a par with the 'styles' of the past...," i.e. contemporary architecture was not used as *the* modern expression, but simply as the latest addition to the catalogue of styles: "Modern architecture cannot be served by syncretist acceptance. Either it is a new way of light which demands conversion, or it is merely an impediment in the growth of taste in revivalism."[38] He continued that many young men in Europe who were interested in becoming "modern architects" have returned to the full apprenticeship sys-

33. Joseph Esherick, "Architectural Education in the Thirties and Seventies: A Personal View," Spiro Kostof, ed., *The Architect,* op. cit., pp. 264 and 272.

34. *The New York Times,* January 13, 1936.

35. "Jan Ruhtenberg Appointed at Columbia," *Pencil Points,* 15 (supplement, 1934), p. 15-16. Rohdenburg, *A History,* p. 38, writes that Ruhtenberg attended the Bauhaus, but his name does not appear among Bauhaus students (see Hans M. Wingler, *The Bauhaus,* Cambridge, 1969, p. 615 ff.). According to Philip Johnson (interview with author July 20, 1981) he had been responsible for bringing Ruhtenberg to this country. Despite the claim that he was of "Swedish parentage" (see *Pencil Points,* Ibid.), Johnson insists that Ruhtenberg was German. Johnson believes that Ruhtenberg found it more expedient during the Nazi period to pretend that his nationality was not German. His "association" with Mies was not as an apprentice, but as a volunteer, according to Johnson. Further, Ruhtenberg's association with the Museum of Modern Art, also listed in *Pencil Points,* is spurious as well says Philip Johnson, who was at the Museum of Modern Art in the early thirties.

36. Interview by author with Theodor Rohdenburg, May 26, 1981. The same type of transparent model was recommended by Eugene Steinhof, an Austrian, in "A New Way to Teach Architecture," *American Architect,* 142 (July 1932), pp. 22-23.

37. Associated Collegiate Schools of Architecture, minutes, second session, 23 (May 4, 1936), pp. 5-6.

38. Henry-Russell Hitchcock, Jr., "Architectural Education Again," *The Architectural Record,* 68 (April 1930), pp. 445-446.

tem as a way to avoid the conservative schools altogether. At the same time, he cautioned, while the apprenticeship system would allow a student to search out a modern master, its stress on architecture as a craft may not be suitable for the complexities of modern construction and the size of American architectural offices.

What really seems to have turned the tide away from the abstract programs of the Beaux-Arts system was not so much the Museum of Modern Art's exhibition and the publication of *The International Style* in 1932, but the unavoidable realities of the Depression. By 1936, a study group on architectural education (led by Arthur Loomis Harmon) found that the professional life of architects had undergone a radical change: "The architect must now be a counselor to financial houses as to the rehabilitation and maintenance of their properties, and interpreter of building laws to real estate, an advisor of welfare under relief projects..."[39] A growing awareness that architectural education could not go on as before is clear from discussions of this subject throughout the thirties. George Herbert Gray, the Director of the New England Division of the A.I.A. wrote in "The Schools and the New Architecture", published in *The Octagon* in 1933 that "it is pretty generally agreed, that, viewed historically, we are in a period of transition, and some think a major period, fully as significant as the renaissance which followed the middle ages."[40] He found that with the current drafting room methods students became too "set in the habit of thinking in two dimensions." As a cure he suggested the use of models and the study of buildings, both completed and in the process of construction. E. Raymond Bossange, the Dean of the College of Fine Arts and the Director of the Department of Architecture at New York University, also believed that architecture was in the midst of a great new development. But, unlike Gray, he did not compare the thirties to the Renaissance: "This is one of the most significant periods in the history of architecture. It is comparable in importance to the Greek and Gothic periods." The current changes that would, in time, produce a "third great architectural system," he wrote — again agreeing with Gray — could be helped along by the use of models, encouraging "greater appreciation of solid form."[41] George H. Edgell, dean of the school of architecture at Harvard before Hudnut, responded to Gray's call for a more practical education, by stating that: "One of the great difficulties at present is the result of the depression...the difficulty of getting a job is not only a serious matter economically for the student, but prevents his getting office experience when he should be getting it, even during his period of education."[42]

In 1937, Everett V. Meeks, Dean of the Yale School of Architecture, in an article on "Foreign Influences on Architectural Education in America" that continued the debate on architectural education begun by Gray in 1933, was one of the few educators who did not reject the Beaux-Arts method as outmoded. Nevertheless, he conceded that in contrast to the more than one hundred American students who were at the Ecole in Paris when he studied there: "Today I doubt if there are two or three men there." He went on to

39. This was reported by Prof. William Sanders of Columbia to a meeting of the A.C.S.A, minutes, May 4, 1936, p. 7.

40. *The Octagon,* 5 (February 1933), p. 10. This article had been prepared as a paper for a forum on education that did not take place. Gray invited the dean of the school of architecture at M.I.T., Harvard, and Yale to respond. The latter two did in 1937.

41. "Changes in Architectural Education," *Pencil Points,* 14 (July 1933), pp. 309-310.

42. "The Schools and the New Architecture," *The Octagon,* 5 (May 1933), p. 6.

attribute the change entirely to the Depression: "Of course the great factor in education, as well as in the profession, which has made us sit up and take account of stock has been the depression and the resulting era of utilitarianism in architecture."[43] Also in 1937 the Princeton School of Architecture sponsored an Architectural Round Table at which both architectural education and modernism were addressed. George Howe questioned the teaching of architectural history from the past to the present. He suggested that it be taught in reverse sequence "in order that we might be sure to bring contemporary life and its problems adequately to the attention of the students." In his own experience "starting out with Rameses one rarely got to Rockefeller."[44] Later in the conference Ely Jacques Kahn, architect of many Art Deco office buildings, annoyed Howe by "not speaking with sufficient disrespect" of historicizing buildings. On the defensive, Kahn claimed that any work is modern "if it really worked and had charm and showed a mastery of the use of . . . materials. . . . Why go into all this frenzy of cantilevered buildings and insist upon doing something stunty?" Kahn asked the graduate students, if the Princeton campus were to be completely destroyed, whether they would want it rebuilt by a modernist. The yeas drowned out the nays. "It was clearly evident throughout the conference that the sympathy of the student is all with the modern movement."[45] Thus, the debate over Beaux-Arts versus modernism was in full swing and already moving in the direction of the latter before Gropius arrived at these shores.

It is obvious that a new sentiment was in the air throughout the thirties, but how much difference did the new curriculum at Columbia make in the end? Hudnut left only a year after the changes were instituted to assume his deanship at Harvard. Jan Ruhtenberg left the following year, 1936, to start his own office. Max Abramovitz, who had taught design at Columbia from 1930–1932 and then was at the Ecole on a fellowship for two years, on his return from Europe in 1934 found that everybody at Columbia was still "teaching the same thing that I'd taught two years before."[46] However, the changes had only just been made and Abramovitz's opinion is, for that reason, not a reliable assessment of the success of the new curriculum. Theodor Rohdenburg, who was a student from 1933 until 1937 does agree that the changes were not as thoroughgoing as they were to be at Harvard later in the decade only because Hudnut was in charge at Columbia for too short a time.

In one year very little could be accomplished. And although Hudnut instituted a new curriculum, most of the same teachers were on the faculty before and after 1934. Harvey Wiley Corbett, the Beaux-Arts trained architect, taught design before and after the change. Talbot Hamlin, the school's great teacher of architectural history, was at Columbia from the twenties onward. In 1933 he had written an essay in *The American Architect* attacking modernism called "The International Style Lacks the Essence of Great Architecture,"[47] a theme he was to continue in many of his later writings. Nevertheless, despite a teaching staff that was still part of the Beaux-Arts tradition, Rohdenburg remembers that by

43. *The Octagon,* 9 (July 1937), p. 41.

44. This phrase of George Howe's was probably inspired by Charles Harris Whitaker's popular *The Story of Architecture: From Rameses to Rockefeller,* (New York: 1934).

45. W. Pope Barney, "Premises and Conclusions at the Princeton Architectural Round Table," *Architectural Record,* 82 (September 1937), pp. 58-60.

46. Interview: Max Abramovitz by Richard Oliver, March 19, 1981, typescript, p. 19, GSAP Archive.

47. *American Architect,* 143 (January 1933), pp. 12-16. For a discussion of Hamlin's writings see Kenneth Frampton's essay.

Fig. 12 Design Project, 1937–38, Filippo Rovigo *(1937)*. Photo: Avery Archives.

1937 most of the student projects were done in a more or less modern style.[48]

One other important change initiated by Hudnut but one that did not take full effect until after his departure from Columbia was a greater emphasis on city planning as a discipline. In 1935, while Hudnut was still at Columbia, Henry Wright and Werner Hegemann were hired to teach courses on town planning. Wright was well known in America for his design (with Clarence Stein) of Sunnyside Gardens, New York, and Radburn, New Jersey. Hegemann had been an established author and editor of architectural and city planning publications in Germany and in the United States. He had also been a partner of Hudnut's from 1916 to 1921. But both Wright and Hegemann died within a year of their appointment to the faculty. Following Wright's and Hegemann's deaths in 1936, Columbia called on Sir Raymond Unwin and Carl Feiss to continue the program in town planning. During this period Carol Aronovici also taught planning courses in the School of Architecture's extension program. Though Columbia had some sporadic courses in city planning much earlier, it began to offer a graduate degree in Planning and Housing in 1937, one of the earliest such degree programs.

Wright, through his association with Stein and Lewis Mumford in the Regional Planning Association of America, was closely allied with principles of English garden-city planning. Unwin, of

48. Interview: Rohdenberg by Author, May 26, 1981.

course, was the major practitioner of the English garden-city movement. Hegemann was, to a large extent, a follower of Camillo Sitte's romantic, psychological, and experiential approach to urban problems. In contrast to Harvard, which hired Martin Wagner, the socialist planner who had been responsible for helping to organize low-income housing cooperatives in Germany and who had been chief city planner of Berlin, and in contrast to the Illinois Institute of Technology, which hired Ludwig Hilberseimer, who had taught planning courses at the Bauhaus under Hannes Meyer and later Mies, Columbia's urban planning program seemed to perpetuate the politically more utopian and romantic anti-urban attitude of the late nineteenth century. Nevertheless, it was to be just such notions which in a very watered-down form after World War II were to make a much greater impact on the development of American suburbia than the more rationalist urban concepts of Wagner or Hilberseimer. The picturesque garden-city certainly had more popular appeal than twentieth-century ideas of urbanism. And, as the garden suburb stripped of its social framework, it was more readily adaptable to the laissez-faire approach of the American private developer.

In 1937 Leopold Arnaud was named the new Dean. Arnaud belonged to Columbia's old guard. He had graduated from the School in 1919 and subsequently attended the Ecole. During the later twenties he worked for the large New York firms of Warren & Wetmore and Voorhees, Gmelin & Walker. The new curriculum, adopted in 1934, was virtually abandoned in 1937.[49] During this period Donald Fletcher taught design courses. Fletcher as late as 1947 published a book on architectural design with *Vive l'Ecole!* on the dedication page.[50] But despite the apparent retreat from modernism concerning the curriculum and teaching staff, Jan Pokorny, who began as a student in 1940, recalls that most of the student projects were nevertheless done in a modern idiom[51] *(fig. 12)*. It seems that like the students at Princeton, who would have rebuilt the campus in the International Style, the younger generation at Columbia also was moving in the direction of modernism, despite the retrenchment on the part of the faculty. In fact, the older generation of architects teaching and practicing in the late thirties, even men who had earlier accommodated themselves to the more florid forms of Art Deco, was going back to a severer kind of classicism. The hulking gray mass of Harvey Wiley Corbett's Criminal Courts Building in Manhattan of 1939 *(fig. 13)* is a good example.

Morris Lapidus, who started to practice independently in the thirties, did not pass through this period of transition with ease: "I began to do things in the Bauhaus manner. I worked for a number of years in that style, and that was my most unimpressive work... It gave no latitude to do anything."[52] Instead, he turned to an eclectic mixture of Beaux-Arts, and Art Deco, with occasional touches of International Style features. Despite his rejection of the International Style, he was greatly inspired by the semicircular ebony wall in Mies' Tugendhat House.[53] He may not have adopted the general vocabulary of the International Style, but he did copy its more sensuous details. He became a specialist in the redesign of

Top: fig. 13 Criminal Courts Building, New York, 1939, Harvey Wiley Corbett. Photo by Cervin Robinson.

Above: fig. 14 Shwobilt Store, Tampa, 1936, Morris Lapidus *(1927)*. Photo: Morris Lapidus.

49. Rohdenburg, *A History,* p. 36.

50. Donald Atkinson Fletcher, *Introduction to Architectural Design,* (New York: 1947).

51. Interview: Pokorny by Author, May 26, 1981.

52. Interview: Lapidus by Oliver, p. 13.

53. Ibid., p. 28 and Cook and Klotz, *Conversations,* p. 149.

a series of elegant stores *(fig. 14)*, characterized by his use of biomorphic forms, decks with cut-outs, and thin, columnar elements.[54] Lapidus had originally come to Columbia because he was interested in doing stage design and, even if he never officially became a stage designer, as an architect he did become the master of set design.

Lapidus had a chance to do his biggest set design when he received the commission for the Fountainebleau Hotel in Miami Beach *(fig. 15, 16)*, completed in 1952. It was also his first independent building. Lapidus came up with a palace style via Busby Berkeley.[55] Because of his thorough Beaux-Arts training he always remembered how to use ornament and rich materials. His design of this period in many ways seems to anticipate Robert Venturi's later theories. But where Venturi was to insist on the inclusion of many high-art elements along with commercial imagery, producing intellectual statements, Lapidus was more hedonistic. He used popularized images of grand design. The chandeliers, the marbles, and the grand staircase that leads nowhere are the props of an aristocratic life as they had been transmitted through school projects. This was not French Provincial, but Versailles-cum-Buckingham Palace on the Lido, a fantastic stage-set for guests who wanted to forget the drabness of Brooklyn or the Bronx.

The period of transition in the thirties from the Beaux-Arts educational system to one that embraced European modernism was not an easy one, nor did the change occur with dramatic speed. Harvard was to be the exception; most architectural schools, like Columbia's, did not make the same clean sweep of the past. It was largely the Depression that forced the issue to a head.[56] The International Style had evolved under conditions of economic exigencies from Adolf Loos' demand for less ornament to the low-income housing estates of the twenties. Its frugality seemed more appropriate in the thirties than the idealized, stately Beaux-Arts schemes. For students who had been trained in the latter method, the conviction that the new style was necessarily better was not always present. There were some architects, such as Morris Lapidus, who, to be sure, had arrived at a personal and popular style via Art Deco and the more sensuous South American version of the International Style, but who never quite gave up their first training in producing an architecture of entertaining richness. As William Ward Watkin predicted accurately in 1931: "The nature of our modernism, when it comes, is evidently to be moderated by our conservative tradition."[57]

Top: fig. 15 Fountainebleau Hotel, Miami Beach, 1952, Morris Lapidus *(1927)*. Photo: Morris Lapidus.

Above: fig. 16 Fountainebleau Hotel, Miami Beach, 1952, Morris Lapidus *(1927)*.

54. "40 Years of Lapidus at Miami University," *Interiors*, 126 (November 1966), p. 12.

55. Alan Lapidus, "The Architecture of Gorgeous," *Design and Environment*, 4 (1973), pp. 22-25. See also Mary Josephson, "Architecture: Lapidus' Pornography of Comfort," *Art in America*, 59 (March – April 1971), pp. 108-109.

56. Joseph Hudnut, "Architecture Discovers the Present," *The American Scholar*, 7 (Winter 1938), pp. 106-114. See also Meeks, "Foreign Influences," on this point.

57. Watkin, "Impressions of Modern Architecture."

History IV
1933–1935

Judith Oberlander

Joseph Hudnut. Photo: Harvard University
Graduate School of Design.

O n February 6, 1933, President Butler informed Joseph Hudnut that he had been appointed Acting Dean of the School of
Architecture, effective July 1, 1933.[1] This appointment was upon
the recommendation of William Boring, who had requested and
received a leave of absence from his duties as Dean. The next day,
Hudnut responded, noting that by the following fall term, he
would present to Butler

*a program for the development of the School of Architecture...based upon
a careful study not only of conditions within the School and in the field of
architectural education but also of the situation confronting the profession of
architecture as a whole.*[2]

Joseph Hudnut was born in Big Rapids, Michigan, on March
27, 1886.[3] He was educated at Michigan Military Academy prior
to studying architecture at Harvard (1906–1908) and the University of Michigan where he received his B. Arch. in 1912. In 1916
Hudnut began studies for the Master of Science in Architecture at
Columbia and graduated as the Alumni Medal recipient in 1917.
During the First World War he served in Italy and upon his return
in 1919 he practiced architecture in New York City. Associated for a
while with Werner Hegemann, he worked on city planning projects for Milwaukee and Reading, Pa., and he designed industrial
housing and churches.[4]

Prior to his return to Columbia as Professor of Architectural
History in 1926, Hudnut taught at the Polytechnic Institute in
Auburn, Alabama (1913–1917) and at the University of Virginia
(1923–1926), where he also directed the McIntire School of
Fine Arts.[5]

Hudnut moved quickly to change the focus of the School to
reflect the times and his own educational philosophy. He initiated
changes in the curriculum, hired new faculty and visiting critics,

1. Nicholas Murray Butler to Joseph Hudnut, 6 February
1933, Central Files, Columbia University (hereafter Central Files).

2. Hudnut to Butler, 7 February 1933, Central Files.

3. Hudnut died on January 16, 1968, in Dover, Massachusetts. See obituary in *The New York Times,* 17 January
1968, p. 47.

4. Curriculum vitae of Joseph Hudnut, Central Files.

5. Ibid.

and sought to develop a new relationship between the School and the profession, then in turmoil as a result of the Depression which had sharply reduced work for architects across the country. Talbot Hamlin commented on the profession's new sense of social responsibility:

In the enforced leisure of the depression the architect has begun to think of the value of his training to society as a whole; he has begun to apply his creative talent to housing, to city planning, to the problems of social recreation...he is beginning to realize how deeply the great dilemmas of poverty and wealth are implicated in his work.[6]

In addition to the Depression, two other factors contributed to the profession's sense of unease: the impact of European modernism, and the introduction of new materials and building techniques.

Education for contemporary society was Hudnut's primary goal and in his view, if this was to occur, radical changes were required. In his first annual report on June 30, 1934, Hudnut wrote:

The schools of architecture have a prescriptive part in the formation of an architecture of the future...We must believe that it is not only a part of our work to give our students a technique which shall be useful and salable, but we must also strive to make them fit to apprehend a new and vastly wider responsibility than has hitherto characterized the architect. The young architect must leave our halls not only equipped with a basic understanding of his new technology, but he must be resolute to use that technology for the reconstruction of our human environment.[7]

In seeking change, Hudnut enjoyed the support of President Butler, who had appointed a committee of architects to report on the School, comprised of Charles Butler, Wallace K. Harrison, William F. Lamb *(Columbia, 1906)*, Ralph Walker, and chaired by Grant La Farge.[8] The committee observed that there are two general types of architecture schools, the one, *Stylistic*, the other *Organic*, and felt that Columbia's School should evolve from being an example of the former to that of the latter. They sharply criticized the *Stylistic* type:

it dwells essentially in the past in that it assumes that a student, not yet awake to the sense of himself as an architect, will by the study of historic styles, by learning certain of their "elements," academically determined to be "correct," thereby in some mysterious manner become able to achieve personal expression in terms of his own day.[9]

In contrast, the committee praised the *Organic* type, which it thought was the exact opposite of the *Stylistic*:

It begins with the belief that the approach to the study of architecture is best made through the practice of architecture. That is, that however simple may be the exercises of the beginner, they shall deal with actualities, with fundamental principles. In doing this it places confidence in the intelligence of the student, in his desire to learn, his ability to do so quickly once he feels himself to be engaged with reality.[10]

To accomplish the reform of the School, the committee recommended a series of changes. It felt that:

6. Talbot Hamlin, "The Architect and the Depression," *The Nation,* 137 (August 9, 1933), p. 154.

7. Hudnut to Butler, 10 July 1934, with report attached, Central Files. The report was regarded as sufficiently important and newsworthy to be published in the architectural press. See "Report of Dean Hudnut, June 30, 1934," *Architectural Forum,* 62 (February 1935), p. 167.

8. In 1915, the Trustees of the University established a Committee of Visitors to advise and guide the School. By 1933, its role had become loosely defined and this prompted President Butler to redefine its purpose and to appoint new members to the Committee. In their report to Butler on May 1, 1934, the committee members stated their objective as: *a School of Architecture that shall be abreast of present day conditions and shall prepare its students to meet them, to participate in them as an active force, rather than to be the product of preparatory methods and theories based upon social conditions obsolete or obsolescent and therefore devoid of living reality.*

Thus it is clear that members of the profession sought a change in educational methods as much as Hudnut did. See, *Report of Committee on Columbia School of Architecture,* May 1, 1934, Central Files. The report, too, was published in the professional press. The "The Architects' Committee Reports on Columbia's School of Architecture," *Architectural Forum,* 62 (February 1935), p. 163.

9. *Report,* May 1, 1934, Central Files.

10. Ibid.

the student should not be forced to learn any set of systems of architecture, such as the "orders," but should be shown the principles of thought which go to make beauty... that considerably more emphasis be placed upon the social aspect of architecture, not only relating to so-called "low cost housing" which is in the limelight today, but also to various other problems which the student will have to face in later years in the practice of his profession... [and] that the School of Architecture be moved from its present quarters and placed downtown, whenever that may be practicable.[11]

Hudnut found himself "heartily in accord with the recommendations made by this committee," and noted to Butler that the very process of transition from a "stylistic" to an "organic" school which had already been under way "ought to be greatly accelerated."[12]

Emphasis on a wider social consciousness and upon technological progress became important components of the School's educational philosophy under Hudnut's administration. Furthermore, he felt that it was the duty of the School to respond to the changing role of architecture and to endeavor to meet its future needs. While, in his opinion, students would not be too harsh on the educational system if it failed to understand what lay ahead, Hudnut claimed that:

there is only one procedure which they will not forgive, and that is an entrenchment behind the walls of tradition and habit, where, heedless of their urgent necessities and deaf to the human anguish around us, we give no thought to that new environment in which they are to live.[13]

Beginning with the academic year, 1934–1935, Hudnut introduced the following changes: studios comprised of students in all grades of design; the elimination of competition in design; the option to take courses in economics, social sciences, and business; and the replacement of cast drawing by life drawing.[14] The curriculum initiated by Hudnut to a large extent resembled that of the German *Techniche Hochschule* because of its emphasis on the technical aspects of architecture.[15]

Although the problem method of instruction was retained, competitions were discontinued since Hudnut felt that individual guidance for each student was an essential component of the program. The problems given in the studios were of two types — major problems which were individual, non-competitive and of indeterminate length; and sketch problems which were done in a group, judged on a competitive basis and executed within a limited period of time, usually eight hours. Within each major problem there were three stages: the establishment of the program, prepared by the master or student; preliminary studies; and presentation. A radical change from the previous curriculum occurred at the completion of the problem when the appraisal of a student's work took into account the entire work of the semester, instead of merely the final presentation.[16]

The sketch problems were given every two weeks and corresponded to the students' progress. There were two groups: Class A

11. Ibid.

12. Hudnut to Butler, 10 July 1934, Central Files.

13. "Columbia Reorganizes Teaching of Architecture," *Architectural Record*, 76 (July 1934), Back of Frontispiece.

14. Hudnut to Butler, 10 July 1934, Central Files. See also, *School of Architecture, Bulletin of Information, 1934–1935.*

15. "Columbia Changes Her Methods," *Architectural Forum*, 60 (February 1935), p. 168.

16. Ibid.

for those who had already completed eight problems, and Class B for those who had not. Each problem was announced a week in advance so that research could be completed.[17]

Within the restructuring of the curriculum, the courses themselves also changed to reflect the new educational philosophy of the School. Courses such as "Shades and Shadows," Analytique" and "Descriptive Geometry" were replaced by "Life Drawing," "Sketch class and water color" and a drafting course, "Descriptive Geometry and its applications." Other courses were given on an elective basis: "Modern Sculpture," "Building Construction," "Urbanism," "Critical Writing," "Business Law," "Principles of Economics," "The Aesthetics of Architecture" and "Contemporary Architecture."[18] In order to offer these various elective courses, Hudnut arranged for members of other faculties to teach in the School of Architecture.

In 1934, Hudnut made one new appointment to the architecture faculty. Jan Ruhtenberg, a disciple of Mies van der Rohe, was hired as Associate in Architecture in 1934 and taught courses in Architectural Design until 1936 when he left for professional practice.[19] Ruhtenberg was hired to replace Lemuel Dillenback, who had been asked to resign. In 1929, Hudnut had urged Boring to reorganize the courses in design, and to do so by hiring Dillenback. Hudnut "was greatly impressed by reports of the vigorous and successful organization and administration of the work in design at the University of Illinois" under Dillenback's direction. The Beaux-Arts Institute of Design had recognized Dillenback's work by awarding to Illinois its medal for unusual excellence. Subsequently, Boring hired Dillenback to be Professor of Design. But Hudnut further observed "shortly after Dillenback's appointment that, however able he might prove to be as an administrator, he failed to demonstrate those qualities of scholarship which are obviously essential for a man who is to form the taste of future architects." As a result, Boring "repeatedly requested the appointment of a second Professor of Design who might bring to the School some of the qualifications which were obviously lacking in Professor Dillenback." After becoming Acting Dean, Hudnut requested and received Dillenback's resignation, and the latter remained at the School until August, 1934, when he accepted an appointment as Professor of Design at Syracuse University, receiving in the process a year's salary for leaving. Dillenback was the only senior member of the faculty other than William Bell Dinsmoor, and by removing him, Hudnut was effectively able to eliminate any serious reaction to his proposed changes.[20]

Hudnut felt that the School "ought to have more frequent and more important contacts with the profession of architecture," and to this end he established a Panel of Jurors, a list of twenty-five architects, many of whom were leading members of the New York architectural community. Among them were Chester Aldrich *(Columbia, 1893)*, Harvey Wiley Corbett, Harrie T. Lindeberg, Clarence Stein, George Howe, Louis Ayres, Julian Levi *(Columbia, 1897)*, and Egerton Swartwout. These men were invited to serve on School juries that were held twelve times a year, and the infor-

17. Ibid.

18. School of Architecture, Bulletin of Information, 1935—1936.

19. Hudnut to Butler, 12 June 1934, Central Files.

20. Hudnut to Frank Fackenthal, 27 September 1934, Central Files.

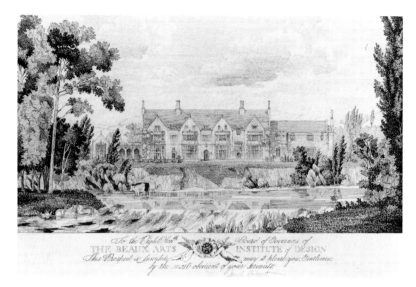

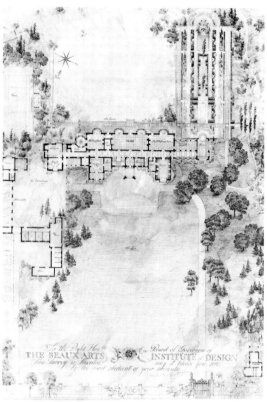

A Country House, 1917, Joseph Hudnut *(1917)*.
Photo: Avery Archive.

mality of the occasions allowed them to have "many opportunities to know at first hand the work of our students and to talk over school problems with members of the faculty." However, the faculty and the visiting architects continued to evaluate student work with the students themselves not permitted to attend or to explain the work.[21]

Hudnut obviously had the support of Butler and the Trustees for the changes he was making, because he was appointed "to be Dean of the Faculty of Architecture from July 1, 1934 during the pleasure of the Trustees, without change of salary."[22]

As part of his endeavor to directly involve the School in the affairs of the profession and the city, Hudnut proposed to Butler "that the University undertake a survey of the City for the purpose of making recommendations in respect to sites for Housing Projects…in cooperation with the Regional Plan Commission and also with the Slum Clearance Committee.[23] This effort, which was approved by Butler, also had the support of Robert D. Kohn *(Columbia, 1890)*, then Director of Housing for the Federal Emergency Housing Administration.

One of the most important aspects of Hudnut's reorganization of the School was the establishment of a Town Planning Studio, which was to offer

practical and theoretical courses in the reorganization and extension of city plans, the planning of building sites, the design of housing developments and of civic facilities for recreation, and in related fields of architectural design.[24]

The course of study was proposed to be parallel with architecture, allowing the student to specialize in town planning.

Hudnut applied to the Carnegie Corporation for funding for the Town Planning Studio.[25] While waiting for financial support he was able to convince Butler that he should begin the course in the spring of 1935. With the approval of Butler, Hudnut brought to the School, "unquestionably the most competent authority" in the field, Henry Wright.[26] Wright was hired not only to provide ad-

21. Hudnut to Butler, 11 November 1933, Central Files.

22. Butler to Hudnut, 7 May 1934, Central Files.

23. Hudnut to Fackenthal, 28 November 1933, Central Files.

24. Hudnut to the President and the Trustees of the Carnegie Corporation, 19 November 1934, Central Files.

25. Hudnut to Butler, 21 January 1935, Central Files.

26. Ibid. See also, Henry Wright, *Notes Relating to the Teaching of Town Planning in a University,* Central Files.

vanced instruction in town planning, based upon his experience in Sunnyside, Queens, and Radburn, New Jersey, but to foster the development of the School as a research center in the field. One benefit of the course would be "the introduction into the field of architecture of a limited number of men sensitive to form and mass in relation to topography, sunlight, the interplay of man's relationships and an understanding of the basic principles of site engineering." Wright proposed that the problem method be used in the course, although he felt that "these problems need not be competitive, but they would frequently be collaborative in order to develop the interrelated aspects of the subject."[27]

Wright began work in the spring of 1935 on two projects: he gave instruction in the Town Planning Studio, and he conducted the Hamilton Heights Study.[28] Hudnut saw many benefits from the Hamilton Heights Study:

we shall furnish a most valuable experience for our advanced students, and we shall have made a fortunate beginning in the development of our plan for the expansion of the School. We shall, at the same time, make a practical contribution towards the welfare of our neighbors to the north, and perhaps shall assist in the prevention of that deterioration which is threatened in this fine, residential section of the City.[29]

Another well known city planner was brought to Columbia in February, 1935 to assist Wright with the Town Planning Studio. Werner Hegemann, a German planner and former editor of *Staedtebau* and the *Wasmuths Monatshefte für Baukunst* from 1924–1933, was hired upon the recommendation of Hudnut.[30] Hegemann taught a seminar on the Plan of the City of New York which included an analysis of the City's Regional Plan and provided the opportunity to examine an actual plan in process of implementation.[31]

While Wright was conducting the Hamilton Heights Study, Hegemann directed a fourth-year design studio that undertook the design of a small residential park for inexpensive houses.[32] The intention of the project was to devise a plan for a fifty-three acre site in Port Chester, N.Y. The site — an estate known as "Greyrock" — was twenty miles east of New York City on the western shore of Long Island Sound and therefore a desirable location for residential use. Prior to Columbia's involvement with the site, the New York Regional Plan Association had investigated its potential use as parkland with some housing for various income groups. In keeping with the School's emphasis on actual projects, this study involved a specific site, demanded a realistic budget and cost analysis for the post-depression market, and an architectural design which was appropriate to the program — a two bedroom house to cost approximately $6,000 including the land. As simple expressions of their interior layout and modern character, the houses were designed to encourage free circulation between the interior and exterior as well as within the building, and a number of designs had flat roofs with large areas of fenestration.[33]

Both Wright and Hegemann died in 1936 while the Town Planning program was in its infancy.[34] The following year the planning

27. Wright, *Notes*.

28. The latter was a survey and report of the area lying west of St. Nicholas Avenue between 125th Street and 155th Street, completed with the support of an advisory committee consisting of representatives of the Regional Plan Association, the Hamilton Heights Association, and the Russell Sage Foundation. The report included recommendations *respecting the means by which this area could be protected and improved, both in respect to living conditions and in respect to recreational areas and the organization and distribution of institutions. Traffic conditions, commercial facilities, and the problems of health and education [were] considered* (Hudnut to Butler, 21 January 1935, Central Files). See also, Hudnut to Butler, 23 January 1935, Central Files.

29. Hudnut to Butler, 21 January 1935, Central Files.

30. Werner Hegemann's appointment was made possible by a generous group of friends who established a fund for his salary (Hudnut to Fackenthal, 31 January 1935, Central Files).

31. Hegemann voluntarily left Germany in 1933 to settle in the United States. He became a visiting professor of city planning at the New School for Social Research prior to his appointment at Columbia.

32. "A Small Residential Park for Inexpensive Houses," *Architectural Forum*, 62 (May 1935), p. 478-483; and Werner Hegemann, "The Planning of Greyrock," *Architectural Forum*, 62 (May 1935), p. 484-498.

33. Ibid.

34. Henry Wright died on July 10, 1936. See obituary in *The New York Times*, 11 July 1936. Werner Hegemann died on April 13, 1936. See obituary in *The New York Times*, 14 April 1936.

courses were continued by Sir Raymond Unwin and Carl Feiss, while Carol Aronovici gave courses on housing and urbanism in the Extension Program. The establishment of a planning program at Columbia made it one of the first universities to offer such a program. To a large extent, this was due to Hudnut's desire to relate education to the field of practice and provide the students with "a wider experience with problems relating to the organization and expansion...of our cities."[35]

Like Boring before him, Hudnut wanted to establish a postgraduate and research center at the School. On February 6, 1934, Hudnut sent his proposal for an Institute of Urbanism, modeled on the *Institut d'Urbanisme* in Paris, to the Secretary of the University, Frank Fackenthal. The purpose of the Institute was:

to carry on research relating to the immediate problems of the City of New York, such as administrative organization, economic and social development, and the physical facilities for urban life.[36]

Hudnut envisioned that from ten to twenty instructors from the various faculties of the University would constitute the staff of the Institute, that several fellowships would be available for students, and that the facilities would include several lecture rooms, seminar rooms, a drafting room, offices, and a small library. Like many of Hudnut's proposals, this was not realized, in part because of his departure to Harvard in 1935. Nevertheless, its proposed purpose and structure further confirm Hudnut's essential goal of reintegrating the School with the real concerns of the larger world and of New York in particular.

The changes which Hudnut proposed and those he was able to enact were the subject of much discussion within the profession, at other schools, and in the professional magazines. Some conservative critics like H. Van Buren Magonigle simply ridiculed Hudnut's pronouncements about the new and wider responsibilities of the architect.[37] Other critics like C. Matlack Price presented a more thoughtful appraisal of Hudnut's reforms, calling them "the beginning of a new *rapprochement*":

In an age when so much established precedent in so many fields is being challenged, re-examined, and made over, it should not be surprising that architectural education finds itself in need of a new orientation, a new set of ideas. The challenge comes alike from today's students and from their prospective employers.... The present vastly accelerated tempo of architectural thought and performance makes the difference between its teaching and practice disturbingly apparent. It is in this that lies the challenge to the schools and universities, rather than in the essential rightness or possible error of the whole doctrine of modern architecture.[38]

For reasons which remain unknown, Hudnut did not stay long at Columbia before accepting the position of Dean of the Graduate School of Architecture at Harvard.[39] George Edgell was to retire as that school's dean in 1935 and Hudnut was approached by President James Conant of Harvard. When Butler learned of Harvard's offer, he wrote immediately to Hudnut:

Naturally, I hope we may take it for granted that while appreciating to the

35. Hudnut to Butler, 21 January 1935, Central Files.

36. Hudnut to Fackenthal, 6 February 1934, with attached *Memorandum: Proposed Institute of Urbanism for Columbia University,* Central Files.

Hudnut's interest in an Institute of Urbanism, and his later working relationship with Walter Gropius at Harvard have formed the basis of a rumor that Hudnut wanted to bring Gropius to Columbia. According to Winfried Nerdinger, Gropius, while in England in the early 1930's and out of work wrote to various educational institutions in the United States seeking employment. He did so at the suggestion of A. Lawrence Kocher, an editor at the *Architectural Record.* The only institution to express interest was Columbia's School of Architecture, or rather Joseph Hudnut, then Acting Dean. This is confirmed in a letter from Gropius to Pierre Jay, 20 June 1934, held in the Gropius Archives, Houghton Library, Harvard University. However, Ise Gropius, in a telephone conversation in June, 1981, claimed that Gropius never had any intention of coming to Columbia because he felt that Columbia was not an adequately influential institution.

Hudnut may have had Gropius in mind for one of two positions. The first was that of Professor of Design, a position then held by Lemuel Dillenback, whom Hudnut wished to replace. The second position was as Director of the proposed Institute of Urbanism. Gropius, who always argued for an interdisciplinary approach to architectural problems might have been an ideal director.

A full account of the relationship between Hudnut and Gropius must await publication of Reginald Isaac's history of the Graduate School of Design at Harvard.

37. H. Van Buren Magonigle, "The Upper Ground: Being Essays in Criticism," *Pencil Points,* 16 (January 1935), p. 17.

38. C. Matlack Price, "The Challenge to Architectural Education," *Architecture,* 70 (December 1934), p. 311-315.

39. The key reasons for Hudnut's departure to Harvard must remain speculative for now; it may have been merely a question of salary, as Columbia had not increased Hudnut's salary when he was appointed Dean, and Harvard undoubtedly made a better offer. It may also have been based upon Hudnut's perception of each of the university presidents. Nicholas Butler of Columbia was soon to retire, and unlikely to initiate any major reforms; James Conant of Harvard, on the other hand, was younger and was eager to enliven all the various parts of Harvard University. As a result, Hudnut may have felt that Harvard was the place where he could more fully realize his goals for architectural education.

*full the compliment, you will not dream of changing your academic rela-
tionship. We are looking to you here to plan and to carry through, during
the next few years, a truly forward facing and constructive program for the
development of architectural education in all its forms and phases, which
will be backed by the resources, the contacts and the opportunities which
Columbia University and the City of New York alone can offer.* [40]

Hudnut responded four days later:

*I could not think for a moment of leaving Columbia unless there were
offered me elsewhere an opportunity of a very exceptional nature indeed. I
did not believe until recently that such an opportunity could exist, but the
plans for the work at Harvard which President Conant has explained to
me are, to say the least, arresting and I feel that I must give them careful
consideration.* [41]

Although Hudnut did not remain long enough at Columbia to
fully solidify the curricular and administrative changes he had begun, he nevertheless had outlined a series of long-term changes in
his Dean's Report of 1934. These included: the establishment of a
professional course in landscape architecture; a course in urbanism, housing and the planning of cities; professional courses in the
industrial arts; a professional course in interior decoration embracing both theoretical and practical instruction; and the strengthening of graduate courses "so that Columbia may become the most
important center for this work in the United States." [42] Of all the
changes envisioned by Hudnut, the most radical dealt with the
administrative structure, the location, and thus the purpose of the
School:

*The School of Architecture, now expanded into a School of Design in
which all the activities in plastic design are correlated, should be moved to a
site near the center of the artistic and professional center of New York City.
The School should then be given an autonomy as complete as is practicable. It should be directed by a Board of Architects who should be free to
determine its policies and develop a technique of instruction free from the
limitations imposed by university organization and collegiate tradition.* [43]

In his short tenure as Dean of the School, Hudnut had managed
to create at least a new image of what architectural education
should become, and he had been able to institute as far-reaching
changes as possible within the constraints of time, faculty, and
budget. Hudnut surely understood that the changes he envisaged
could not be accomplished quickly, and thus it is a criticism neither
of Hudnut nor of his changes to say that his departure to Harvard
left the School in a state of some confusion. The old pedagogy had
been discredited, and a new pedagogy to take its place had not yet
been fully instituted.

40. Butler to Hudnut, 31 May 1935, Central Files.

41. Hudnut to Butler, 3 June 1935, Central Files. Hudnut resigned three days later on June 6, 1935 (Hudnut to Butler, 6 June 1935, Central Files).

42. Hudnut to Butler, 10 July 1934, Central Files.

43. Ibid.

In Search of an Order to the American City: 1893–1945

M. Christine Boyer

With the emergence of the vast American metropolis after the Civil War, two new dilemmas of modern society became apparent: how to control and arrange the spatial growth of these giant cities in order to improve and normalize the spatial whole so that it would efficiently support industrial production as well as the development of civilization; and how to discipline and regulate the urban masses, in order to eradicate the dangers of social unrest, physical degeneration, and congested contagion which all cities seemed to breed.[1] These questions of order and discipline forged a new relationship between the architectural adornment of urban space and the scientific treatment of spatial development. This new relationship, in turn, called forth the process of city planning.

As we shall see, however, because this process was blatantly utopian, anti-historical, and anti-urban, it never achieved a radical realignment of either the city or the urban populace. Its strategies and tactics represented a cumulative set of failures, each struggle bringing forth yet another reform from the City Beautiful movement to Comprehensive Planning, to Zoning, to Housing and then to Regional Planning before the process of physical planning was eventually abandoned. As part of the New Deal reforms in the 1930's, the Federal Government began to absorb planning into its bureaucratic structures. It is then that we find city planning absorbed in another objective: how to plan and facilitate rational strategic decision-making for governmental policies.[2] The nineteenth-century ideal of a perfectly planned and ordered city was forgotten by 1945 (abandoned in part because of the utopian, anti-historical and anti-urban nature of physical planning). In the process, American city planners from 1893 to 1945 passed through the metropolis, marked, manipulated and improved its spatial order without historically understanding or physically admiring it. Their final solution was to abandon it.

The story of this quest for an order within the American city can be told by focusing on the dialogue of four prominent city planners: George Burdette Ford, Carol Aronovici, Henry Wright, and Carl Feiss. Each one was not only instrumental in the definition and promotion of a discourse about city planning, but they were associated as well with the School of Architecture at Columbia University between the years of 1912 and 1945.[3]

A PICTORIAL ORDER:

By this great object lesson at Chicago, any thoughtful mind may learn that order and congruity in the architecture of our city streets are not necessarily monotony and wearisome iteration, but may be obtained by mutual concessions, resulting in an effect of concord without detriment to any desirable quality of individual distinction.

Henry Van Brunt, "The Columbian Exposition and American Civilization" (1893)

Our battle... is not so much against a definite or an established order of things as it is against chaos.

Fred Ackerman, Seventh National Conference on City Planning (1915)

1. For a full treatment of the multiple roots of American physical planning from 1890 to 1945 see M. Christine Boyer, *The Order of the American City* (Forthcoming The MIT Press, 1982).

2. For a discussion about the increasing levels of rationalization see Jurgan Habermas, Introduction, *Theory and Practice* (Boston: Beacon Press, 1973).

3. George Burdette Ford (1879–1931) trained as an architect in the U.S. before studying at the Ecole des Beaux-Arts. He quickly turned his interests to the new field of city planning where his projects spanned the city beautiful movement, the progressive tenement house reforms, comprehensive physical planning, and congestion and zoning schemes, before moving to regional planning in the 1920s.

Carol Aronovici, Ph.D. brought an interest in social science survey techniques to the process of city planning. As general secretary to the Suburban Planning Association in Philadelphia in 1914, he was most interested in providing low-cost housing for home ownership in the suburbs, an interest which he combined with regional planning in the 1930s.

Henry Wright (1878–1936) trained as an architect in the U.S. He held an early interest in community and site planning, becoming the architect, along with Clarence Stein, for the new towns of Sunnyside N.Y. and Radburn N.J. A member of the Regional Plan Association of America, he was responsible for the report on Regional Planning in New York State submitted to the New York State Commission of Housing and Regional Planning. His continual advocacy of group housing and the evolution of this housing type are well documented in his book of 1935, *Rehousing Urban America*. Along with Carol Aronovici, he started the Housing Study Guild which later influenced the development of the Division of Housing and Planning at Columbia University in 1935. Carl Feiss, an architect and city planner, along with Sir Raymond Unwin continued the work of Wright at Columbia in 1936. By 1937 the school offered an M.S. in Planning and Housing. Feiss remained at Columbia until 1942.

Architectural critics considered the nineteenth-century American city to be inhuman and ugly, a chaotic juxtaposition of good, bad and indifferent architectural styles, each competing to achieve notoriety by boldness in height or in ornamental pretension. The pictorial triumphs of the Chicago World's Fair of 1893, with its landscape plan and common module for the ensemble, became an object lesson for American architects. It taught them the value of architectural scholarship and strict subordination to a singular sense of order serving as a timely corrective to the national tendency to experiment in design.[4]

But Montgomery Schuyler took a more critical view of the Fair's lessons. He warned the architect, so recently provided with the opportunities in photography to reproduce and to copy whatever appeared admirable or striking, that he must learn to admire correctly. He must not be misled to reproduce or to imitate the successes of the Fair for its purpose, he claimed, was one of illusion: the buildings were not work-a-day but holiday structures, a triumphal stage setting for an unparalleled spectacle.

It is essential to the illusion of a fairy city that it should not be an American city of the 19th century. It is a seaport on the coast of Bohemia, it is the capital of No Man's Land. It is whatever you will, so long as you will not take it for an American city of the 19th century, nor its architecture for the actual or the possible or even the ideal architecture of such a city.[5]

Few American architects heeded this warning, for the spatial chaos of the city was seen as the problem of controlling growth, restoring order to the arrangement of buildings, separating and dividing uses as answer to "things out of place." To aid them in their attempts, the early city improvers sought an adequate symbol which would express their ideals of order and beauty and found this in the "White City" of the Fair. As John B. Walker expressed the hope of the times,

Who believes that the people of the second half of our century will be content to live in those abominations of desolation we call our great cities... brick and mortar piled higgledy-piggledy, glaringly vulgar, stupidly offensive, insolently trespassing on the right to sunshine and fresh air, conglomerate result of a competitive individualism which takes no regard for the rights of one's neighbors?[6]

City after city adopted the crusade of the City Beautiful, embellishing their order with civic centers, diagonal boulevards radiating from monumental nodes, majestic new libraries, railroad stations, museums and auditoriums until it was proclaimed that "...if it was said (of earlier times) that 'all roads lead to Rome' so now it may be said that all city plans refer to the Columbian exposition...that dream of a White City."[7] This was the architecture of the ceremonial, the power and might of America at the advent of its own imperial age made manifest through imitation of empires past. These Beaux-Arts illustrations detached fragments of the European city from their historical tradition, as luxurious inserts in the still chaotic city

4. William Coles (ed) *Architecture and Society, Selected Essays of Henry Van Brunt.* (Cambridge, Mass.: The Belknap Press: 1969), pp. 233-234.

5. Montgomery Schuyler, "Last Words About the World's Fair," *Architectural Record,* 3 (January – March, 1894), pp. 556-574.

6. John B. Walker, "The City of the Future," *Cosmopolitan* (September 1901).

7. J. H. McFarland, "The Growth of City Planning in America," *Charities and the Commons* (February 1, 1908).

structure. A plurality of copies stood in the place of a unique experience, like designs for a utopian vision that could be purchased ready made. This is what the critic Walter Benjamin termed the "metaphysics of the present," where only the trivialized work of art can reach a public, its "aura" lost in the mechanical reproduction that makes the object accessible to mass consumption. By dispensing with an authentic historical and urban score, a montage of civic structures and ornaments was offered to quench a public's thirst for an ideal order.[8]

CREATING A TAXONOMY OF URBAN SPACES:

...amid such vast and varied (urban) centres, such a crowded phantasmagoria of life, how shall we agree upon any orderly method of observation and description, such as that required in each and every department of science?

Patrick Geddes (1908)

The Social Survey is a process of qualitative and quantitative analysis of our social environment both in the past and in the present in order to make possible the visualising and the actual creation of practical utopias.

Carol Aronovici, Social Legislation and the Survey (1910)

In addition to the dilemma of physical disorder, there were social problems which thwarted what could have been an ideal order for the American City. The city was considered a dangerous and pathological environment which deformed the lives of the masses. Early in the nineteenth century, a concern with public health and welfare provided the rationale for a new type of intervention in urban space. It was carved up into a taxonomy of cellular sections: noxious uses were banned from residential quarters, tenement districts were surveyed for disease and congestion, the sanctity of the private home was invaded to normalize child development.[9] Under this management strategy for spatial order, there was no need for ceremonial displays of power because a medicalized space gave rise to a control by public inspectors, the details and fluctuations of the population were exposed to constant monitoring.[10]

This nineteenth-century surveillance of the urban masses produced a new form of knowledge through the use of commission inquiries, social surveys and statistical procedures. Planners used these new applications of science and technology to examine the American city. Rather than seek to impose an architectural order upon the urban fabric, they sought a technical regulatory control within the fabric of the city, a scientific knowledge or program that would discipline, that is improve, transform, correct and control, the threatening urban masses amid chaotic spatial disorder.

Patrick Geddes stated in 1908 that to physically plan our cities an adequate collection of maps was needed, then a detailed survey of their geographical and historical development, their industrial conditions, their advantages and defects, and the condition of their future development. Geddes proposed to define an immediate impression of the present through survey

8. Walter Benjamin, "The Work of Art in the Age of Mechanical Reproduction," *Illuminations*. trans. Harry Zohn (New York: Schocken Books, 1969), pp. 217-251.

9. For an in-depth treatment of the 18th century medicalization of space see Jacques Donzelot, "The Preservation of Children," *The Policing of Families,* trans. Robert Hurley (New York: Pantheon Books, 1979), pp. 9-47; and Michel Foucault, "The politics of Health in the Eighteenth Century," in Colin Gordon, ed. *Power/Knowledge* (New York: Pantheon Books, 1980), pp. 166-182.

10. For a full explanation of Foucault's treatment of disciplinary structures see, Michel Foucault, *Discipline and Punish: The Birth of the Prison,* trans., Alan Sheridan (New York: Pantheon Books, 1977).

returns and statistics, the plan, and the programmed estimate. It was time to dwell upon the city's geographic factors for, he thought, they deeply underlie, in fact largely determine the health and efficiency of the people.[11] Carol Aronovici followed Geddes' dictum in America. He felt that the social survey must build up a science of social organization and that municipal corruption and moral decay could be controlled by the scientific diagnosis of social and political institutions.[12]

George Ford also shared Aronovici's faith that scientific precision would control urban disorder; he proclaimed that the capricious art of city development was turning into a respectable exact science.[13] City planning was

rapidly becoming as definite a science as pure engineering. The best plan for the development of a city can be determined upon in advance as clearly as the plans for a bridge or for a reservoir. It is also solely a matter of proceeding logically from the known to the unknown in city planning. . . . [there is] the necessity for a careful analysis of conditions. The requirements must be first definitely determined upon. Then these should be separated into several classes according to their urgency, ranging from the immediate and imperative through the desirable to the more remotely advantageous. Working in this way one soon discovers that in almost every case there is one and only one logical and convincing solution of the problems involved.[14]

As Ford clarified in 1912, city planning had changed its objective from an initial emphasis upon the location and grouping of major civic and public buildings in displaying the dignity and majesty of the corporate city to a focus on the living, working and recreational areas of the people. Only after city planning embraced these concerns, Ford claimed, would comprehensive planning truly begin.[15]

The social survey linked to comprehensive planning held an instrumental attitude toward urban space: to reorder the city form and to discipline its populace implied the imposition of a scientific program upon the built environment. Surveying techniques would leave no zone of darkness, every detail would be exposed to the light of disciplined study and control. Analysis would naturally lead to a prescription for a new moral and physical order. Dividing the city into a typology of functional cells, reassembling these parts into an efficiently operating whole through comprehensive planning meant that the ideal urban order was rendered as a mechanical city. The planner became the technical efficiency expert. To believe in the value of rational organization and the scientific approach was a negative stance, both anti-historical and anti-urban. The planner became responsible for eliminating both the contradictions and the historical continuities of urban reality and for constructing instead an abstract mathematical or statistical order.

HOUSING FOR THE MASSES

The city's primary function: a place where people live concentratedly. To live they must work and they must play. . . Any city development which

11. Patrick Geddes, "The Survey of Cities," *Sociological Review* (January 1908); and Geddes, *City Surveys for Town Planning* (Edinburgh: Geddes and Colleagues, 1911).

12. Almost every book and article which Aronovici wrote contained a methodological treatment of survey techniques. See for example, Carol Aronovici, Ph.D. *The Social Survey* (Philadelphia: The Harper Press, 1916); and Aronovici, *Housing the Masses* (New York: John Wiley and Sons, Inc., 1939).

13. George B. Ford, "The City Scientific," *Proceedings of the 5th National Conference on City Planning* (Chicago: Illinois, 1913).

14. Ford and Aronovici were among a dozen planning consultants who, since the early 1900s, had been co-partners of planning firms, collaborators on planning projects, co-authors of books and articles, and co-participants on improvement committees and in annual housing and planning conferences. All of these men collectively defined a location for the discourse on planning the American city. The skills of the architect, the landscapist, the traffic expert, various kinds of engineers, lawyers and real estate investors, working together defined the process of city planning.

15. George B. Ford, "Digging Deeper in City Planning," *American City*, 6 (1912), pp. 557-562. For further clarification of Ford's early comprehensive plans see, George B. Ford and E.P. Goodrich, *Preliminary Report of the City Plan Commission, Newark, N.J.* (June 1, 1912); and Ford, "Recreation, Civic Architecture, Building Districts and General Summary of Present City Planning Needs," *Development and Present Status of City Planning in New York City* (1914), pp. 52-76.

does not take due cognizance of [life, work and play] is not only unscientific, it is criminal. It is a distinct betrayal of trust.

George Ford, Digging Deeper in City Planning (1912)

Juxtaposed against the comprehensive control of the metropolitan whole was the concern with the minimal living unit: the single family home and the model tenement.[16] As early as 1909, Ford wrote that the character and design of housing for the masses affect the happiness or unhappiness, the uplifting or debasing, the goodness, usefulness and helpfulness of a person's life or its disintegration into useless and immoral behavior. The problem for our cities and the moral lives of its inhabitants, he noted, was the fact that very few architects were involved in the design, production or promotion of model tenement homes.[17] The architect, Ford observed, should become intimately involved with these issues: fireproof construction, contagion, burglary, light and air, sanitary needs, and the care and rearing of children.[18]

Aronivici held an opposing position for he felt too much emphasis had been placed on housing for the masses. Twenty-five years of tenement house legislation saw the establishment of minimum housing standards for a mere 10% or 12% of the population in need of housing.[19] If one wanted to speak in 1914 of housing as a factor in the social, moral and economic progress of the nation then the housing solution should provide an alternative for those who could afford but cannot obtain adequate housing. Through intelligent planning, "utopia will be realized in the suburbs."[20]

A discourse began on the failures of the American City which reached a crescendo in the 1920's and 1930's. Aronovici believed that the ultra-urbanization of all human activity was a proven failure. An exodus into the splendid metropolitan areas surrounding the decadent core would hopefully be the trend of modern society.[21] In 1920 he outlined the basic problems which underscored the need for a housing policy. First, the housing environment constituted a considerable factor in the mental and physical characteristics of individuals.[22] Overcrowding that exposed the individual to the gaze of others led to a laxity in needed moral standards and rules of conduct.[23] The difficulty in securing transportation to a new place of work was the reason why so few Americans were homeowners, he claimed. Thus homes and industry must be re-distributed to reduce traveling time.[24] Most importantly, to protect and promote the value of homeownership, American cities would need a way to regulate and control land prices as well as a method to safeguard against the future deterioration of property values.[25] The failure to regulate the heights of buildings, the absence of building codes, the invasion of whole districts by large immigrant groups considered undesirable by older residents and the refusal to protect homogeneous neighborhoods and uniform building styles, all led to the deterioration of land values and the discouragement of long-term investment in homes, with their consequent adverse effects on the creation of good citizens.[26]

The Future Tower City.
Drawing by E. Maxwell Fry.

16. For an early treatment by Henry C. Wright see "Transit and Housing," *Proceedings of the National Housing Association* (Cincinnati: 1913).

17. George B. Ford, "The Housing Problem I-V" *The Brickbuilder,* 18 (1909), pp. 26-29, 76-79, 100-104, 144-147, 185-189. Not only had Ford's thesis been on the tenement house problem, he also chose to reside in a model tenement house, the Phipps House No. 1, almost from its opening.

18. Ford based his own concerns on a published account by Dr. E.R.L. Gould by the U.S. Bureau of Labor in 1895, in which Gould spoke of the four requisites of model housing being "privacy," "health," "safety," and "comfort."

19. Carol Aronovici, "Housing and the Housing Problem," and "A Housing Survey," *The Annals of the American Academy of Political and Social Science,* 51 (January 1914), pp. 1-7; 125-131.

20. Carol Aronovici, "Suburban Development," *The Annals of the American Academy of Political and Social Science,* 51 (January 1914), pp. 234-238.

21. Ibid., p. 238.

22. Carol Aronovici, *Housing and the Housing Problem* (Chicago: A.C. McClurg and Co., 1920), p. 17.

23. Ibid., p. 15.

24. Ibid., p. 17.

25. Ibid., p. 62.

26. Ibid., p. 71-72.

The construction of tenements in the city and single family homes in the suburbs was a tactic with which to mold the urban masses, thinly veiling a concern with public morality and social concern evolved out of the nineteenth-century philanthropic reforms which utilized model housing as the means to transmit certain moral precepts and behavioral habits to the urban masses. The woman was given a new weapon, and instructed on how to use it: a hygienic, spacious and efficiently-run home would stop the dissolution of the family. Model housing would also eradicate the slums, and with them their function as a retreat from the scrutiny and the control of society. Hence Ford placed his emphasis upon hygiene, safety and child-rearing. But housing would also be used to strengthen the public order. Homeownership would make good citizens, as Aronovici suggested: the urge for political protest was moderated under the threat of losing one's home.[27]

Still, comprehensive planning and housing reforms soon appeared to fail. Speculative real estate practices and the money economy were said to stand in the way of their success. So we find that an increasing social alienation and technical abstraction in the fragmented city of the 1920's enabled the planners to direct their concerns to perfecting a quantifiable order through zoning.

ZONING

Districting would keep the vampire from sucking the life blood out of his neighbor.

George Ford, City Building by
Coercion or Legislation? (1916)

The origins of American City slums lie in the inequalities of city planning. Skyscrapers next to mean business blocks, palaces next to hovels will be unknown under more rational city building.

Harvey W. Corbett, What the Architect
Thinks of Zoning (1924)

Once again a technical device was proposed to solve the problems of the American City. George B. Ford was one of the earliest supporters of the concept of districting or zoning. In 1914, he noted that there were areas of New York City where five to six thousand people were living in one block in crowded six story tenements while three quarters of the city's land remained unimproved. The state tenement laws and the City building and sanitary codes tried to alleviate some of the worst conditions but still private property across the city was developed in a haphazard fashion.[28] Momentum to limit the height, bulk and arrangement of buildings throughout the city gathered slowly, until a dramatic example of the need for control arose.[29] Garment manufacturers and jobbers daily clogged Fifth Avenue between the hours of twelve and two. As a result, land values between 23rd and 34th streets declined by half and the high-class retail values dropped to those of manufacturing levels. Big lenders, such as the insurance companies and the savings banks announced that they would no longer consider loans to manufacturing buildings in the district.

27. Donzelot, *The Policing of Families,* pp. 40-41.

28. Ford, *Development and Present Status of City Planning,* p. 66.

29. The New York City Board of Estimate and Apportionment appointed The Heights of Buildings Commission in 1913 and one year later the Commission on Building Districts and Restrictions. Ford served on both these commissions, as Secretary and Director of Investigation of the former and consultant to the latter. Ford, *Development and Present Status of City Planning,* p. 72. A comprehensive zoning ordinance was passed in New York in 1916.

All of this waste could have been avoided, Ford maintained, if the city had created a zoning plan twenty years earlier. Aronovici agreed; the loss of twenty-one million dollars in property values along Fifth Avenue near 23rd Street was a good illustration of the damage rued because a city refused to zone.[30]

Credit had been given to George B. Ford for first visualizing the zoning envelope within which the architectural form of tall buildings would have to lie,[31] but it was Harvey Wiley Corbett, another professor at Columbia's School of Architecture, with the aid of delineator Hugh Ferriss, who imagined its full potentiality.[32] Zoning, or so it was hoped, would direct architecture into the proper channels of expression. The common complaint was that architecture schools failed to train architects on how to interpret public values and how to transform them into art. For these reasons, Irving Pond argued, zoning commissions were needed to point the way.[33]

Aymar Embury II and Corbett both believed that the 1916 New York Zoning Law ordinance would bring about a uniform cornice line at the setback limit, smoothing out the jarring effects of individual competition along the street facade. Cupolas, spires and towers were expected to cluster above and behind the setback line as long as they did not exceed a diagonal drawn through the center of the street and resting on the limiting height of the cornice line.[34] Corbett explained that in order to allow light to permeate the conical form of the envelope, courts had to be cut from the outside into the building bulk. For structural and economic reasons, the tower allowed to reach to infinity on at least 25% of the lot had to be moderated and the setbacks balanced at distances which offered reasonable floor areas. The design of high buildings had been inverted with the passage of the zoning decree: instead of proceeding from plan to section and then elevation, now the architect composed the overall shape, then the facade and finally moved inward to the plan. As well, the zoning ordinance made small buildings on small lots uneconomical, and forced the developer to consolidate lots and to construct massive structures. Corbett believed that since economics would force every developer to build to the allowable density, the development of the city and the burdens of taxation would be equitably distributed. These in turn would more evenly distribute the volume of traffic upon the street.[35]

Because the city was a gigantic machine in the minds of the planners, the cellular division of land uses into functional zones and the reduction of architectural design to regulatory procedures became permissible strategies. The city, its land and architecture were subjected to the technique of mechanical optimization. As the tempo of change in the machine city accelerated, the mathematics of zoning was expected to correct all the city's malfunctions. Zoning represented the promise of scientific progress; technical efficiency experts would manipulate and manage the order of the city. Zoning took the country by storm.[36] Yet a gap emerged between the techniques of regulatory control and the aesthetic form of the city, in part because zoning

A Study of the New York City Zoning Law of 1916. Drawing by Hugh Ferriss.

30. Ibid., p. 70.

31. George B. Ford, "City Planning by Coercion or Legislation?" *American City* (April 1916), pp. 328-333; and Carol Aronovici, *Housing and the Housing Problem*, p. 83.

32. George B. Ford, "Preface," *Building Height, Bulk, and Form: How Zoning can be used as a protection against uneconomic types of buildings on high-cost land.* (Cambridge, Mass.: The Harvard University Press, 1931).

33. Harvey W. Corbett, "Zoning and the Envelope of the Building," *Pencil Points*, 4 (April 1923), pp. 15-18; and Hugh Ferriss, *The Metropolis of Tomorrow* (New York: Ives Washburn, 1929).

34. Irving Pond, "Zoning and the Architecture of High Buildings," *Architectural Forum*, 25 (October 1921), pp. 131-133.

35. Aymar Embury II, "New York's New Architecture: The effect of the Zoning Law on high buildings," *Architectural Forum,* 25 (October 1921), pp. 119-124; and Corbett, "Zoning and the Envelop."

36. Corbett, "Zoning and the Envelop."

did not by itself present a particular aesthetic vision of the city, only a normative, regularized form.

Caught up in an immense real estate boom, by the late 1920's skyscraper after skyscraper dominated the city's skyline and suburban tract towns sprawled along the major highways and railway lines. If zoning was going to create a new rational urban order in the 1920's, by the 1930's the realities of jammed up traffic lanes along canyon streets lined with monstrous buildings no longer appeared so heroic. Escape by the automobile appeared to be the only solution.[37]

THE REGIONAL ESCAPE

Scientific City Planning will begin only when our confidence in the city of today will have come to an end.

Carol Aronovici, The Survey (1932)

From the top of bankrupt skyscrapers on bankrupt land, the detail of the cities was lost. Man takes pride in the heights he has created, but a sound community is not built on the vertical escape from reality.

Carl Feiss, One Nation Indivisible (1940)

George Ford, Carol Aronovici, Henry Wright and Carl Feiss — each one had a tendency to propose a regional escape

Suggestion for arrangement and setbacks of apartment groups in New York City, George B. Ford. Drawing by Arthur J. Frappier.

37. In 1922 it was reported that 20 enabling acts, 50 ordinances and nearly 100 zoning plans were in progress. By 1925, 368 municipalities had passed zoning ordinances; and by the end of 1930 more than 1,000. U.S. Department of Commerce. *Zoned Municipalities in the U.S.* (Washington: U.S. Government Printing Office, 1931).

when he was overcome by the blighted urban environment, the over-speculative and congested city. As early as 1923 Ford asked whether it would not be better to retard the city's intensive growth and to force it to spread out or decentralize into the surrounding region.[38] Aronovici was not so sanguine, and warned that the suburban areas might remain vassals of the great city which would keep a hold over whatever new life these people had sought. The new regionalism of the 1920's aimed to break this control and to create areas of local autonomy in which the central core would play the role of specialist to socially and economically independent communities.[39]

In the depression of the 1930's, urban real estate began to be a burden to its owners and a menace to municipalities. The building industry collapsed, all municipal improvements stopped, agricultural productivity declined, and more than five million people lived on less than subsistence level. These calamities brought a quarter century of community planning to a standstill. Aronovici noted that planning as we have seen it in terms of the layout of highways, the provision of parks and recreation areas, the design of civic centers, the establishment of zoning controls, no longer made sense. Now cities must reach out into the regional areas from which they took their raw materials, collected their water, and harvested their food. They must learn to plan for their survival on the basis of soil conditions, climatic ranges, diversity of natural resources, and the distribution of waterways.[40]

Planners obsessed with the movement of freight and human beings had piled up huge debts for public highways and public transit systems: an emphasis which simply sped up the obsolescence of houses, apartments, offices and manufacturing plants in the center of the city. The radio, the telephone, television, highways, and the impending promise of air travel, Aronovici observed, made the city largely a tradition devoid of the conveniences of modern efficient living. We need, he continued, a complete re-evaluation of the central city: a junking of what is obsolescent and a replacement of the economic and individual functionalism of the past.[41]

Henry Wright also saw regional planning as the solution to the 1920's orgy of land speculation which had left every metropolitan region with both a surplus and a slack in its land development.[42] He compared city building to the art of weaving. So he complained, we had planned the 'warp,' our important lines of transportation too far in advance of the 'weft' thus making the urban pattern sag and pucker, stitches had been dropped and the important binding process neglected. Left behind, the blighted areas of the city were the great mass of misshapen, puckered, raveling and worthless fabric.[43] Implicit in Wright's community plans during the 1920's, was the ideal of single family home ownership, but in the depression of the 1930's he foresaw that some form of 'group housing' had to be the solution, and it was this form which he envisioned as replacing the blighted areas of the city.[44] Replacement, however, should be done by operating companies with the power to acquire large tracts of land in the

38. Harvey Corbett, "The Skyscraper and the Automobile have made the Modern City," *The Architect and Building News*, 173 (January 1914), pp. 27-28.

39. Ford felt that regional cooperation in 1923 was the only solution for problems which were common to the whole area. For example, without such coordination, towns were passing zoning ordinances which strangled the outward growth of the central city; thoroughfares were not planned so that intercommunication between communities was inefficient. Trolleys and buses, bridges and viaducts, sanitary and electric systems, waterways and aviation needs all required coordination through a regional plan. As consultant to the New York Regional Plan, Ford was responsible for an empirical study of the middle-New Jersey area. He proposed the development of a linear city to straddle the railroad line accompanied by improved commuter rail facilities and upgraded automobile highways. George B. Ford, "Regional and Metropolitan Planning Principle, Methods, and Co-Operation," *Proceedings of the 15th National Conference on City Planning* (Baltimore: 1923).

40. Carol Aronovici, "Let the Cities Perish," *The Survey*, 68 (October 1931).

41. Carol Aronovici, *"Regionalism: A New National Economy."* *Columbia University Quarterly* (December 1936).

42. Aronovici, "Let the Cities Perish."

43. Planning, Wright advised, must now be used to delimit as well as to expand. Regional Planning must determine what the actual needs and absorption abilities of the city really are and what can be done with the growing dry rot at the center of the city. Henry Wright, "To Plan or Not to Plan," *The Survey* (October 1932), p. 468.

44. Henry Wright, "City Planning in relation to the Housing Problem," *Proceedings of the 24th National Conference on City Planning* (1932).

suburban regions, while the blighted cores must be put to other uses.[45]

Planners of the 1930's cumulatively turned their backs upon the disorder of the city. They saw economic depression and the approaching urban insolvency as a special disease imposed upon the city by speculative over-materialistic businessmen and the American faith in competition by size alone. American cities, those critics complained, had passed through their period of growth and development, and were now face to face with the problems of mature civilizations: "arrested circulation," "auto-intoxication," followed by "local congestion" and "community scurvy" were the danger signs of this "national arteriosclerosis."[46] The quest for a spatial order to the American city was abandoned: first by the regional planners in search of a harmonious new life to be achieved by organically balancing new communities with regional resources; and then by the housing experts who claimed there was nothing to preserve in the obsolescent cores of the city. No longer interested in the historic urban centers, the planner moved to Washington to join hands with public administrators within New Deal bureaucracies. The lawyers, the real estate developers, and local politicians were left behind to put together the last pieces of what would become known as the Urban Renewal game. A city of fragmented voids and textual insertions, new oases representing cultural and civic centers, or housing and office tower projects would be the inadvertent result.

45. Henry Wright, "Are we Ready for an American Housing Advance?" *Architecture,* 67 (June 1933), pp. 309-316; Wright, "Housing — Where, When, and How?" *Architecture,* 68 (July 1933); and Wright, *Rehousing Urban America* (New York: Columbia University Press, 1935). Group housing abandoned the lot line and eliminated the narrow side lots, enabling a continuous perimeter building along the street. Each structure was one to three stories high, with broad fronts and narrow depths. Most of the open space was pooled into common lands. Sunnyside NY and Radburn NJ, both planned by Wright and Clarence Stein, are examples of this group plan. See Wright, "City Planning in relation to the Housing Problem"; and Wright, *Rehousing Urban America.*
At Wright's untimely death in 1936, Carl Feiss and Sir Raymond Unwin were both responsible for continuing the emphasis on regional planning and group housing at Columbia University. Sir Raymond Unwin had been architect for Hampstead Garden Suburb Trust in 1906. His overriding principle, "Nothing gained by overcrowding," was still evident in the 1930s through his advocacy of groups of low density garden suburbs surrounding a central city nucleus. Unwin had been a frequent visitor to American city planning and housing conferences from the early 1900s and had also been an active consultant during the 1920s to the Regional Plan of New York. See Raymond Unwin, "The Overgrown City," *The Survey* (October 15, 1922); "America Revisited — A City Planner's Impressions," *American City* (April 1923) and "Urban Development: The Pattern and Background," *Journal of the American Institute of Planners,* 1 (September – October, 1935), p. 45.
Feiss also continued the emphasis on group housing which Wright had started, adding an historical context for this American tradition. In the aftermath of New Deal Planning and with the approach of World War II, many Americans were reacting negatively to the planning concept. It was Feiss's role to remind us that planning new towns in relationship to suitable population size and natural resource allocations went back to colonial times. It was only the industrial revolution in the 19th century which swamped the concept of town planning and produced the ugly, dirty, noisy and congested metropolitan monstrosity. Then after World War I, the automobile offered a cheap escape from the city and the modern suburb indiscriminately spread into the countryside. Years of suburban boom followed leaving the center of the city to fester and die. But this, for Feiss, was a natural adjustment of the nation simply settling down to work with the machine age and not a matter of planning. Now, he advised, we must settle down to rebuild not only new towns but to rehabilitate the center city as well. See Carl Feiss, *Survey of Planning and Housing Education in Institutions of Higher Education in the United States* (New York: National Association of Housing Officials, 1937): "One Nation Indivisible," *Survey Graphic,* 29 (February 1940); "The Heritage of Our Planned Communities," *Journal of the Society of Architectural Historians,* 1 (July – October, 1941), pp. 27-32; "History and the Modern Planner," *Journal of the Society of Architectural Historians,* 3 (January – April, 1943), pp. 7-10; and "Housing and the Urban Esthetic," *Magazine of Art* (November 1944), pp. 258-262, 278.

46. Robert A. Lesher, "National Arteriosclerosis," *The Survey* (October 1932), p. 456.

Leopold Arnaud. Photo: Columbia University.

History V:
1935–1959

Diane Boas

Following his decision to depart for Harvard in 1935, Joseph Hudnut promised to help President Butler and his Advisory Committee to choose his successor as Dean of the School. In a memo to Butler, Hudnut considered Ellis Lawrence, Dean of the School of Architecture at the University of Oregon to be "the best man among those who are available," and Roy Childs Jones, Acting Dean of the School of Architecture at the University of Minnesota, "one of the outstanding men in the field of education. He understands the Modern Movement and is sincerely in sympathy with it." Also listed in the memo was Kenneth Stowell, the editor of *The Architectural Forum;* Ralph Walker, progressive New York City architect; and Wallace K. Harrison, one of the designers of Rockefeller Center and a man who in Hudnut's view "is always the champion of the intellectual forces in architecture — and would be strong as an administrator." At the head of Hudnut's list was his former assistant, Leopold Arnaud, "a man of excellent judgement, careful and systematic in his habits and thoroughly dependable." Hudnut wrote that:

Arnaud could take over as acting Dean, the direction of the School until such time as a permanent appointment could be made. Mr. Arnaud lacks experience in responsible positions. In my judgement he is fitted for greater responsibility, but naturally this judgement should be tested by experience. Mr. Arnaud has not a wide reputation, is not well known in the profession, but this is in some ways an advantage since he has not become identified with any of the many groups into which the profession is divided. [1]

Butler postponed his decision and instead appointed a three-

A Redevelopment of Greenwich Village, ca. 1946, designers unknown. Photo: GSAP Archive.

1. Joseph Hudnut to Frank Fackenthal, 7 June 1935, Central Files, Columbia University (hereafter Central Files).

man Committee of Administration comprised of Cecil C. Briggs, professor of drawing, Jan Ruhtenberg, professor of design, and Arnaud as chairman.[2] The three-man committee did not function well together, and on February 3, 1936, Arnaud was appointed Acting Dean, in part due to the urging of the existing Advisory Committee chaired by Grant La Farge.[3]

Arnaud's conservative views on architecture seemed to be a reversal of the policies established by Hudnut, and in due course, Hudnut was approached for opinion and advice by Butler and Fackenthal:

I do think it important that we avoid an impression of reaction. Everyone thinks of Columbia's School as one in the front rank of progressive schools; it would be a pity to lose that position. I wish that Arnaud would make at this moment a clear and vigorous statement of his ideas.[4]

In a second letter to Fackenthal, Hudnut observed:

I think that much of the existing confusion of thought in respect to the Schools of Architecture comes from a failure to distinguish clearly between theories of design and theories of education. I believe, for example, that a school like Columbia should be hospitable to all theories of design; but I think it should have a firm and clearly expressed educational policy based upon consistent theory. You may have both liberal and conservative instructors in your faculty, but you ought to know definitely whether (for example) you are in favor of competitions or against them. Most architects judge the schools not by their educational ideas (of which they usually know nothing) but by the kind of buildings designed by the instructors and students.[5]

The conflict between Arnaud, his faculty, and the Advisory Committee continued, and as a result Hudnut returned to New York to discuss matters with Arnaud. He came away discouraged about Arnaud, writing to Butler:

I think he is sincere in his desire to serve the school, but I think he is lacking in the breadth of view and in experience with people. He is more like a 'head clerk' than a Chairman of the Board.

So far as his views about architecture and the teaching of architecture are concerned, I think they are reasonably liberal and I see no reason to quarrel about them. I urged him to make his position clear about these matters and he has promised to do so — in his own way, of course. I think everything will be alright if you appoint as professor of design an architect of unquestioned reputation, fairly liberal in his views, and with distinction in manner and speech. Let Arnaud be 'General Manager' for such a man. Let it be understood... rather than expressed, that the new professor has the confidence of the President and that he (Arnaud) is expected to support him.[6]

Despite this rather sharp appraisal, Arnaud continued to gain favor with the Advisory Committee, particularly C. Grant Lafarge. Arnaud had already demonstrated his commitment to the School and his personal demeanor promised order and good taste. It would be precisely his suitability and dedication that would make him difficult to unseat. On July 1, 1937, Arnaud was appointed Dean, a position he held until 1959, thereby extending

Community Planning Study, ca. 1946, designers unknown. Photo: GSAP Archive.

2. These three men had different views on architectural education. In a letter to Butler, Briggs urged that the School be divided into three closely knit departments — Theory and Design, Graphic Representation, and Architectural Engineering — and felt that:
the School should have actual site projects, being built, contracted, financed and sold in the interest of the university, where complete office practice would be required for the student in connection with the construction courses. What technical school can be complete without a real proving ground? (Briggs to Butler, 27 January 1936, Central Files).

3. Arnaud to Butler, 4 February 1936, Central Files.

4. Hudnut to Fackenthal, 16 February 1936, Central Files.

5. Hudnut to Fackenthal, 17 March 1936, Central Files. This remark by Hudnut does much to dispel the idea that he was a zealot about modern architecture. It appears that his own attitude toward the content of architecture itself was more catholic than indicated by his sweeping revisions of the School's methods during his tenure.

6. Hudnut to Butler, 24 March 1936, Central Files.

what was originally a temporary administrative appointment into a twenty-four year tenure.[7]

Arnaud was born in New York City in 1895 not far from Columbia at 139th Street and St. Nicholas Avenue in a house built by McKim, Mead and White. His mother was a native New Yorker while his father was Spanish born. As his father's business took the family abroad, Arnaud grew up in Latin America and Europe. During his teenage years the family lived in Paris where he attended the Lycee Janson de Sully of the Sorbonne from which he graduated in 1914. In the fall of that year he entered the Columbia School of Architecture. Like most other young men, Arnaud interrupted his studies to enlist in the U.S. Army where he served from 1917 to 1918.[8]

Arnaud returned to Columbia where he received his Bachelor of Architecture in June, 1919. That August, he enrolled at the Ecole des Beaux-Arts where he finished his schooling in the *atelier* of Monsieur Heraud. He returned to New York City in 1924, where he worked at Warren and Wetmore for four years and at Voorhees, Gmelin, and Walker for three years. By the early 1930's the harsh economic realities of the Depression caused a sharp drop in architectural commissions. Consequently, Arnaud sought a more secure future as a teacher of architectural history and rendering at Columbia. Concurrently, he attended courses for his M.S. degree which he received in 1933.[9]

When Arnaud became Dean in 1937, Franklin Delano Roosevelt's New Deal had been in effect for four years. Although characterized by a distrust of vast concentrations of wealth and a desire to improve the lot of the less fortunate, these social stirrings were not new in American political history. What was new about the New Deal was its emphasis on the dynamic role of the Federal government and on the regulatory role of the state.[10]

During the worst years of the Depression, home building virtually ceased and most architectural offices closed. Architects benefitted under the New Deal's increased building campaign as private practitioners were given a major portion of government work. Under FDR, the Wagner Steagall Housing Bill (passed in the spring of 1937), the FHA, the WPA, and the PWA programs were all coordinated to confront America's most urgent housing problem: providing low-cost housing for low-income families. These new Federally-funded projects required architects to work as members of teams that included planners, sociologists, and other technicians. Changes in the practice of architecture influenced Arnaud's goals for architectural education. Arnaud endorsed the training of general practitioners who, provided with a broad educational background, would be equipped to complement the efforts of other professionals.[11]

A clear and vigorous statement of Arnaud's ideas on architectural education was not forthcoming, as Hudnut had hoped. Instead, an article entitled "History and Architecture" printed in the *Columbia University Quarterly* in December, 1936, can be read as the first published, albeit covert, declaration of Arnaud's conservative ideals. This article contains the four main "middle-of-the-road" themes that Arnaud would reiterate in all of his later

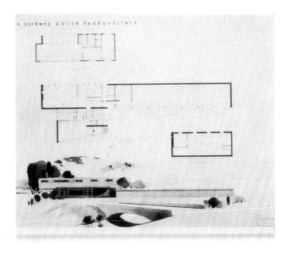

Top: A Parkway Police Headquarters, ca. 1954, designer unknown. Photo: GSAP Archive.

Above: A Clock Shop, ca. 1946, designer unknown. Photo: GSAP Archive.

7. Butler to Arnaud, 10 February 1937, Central Files.

8. Diane Boas, "Notes on Leopold Arnaud," Avery Archives.

9. Ibid.

10. Dexter Perkins, *The New Age of Franklin Roosevelt* (Chicago: University of Chicago Press, 1957).

11. Ibid.

essays: the defense of the study of history and a lament over the loss of ornamentation and craftsmanship; the emphasis on the evolutionary nature of styles; the importance of taste and a sense of beauty; and the need to respond to the needs of the majority.[12]

In a review published in the *Art Digest*, January 15th, 1936, Arnaud struck more of a balance between his conservative ideals and modern demands.

Architectural students, Prof. Arnaud explained, will be trained to meet the problems which are arising from the transition from depression to recovery in the building industry.... The major change in the school affects the correlation of architectural construction and architectural design and the method of teaching these subjects. So called 'paper design' has been substituted by design closely related to reality and the school will avail itself of the outstanding architectural opportunities which exist in the City of New York. Effort has been made to correlate architecture with the other arts, not only to broaden the student's cultural knowledge but also to demonstrate the working possibilities that result from this intimate relation.... The general policy of the school will be to produce not draftsmen but well rounded architects, creative artists capable of carrying on the ideals and traditions of the profession and sound thinkers well versed in the modern needs of the practice.[13]

Arnaud's early influence as head of the School came not through a commanding ideological statement, but by a quiet consolidation of the curriculum. Starting with Hudnut's program of courses in 1934–1935, by 1936–1937, Arnaud had organized a curricular structure that would remain unchanged for a quarter-century.[14] He explained this curriculum in 1939, at a lecture delivered to The Architectural League on the occasion of a League exhibition of the work of the School:

We subdivide the instruction into four general categories: design, construction, history and theory, and drawing.

It is a question whether design can actually be taught. The best that can be done is to show the student a method of procedure or way of study; to develop his artistic sense and his facility in composition — both in plan and elevation; and to show him how to interpret a program. The method used is still the old method which has proven to be most adequate, namely; the 'problem method,' in which the student can develop his own ideas and receive individual and careful criticism from his master. We are careful to allow the student to develop individually, and do not force upon him any definite type or 'style' of design.[15]

Design formed the core of the curriculum, and the other three elements were meant to reinforce design:

Instruction in construction is carried on parallel with the instruction in design, and... each problem in design is also considered as a problem in construction, and the work is criticized by the instructors in construction as well as by the instructors in design.... the architect can learn much from the study of history. He not only becomes acquainted with the materials used by men of the past and with their methods of building, but also sees how they have solved their problems in relation to the economic and social conditions of their environment.[16]

12. Leopold Arnaud, "History and Architecture," Columbia University Quarterly, 27 (December 1935), pp. 409-414. The themes in Arnaud's essay constituted the key points on which more conservative educators like Arnaud and more progressive educators like Gropius and his followers would base their criticism of each other. Again and again, Arnaud raised the issues of ornament and craftsmanship to attack the coldness of the "new" style and as a basis for a return to historical study. Doubtless Arnaud was familiar with the precepts of the Bauhaus and the International Style, but for him modern objects and buildings of merely functional beauty were anathema to his own perception of beauty in the arts. See, Walter Gropius, "Education Towards Creative Design," American Architect, 150 (May 1937), pp. 26-30.

Defending the importance of the study of history, Arnaud explained his belief that the history of architecture combines the development of civilization with that of structure; it is not merely a tabulation of the sequence of styles, but includes an analysis of the reasons — social, political, racial and regional — that caused the differences in the manner of expression. Consistent with his belief in the cyclical evolution of styles he insisted that the extremists did not seem to realize that modernism was only in its very early stages and that the invention of machines did not necessarily imply that ornament would be banished forever. He espoused a belief that students should be encouraged to cultivate taste and discernment; and that the study of beautiful buildings from the past would enable the student to absorb and to develop a sense of beauty. And finally Arnaud discussed the importance of designing an educational program to fit the needs of the "average" student — the middle range of students who would constitute the majority of the profession.

13. "A Review of the Field in Art Education," The Art Digest, 10 (January 1936), p. 26.

14. Typical Program 1934–1935, FIRST YEAR:

FIRST YEAR		
Architectural Drawing:	Elements of classic architecture	3
Architectural drawing:	Shades and shadows	2
Theory of architecture:	Plan and composition	2
Building construction:	Statics	3
History of architecture:	Greek	3
Drawing and Painting	Preparatory	2
Architectural drawing:	Analytique	*
Architectural drawing:	Rendering	2
Theory of architecture:	Plan and Composition	2
Building construction:	Strength of materials	3
History of architecture:	Roman and Byzantine	3
Drawing and Painting	Life drawing and composition I	2

SECOND YEAR:

Architectural design:	*Projets*	*
Architectural drawing:	Descriptive geometry	2
Theory of architecture:	Plan and composition	2
Building construction:	Mechanical equipment	3
Building construction:	Mechanical equipment	3
Drawing and Painting	Life drawing and composition II	2
Architectural design:	*Projets*	*
Architectural drawing:	Perspective	2
Theory of architecture:	Plan and composition	2
Building construction:	Methods and problems	4
History of architecture:	Medieval	3
Drawing and Painting	Life drawing and composition III	2

THIRD YEAR:

Architectural design:	*Projets*	*

Courses in theory also supplemented design:

Beginning with the study of elements — doors, windows, walls, and the like — the work proceeds with analyses of spatial arrangements, sequences, proportion, rhythm, and scale. The Student investigates various types of buildings for their specific requirements;.... He studies individual theories from ancient times to the present, and sees how these theories affected the architecture of the authors and of his contemporaries. This is particularly important in the present period, since there are many conflicting theories which influence contemporary design.[17]

Finally, Arnaud observed that because architects must express their ideas by delineation, drawing was included throughout the course, "to develop their dexterity of expression in various media and in color, and also to develop their imaginative qualities."[18]

Arnaud also revealed his goal for the School, as expressed in his curricular structure:

We prepare the student so that upon graduation he will be of immediate use as an assistant and collaborator; but our chief aim is to give him a broad background, to show him a way of study, and to interest him in the various subjects of his profession so that he will have the necessary equipment and flexibility to develop and to become a versatile and capable creative artist in his own right.[19]

By 1940, Arnaud was able to report that the entrance requirements to the School had been reduced from 60 credits to 30 credits, transforming what had been a six-year program (two and four) into a five-year program (one and four) that was in direct competition with the five-year Bachelor of Architecture program popular at many schools across the country.[20]

Arnaud never hired a strong individual design critic, as Hudnut had suggested to Butler, to give guidance to the design philosophy of the School. Instead, he surrounded himself with teams of lesser-known designers whose views and backgrounds were similar to his own. The first of these, the team of Donald Fletcher, John C.B. Moore, and Edgar Williams, was hired in May 1936.[21] In their studios the three taught the formal principles of design, echoing the traditions of the Ecole but applying them to contemporary problems. Solidly supported by a conservative staff Arnaud invited such modernists as Richard Neutra, Alvar Aalto, Amadee Ozenfant, George Grosz, Nelson Bennett, Eric Mendelsohn, Stewart Davis, Buckminster Fuller, and Serge Chermayeff to give lectures at the School.

Arnaud continued to support one of Hudnut's most important projects: the four-year long course in Town Planning and Housing Studies, begun in 1935 aided by a twenty-four thousand dollar grant from the Carnegie Corporation. The work was designed to prepare the architect for leadership in community development. At the program's inception Arnaud explained that:

the present momentary swing again toward a new suburban spread carries with it the possibility of repeating previous foolish practices in urban housing. Emphasis will be on the study and appreciation of the external relationships of building masses and community organization. All students

Theory of architecture:	Advanced composition	3
Building construction:	Theory of modern structures	3
History of architecture:	Renaissance	3
Drawing and Painting	Architectural sketch class	2
Sculpture	Modeling	2
Architectural design:	*Projets*	*
Theory of architecture:	Advanced composition	2
Building construction:	Theory of modern structures	3
History of architecture:	Baroque	3
Drawing and Painting	Water Color	2
Sculpture	Modeling	2
FOURTH YEAR:		
Architectural design:	*Projets*	*
Building construction:	Financing: organization	2
Elective courses		6
Architectural design:	*Projets* and thesis	*
Elective courses		6

Typical Program, 1936–1937, FIRST YEAR:

Introduction to design	6
Materials and methods of construction	2
The architecture of New York City	2
History of Greek architecture	3
Descriptive geometry and its applications	6
Statics	3
Strength of materials	3
Drawing and painting	4
SECOND YEAR:	
Architectural design	10
Theory of architecture	4
Methods of construction	8
History of Roman architecture and of medieval architecture	6
Mechanical equipment of buildings	3
Drawing and painting	4
THIRD YEAR:	
Architectural design	10
Theory of architecture	4
Structural design and planning	6
History of Renaissance and of baroque architecture	6
Drawing and painting	4
Sculpture	4
FOURTH YEAR:	
Architectural design	5
Thesis	5
Financing and organization of building operations	2
Elective courses aggregating 12 points (see page 25)	12

15. Leopold Arnaud, "The Education of the Architect as We See it at Columbia," *The Bulletin of the Beaux Arts Institute of Design,* 16 (December 1939), pp. 2-3.

16. Ibid.

17. Ibid.

18. Ibid.

19. Ibid.

20. "Report of the Dean of the School of Architecture," 30 June 1940, Central Files.

21. Donald Fletcher received a Certificate in Architecture from Columbia in 1920, after which he attended the Ecole des Beaux-Arts. After returning to New York, he practiced

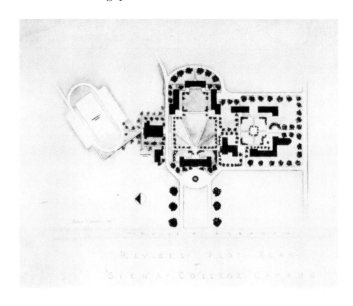

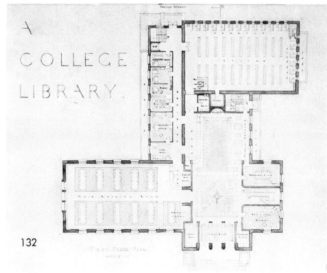

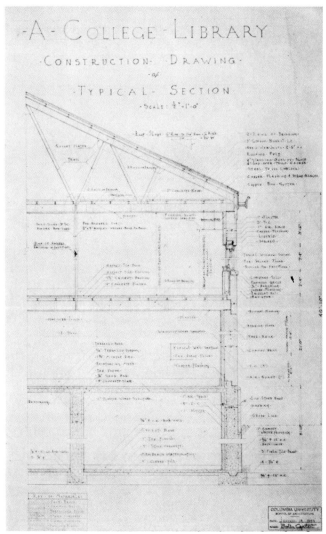

Clockwise from top left: A College Library (plan, site plan, perspective and construction details), 1943, designer unknown. Photo: GSAP Archive.

in the third and fourth years at the school will be required to take some of their studies and other elective work in the Town Planning Studio. [22]

Henry Wright was chosen to be the first director. Born in Lawrence, Kansas, Wright graduated from the University of Pennsylvania in 1901, and from the start made housing and town planning the focus of his career. Throughout his life his primary commitment was to provide adequate housing for low income families. [23]

Wright died suddenly in the summer of 1936, after only three semesters at Columbia. Following his death, Carl Feiss and Sir Raymond Unwin became Co-Directors. Feiss had been an instructor in City Planning under Wright since April, 1936. He left Columbia in September, 1942, for a position as Director of the City Planning Commission in Denver, Colorado. [24]

In July, 1936, Coleman Woodbury, Director of the National Association of Housing officials, sent a letter to Arnaud recommending Sir Raymond Unwin as Wright's successor: "as the man who combines most effectively technical ability and experience in planning and housing with an extraordinary knowledge of their political and economic implications." After his first visit to America in 1922 at the invitation of the Russell Sage Foundation, Unwin came frequently to lecture and to attend conferences on housing and city planning. He lectured at M.I.T., Cornell, and other American institutions before being named Visiting Professor of Architecture at Columbia in 1936. Unwin died at the age of 76 in June 1940. [25]

In 1935, Arnaud established an interdisciplinary studio, the Scenic Design Program, established in collaboration with the Juilliard School of Music under the direction of Frederick Kiesler. Kiesler gave a series of lectures and under his direction architectural students designed and executed sets and costumes used in several operatic performances. According to Arnaud this arrangement enabled the musicians to acquire a better understanding of the work of the scenic designer and permitted the architect to familiarize himself with the practical possibilities of color, lighting, and stagecraft in general. [26]

From 1937 to 1941 Kiesler ran his Laboratory of Design Correlation to the study of pure form and application to architectural design and industry. This course was an alternative to one of the architectural design studios that led to the M.S. degree. The appointment of Kiesler was clearly Arnaud's response to Hudnut's appointment of Gropius at Harvard. Arnaud recognized that Gropius would become influential in the field of applied design and he was anxious to establish his own course in Contemporary Design. Kiesler, although a romantic and innovative designer, never enjoyed a great following, and on one occasion, he perturbed the administration when his studio spent an entire semester on the design of a bookcase. As students became interested again in traditional coursework, enrollment in Kiesler's classes diminished.

In the years after Arnaud became Dean in July, 1937, he faced a series of crises caused mainly by world events. By the early 1930's the Depression had reduced the School to one quarter its normal

in various architectural offices. He spent four years teaching at the Pratt Institute before coming to teach at Columbia. Arnaud regarded him as "progressive in his ideas..." (Arnaud to Fackenthal, 15 May 1936, Central Files).
John Crosby Brown Moore graduated from Harvard University in 1918, after which he studied at Columbia for three years before attending the Ecole des Beaux-Arts. He was the architect of a building at the Chicago Fair of 1933 which was favorably received, and Arnaud regarded him "as one of the most promising younger men with decided 'contemporary' tendencies" (Ibid.).
Edgar Williams graduated from M.I.T. with a B.S. in 1908 and an M.S. in 1909. He was a Fellow of the American Academy in Rome in 1912, and later was a Trustee of the Academy. He was a well-established architect before coming to Columbia, and in a letter of 12 December 1935 to Fackenthal, Arnaud had even recommended that Williams be considered for the Deanship (Ibid.).

22. Arnaud to Fackenthal, 1 February 1937, Central Files.

23. Prominent as an architectural educator and internationally known, Wright made his reputation through his garden city projects of Radburn, New Jersey; Sunnyside, Queens (together with Clarence Stein); and Chatham Village, Pittsburgh. He was a fellow of the A.I.A. and at one time Chairman of the City Planning Association of St. Louis, Missouri and later Chairman of the Committee of City Planning of the A.I.A.
In 1933 he was a consultant for the Housing Division of the PWA at Washington, D.C., and in that same year founded the Housing Study Guild. Mr. Wright was one of a group of experts appointed in 1934 by the National Association of Housing Officials to tour the U.S. and observe housing progress made in various cities.

24. Feiss received his M. Architecture from the University of Pennsylvania in 1931. That year he was made Research Fellow in City Planning and studied under Eliel Saarinen at the Cranbrook Academy of Art, Bloomfield Hills, Michigan, for two years. From 1933 to 1935 he practiced in Indianapolis and Cleveland doing architectural work and site planning. In 1935 he went to M.I.T. as a Graduate City Planning Research Scholar and Instructor in Construction. He received his Master of City Planning from M.I.T. in the summer of 1936.

25. Born in 1863 in Rotherham, Yorkshire, Unwin was educated at Magdalen College, Oxford, where his chief interest was engineering. He began studying architecture only when he was thirty-three. He earned his national reputation in England shortly after the turn of the century as chief designer of Letchworth, the country's first garden city. Following that, he laid out Hampstead Garden Suburb, five miles north of London, and planned numerous model towns throughout England.
In the fall of 1934, Unwin headed a committee of foreign experts which made suggestions for low cost housing to President Roosevelt after a six-week tour of the country. Unwin was a tireless advocate of low cost housing and slum clearance as a means of economic and social betterment. Private enterprise he believed to be incapable of providing low rent housing on the scale and at the cost that was necessary. He urged a government-funded housing program based on yearly subsidies rather than a lump sum grant. He criticized the Wagner Housing Act under which local housing authorities lacked the flexibility in the application of subsidies to specific houses and at specific periods of time.

26. During the 1920's in his native Vienna, Kiesler conceived of the two ideas that were to make him famous: the Endless Theatre and the Endless House. The theatre comprised an integrated playing and seating area consisting of a series of elevators, passageways, and shifting lights which Kiesler hoped would give drama a limitless range of staging possibilities.

size. Just as attendance began to rise, World War II began. The whole campus, as was true of others across the country, was converted into training facilities for the war. For the duration of the war, the School offered an accelerated program of study allowing the student to fulfill the degree requirements in a minimum time of two years and eight months instead of the standard four-year period. Two courses in the application of camouflage to industrial buildings were taught. There were special drafting classes to prepare civilians entering the Curtis Wright Aircraft Plant in New Jersey.[27]

During the war the student body consisted primarily of women, men with 4F deferments, and foreign students. The field of architecture has always been slow to accept women into its ranks. Even during the war when women comprised at least one half of the student body, no effort was made to encourage them in their career decisions. Arnaud was considered to be especially unhelpful to women, even by the standards of the day. In spite of the obstacles, women did graduate from the School and several went on to become successful architects, among them Natalie De Blois (1944)[28] and Judith Edelman (1946).

In the summer of 1941, New York University announced that it would phase out its course in architecture, and as of October, 1941, would receive no new students. Arnaud observed in a letter to Butler that:

the New York metropolitan area, with over seven and a half million inhabitants, had no school where a young man could prepare himself for the State examination in architecture by working during the day and following professional courses at night.[29]

This presented Arnaud with the opportunity to revive the Evening Program in the School, with its many advantages, "not the least being that it allowed young men to parallel their studies with practical work."[30]

In the fall of 1942, the School offered an evening degree program of seven years duration. To enter the program, the student had to present 30 credits of pre-architectural courses. The School's course was structured so that in one year, the evening student took only half as much work as the day student. Thus, the evening student took six years to complete the first three years of the day program. Finally, the evening student was required to take the last year in the day course.[31] The evening students were a more heterogeneous group and, on the average, older, with considerable "real world" experience. Their infusion into the last year of the day program was regarded by many as producing desirable and healthy interaction.[32] During the 1940's and 1950's, the Evening Program flourished, numbering as many as ninety students a year, which included minority, foreign-born and women students.[33]

An increase in enrollment was predicted to begin following the demobilization of servicemen after the conclusion of the war. Thus, as early as 1943, Arnaud was urging the University to consider a new building for the School:

This building should house not only the School of Architecture with its

In 1926 Kiesler came to New York City to direct an exhibition of international theater techniques at Steinway Hall. He decided to stay and become director of scenic design at the Juilliard School of Music.

27. Arnaud, "Forty-Five Years at Columbia University," p. 4. Interview: Natalie De Blois by Author, 1 July 1981.

28. Upon graduation from Columbia in 1944 (to which she had won a scholarship in 1940) and a brief period of employment with the firm of Ketchum, Gina & Sharpe, Natalie De Blois (1921–) joined the newly established New York office of Skidmore, Owings & Merrill. Her first project with SOM was the bath houses for Jones Beach, Long Island. Shortly thereafter, in 1946, whe was made a senior designer and in 1948 she became basic design coordinator for the Terrace Plaza Hotel in Cincinnati, working with Louis Skidmore and William Brown. As a Fulbright fellow in 1951, De Blois entered the *Atelier Mardeof* as a third-year architectural student at the Ecole des Beaux-Arts. While in Paris, she served as senior designer under the direction of Gordon Bunshaft for SOM's Consular-Amerikahaus program. Throughout her tenure with the New York Office, De Blois worked with Bunshaft as senior designer. From the time she returned to New York and SOM in 1952, De Blois played a crucial role in a number of important projects, including: Lever House (1952), the Connecticut General Life Insurance Building, Bloomfield Connecticut (1957), the Pepsi-Cola Headquarters Building (1959), and the Union Carbide Building (1960). Under the aegis of the American Institute of Architects Task Force on Women, De Blois participated in a project aimed at uncovering the prejudices faced by women architects. Following a year of research, writing and teaching, in 1974, she joined the Houston firm of Neuhaus & Taylor as Senior Project Designer.

29. Arnaud to Butler, 25 February 1942, Central Files. In 1917, Columbia had instituted a dual course in architecture: students could attend eight years of evening study and receive the Certificate of Proficiency, or they could attend four years of day study and receive the Bachelor of Architecture. Changes in the registration laws in New York State in 1936 required that all candidates for examination for license to practice be graduates of recognized institution. Columbia's Certificate holders were not, technically, graduates of the University, and so the School discontinued the evening program. As a result, 175 students left Columbia to enroll at New York University where they could obtain a degree for evening work.

30. Ibid.

31. Ibid. See also, "Report of the Dean of the School of Architecture, 1942–43," 30 June 1943, Central Files, p. 6.

32. Memorandum: Jan Pokorny to Richard Oliver, 20 August 1981, Graduate School of Architecture and Planning Archives (hereafter GSAP archives).

33. Led by Professor William A. Hayes and George M. Allen, the program offered a work-study alternative to these talented, often older, and highly motivated students. George Nelson and Henry Wright, the famed first editors of "Architectural Forum," were faculty members. Other names which come to mind include Minoro Yamasaki, Charles Warner *(Columbia, 1938)*, Danforth W. Toan *(Columbia, 1949)*, George Lewis, Lo-Yi Chan, Paul Mitarachi, Gerhardt Kallman, Max Bond, David Glasser *(Columbia, 1961)*, Michael Harris, Charles Winter *(Columbia, 1955)*, Richard Bender, Simon Schmiderer, and Ervin Galantay...With the essential and continued support of the full-time faculty the program provided an early and significant experiment in continuing and/or graduate education and an alternative approach to architecture at Columbia.

Over the years the program won the respect of the profession and visiting evaluating committees for its form *various sub-divisions, and the Avery and Ware Libraries, but also the Department of Fine Arts and Archeology and the Fine Arts Library, and might conveniently include space for the classes for the drama as well. To be quite ideal, this building should also include one or even two auditoriums, so greatly needed on the Campus.* [34]

Part of the rationale for a new building was that the School had grown, "to include an important division of Planning and Housing, instruction in Landscape Architecture, numerous coordinated classes in the creative arts — drawing, painting, sculpture, engraving and the like." The Laboratory of Design Correlation had been discontinued during the war, but was expected to be re-established. And, of course, the evening classes were expected to grow. But Arnaud observed that Avery Library, too, had grown to over 45,000 volumes and was acquiring nearly one thousand new volumes a year. Closely allied to Avery Library was the Fine Arts Library. Arnaud appears to have been making a bid to consolidate various departments and facilities into one school concerned with the design and study of the environment in broad terms. [35]

In "Training Architects for the Future," Arnaud cast his projections for the immediate future of the architectural profession:

It can be assumed that in the post-war era the architect will build for a community or a group. Consequently, his client will not be an individual, and the architect will function as a member in a team of specialists. [36]

He went on to explain that although design would remain the nucleus of an architectural student's studies, the student must have a knowledge of technology and sociology to enable him to collaborate with a variety of civil authorities. This view of the future of professional practice explains Arnaud's approach to training the qualified practitioner. By 1943, in "Buildings the Future Will Demand and Materials for Building them," Arnaud enthusiastically embraced the potential of modern materials and methods. [37]

He praised new developments in the field of plastics and glue, the building potential of the parabolic arch, the advantages of prefabrication, panel heating and piped light. He concluded in speaking of the role of the architect:

While retaining his capacity to conceive in terms of design, it will be equally imperative that he have a thorough knowledge of structural and mechanical requirements. . . . Furthermore, it will be the unique mission of the architect to transcend method and mechanization, and to infuse into architecture those intangible qualities which will make the buildings of the future fit for the use of human beings. [38]

In two articles published in April, 1948, and July, 1949, Arnaud endorsed his post-war curriculum. [39] The structure of the curriculum he described reiterated his policies of the 1930's: the balance between design, construction, history and theory, and drawing. In the design courses, Arnaud personally reviewed all studio programs for sequence, content, and language. The first

and content. For the students there was an extraordinary degree of flexibility — ahead of its time — allowing them to spend some years in the day school to move back and forth between classes in the evening program and the day school, and to have access to the same faculty who gave a full measure of dedication to both the evening and day school curriculum (Memorandum: Pokorny to Oliver, 20 August 1981, GSAP archives).

34. "Report of the Dean," 30 June 1943, Central Files.

35. Ibid.

36. Leopold Arnaud, "Training Architects for the Future," *Pencil Points,* 23 (June 1942), pp. 287-288.

37. Leopold Arnaud, "Buildings the Future Will Demand and Materials for Building Them," *Pencil Points,* 24 (January 1943). In 1940, Arnaud reported that the School had held a one-day conference on "Plywood," the "first in a series on modern materials and modern uses of traditional materials." (Dean's Report, 1939–1940, Central Files).

38. Arnaud, "Buildings the Future Will Demand."

39. Arnaud, "How Architecture is Being Taught," *Journal of the A.I.A.,* 10 (April 1948), pp. 149-153. Arnaud, "Training the Architect at Columbia University," *Empire State Architect,* 9 (July–August 1949), pp. 13-15.

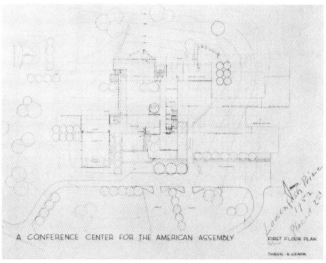

A Conference Center for the American Assembly, perspective and plan, Emil Kempa *(1952)*. Photo: GSAP Archive.

year was devoted to elementary design problems, including actual but simple buildings.[40] The second year included buildings of greater complexity, and the student would have to present written and graphic program analyses, an architectural scheme, and a constructional analysis.[41] The third year dealt with community problems, and often the subject of a program would be a comprehensive suburban development of an actual site, reflecting contemporary professional practice.[42] The fourth year began with a complex program for a major, often public building,[43] and concluded with a thesis, composed of a written program, building scheme, drawings, and cost analysis, all completed by the student.[44]

The construction courses were expanded to include the study of the theory and practice of building, mechanics of materials, calculation of structural members, and mechanical equipment such as heating, ventilating, plumbing and electrical appliances. To supplement work in the classrooms, students made numerous visits to factories to study the fabrication of materials, and to buildings during the process of construction to study the methods being used.[45]

During the summers, students were assisted in finding work. In 1955, a program entitled Imaginative Building was proposed as an alternative to regular summer jobs. It was a laboratory course consisting of a number of preparatory sessions during the Spring session followed by five continuous weeks of field work at Camp Columbia during the months of June and July. Students working in teams under the guidance of instructors and consultants designed and actually built small structures of an imaginative and experimental nature. These structures were designed to fit in with the building program of Camp Columbia and became the property of the Camp. The Directors of the program were Arnaud, Bruno Funaro, W.J. Hennessy, and Mario Salvadori.[46]

In the late 1940's; Arnaud appointed several new staff members. From his curriculum vitae alone, Percival Goodman, a recipient of the 1925 Paris Prize seemed to resemble the majority of Arnaud's faculty. Goodman's writings and political activities soon revealed

40. In 1946–1947, first-year programs included *A Beach Cottage, Quarters for Country Club Help* (at an actual club in Rockland County, New York), *A Clock, A Lighthouse, A Movie Theatre Entrance, A Flower Market, An Expressive Form, A Non-Representational Form.* In 1957–1958 first-year programs included *An Optical Shop, A Study in Mass, A Study in Lines and Planes, A Garden Shelter, A Bus Stop in a National Park* (Program Statements, GSAP Archives).

41. In 1946–1947, second-year programs included *A Doctors' Building, A Ferry Landing, A Country Inn* (a prototype inn to be built by the Park Commission), *A Military Chapel, A Shelter.* In 1957–1958, second-year programs included *A Hunting and Fishing Camp, A Building for the display of "Mayflower" and related exhibits, A Parkway Police Headquarters, A Truck Transfer Depot* (Program Statements, GSAP Archives).

42. In 1946–1947, third-year programs included *A Community Center for Rockingham Park, New York, Country Club Lounge, Housing Development at Rockingham Park* (development of a suburban estate), *A House, Country Residence with attached Handcraft Facilities, Dairy Farm Group, A Small House, A Retreat.* In 1957–1958, third-year programs included *A Community Cultural Center, A Residential Subdivision, A Youth Center, A House in a Controlled Development* (Program Statements, GSAP Archives).

43. In 1946–1947, fourth-year programs included *A Trade School,* and *A United States Legation in a South American country.* In 1957–1958, fourth-year programs included *Outdoor Areas for a Small House,* and *A United States Embassy in a North African country* (Program Statements, GSAP Archives).

44. In 1948, graduate students in planning prepared a study of traffic and park systems for the villages of Tarrytown and North Tarrytown, at the request of the villages. The completed work was exhibited in the Tarrytown Library, and an evening presentation to the citizenry was made (Dean's Report, 30 June 1948, Central Files).

45. Arnaud, "How Architecture is Being Taught"; Arnaud, "Training the Architect at Columbia University."

him to have inclinations toward the radical left. In his studios Goodman tried to instill in his students a social awareness and the ability to ask *why* a building should be built rather than the more usual query of *how* it should be built. He tailored the Master's Program to fit the interests of his students, allowing foreign students to devise programs pertinent to their native countries.[47]

Mario Salvadori shared Goodman's concern that there should be a social imperative as well as a scientific rationale behind constructing a building. Salvadori emphasized the danger of separation between the architect and the engineer in the twentieth century, and felt that the solution lay in collaboration between small groups of experts. Salvadori argued that today's architect should be the equivalent of the fifteenth-century humanist combining technological background with imagination. In his classes Salvadori held up men such as Pier Luigi Nervi, Edwardo Torroja, and Felix Candela as examples of men who were at once engineers, architects, contractors, and businessmen.[48]

In 1954, Arnaud appointed James Marston Fitch as successor to Talbot Hamlin in the Historian's Chair. Since 1948, Fitch had been teaching Theory of Architecture in the School of General Studies. He placed architectural history in a sociological and technological context rather than describing it as a stylistic progression, and in this sense he shared Arnaud's view of history.[49]

In 1957, Arnaud hired Jan Hird Pokorny *(Columbia, 1940)* to succeed Bruno Funaro as the Director of the Evening Program. Pokorny had been a Visiting Critic at the School intermittently from 1946 to 1957. Arnaud believed that no administrator should be totally removed from teaching, and so Pokorny also taught courses in technology and modern materials.[50]

In 1950 Arnaud continued to defend the Beaux-Arts system of education, even in the face of such commentary as that by Carl Feiss:

There is almost nothing in the tattered remnants of our Beaux-Arts atelier system in formal architectural education which relates the drafting table to the modern world.[51]

Arnaud believed that the fundamental tenets for the teaching of architecture in the French schools were the same as in any good school: to teach the student to analyze social requirements and then have the artistic ability to translate the requirements into a workable and aesthetically pleasing plan and elevation. Making a building work functionally was essential but not sufficient in and of itself. Still, he had reservations about the Beaux-Arts system:

The unfortunate point, it seems to me, is that it was thought possible to transplant to this country a method of teaching essentially foreign to us. The sad and curious fact is that there are intelligent people who are vociferous in condemning the so-called French system yet they are willing to accept this or that other system, which is just as alien to our needs, under the pretext that it is 'modern.'[52]

Statements like this made Arnaud seem reactionary, but in fact, the School was catholic enough to accommodate a broad variety of students and professors. However, the lack of strong ideological

46. Leopold Arnaud, "Proposal of a New Summer Course to be Given Jointly by the Faculties of Architecture and Engineering at Camp Columbia," 15 November 1955, Central Files. The idea for such a program reflects the influence of the Bauhaus and the experiment at Black Mountain College, North Carolina, where students built many of the main campus buildings.

47. Interview: Percival Goodman by Author, 19 May 1981. After returning from Europe in 1929, Goodman opened an office in New York City with the painter/designer J. Franklin Whitman. The firm's first commissions were interior designs for department stores. Goodman is best known as an architect of synagogues and as a teacher and writer on architecture and town planning. In 1947 he wrote *Communitas* with his brother Paul and in 1977 he finished *The Double E.* He taught at New York University before its architecture program was discontinued, and then came to Columbia in July 1946, where he remained for twenty-five years.

48. Salvadori was educated at the University of Rome from which he received his doctorate in Civil Engineering. Moving to America he became a lecturer with the rank of professor at Princeton and lecturer and later professor at Columbia in 1940 and 1960. He is co-author of three engineering books and author of articles published in America, England and Italy. In New York he set up an office with Paul Weidlinger as consulting engineer. See Mario Salvadori, "Technology in Architecture: A Contribution and a Challenge," *Architectural Record,* 128 (September 1960), pp. 238-240.

49. Fitch was known for his professional achievements. He had held editorial positions with *Architectural Record, Architectural Forum,* and *House Beautiful.* His book, *American Architecture: The Forces that Shape It,* published in 1948, had won wide acclaim. See James Marston Fitch, *American Architecture: The Forces that Shape It,* (Boston: Houghton Mifflin Co., 1948).

50. Jan Hird Pokorny was born in Czechoslovakia and studied at the Polytechnical University of Prague, where he was graduated as "Engineer-Architect" in 1938. He practiced architecture in Czechoslovakia, where he designed a mountain hotel in Moravia, won the 1939 Housing and Office Building Competition, and executed rapid transit studies for the city of Prague. He came to the United States where he received the Master of Science in architecture from Columbia. He was with the architectural firm of Leo M. Bauer, Detroit, and then with Skidmore, Owings & Merrill as a designer. After becoming an American citizen, he opened his own architectural firm in New York, completing a number of distinguished buildings in and around New York City. Since the Evening Program was disbanded, Pokorny has taught courses in both architecture and historic preservation.

51. Carl Feiss, "Out of School," *Progressive Architecture,* 30 (September 1949), p. 12.

52. Arnaud, "Columbia Dean Recalls This Century Brought Beaux-Arts Schools to United States," *Progressive Architecture,* 31 (January 1950), p. 9.

guidance from Arnaud diminished the School's role as a participant in the development of a modern American architecture, as it
was conceived, for instance, at Harvard under Gropius, or at Penn
under Kahn. As Arnaud's tenure extended for a longer and longer
period of time, it became clear that he tended to resist new ideas
and that he was unlikely to be innovative. The stability which
Arnaud had undeniably brought to the School seemed more and
more to represent a form of stagnation. By the mid 1950's,
rumblings of dissatisfaction began to be felt among the faculty and
students. Having invested so much of his life in the School,
Arnaud became paranoid about a plot to gracelessly remove him
from the Deanship. Certainly Arnaud was overworked and was
not averse to relinquishing many of his responsibilities outside the
School. His duties had multiplied to an insupportable extreme and
he was quite simply over-extended: he was Director of the School
of Painting and Sculpture, Director of the School of Dramatic
Arts, Director of the Casa Italiana, active on nineteen University
committees, and represented the University in eight countries in
Latin America and five in Europe.[53] Due to both real and imagined
pressures, Arnaud retired from the Deanship at the end of the
academic year 1958–1959.

In his final report to the University on June 30, 1958, Arnaud
took stock of the School, and by implication his accomplishments
as its Dean:

*Practically all of our graduates found immediate employment at good
salaries without difficulty, and from reports received the employers were
well satisfied with the training our students had received.*

*Our School at Columbia continues to attract a goodly number of
applicants for admission, and our reputation both at home and abroad, as a
center for serious and thorough professional training continues to be
enviable. . . .*[54]

Arnaud also observed that the School had a student body of
diverse geographic origins, including a large proportion of foreign
students:

*This, of course, makes a stimulating and diverse group of students with
many interests in common, but with sufficient differences of background and
tradition to make an exciting and cosmopolitan center which is one of the
great attractions of our School at Columbia.*[55]

Arnaud concluded on a personal note:

*Having entered Columbia in September, 1914, I may say that with the
exception of a five year period for advanced study in Paris, France, I have
been active at Morningside for about forty-five years. These years have
passed quickly and on the whole pleasantly. Now it is time to turn to other
activities.*[56]

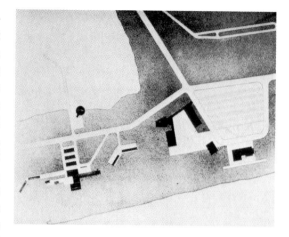

A Resort Hotel, ca. 1954, perspective and plan,
designer unknown. Photo: GSAP Archive.

53. Arnaud, "Forty-Five Years at Columbia," p. 8-9.

54. "Report of the Dean of the Faculty of Architecture
for the Period 1 July 1956 Through 30 June 1958," Central
Files, p. 1.

55. Ibid., p. 2.

56. Ibid., p. 9.

The fundamental thing in judging the work of a bourgeois intellectual is not to determine whether it includes reactionary elements or not; rather one must ascertain whether these elements constitute a universe in expansion or in contraction.

Tomás Maldonado[1]

Slouching towards modernity: Talbot Faulkner Hamlin and the architecture of the New Deal

Kenneth Frampton

As far as architectural ideology is concerned, the changing ideas espoused in the Columbia School of Architecture between the two World Wars seem to find a certain reflection in the career of Talbot Faulkner Hamlin (1889–1956) who was, so to speak, born into Avery Hall, since he was the son of A.D.F. Hamlin, Professor of Architecture at Columbia until his accidental death in 1926. The younger Hamlin seems to have accepted his destiny from the outset, translating, at the tender age of twelve, Pliny's letter on the Laurentine Villa, travelling to Europe and Turkey with his father in 1909 and entering the School of Architecture at Columbia in the following year. Hamlin junior enjoyed all the privileges that a liberal scion could expect to receive at the turn of the century. Educated at Amherst and then at Columbia, he was to publish his first book, *The Enjoyment of Architecture* in 1916, and to start teaching in the University extension course by the time he was twenty-seven. Four years later, he became a partner in the established New York firm of Murphy and Dana, which in 1925 became the practice of McGill and Hamlin.

Where Hamlin's early experience with Murphy and Dana familiarized him with the design of "mass-produced," semi-detached suburban houses, in either a vaguely Arts and Crafts or Colonial style, his personal expression as an architect only emerged with the institutional work that McGill and Hamlin achieved after 1925, above all, in the collegiate Gothic of New Rochelle College, New York, and in the chunky, massive proportions of a number of churches designed for Brooklyn and elsewhere, including the National Shrine of the Little Flower in Royal Oak, built in Michigan in 1926, a commission which was reminiscent of the bold massing employed by the eclectic architect Bertram Goodhue, whose exotic, post-San Diego Exhibition manner Hamlin greatly admired. For his own part, Hamlin, the architect, remained an uncertain eclectic throughout his life, his work being indistinguishable from many other traditionalists who tentatively posited a Neo-Gothic or vaguely Arts and Crafts, "liberal" style as a way of transcending the pompous elitism of the Beaux-Arts system in which they had been trained. Nostalgic for the probity exhibited by the American Colonial vernacular, Hamlin admired, like many other architects of his generation, the private fitness of the clapboard houses of Salem, together with the public dignity of the architecture of the Jeffersonian Enlightenment. For Hamlin, as his critical career advanced, the guarantee of civic well-being seemed to radiate almost as an unfulfilled promise from the profiles and forms of the American Greek Revival. Like Lewis Mumford, he felt that this American idyll had been destroyed by the industrialism that followed the conclusion of the Civil War.

Talbot Faulkner Hamlin.
Photo: Columbia University.

1. Quoted in Roberto Segre's review of Maldonado's book, *Design Nature and Revolution* in *Arquitectura Cuba 34* (1973).

Despite his admiration for the work of McKim, Mead and White, the full rhetoric of the Beaux-Arts always seems to have caused Hamlin a certain embarassment at both an artistic and socio-cultural level, although it is clear that he acknowledged that the institutions of the state and the aspirations of the developing continent still required representation by some form of suitably eclectic, if not academic, monumentality. Despite this nostalgia for Neo-classic monumentality Hamlin refrained from such a rhetoric in his practice. In general he veered towards the Neo-Gothic although he was not beyond experimenting on occasion with styles which were close to the Art Deco or the Modern; first, in a competition for a provincial airport and then, in a seaside villa designed for Paul Fancher in 1933, where flat roofs, cubic shapes and steel fenestration brought him ostensibly close to the International Style as this had been celebrated by Henry-Russell Hitchcock and Philip Johnson in their famous exhibition of that title, staged at the Museum of Modern Art in 1932. This, of course, could hardly be considered daring since aeronautical and maritime subjects had, like factories, long been regarded as suitable subjects in which to express an uninhibited modernity. However, it is not inconceivable that Hamlin would have embraced international modernism, something along the lines of George Howe, had he continued to practice after his appointment as director of the Avery Library in 1934.

The Avery Librarianship, which he occupied with distinction for twelve years from 1934 until 1946, resolved a perennial conflict in Hamlin's personality; the split that had arisen between his appointed vocation as a professional architect and the indisputable fact that he was rapidly becoming, despite his practice, one of the most prolific writers of his generation. Moreover, while Hamlin published seven works of book length between 1934 and his death in 1956, he was, in his daily critical capacity, a kind of public conscience whose relative absence in the world today is to be deplored. Thus, apart from his growing reputation as a scholar and a critic, his most important role during the New Deal, which lasted throughout his tenure as Avery Librarian, was that of functioning as a kind of intellectual guardian of the public weal. This is also reflected in his thirteen-year-long association with the U.S. Housing Authority Architectural Advisory Committee, of which he was a member from 1941 to 1954, and wherein he functioned as a committed protagonist of social reform. In fact, his faithful devotion to Roosevelt's legacy in the field of Federal welfare housing was sufficient for the editor of *Who's Who in America* to characterize him as a socialist.

Like Mumford and Raymond Unwin, to whom he was spiritually affiliated, Hamlin sought throughout his life to arrive at a balance between the intrinsic virtues of urban civilization and the broader socio-ecological benefits of decentralized development. Heinrich Tessenow's polemical book, *The Provincial City and Craftsmanship,* of 1918 would have been a summation of his ideal, although it is extremely unlikely that Hamlin even casually perused this work for no copy has ever been held in Avery Library.

But the cultural model which Hamlin rather tentatively tried to formulate was already there in Tessenow, who following Paul Mebes' pro-Biedermeier text *Um 1800*[2] of 1907, projected the anti-industrial ideal of the small provincial city which, in theory, would combine the civic virtues of political independence with a craft-based expression related to the evolution of an authentic regional style. Such a style for Tessenow was fundamentally Biedermeier, whereas for Hamlin it was the American Greek Revival — the subject of his most scholarly works. Like Morris and Carlyle before him, Tessenow confronted the vexed issues[3] of divided labor and cultural alienation in industrialized society; questions which Hamlin was loath to formulate in such abstract terms, for he was certainly no latterday Pre-Raphaelite nor a critic of post-Hegelian persuasion.

Nevertheless, Hamlin's commitment to the culture of the public realm is borne out by his lifelong ambivalence towards the urban dispersal implicit in the process of suburbanization, while his reservations about *avant-gardist* abstraction in architecture stemmed, at least in part, from his recognition that architectural culture in a true democracy should by definition, be a culture accessible to the people as a whole. Much of this may be construed from his revealing reviews of the works of others, even if he failed to formulate this position in unequivocal terms. Thus, while recognizing and admiring the socio-cultural arguments advanced in favor of a decentralized economy by Percival and Paul Goodman in their book *Communitas* of 1947, Hamlin was nonetheless to take exception to their specific advocacy of urban dispersal when he wrote of the authors' apparent misunderstanding of the ideals, of both the garden city and the satellite town to the effect that:

neither was conceived as a mere dormitory suburb. The entire concept of the garden city depends on integrating industry, agriculture, and residence, and both Letchworth and Welwyn were designed to be self-supported by means of local industries. It was only an accident of the monstrous growth of London that Welwyn, despite its flourishing industries, became a dormitory suburb.

Hamlin was as convinced as Camillo Sitte and Unwin before him, that the civic virtue and soci-cultural identity of the garden city must derive, in representational terms, from the density and subtlety of its urban form. Thus, as resident editor for *Pencil Points* in the early 1940's, Hamlin wrote of the future development in post-war America in the following terms:

Whatever may be the changes which the after-war period will bring, one, I think, is sure: the greater and greater importance of community subdivision and site planning in the architect's field. If, for example, prefabrication and standardization of residential units should become common — a not unlikely technical development — the aesthetic effect and the usefulness of the new community are bound to result much more from the relationships between the units than from the units themselves. One can see this fact very clearly in certain rare suburbs of today where careful handling of site composition makes an attractive residential center even out of commonplace houses; one may see the reverse as well in places where quite lovely

"I think he's walking out with the plans of our three industrial jobs under that beard."

Photo: *Pencil Points,* 1941.

2. I mention these German texts to remind the reader that there were parallel post-English Arts and Crafts movements which were developing in continental Europe prior to the First World War. Hamlin's affinity for and experience with craft production was fairly extensive including a brief period as a freelance designer for the New York craft firm of Rambusch. I am grateful to Steven Bedford for revealing this connection.

3. For Hamlin, the American Greek Revival and the triumph of provincial culture were one and the same. In his study *Greek Revival in American Architecture* of 1944, Hamlin documented the work of those architects who, in the short span between 1820 and 1860, were able to embody the substance of a classical urban culture; men such as Benjamin Latrobe in Washington and Charleston, S.C., William Strickland in Nashville, Tennessee and Charles Bulfinch in Boston, to mention only a few.

For Hamlin, the Greek Revival was the last moral American style, although even this was not immune to the structure of his critical spirit. Thus in comparing the Greek and Gothic revivals, Hamlin wrote: "The Greek Revival, too, was often guilty of much the same error, stuccoing brick to symbolize stone, and using wooden columns in most...of its domestic work" (p. 333). At the same time, Hamlin was well aware that rapid expansion and industrialization, in the last half of the nineteenth century, had been largely responsible for the destruction of this urbane and urban style, and thus we read of its demise:

This emergence of the millionaire was as fatal to the artistic ideals of the Greek Revival as were the speed, the speculation, and the exploitation that produced him. He travelled abroad in luxury, he lived at home in a plethora of things bought... He was profoundly envious of culture, but he could not understand the deep roots of the American culture which had preceded him. He wanted change, he envied Europe; what architecture was possible for such a man but eclecticism (p. 335).

buildings have their effect lost and destroyed by monotonous or uncomposed groupings.

The late Sir Raymond Unwin recognized the permanent importance of this kind of mass or site composition to a high degree, both in his book, Town Planning in Practice, *and in his executed work with Barry Parker in Hampstead and elsewhere in England. Hampstead I know well. Its little cottages, its row houses and semi-detached villas are not in themselves exciting architectural achievements: yet, because of their arrangement, the pleasant courts, the preservation of old trees, the careful study of road widths, and the design of road intersections so that vistas shall always be interesting, Hampstead Garden Suburb is one of the most continuously attractive, inviting, and beautiful suburban communities in the world. It is not formal, but it is all definitely composed. It is not a grand plan in the Beaux-Arts tradition, but it is very definitely a grand plan in the most human way, in which every part exists because of its relation to the other parts. The whole design is conceived in three dimensions; and the relationships between the central square, with its two churches, and the roads, curving and straight, which lead out of it, with the building sizes and placing along the roads, are all one integrated and subtle conception. Much the same is true of large portions of the garden city Welwyn. It is true also of the best German site planning, such as Ernst May's beautiful Frankfurt suburb, Romerstadt, which so charmingly swings around the curving hillside on which it is placed. There is hardly a suburb or town of recent design in the United States which shows these qualities. Even the best of the American site plans still seem full of loose ends; they tend either to monotonous regularity or to a kind of straggling lack of integration. Only here and there, as in the Buhl Foundation groups in Pittsburgh, or in the select few of the government housing groups, do these qualities of integrated composition and individual interest of view occur.* [4]

I have cited Hamlin at length, here, in order to demonstrate something of the tenor of his opinion with regard to future forms of urban development and land settlement, although one may register surprise at this passage, in as much as it implicitly criticizes, by omission, what had then been achieved in Radburn and in Sunnyside Gardens by such distinguished New Deal planners as Clarence Stein and Henry Wright — Wright even serving as a member of the faculty until his death in 1936. And while Hamlin does not go so far as to cite the Greek Revival as the only enduring representational style appropriate to democracy, he nonetheless suggests both here and elsewhere that the people need to acknowledge their identity and social cohesion through a collective acceptance and celebration of urban form in terms of style. Hence the stress placed in the above text on Hampstead Garden Suburb's central square and its two churches.

The issue of appropriate representation was a recurrent theme in Hamlin's thought as is borne out by his unequivocal admiration for Goodhue's Nebraska Capitol, Feilheimer's Cincinnati Railroad Station, and Hood's Rockefeller Center, all three of which remained for him enduring examples of an appropriate twentieth-century monumentality. This factor also accounts for his lasting appreciation for something so rhetorically Neo-classical and Beaux-Arts, as Chicago's Columbian Exposition of 1893. In

4. Talbot F. Hamlin, "Communities and Architects in a Post War World," *Pencil Points*, 22 (March 1941), pp. 173-174.

his 1941 review of the first edition of Siegfried Giedion's *Space Time and Architecture* it is significant that he takes the Swiss historian to task for having accepted the Prairie School account of what they retrospectively conceived as the destruction of American architectural culture at the hands of international capital and Daniel Burham's worldly architectural acumen:

Giedion falls into the usual "modernist" error of misjudging the influence of the Chicago World's Fair of 1893. Protest about it as we like, millions of people loved it, and it gave to them a vision of something for which they were starved. Instead of mere unthinking condemnation, would it not be well for the true historical critic to examine what qualities in it made it so loved? The people saw a designed whole, carefully composed according to a brilliant general plan; they saw a group carefully related to its site by adroit use of water and the lake; they saw order. If they mistook the order, which delighted them, for the 'orders,' so misused in the buildings, should not the reasons for this error also be studied? [5]

Unlike Joseph Hudnut, who was possibly to the left of Hamlin at least as far as modernism was concerned, or Leopold Arnaud who was patently to the right in almost every respect, Hamlin came to terms with modern architecture only gradually and even when, in the last two decades of his life, he had more or less accepted the genre, he did so with a measure of assent that was always implicitly tinged with reservations. This much may perhaps be most clearly perceived in Hamlin's uneasy attitude towards Le Corbusier of whom he was, at first, sharply critical and whose position he came, by degrees, to accept only at the level of some of the theoretical premises involved. Thus, in a review of Frederick Etchells' translation of Le Corbusier's *Towards a New Architecture*, which Hamlin contributed to *The Nation* in 1929 we find him writing that:

Le Corbusier's book has long been known in the original French to students of modern art movements and one cannot but be glad that it is now rendered available to all readers. It is a stimulating book, a breathtaking book, a question making book, more fruitful of discussion than of opinion. It is exciting as a modern newspaper is exciting, written out of hot enthusiasm pure propaganda. Refreshing to the last degree in its analyses of Roman, Greek and Renaissance work; cutting and sound in its grasp of 'the illusion of plans,' full of a self confident austerity, almost Franciscan, it nevertheless, by some psychological perversity, succeeds in developing, out of its clarity, its keeness and its idealism designs of a fantastic and monotonous ugliness, towns of rectangular harshness and interiors like the inside of an operating room. It is a disturbing book because so completely doctrinaire and yet so persuasive. Its deification of machinery and machine forms implies to them a beauty which they may not possess or possess only spasmodically and by accident. It is characteristic that on the last page the last two lines are 'Architecture and Revolution,' and beneath that a picture of a briar pipe. [6]

Seven years later Hamlin had hardly changed his opinion when he wrote the following appraisal of Le Corbusier's first public appearance at Columbia University in the fall of 1936; a notice which, incidentally, displays his consummate skill as an essayist.

5. Talbot F. Hamlin, see Giedion Review, 1941. *The Nation.*

6. Talbot F. Hamlin, *The Nation,* (March 1929).

To those who know his books, especially Vers une architecture *(translated as* Towards a New Architecture, *published in New York in 1927)*, Precis d'une architecture moderne, *and the recent* La Ville radieuse, *there was perhaps little specifically new; yet the dynamic power of his personality — so well expressed in his tall spare form and his long well-modeled head, — the beautiful organization of the material, and especially the swift, nervous drawings with which he deftly and clearly illustrated his points added immensely to the vividness of his theories. Much, that, written in cold print, may look strained and strident, in the lectures came over merely as pointed and forceful.*

This is not the place, or the moment, for an extended criticism of Le Corbusier's ideas. Yet one thing must be said: Of his sincerity, of the power and discipline of his mind, of the logical — rigidly logical — character of his thinking, these lectures leave no possible doubt. Starting with the premises he assumes, it seems difficult to arrive at any conclusions except those he sets forth. It is this quality, rather than the buildings he has designed, which has made him undoubtedly one of the three or four most important individuals in the architectural world of today. It is precisely in this logical character that his greatest lack is inherent. Like most thoroughly logical persons, he tends to oversimplification; of a dozen possible premises, he chooses perhaps but three to build on — and these three are not always the most important. This was especially evident in the lecture on city planning; in the premises he assumed, and in those which he neglected to assume, there was implied a whole philosophy (or perhaps a lack of philosophy) of human life, its real aims and its actual functioning, that was, to say the least, susceptible of much questioning and not a little disagreement. Nevertheless, the present confused world has deep need for much more such keen thinking as Le Corbusier's.[7]

The fact is, of course, that Hamlin vacillated in his opinion of Le Corbusier and it was just this evasiveness which finally brought him into disfavor in the 1950's with a younger and more militant generation of critics. He was however to make his distaste for Le Corbusier's architecture quite explicit for he unequivocally condemned the Villa Savoye in petite bourgeois terms when he wrote of it as being a "space in which it is literally impossible to form a single intimate conversational corner." It is surprising nonetheless that not once did Hamlin recognize the Beaux-Arts not to say Neo-classical principles lying beneath much of Le Corbusier's public work or that, given Hamlin's lifelong love of the sea and ships, he could not bring himself to acknowledge the poetic wit of the marine references incorporated into the figurative elements and details of Le Corbusier's Purist villas. And the reason is perhaps not so hard to find, for as his 1937 Parisian report reveals, what disturbed Hamlin in Le Corbusier, apart from the abstract "totalitarianism" of his form and thought was, above all, the subversive Surrealism that Hamlin sensitively detected as lying just below the surface of the apparently rational style.

Hamlin's conversion to modernism was as slow as it was sporadic. This much seems to be borne out by the varying postures he adopted between his first book of consequence, *The American Spirit in Architecture* of 1926, and 1933, when reacting to the influence of the International Style. Hamlin, despite the scorn that he

7. Talbot F. Hamlin, *Columbia University Quarterly*, 28 (March 1936), pp. 68-69.

had poured on the MOMA show,[8] was already lecturing about the modern movement in architecture and giving favorable notices to such Expressionist works as Mendelsohn's hat factory built in Luckenwalde in 1921. In January, 1933, in a lecture given in Hamilton, Ontario, Hamlin came out against "such weird constructions as Gothic apartments and airports in Spanish Renaissance Mission style" and roundly castigated what he regarded as "postage stamp" designing, largely manifest in the *arriviste* Anglo-Saxon fashion of Stockbrokers Tudor, wherein thin, decorative, half-timbered facades were applied indiscriminately to either balloon-frame or load-bearing masonry structures.[9]

This was a decisive change from the position which Hamlin had implicitly adopted in the mid-1920's when even works as relatively traditional as Louis Sullivan's Wainwright Tomb completed in St. Louis in 1892 or Eliel Saarinen's second-prize entry for the Chicago Tribune of 1922, were still being classified by the young critic as "modernish non-styles" and where in an extensive panorama of American architecture, comprising well over 600 illustrated entries, Frank Lloyd Wright was accorded only a single reference for his Ward Willets house built in Highland Park, Illinois, in 1902. In a survey in which Goodhue's Spanish Colonial manner is warmly received and Grauman's "pre-Columbian" Hollywood Theatre is regarded as an appropriately exotic context for escapist entertainment, Wright is somewhat disparagingly classified as a representative of the American "Secessionist" mode. One has to remember that this assessment was being set into print fifteen years after the appearance of the Wasmuth volumes at a time when Wright had built over forty major works, including, as public structures of consequence, the Unity Temple, the Larkin Building, Midway Gardens, and the Imperial Hotel in Tokyo.

It was to take Hamlin another decade to finally accept Wright in all his greatness and even then, he was unable to persuade such diehards as Arnaud of the validity of his newfound enthusiasm. Interestingly enough, for someone who was concerned with composition but rarely categoric about it, Hamlin's first, almost unqualified, appraisal of Wright began with a reference to the Beaux-Arts principle of subordination, with Hamlin praising Wright for his recently perfected control over this precept, particularly in his recent work, which, as Hamlin put it, had become

surer, less concealed under the sometimes questionable ornament that has in the past veiled the essential simplicity. Now, in the latest work, and especially in the Kaufmann house and the Johnson's Wax Company building, the process has at last completely triumphed. In both there is a new clarity, a new power, a new poetry.[10]

There follows in this analysis of Wright, published in 1938, a panegyric to the Kaufmann house, which Hamlin praises for its single-minded use of the concrete cantilever as the primary, formal and structural device for layering the building into the site. Hamlin was impressed by the way in which this horizontal complex harmonized with the surrounding geological strata, while at the same time affording a relieving contrast to the incessant verticality of the trees. In fact, Hamlin was to rest the burden of his critical approval

8. Talbot F. Hamlin, "The International Style Lacks the Essence of Great Architecture," *American Architect*, 143 (1933).

9. See newspaper cutting Hamilton Ontario, TFH Collection, Avery Library, Box 3, item 3:g.

10. Talbot F. Hamlin, "F.L.W. — An Analysis," *Pencil Points*, 19 (March 1938), pp. 137 & 139. See also Hamlin's review of Wright's *Architecture and Modern Life* in *The Nation* (1937).

of Wright on the latter's use of structural invention as the primary unifying device. And yet, as in the Kaufmann house, the Johnson's Wax complex is applauded not only for its structure but also for the subordination of the parts to the whole:

The general framework of the plan is merely a series of these circular mushroom columns arranged on a simple pattern of square bays. The corners are all rounded — again the circle idea. The ventilation shafts are circular. Played into this is the mezzanine gallery, and above that the penthouse, with executive offices; and in all the elements of these the circular corner reigns, as though the larger element — the greater melody — were repeated here in a different key and with a different but related rhythm. Again the analogy of musical counterpoint is felt.[11]

In general Hamlin seems to have welcomed Wright's Broadacre City, particularly for its implicit policy of agrarian reform, as expanded on at length by Wright and Baker Brownell in their joint text *Architecture and Modern Life* of 1937. But aside from the questionable grass roots politics involved in this proposal, about which Hamlin remained characteristically naive, the reluctant modernist also seems to have liked the accompanying eurhythmics of Wright's new found "organic form," and it is a testament to Hamlin's fastidious, not to say puritan sensibility, that where he had been generally repelled by the Eldorado exoticism of Wright's Prairie Style decor, he was just as captivated by the veracity and structural authenticity of Wright's Usonian "streamlined" form. Only at one juncture did Hamlin have reservations about Wright's work of the mid-1930's and this concerned his obsessive introduction of the hexagon as a planning module, above all in the Hanna house built at Stanford, California in 1937, about which Hamlin entertained doubts, on the grounds of its anthropomorphically non-normative nature or as he put it, "the making of a hexagonal bed offers difficulties to those who sleep with their arms and legs flung out, who would do better on a star-shaped than on a hexagonal couch."

All this ebullient enthusiasm for Wright again becomes muted in Hamlin's magisterial *Forms and Functions in 20th Century Architecture* of 1952 where, subject presumably to Arnaud's implicit stricture, Wright's remarkable achievement is once again almost begrudgingly acknowledged and while Hamlin praises the intelligent sequential planning of both the Unity Temple and the Imperial Hotel, he does so in such a way as to stress Wright's dependence on the precepts of the Ecole des Beaux-Arts.

Hamlin's growing enthusiasm for modernity, in both a social and aesthetic sense, reaches its apotheosis in 1937, on the occasion of the *Exposition Universelle*, staged in Paris in that year, when he writes in glowing and romantic terms of the way in which he was overwhelmed by the monumental use of light and water.

At night, the exhibition is at its best. One should enter by the Trocadero Gate, past the great green column of international peace, and over the wide terrace where the old Trocadero once stood. One comes suddenly to its edge, a sheer, cliff-like drop and, below, sees the sloping walks and terraces and stairs — magnificent great flights — that surround perhaps the most beauti-

11. Talbot F. Hamlin, "F.L.W. — An Analysis," *Pencil Points*, 19 (March 1938), pp. 137 & 139. See also Hamlin's review of Wright's *Architecture and Modern Life* in *The Nation* (1937).

ful and astonishing fountain ever built. At its top, just beneath one, twenty great nozzles inclined upwards about twenty degrees, arranged in four banks of five each, shoot out a great sheaf of white water two hundred feet, to fall in a continuous roar into the long basin below. . . Beneath, in the great basin, similar jets form a colonnade on the sides and between them sheets of water sprout transversely across the pool. The whole is lighted by carefully concealed spots and floods and by underwater lights; as one watches their extraordinary display of graceful power — its emotional effect is tremendous — suddenly, yet gently, the colors change — now pale blue, now green, now violet, now pink. Framing — in this central fountain are broad banks of grass, vivid green and fresh from the continual spray, then wide walks thronged with crowds whose noise is devoured and hidden by the rush of waters, and the thick trees half hiding the many national buildings behind them. . . . At the Quai, the Trocadero gardens are closed by the long masses of the Russian and German buildings which are placed with true Gallic wit to glare at each other across the main axis. . . . Beyond, rises the Eiffel Tower, now a black ghost, with purple shafts of light rising vertically to enframe it, now glowing dull red, now dull green, while the soffits of its four great arches are bright with green and blue and white neon tubes. All this color lighting is as subtle, as delicate, as it is impressive; the object has been to produce beauty rather than to astonish; yet the result is breathtaking. [12]

That Hamlin perceived something more unifying in this exhibition than the central Neo-Baroque summation achieved by this rhetorical Beaux-Arts waterscape is borne out by a later passage in which he suggests that this highly differentiated, yet ideologically harmonious exhibition — unified perhaps by a common innocence and conviction — could well be the product of a new consciousness and socio-technical capacity; the collective international evidence let us say of a process of modernization which was then taking place all over Europe despite the world-wide depression. Of this Hamlin wrote:

There is little in the fair which one could term frankly "International Style," with the possible exception of the Swedish building (the stupid exterior of which conceals a host of interior facilities), yet the fair has style. Perhaps this is the most significant achievement: that here in 1937 is a host of buildings differing enormously in plan, conception and detail; each one free and in its own way creative; and yet each helps the next; all seem part of one movement, one great design, one culture. Those which one must except from this blanket statement are all expressions of basically different cultural ideals (Germany, Russia in part, Italy in part and Romania and Egypt). . . . Perhaps this new harmony is a real thing; perhaps it is more than momentary, and expresses a real internationalism that gives point to the enormous and moving tower of peace.

While the Spanish Civil War and the invasion of Czechoslovakia were to prove Hamlin unduly optimistic about the promise of international social democracy, the buildings assembled on the banks of the Seine afforded him an occasion on which to take stock of a kind of eclectic modernism — a non-doctrinaire "style" which in 1937 could be construed as possessing universal relevance. In this way, both the methodology and the content of his Parisian report

12. This and the following passage are both taken from a manuscript of Hamlin's which evidently remained unpublished. See TFH Collection, Avery Library, Box 3, items 3.1 & 3.7.

anticipated the substance and the structure of his encyclopaedic
Forms and Functions of 20th Century Architecture.

It is worth noting, in passing, what it was that Hamlin felt to be
of cultural import during these last years of world peace prior to
the outbreak of the Second World War, since his critical choice,
together with his equally critical censorship, affords us some idea
as to what the pedagogical ideology of Columbia was like during
the New Deal period. It is clear not only from this unpublished
report but also from the unpublished sketches which accompany it
that the secretly whimsical side of Hamlin's personality could not
resist the superficial Neo-rococo of the *Pavillon des Arts Feminins* or
the streamlined Art Deco manner of the *Pavillon de St. Gobain*
which Hamlin rated as the best building in the whole exhibition. In
both instances, the decorative and the sensational as revealed by
surface treatment and light were given priority, and it was this
same emphasis on revetment which was to color Hamlin's overall
concept as to what kind of normative modern architecture would
be appropriate in a social democracy. That is to say he was
apparently incapable of evaluating any of the exhibition buildings
as total works from their structural and formal concept to their
sequential order or their metaphorical significance to their material
finish. Thus with few exceptions the buildings in the *Exposition
Universelle* are valued either for their material brilliance or for their
spatial order or for their structure or even, here and there, for all
three, but it is significant that an idea of the total building never
truly emerges either in Hamlin's writings or in his sketches. It is as
though Hamlin's critical perception was becoming atomised, so
that one might separately appreciate, as Hamlin did, the detailing
of Alvar Aalto's Finnish Pavilion and even its spatial order, but
strangely enough never the whole work, with its narrative
meandering promenade, its metaphorical configuration and its
typological allusions. While well aware that its double atrium
parti — one open, one roofed over — was a reference to Roman
culture, Hamlin could not take the more demanding step and
recognize that its overall composition was a metaphor not only for
the traditional Nordic farm complex, but also for the aggrega-
tional form of a typical Karelian village. And what was the case in
Hamlin's attitude to the Finnish Pavilion applied with equal force
to his appraisal of other buildings, such as Krejcar's Czechoslova-
kian Pavilion which, while appreciated for its structure and
circulation, was never evaluated as a whole.

In retrospect the most shocking aspect of Hamlin's essay on the
Exposition Universelle is the quite important works which he passed
over without comment. Thus while he appreciated (in retrospect)
the structural brilliance of Le Corbusier's *Pavillon des Temps
Nouveaux,* he was not touched in any way by its equally remarkable interior. At the same time there were at least two works of
canonical import about which he was to remain inexplicably silent;
Junzo Sakura's quite seminal and prophetic Japanese Pavilion, and
Jose Luis Sert's delicate and politically sensitive Spanish Pavilion,
wherein Picasso's *Guernica* was exhibited for the first time. About
all this Hamlin tells us nothing.

During the Second World War a great deal of Hamlin's spare

energy was expended in trying to improve the general standard of
the welfare and defense related housing built under the auspices of
FPHA and during these years, as an adviser to the U.S. Housing
Agency, he endeavored to evolve more effective methods for the
evaluation of housing quality. In this, he was unquestionably part
of a major national effort to raise the standard of New Deal housing involving such early protagonists in the field as Albert Mayer,
Henry Churchill, Douglas Orr, William Lescaze, George Nelson
and Vernon deMars. Hamlin's most substantive contribution to
this effort was the "model" evaluation that he produced of the
Pioneer Homes project which had been completed by the Syracuse
Housing Authority in 1939 and which was later the subject of an
extensive analysis, formally submitted by Hamlin, in June 1944.
The housing experience that Hamlin had gained in the firm of
Murphy and Dana stood him in good stead, for this firm designed
government housing in America in the last years of the First World
War; above all in the Arts and Crafts model settlement that they
built for the United States Department of Labor at Waterbury,
Connecticut in 1918. That Hamlin had had direct experience in the
design of housing is borne out by the comprehensiveness and
precision of his Pioneer Homes report. Hamlin was against a
purely statistical evaluation of housing and true to his Unwinian
upbringing he was generally disturbed by the tendency towards
extremely dense development, frequently perpetrated in some of
the early New Deal developments, although this was not the case
in Syracuse. Similarly, in contradiction to the accepted norms of
economical housing practice, Hamlin remained convinced that the
widest possible variety of unit types should be employed in order
to avoid visual monotony. Hamlin, like Mumford, also attached
great importance to the integration of landscape into housing and
today his all but forty year old strictures against certain pernicious
practices have an uncomfortable ring of *deja vu*. Reading Hamlin's
Syracuse report after all these years, one is struck by the fact that
little has been learnt by American society as to the accommodation
standards it should be willing and able to provide for the poorer
strata of its population. Thus we find Hamlin writing critically of
the Pioneer Housing development:

*Originally, paved play areas supposedly for little children were furnished
close to apartments, wherever apartments occurred. They are surfaced with
black-top and surrounded with high galvanized iron wire fences. . . . At the
present time they are not used and in all our visits to the project the only use
we saw made of any of these play areas was three little girls playing house
in the shadow of an apartment. This is not surprising. I can see no reason
whatsoever why children should want to use such unappetizing, hot, and
ugly spaces and I believe that in all future projects any attempts to force
children into such play areas should be both impractical and inhuman.*[13]

Hamlin the liberal-socialist is also detectable in the virulence
with which he opposed the industrial zoning and waste disposal
areas projected by Robert Moses in his plans for the future development of Staten Island. Thus we find Hamlin, in October,
1951, writing in support of a local protest group:

13. See correspondence in TFH Collection, Avery Library,
Box 4, item 4.2.

It is the kind of thing which is bound to happen until the re-planning of Staten Island is approached from the realistic and not the diagrammatic point of view. The present street pattern indicated on the official map is a disgrace to human intelligence, and the zoning that exists is incoherent and without real meaning because it is based on a consideration of flat maps and arbitrary percentages rather than on any careful investigation of the site itself.[14]

As Dean Leopold Arnaud endeavored to make clear in his intro-duction, the intention behind the publication of the four volume *Forms and Functions of 20th Century Architecture* was to recast for the second half of the century, Julien Gaudet's *magnum opus,* his *Elements et theories de l'architecture* of 1902, which had been the summa-tion of the precepts and practices of the Ecole des Beaux-Arts at the turn of the century. Arnaud's preface adumbrated the evolution of Humanist theory in terms of a series of canonical texts which had appeared at intervals of about a century; a heritage within which this work was now being advanced as a legitimate heir. The intro-duction reiterated the classical succession in architectural theory, Vitruvius, Alberti, Vignola, Palladio, Blondel, Gibbs, Chambers, Durand, Guadet, and now, fifty years before its time due to the apocalyptic transformations wrought by industry, Hamlin. In a spirit of catholic revisionism there was more than an implication in Arnaud's introduction that if theory must be re-written then it had better be reformulated as a new canon under the auspices of the academy. *La academie est mort, vive la academie!*

But what of course secretly perplexed Arnaud and more impor-tantly Hamlin was, what would be the appropriate taxonomy to employ in classifying the heterogeneous architectural experience of the past fifty years; not that either Arnaud or Hamlin publicly admitted this difficulty. The theoretical breakdown employed by Guadet and even more categorically by Durand was simply to be modified by Hamlin so as to accommodate modern circumstances without bothering too much about the epistemological questions involved, such as the normative relations which should obtain between the general and the specific, or the issue as to what finally is the prime mover of the art. It is interesting how this unsystema-tic upgrading of Guadet enabled Hamlin to evade the issue as to what was the appropriate methodology by which the art of ar-chitecture should be now practiced.

And here one must remark on Hamlin's most paradoxical de-parture from the procedure adopted by Guadet, namely, the sup-pression of any methical discussion of the principles of compo-sition, that is, the precepts by which the order of the whole was to be assured. Such was the myth of the functionalist *demiurgé* that the ethos of the New Deal regarded the very notion of composition as taboo, as a subjective undertaking lying beyond the limits of re-spectable discourse. Instead it posited, as prime mover, the biolog-ical or the organic, which meant for Hamlin and others the neces-sarily convenient disposition of a building's "organs"; a process which was vaguely conceived as conforming to the precepts of Anglo-Saxon scientific empiricism. That there could indeed be a *dialectical* relationship between form and content, as Le Corbusier had attempted to demonstrate with lucidity throughout his life,

14. See correspondence in TFH Collection, Avery Library, Box 4, item 4.1.

was generally denied by Anglo-Saxon theoreticians such as Hamlin and John Summerson, the last proving, by the process of logical exclusion, the impossibility for such a dialectical generation of order, in his by now famous address of 1957 entitled *The Case for a Theory of Modern Architecture.*[15]

Unlike Guadet for whom *les principes directeurs et les grands regles de la composition* were to be the main orienting principles already set out as such at the beginning of his theory, Hamlin refused to deal directly with the issue of composition and embraced instead a taxonomy that comprised a series of constituent elements, which somewhat inconsistently varied from fragmentary spatial episodes drawn from randomly chosen works to basic building components such as doors, windows, columns, piers, beams, ceilings, floors, arches, vaults, etc. Only in volume two did he attempt to deal with the overall problem of composition but then he tended to approach the subject largely in terms of internal spatial "narratives" structured about the concept of a progress. And if the dialectic of "route and goal," related possibly to the theories of Dagobert Frey, was the main principle of hierarchic unity adduced by Hamlin, his other basic theoretical precept was the decidedly naturalistic notion that style should emerge spontaneously as a consequence of using certain materials and employing a particular technology.[16] He did of course occasionally allude to the received wisdom of gestalt psychology such as, "apparently the human imagination finds it difficult to relate more than five units in one composition" or,

The attractive value of the center of balance has already been referred to in passing. The ordinary person tends unconsciously to walk towards such a center. This is the secret of much of the world's best planning, and it is as true of the design of houses as it is of monumental buildings.

Thus at no point does Hamlin deal with the issue of form or order in a comprehensive way but only as a series of open-ended principles, such as complexity, rhythm, proportion, color, texture, etc. that may have this or that detailed effect on the appearance of the whole. In fact one could claim that Hamlin chose to abandon the *public* destiny of architecture to its pluralist fate, particularly when one compares his general theory to that of Guadet, who was to devote a whole long section of his work to the appropriate articulation of the representative threshold or *le vestibule.* Aware that the traditional monumental destiny of architecture had been disrupted by the demands of industry and by the supposedly populist context of the modern welfare state, Hamlin was just as incapable of discerning the heterogeneous principles of modern composition as he was unwilling to reformulate the precepts of the academy. As Colin Rowe wrote in his review of *Forms and Functions...*:

Preoccupied with the 'principles of composition' neither the author nor the editorial board of this treatise seem to have enjoyed any direct experience of the compositional schemes which derive from Cubist painting by way of Constructivism and the Dutch De Stijl group. Mr. Hamlin reproduces two paintings by Mondrian and comments on their significance for such architects as J.J.P. Oud and Mies van der Rohe; but he does not seem to be

15. See John Summerson, "The Case for a Theory of Modern Architecture," *Journal for the Royal Institute of British Architects,* 64 (June 1957), pp. 307-313.

16. In *Forms and Functions of 20th Century Architecture,* Hamlin wrote:
We cannot judge the excellence of a group [of buildings] on the sole basis of whether it is formal or informal. At the present time the informal trend dominates. We have become so thoroughly imbued with the idea that organic forms based essentially on natural functions are assymetrical that we are often blinded to the equally valid truth that some problems are formal in their very nature." (2, p. 571).

aware of how radically Mondrian's system of composition differs from all previous examples, nor how catalytic in the evolution of modern architecture was Van Doesburg's influence in the early 1920s. He fails completely to make clear how absolutely opposed were the compositions of De Stijl and Constructivism to the principles of Guadet and his generation.[17]

Rowe goes on to note how Hamlin assumes that there is a "naturalistic" basis to all form and how he refuses to acknowledge even the possibility of ideological intent in the process of design and yet as Rowe remarks,

to select the Customs House at New Bedford, Massachusetts, as an illustration of "style resulting from materials," from "granite detailed to express its strength and natural origins," is less than half the explanation of a building in which the most unpracticed eye can detect the predominant influence of the internationally diffused neo-Classical ideal.... Mr. Hamlin is confident that "the historical style of the twentieth century is being inexorably developed... by many forces — economic, sociological, industrial, political...," that "we are expressing our culture, whether we will or no; just because we are architects living at a certain time and in a certain place...," but he is not willing to go further. He examines results but not motivations, and from a reading of this treatise one might think that the twentieth century is being defined largely by external pressures, since so little attempt is made to define its internal, specifically architectural initiative.[18]

Frederick Gutheim was equally categoric and critical in his otherwise gentlemanly review that appeared at the same time. He wrote:

Twenty years ago Hitchcock and Johnson first tried to formulate a description of modern architecture in their pioneer study, The International Style. *Theirs was a fully doctrinaire approach, in terms of which Wright and other romantics — Maybeck, Greene and Greene, and the rest — were completely eliminated, and a set of rules formulated that fit Mies, Gropius and Le Corbusier, but few others. The most creative group of Americans, in the '30's in California, were totally ignored. Figures like Dudok, Mendelsohn, Perret or the elder Saarinen were dismissed. For all its weaknesses of omission...Hitchcock and Johnson took a stand; no one was in doubt where they stood or what they considered good architecture or bad.*

Hamlin's description of modern architecture errs in the opposite direction. Anything goes. On his analysis, any set of architectural ideas can result in a masterpiece. Perhaps it can, in a generous historical perspective; but whether it can more narrowly in terms of an architecture of our own time is certainly a dubious contention, ... perhaps the fairest view of Hamlin's own philosophy is one which recognizes his basic orientation in 19th century liberal thought. He subscribes to the ideals of Morris and Ruskin. He is a democrat, one willing to carry democratic ideas all the way through an industrial society. His ideas on land, labor, capital are liberal. All this equips him to understand and sympathize with those who were in revolt against the architecture of the traditional styles. But his personal taste is a romantic taste, his viewpoint gentle and catholic, and his historical interests and sympathies are so profound one frequently suspects him of disloyalty to his own generation.[19]

17. Colin Rowe, Review of "Former and Functions of 20th Century Architecture," *Architectural Forum,* in *The Art Bulletin* (April 1953), p. 169.

18. Ibid.

19. Frederick Gutheim, "Former and Functions of 20th Century Architecture," *Architectural Forum,* 96 (June 1952), pp. 152-154.

This is certainly a strong accusation and one wonders to what extent it could have been applied to other luminaries on the Columbia faculty during the period. Certainly Arnaud was as catholic if he wasn't quite so liberal but what of Joseph Hudnut, that almost mythic figure, who brought Hamlin into the School proper in 1934, for the purpose of teaching history and whose taste, while not perhaps as liberal or as catholic, was certainly just as romantic, particularly at mid-career, when as Acting Dean of the Faculty he gave the first of the Mathews Lectures under the title of *The Gothic Universitie*. For while Hudnut was to expound with ironic and donnish detachment on the ideological folly of the English Gothic Revival, when, as he put it, "men looked up from their ledgers to catch with a growing certainty the shimmer and stir of antique pageantry" and while he praised, no doubt with Hamlin's approval, McKim's decision to dress the Morningside Heights campus in Roman cornices rather than Gothic spires, he was in his turn a romantic rather than a classicist, for he concluded his otherwise urbane paper with a Futurist image of Columbia University rebuilt "in order to affirm its kinship with the great city at its feet;" an image in part compounded out of Hugh Ferriss' ziggurat metropolis and in part inspired by Antonio Sant Elia's technological vision. "The pattern of my facades," Hudnut wrote,

should repeat the million eyes that catch the sun along the cliff of Riverside Drive; they should confess their harmony with the frail ocean liners in the river below, with the grace of airplanes, with the colossal energy that bent the steel bow of the Hudson bridge against the wall of the Palisades. [20]

Throughout his nine years tenure at Columbia, Hudnut welcomed Germanic modernism in all its aspects, with an intelligence and conviction which was apparently only belatedly shared by Hamlin, although as the years advanced he grew closer to the latter's liberalism. In 1949, when Hudnut published his collected essays, *Architecture and the Spirit of Man*, the fruit no doubt of the often difficult fourteen-year period which he had already spent with Walter Gropius and Marcel Breuer developing the program of the Graduate School of Design at Harvard, Hudnut's views approximated those of eclectic modernism which three years later would inform the pages of *Forms and Functions in 20th Century Architecture*. By the late 1940's the positions of Hamlin and Hudnut were extremely close, with the singular exception that Hudnut categorically refused to accept that in a modern technological welfare state, Neo-classicism could still be adduced or even reinterpreted as the primary representative architecture. Hudnut's reasoning in this regard is worth repeating if for no other reason than that it represents the New Humanist-New Empiricist-Late Bauhaus position with regard to the still-emerging New Deal cultural policy in architecture; a position more or less shared at that time by Anglo-Saxon *emigré* intellectuals as diverse in temper as Serge Chermayeff and Christopher Tunnard. Thus in his provocative piece "The Obelisk of General Washington,"[21] we find Hudnut writing:

In his famous essay, Vers une architecture, *Le Corbusier tells us that the*

20. Joseph Hudnut, "The Gothick Universitie." *Columbia University Quarterly* (March 1934), No:1, p. 9.

21. While Chermayeff was of Russian origin he had in fact been educated in England from the age of 11 onward.

primary geometric shapes are essential to beauty in architecture — without explaining how these are possible in our modern complexity of use or to the inexhaustible variety of our machines.... The buildings of our age will assume, are assuming, a complexity of shape not unlike that of Baroque architecture and yet without that sculptural fluidity or that exultant ecstasy which gave unity to its energetic rhythms; a complexity which may be also, provided we continue with our present speculations into the aesthetics of structure, not unlike Gothic complexity but without that mist of pinnacle and saint which veils the logical surface of the cathedrals.... I have tried to bring my readers not a descriptive or critical analysis of classical architecture but rather a review of those tendencies in this architecture which it seems to me, prevent its use as a language of modernism; its dependence upon a mass and weight inconsistent with our technologies of structure, its basic simplicity of shape which deny the variety and complexity of our buildings, and that abstract and static formalism into which we cannot translate the realism and onrushing temper of our day.[22]

For once, in the light of these remarks, Hamlin and Le Corbusier found themselves inadvertently on the same side of history; the one on account of his perennial Jeffersonian nostalgia, the other for his Late Enlightenment adaptation of the Hegelian dialectic. But the proof of Hudnut's fidelity to a brand of modernism more specific and urgent than that aspired to by Hamlin did not simply reside in this, nor did it derive solely from his historic importation of Weimar culture. Hudnut's modernist loyalty stemmed in the last analysis from his unequivocal support for the structurally expressive architecture of his time; the modern "free style," one might say, which assumed a wide range of formal expression from the Cubistic asperities of Richard Neutra's Lovell House of 1927, to the Neo-Baroque of Oscar Niemeyer's Brazilian Pavilion designed with Paul Lester Weiner for the 1939 New York World's Fair. At times this gamut veered towards coarse, schematic abstraction as in Wallace Harrison's United Nations Headquarters of 1948, at times it aspired to a fairly stringent re-interpretation of local vernacular as in Gropius' brick-faced Harvard Graduate Center of the following year; but in any event this seems to have been the drift of the stylistic range practiced in Columbia University's graduate school during its modernist prime, that is to say, from the time of Hudnut's curriculum reform of 1934 almost up to Hamlin's retirement as Professor of Architecture exactly twenty years later. That the liberal pedagogic consensus would come out in favor of a Cubistic free-style is perfectly understandable, for Le Corbusier was too formalist and Mies too technological and Wright, although possessing the virtues of American origin, was too idiosyncratic.

Hamlin differed from Hudnut not only in his reluctance to advocate any particular modernist style, but also in his nostalgia for an idyllic, if not mythical, America that had long since passed away. Like William Morris in *News from Nowhere,* Hamlin cherished the idea of a normative architecture which would one day be, again, representative of an as yet unborn provincial democracy; that state mythically embodied in Jefferson's America, or rather more precisely that revolutionary promised land to which Benja-

22. Joseph Hudnut, *Architecture and the Spirit of Man,* (Cambridge, Mass.: Harvard University Press, 1949), p. 26.

min Latrobe migrated in 1795, to witness and experience the first fruits of democracy in Richmond and to die twenty-five years later penniless and disillusioned in New Orleans. In *Benjamin Henry Latrobe*, his finest scholarly work, published in 1955, Hamlin wrote, a year before his own untimely death, an epitaph for Latrobe that today might well be applied to himself.

Theoretically he believed in English liberty to the uttermost. He was a passionate supporter of Charles James Fox. Personally he was always a hater of oppression, yet, in practice he saw that democratic action had often resulted merely in schism and futility, and he admired action and results. Evident. . . therefore, are the foundations of a fundamental split in him — a split that at times of discouragement could result in an almost complete cynicism with regard to the effects of political actions, yet a split that never resulted in his abandonment of his basically democratic ideals.[23]

Hamlin isolated two essential and extremely significant features in the life and work of Latrobe; first, that as an English *emigré* he found himself in constant conflict with the perennial American tendency to treat artifacts in terms of improvisation and obsolescence and second, that the fertility of Latrobe's Neo-classicism was grounded in *architectonic* invention. Where the former contributed to Latrobe's ruin — it broke him so to speak on the rock of expediency (he constantly fought to have his lock gates lined with stone instead of timber); the latter brought him close, in such buildings as the Old Supreme Court, to anticipating Louis Kahn, who at the time that Hamlin was working on Latrobe, was already reinterpreting the ethos of Neo-classicism at Yale and Philadelphia. Thus Hamlin, in assessing the final worth of Latrobe's tectonic invention could well have been summing up Kahn when he wrote:

This at once gave his buildings a practical rightness, a reality and a variety that were rare in the United States. It led him inevitably to experiment in different types of construction — particularly in the use of vaults as controlling elements in the design — which raised the best of his work to a plane far above the merely decorative or merely useful.[24]

These words have an admonitory ring today as we stand on the threshold of abandoning the architectonic in favor of scenography.

For Hudnut, towards the end of life, form was the final arbiter in architecture as we learn from the last chapter of his book *The Three Lamps of Architecture* published in 1954. Hudnut refused to accept that there was any necessary contradiction between the architect's commitment to form and welfare provisions of the state. Hamlin on the other hand could never rest content with a hypothetical separation of powers between form and society and so he returned, as an historian, to the only socio-cultural milieu with which his spirit felt at peace, to the mythical republic of the American Greek Revival. Given his pragmatic and otherwise romantic cast of mind he could not even countenance positing for his own time the possibility of achieving a *repetition différente*.

23. Talbot F. Hamlin, *Benjamin Henry Latrobe* (New York: Oxford University Press, 1955).

24. Ibid.

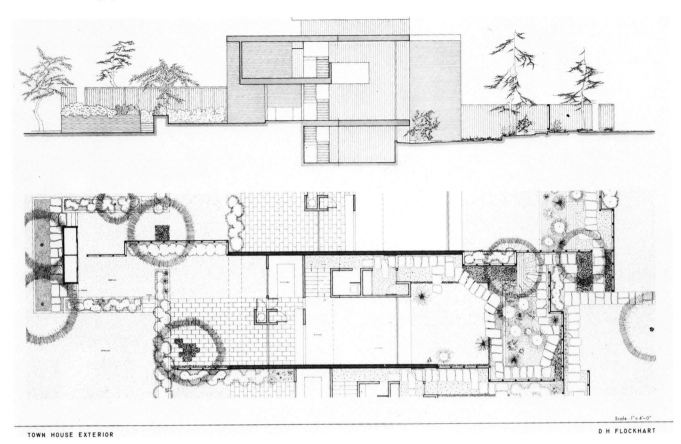

TOWN HOUSE EXTERIOR

Scale . 1" = 4'-0"

D H FLOCKHART

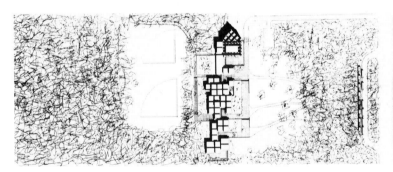

Above: Town House, 1962, Douglas H. Flockhart *(1964)*. 2nd year project Photo: Jan Pokorny.

Middle: K through 6 Suburban School, 1967, John Boerger *(1968)*. Photo: GSAP Archives.

Below: Millar Field Housing, 1967, Thomas Stetz *(1969)*. Photo: GSAP Archive.

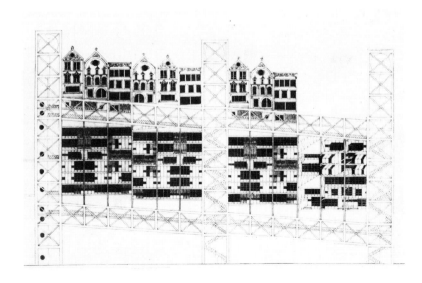

Le Corbusier lectures at the *Four Great Makers of Modern Architecture* series, Spring, 1961. Photo: Jan Pokorny.

History VI: 1959–1968

Richard Oliver

I n the spring of 1958, Leopold Arnaud indicated to President Kirk that he wished to retire at the end of the first semester of the academic year 1958–1959.[1] Accordingly, on July 17, 1958, Kirk appointed a committee composed of alumni Max Abramovitz *(1931),* Morris Ketcham, Jr. *(1931),* Thorne Sherwood *(1936),* Frederick Woodbridge *(1923),* Assistant Dean Kenneth Smith, and Avery Librarian James Van Derpool to seek a replacement for Arnaud. The Committee shared the opinion of Smith who stated that "to overcome the unfortunate reputation under which the School now labors, it needs a head who has a reputation in the profession as an architect and a designer."[2] The Committee took the opportunity to review the status and general direction of the School itself. In their deliberations, two themes recurred:

that [the School] ought to be the finest…in the world, due to its unique location in a great University and in what is unquestionably the architectural center of the country…[and] a general feeling that the Columbia school has never quite lived up to that opportunity or fully taken advantage of that situation.[3]

The Committee held definite opinions on curricular structure, believing that the School "must accept as its first responsibility the offering of the strongest professional curriculum possible leading to the Bachelor of Architecture degree. The development of a strong graduate program should be a concurrent step." The Committee was convinced that "any attempt at an exclusively graduate program without a strong undergraduate school would be a disappointing venture. It would surely have a very limited scope and enrollment and would inevitably become almost

1. Kirk to Arnaud, 23 July 1958, Central Files, Columbia University (hereafter Central Files).

2. Smith to Kirk, 2 May 1959, Central Files.

3. Search Committee to Kirk, 28 May 1959, Central Files.

entirely devoted to architectural history or highly specialized and esoteric subjects." It is clear that the Committee was endorsing as the School's primary role that of training individuals for places in the practice of architecture. As an adjunct to that primary professional obligation, a graduate program would allow qualified students to "pursue research in special fields among which urban planning should have an important emphasis."[4]

To lead the School, the Committee proposed a "two-part affair, requiring an able administrator and policy maker and secondly a director of design." For the head of design, the Committee sought "a man of broad interests and sympathies and not the 'master' type demanding slavish disciples of some one particular facet of architecture. No matter how eminent or well-known, the doctrinaire teacher is not what is envisaged as right for Columbia." The Committee was deliberately seeking an alternative to the direction taken by several of Columbia's sister schools. Columbia would not have an equivalent to Paul Rudolph at Yale, or Jose Louis Sert at Harvard, or Louis Kahn at Penn, men who completely dominated the architectural discourse at their respective schools. The Committee also took a stand against faculty who practiced, noting that the new Dean should be able to raise faculty salaries "to a point where the demands of the School take precedence over those of outside practice."[5]

While the Committee pursued its task of finding a candidate for the Deanship, Kirk and the Trustees addressed themselves to the appointment of an Acting Dean. On January 5, 1959, the Trustees appointed James Van Derpool, a member of the Search Committee, "as Acting Dean of the Faculty of Architecture from February 1, 1959," a choice which met with the approval of Arnaud.[6]

James Grote Van Derpool was born on July 21, 1903. He graduated from the School of Architecture at M.I.T. in 1927 and later attended the Ecole des Beaux-Arts and the American Academy in Rome, followed by graduate study at Harvard. Van Derpool was both an architect and architectural historian. A charter member of the Society of Architectural Historians and a trustee of the American Scenic and Historic Preservation Society, he taught architectural history at the University of Illinois before coming to Columbia University in 1946 as the sixth Avery Librarian.[7]

Van Derpool had no ambitions to seek the Deanship, urging the Trustees to quickly find a replacement for Arnaud. Though Kirk advised him that an interim period was not a time for modification or change, Van Derpool enlivened the School where he could. Among these efforts was a new lecture series that brought important scholars and practitioners to the School, including Buckminster Fuller, Max Abramovitz, and Henry-Russell Hitchcock. Frank Lloyd Wright was scheduled to speak the week of his death.[8]

Yet in his first report, submitted in June, 1959, Van Derpool displayed a broad understanding of the issues facing the profession of architecture and urged that these be kept in mind in the selection of a new Dean. He noted the impact of new structural principles like thin-shell construction and pre-stressed concrete, and he was

4. Ibid.

5. Ibid.

6. Van Derpool to Richard Herpers, 8 January 1959, Central Files; John Mullins to Arnaud, 5 January 1959, Central Files; Arnaud to Kirk, 5 January 1959, Central Files.

7. Press release, 19 January 1959, Central Files.

8. Van Derpool, "Report of the Dean of the Faculty of Architecture for the Period July 1, 1958 through June 30, 1959," p. 7, Central Files.

aware of the diversity of aesthetic approaches to architecture that were then being explored as the International Style was breaking up. He called attention to the distinctly varied objectives of Le Corbusier, Mies van der Rohe, Wright, Edward Durell Stone, Wallace Harrison, and Eero Saarinen, and contrasted all of these men with English "New Brutalism." He observed the uncertain relationships among architects, planners, industrial designers, and structural engineers. Related to this broad understanding of the state of the profession, Van Derpool discussed the role of the School:

We need gifted professors with taste and a firm sense of values to guide the future practitioners. We must provide a vital climate for both faculty and students, one which is conducive to sustained philosophical and practical speculation. We must avoid a premature focusing on any one approach and a frank spirit of inquiry should be promoted.[9]

Apart from proposals for minor administrative changes, Van Derpool proposed three new graduate programs for consideration:

Scholarly investigation of the architectural utilization of new structural techniques — both in their utilitarian and esthetic aspects.

A graduate program for the training of architectural critics, theoreticians, and editorial specialists of a stature that we simply do not possess at the present time.

A national graduate center for the training of the scholarly Preservationist Architect, qualified to handle with scientific and historical accuracy the preservation of the significant buildings and monuments that record the life of our Nation.[10]

None of Van Derpool's suggestions was implemented under his own direction, but of the three, the last was independently developed by James Marston Fitch in the years after 1964 into the program in Historic Preservation.[11]

Van Derpool was Acting Dean for only three semesters, and had no real opportunity to make an imprint on the School. He was a scholarly, essentially academic man, and in the wake of Arnaud's long tenure, opinion once again favored a practitioner-dean. Accordingly, the Search Committee did not seriously consider Van Derpool as a candidate for Dean, but approached such young, distinguished professionals as William Caudill and I.M. Pei, each of whom preferred to remain in his firm rather than to administer a school. From a list of fifty-five potential candidates, three men of diverse qualifications were selected by the Committee to be interviewed for the Deanship: Albert Bush-Brown, the historian then on the faculty at M.I.T.; Henry Kamphoefner *(Columbia, 1931),* the forceful head of the School of Design at North Carolina State University; and Charles Colbert *(Columbia, 1947),* an accomplished practitioner from New Orleans.[12]

Charles Colbert was offered the position of Dean, effective April 1, 1960, in part because the Committee admired his

ability to inspire and stimulate enthusiasm and dedication in young men. He is obviously dedicated to his profession himself and has strong convictions and ideas about architectural education. The Committee is

James Van Derpool.
Photo: Columbia University.

9. Ibid., pp. 1-4.

10. Ibid., pp. 5-6.

11. See Fitch essay elsewhere in this book.

12. Search Committee to Kirk, 28 May 1959, Central Files.

*deeply impressed by his attitude and evident understanding of what the
Columbia School of Architecture might become.*[13]

Charles Ralph Colbert was born on June 23, 1921, at Dow,
Oklahoma. He received a Bachelor of Architecture at the
University of Texas at Austin in 1943, and a Master of Science in
Architecture from Columbia University in 1947. He taught at
Texas A&M University and at Tulane University, and practiced in
New Orleans before assuming the Deanship on April 1, 1960.[14] In
accepting the position, Colbert wrote to Grayson Kirk that he
"considered it absolutely essential that the new Dean visit several of
the better schools of architecture in this country and in Europe
before any changes should be made at Columbia," and that he do
so "while they are in operation, to observe the best in current
practices."[15] After Arnaud's long tenure when the School held to
a steady course, it seemed prudent to Colbert and to Kirk that such
visits should be made. Colbert completed his visits in the late
spring of 1960, before preparing a plan for the revitalization of the
School at Columbia.

In a letter to Jacques Barzun, the Dean of Faculties, Colbert
expressed his goals for the School: "I am convinced that
Columbia's School of Architecture can and should become the
most contributive academic force in twentieth century architecture. To accomplish this, three objectives should be placed before
the School: to prepare the student, to inspire the active professional, and to inform the public at large of the aims of the
profession." He felt four things had to be present to allow this: a
"climate allowing reasonable academic experimentation and
opportunities for real community service projects," "adequate
budget and facilities," "an energetic, spirited, and even inspired
teaching and research staff must be developed...under conditions
where personal objectives are aligned with the direction of the
architectural school as a whole," and last, "outstanding students
must be attracted to the school and challenged to their ultimate
potential."[16]

Some of the themes of Colbert's letter reflected those of the
early 1960's in American society: the call for change and
revitalization, for active involvement in the broad world of affairs,
and for excellence of effort after what was then perceived to be the
lethargy and mediocrity of the 1950's. One theme was not:
Colbert's call for a faculty whose personal objectives were aligned
with the School as a whole seemed to suggest a repression of
individual differences and ran counter both to a long tradition of
intellectual independence for members of an academic community
and to what became a burgeoning individualism in the 1960's.
Colbert's brief tenure as Dean was marked by a sense of high
optimism and an earnest search for new directions in architecture,
and marred by reaction and dissent on the part of the faculty and
students.

Part of Colbert's charge when appointed Dean was to renew the
public image of the School, and to that end he organized a
symposium in 1961 called *Four Great Makers of Modern Architecture.*[17] From March through May of 1961, eight programs, called

13. Ibid.

14. Colbert's curriculum vitae, Central Files.

15. Colbert to Kirk, 4 August 1959, Central Files. Colbert's
list of schools to visit included Harvard, M.I.T., Yale,
Princeton, Penn, I.I.T., the Institute for Design at Ulm,
Germany, the Institute of Technology at Zurich, and the
Institute of Architecture at the University of Venice.

16. Colbert to Barzun, 14 July 1959, Central Files.

17. *Four Great Makers of Modern Architecture* (New York:
Trustees of Columbia University, 1963).

"Cycles," took place, and three special convocations were assembled in the Low Rotunda at Columbia. At two of the convocations, honorary degrees were conferred upon Walter Gropius and upon Le Corbusier. At the third convocation, Mies van der Rohe, who could not attend, was represented by a taped interview. The fourth "Great Maker," Frank Lloyd Wright, had died in 1959. The events surrounding the symposium attracted a wide array of participants and a large audience, and was clearly an important national event in architecture.[18]

Colbert delivered the keynote talk, "Conformity, Chaos, and Continuity," and his description of the purpose of the symposium implied as well his goals for the School:

To these meetings we attach the utmost importance and the highest hopes. Our purposes are several: to honor four pioneers of our profession to whom we owe an immeasurable debt and in the spirit of these men to honor the profession itself, to reaffirm our faith in its controlling and its ordering power without which our threatened civilization could indeed succumb to waste, confusion, ugliness, and violence. And lastly we assemble, humbly and proudly aware of our powers and responsibilities, for an even greater purpose: to call for a critical re-examination of the central issues facing us today and to plead for a new formulation of principles and perspective for the future.

I am not an historian, but a practicing architect and teacher, and I am thus directly and doubly caught up in the uncertainties, the dilemmas, and the challenge of the architectural movement. The general situation of architecture today is a serious one. Our cities and all our human establishments have become so disordered and squalid that most of the visual beauty we find in our human environment is accidental. Certainly, factors have entered over which the architect has no control, if we define architect in the broadest possible sense: not only as the designer of structures, but also as the planner of communities; not only as the draftsman of projects, but also as the realizer, the builder, the entrepeneur; not only as the imaginative artist, but also as the engineer.

What can the architect do? When I said that the forces which endanger not only architecture but human society as a whole are beyond his control and not of his making, I certainly did not mean that he should abdicate. On the contrary, never was there greater need for leadership by architects, leadership not only in social planning and esthetic education, but also leadership in the design of objects in our daily life and in the never-ending battle against shoddy design, shoddy production, and misleading promotion. If we believe that architecture is really the central art, the 'mother' art as it has been called, if we believe that it is the activity which creates order out of space and matter, then that order must animate the small and the large, the seemingly unimportant as well as the decisive.

The architect will, if he can attain that leadership which we demand from him, be a jack of many trades. He will be a Pied Piper and a high priest, a judge, an analyst, a salesman. But whatever he does, he will stand for the qualitative principle and the whole problem, not merely the easy, normative answer. He will not want to sell products, but counsel; he will not process, but create; he will not succumb to his client's demands and to his society, but will reasonably conform with them. He will speak to his client and to society with the voice of logic: the logic of concrete, steel, and

Charles Ralph Colbert.
Photo: Columbia University.

18. Interview: Jan Pokorny by Author, 20 August 1981.

glass, the logic of material in a structure, and, particularly, the logic of spirit.[19]

Although the *Four Great Makers* symposium brought the School much needed public attention, it was essentially a one-time event without lasting effect. Much more important, and substantive, were Colbert's introduction of interdisciplinary study and "real problems," revisions of the curricular structure of the School, and changes in the faculty.

Colbert was most influential at the graduate level in the School. He translated his broad goals into specific policies which stressed interdisciplinary studies, a rational basis for design, collaboration with many of the "real world" participants in the building process, and most especially the introduction of real projects into the academic setting. Students worked on eight such "real" projects during Colbert's tenure, all at the graduate level.[20] Chief among these was a study of the Central Business District of Dallas, Texas. "One Main Place" involved the design of a major grouping of buildings in downtown Dallas — a project which Colbert regarded as in the spirit of Rockefeller Center. The studio project was funded by a large grant from Dallas business interests, and involved a response to actual parameters.[21] In the early 1960's, the idea of students working on complex, mixed-use, urban projects was still relatively new, and Colbert's changes introduced to the School the concept that architectural practice could take new directions.[22]

The graduate program in architecture was developed into three areas of study. "One Main Place" represented one, the study of Central Business Districts. The second was the study of medical facilities, and was arranged as an interdisciplinary course involving both the School of Architecture and the School of Public Health. The third area focused on educational facilities, and was arranged as an interdisciplinary course involving the School and Columbia Teachers' College.[23]

Colbert's belief in interdisciplinary studies was reinforced by three types of faculty appointments. First, he hired individuals other than practicing architects to be adjunct professors, like Douglas Haskell, an editor of *The Architectural Forum,* and Jay Marc Schwamm, a banker; second, he hired practitioners to give courses in the relationship of the architect to a related field, such as "The Architect and the Entrepeneur;" and three, he searched the University for members of other faculties to give courses in architecture, such as Rudolph Wittkower, George Collins, and Edgar Kaufmann, jr., all members of the Department of Fine Arts and Archeology, who gave courses in the School of Architecture.[24]

Colbert's initial revisions in the curriculum were at the undergraduate level. During the academic year 1961–1962, he changed the name and description of various courses in an attempt to have them seem fresh and relevant. For example, "Introduction to architecture" and "Descriptive geometry" were combined to become "Design I: introduction," and "History of medieval architecture" became "History III: special problems in medieval

One Main Place, Dallas, Texas, 1961, Design team: Rudolph Arsenicos *(1962)*, George Chranewycz *(1962)*, Dennis Clark *(1962)*, Sanford Collins *(1962)*, Lynn Cowles *(1961)*, Jane Lyle Piepeveen *(1963)*, George Fasic *(1962)*, Dale Hutton *(1961)*, Ted Litzenberger *(1961)*, Pedro Lopez *(1963)*, Dimitri Porkhayeff *(1963)*, Leonard Schickler *(1962)*, Nathan Sobel *(1962)*, William Sorrentino *(1963)*, Robert Strebi *(1962)*, Narelle Ray Townsend *(1962)*, and Charles Vogelstein *(1962)*.

19. Colbert, "Conformity, Chaos, and Continuity," *Four Great Makers,* pp. 1-5. For a compilation of Colbert's lectures over the years, see Charles Colbert, *18 Talks* (New Orleans: 1969).

20. Colbert to Kirk, 18 March 1963, Central Files.

21. Ibid. See also, Interview: Colbert by Author, 4 February 1981, Graduate School of Architecture and Planning archives (hereafter GSAP archives).

22. Interview: Robert Harper by Author, 25 June 1981.

23. Interview: Colbert by Author, 4 February 1981.

24. Ibid.

architecture." Entirely new courses were offered, like "History I: special problems in the evolution of cities."[25]

To establish an orderly structure of courses and content, Colbert initiated a Committee on Instruction which met weekly and whose job it was to coordinate all courses within the four-year design program and to integrate graphics, structures, theory, and construction with design. This committee was composed of the senior faculty, and Colbert gave it a degree of independence. This was different from Arnaud's tenure when the Dean monitored all courses and design programs for content and even for language.[26]

The structure of the design sequence as it emerged in the academic year 1961–1962 was as follows: the first year was devoted to an introduction to architecture and to design fundamentals; second year was devoted to skills, to the broad question of "how to do it"; third year was given over to visiting critics; and fourth year retained the traditional independent student thesis. The evening program adhered to this sequence, but over the usual seven-year period.[27] The content of the design sequence was also carefully ordered. A second-year project might be a suburban housing project, and the class would spend the whole term on it, considering first the site plan, then the typical street, a unit block, the house itself, the landscape and graphics for the whole project, and as a final recap, the site plan again.[28] Third-year projects were for multi-story buildings and more complex programs such as schools. The fourth-year thesis had to be a "real project," the student was required to seek out and work with a client as the basis for designing a scheme.[29]

Colbert placed his emphasis and his energies in the graduate program, in part because he felt that Columbia should become primarily a graduate school, despite the opinions of the Search Committee that had selected him. As part of that overall strategy, Colbert was intent on phasing out the Evening Program, and did two things to encourage its demise: he transferred Jan Pokorny, the Director of the Evening Program, to the day program; and he moved the program itself out of Avery Hall into the Mathematics Building across campus. The latter had the effect of instilling a sense of camaraderie in the evening students. A year later, Colbert became aware that the better students in the fourth year of the School's program (where day and evening students were enrolled together) were often from the Evening Program. As a result, Pokorny was reinstated as Director and Colbert changed his intentions to phase out the program.[30]

In all of these changes, Colbert was attempting to revitalize the content of the curriculum, the structure of which had not been significantly altered since 1936. Not surprisingly, his efforts were resisted by the tenured faculty. The faculty of the School in 1960 was composed of a number of tenured members, many of whom had been at the School for over ten years, such as Percival Goodman, Albert Halse, Eugene Raskin, and Charles Rieger, together with younger, untenured members like John Fowler and Gerhardt Kallmann. The faculty of any school is at all times a force for continuity in the succession of administrators, and that

25. *School of Architecture Handbook of Information, 1960–1961,* and *School of Architecture Handbook of Information, 1961–1962.*

26. Interview: Pokorny by Author, 20 August 1981.

27. Ibid.

28. Interview: Colbert by Author, 4 February 1981.

29. Interview: Pokorny by Author, 20 August 1981.

30. Ibid.

continuity is often a valuable asset. But when a Dean is hired with a mandate to change a school, that same tenured faculty is often viewed as a liability, as a bastion of "old ways," and this was the case with Colbert and much of the tenured faculty he inherited.

Beginning in the academic year 1961–1962, Colbert assigned his tenured faculty to teach courses different from their usual assignments, and this tended to anger the faculty members who felt, with some justification, that certain perquisites had been taken away.[31] Colbert's intention was to force his tenured faculty to approach coursework in a fresh way, but the inadvertent result was a faculty split in its opinion of the Dean. In addition to the faculty appointments he made for purely interdisciplinary purposes, Colbert was able to hire a number of other new faculty, some as permanent faculty and others as visiting critics. Chief among the former was Edward Romieniec, who had taught at Texas A & M University under Colbert in the 1950's and who had been regarded by students there as an inspiring and influential teacher.[32] Chief among the visiting critics were Ernest Kump, whose Foothill College near San Francisco, redolent of the work of William Wurster, was then receiving much praise, and Harwell Hamilton Harris, well-known in the 1940's and 1950's for his simple, wooden, Craftsman-like houses.

To parallel the changes in the structure and content of the School, Colbert instituted physical changes in Avery Hall. The tables in the drafting studios were pre-arranged in rows before the start of the term, and all the table tops were covered with white material. The fourth-floor hallway became a gallery, and as Cecil Steward, a graduate student in 1960–1961 recalls, "there were exciting exhibits put up in the hallways. Suddenly there was an atmosphere, whether you liked it or not, it was an atmosphere of attention to design."[33]

In starting to revitalize the School, Colbert naturally assumed that it would be able eventually to take a more active and more important role in the architectural decisions of the University. By longstanding University policy, the faculty of the School could not accept University building commissions, nor was the faculty allowed any significant involvement in the awarding of those commissions.[34] This created an awkward situation in which the University desired to have an excellent School of Architecture, but would not allow the members of that School, however talented, to have an effect on University building operations. It was apparent in 1960 that with the construction of Ferris-Booth Hall in 1959, the University was not seeking the best architects for its buildings. This observation was confirmed by the construction of Uris Hall in 1962 and the Law School in 1964. The quality of these buildings stood in striking contrast to the world-famous buildings being commissioned by Yale University at the same time, often awarding commissions to its architecture faculty. Furthermore, these newer, banal Columbia buildings seemed then, and now, to be a dismal departure from the high standards of McKim, Mead & White's original campus.

Although Colbert failed to change this policy, he was able to

31. The feelings of some of the Faculty toward Colbert are covered in letters by Percival Goodman, Alexander Kouzmanoff, and Albert Halse in Central Files.

32. Interview: Cecil Steward by Author, 27 February 1981, GSAP archives.

33. Ibid.

34. The Dean of the School was an *ex officio* member of the University's Advisor Council on Architecture. The Council would offer opinions on University building plans. However, by the time the Council was asked to do so, the program for the proposed building had been approved by the President, an architect had been appointed, and a general site had been selected. Thus, the Council could comment only upon purely formal issues, unrelated to program or site, and on this matter, the Council complained. See Architectural Advisory Council Minutes, 8 January 1963, Central Files.

subvert it in two instances: he appointed Jan Pokorny of the faculty as the architect for a renovation of Lewisohn Hall;[35] and he carried out a controversial study of the Columbia University South Campus as a studio project that was published in booklet form after he had left the School.[36] But in general, Colbert came to feel that the University had undercut his goals for the School by prohibiting its wider role in campus architecture.[37]

Although Colbert assumed the Deanship with the full confidence of the Search Committee and with high hopes of his own, almost immediately his tenure was marked by reaction and dissent, in part because of his autocratic manner and in part because he seemed not able to fully distinguish between the nature of a professional office and that of an academic institution. In search of a new sense of discipline, Colbert issued a handbook of rules that among other things governed the use of radios in Avery Hall, required all drafting stations, including the angle and position of the desk and the type of light, to conform to a single studio-wide standard, and required each student to have "an artistic object" and a name card on his or her drafting board.[38] While at least conceivable and enforceable in a professional office, the students regarded such rules as irrelevant and unduly restrictive in an academic setting, and as a result found them unpalatable.[39] Likewise, Colbert's broad view of professional responsibility to collective society seemed to many to be unrelated to formal issues of any kind. Colbert deplored the aim of the Ecole des Beaux-Arts, "based as it was upon a world of romantic hope and a vanishing social tradition;" he criticized the Bauhaus' "very limited attention to the broader social, political, economic, and organizational changes at work in society;" and in the new, overtly sculptural buildings of the late 1950's, he saw only "unrestrained self-expression" and "effluvium aesthetic philosophies."[40] By focusing so intensely on the broader context of which architecture is a part, Colbert seemed to fail to characterize the more particular tasks and responsibilities which an architect can more reasonably undertake.[41]

Colbert's optimism regarding interdisciplinary work and a revitalized School was not easily translated into a workable curriculum, an appropriate faculty, or a convincing architectural pedagogy. Unable to move forward with the speed and the resolution he could envisage, he appeared to openly disdain the very constituencies he had to inspire, that is, the students, the faculty, the administration, and the alumni. At the Alumni Day Open House on February 12, 1963, Colbert publicly berated the students for not working hard enough, his faculty for not being competent enough, and the administration and the alumni for insufficient support, and he did so in a manner that was regarded as brusque and divisive. This single event unleashed a strong response from faculty, students, and alumni alike and led to Colbert's resignation on April 3, 1963.[42]

Upon Colbert's resignation, Kenneth Smith, the Associate Dean, was appointed Acting Dean until a new Dean could be found.[43] Kenneth Alexander Smith was born on July 16, 1905, in

35. Interview: Pokorny by Author, 20 August 1981.

36. *Columbia University South Campus Study*, GSAP archives. This study was strongly endorsed by the Advisory Council on Architecture at its meeting of 15 January 1963:

It was agreed to make the strongest recommendation possible for a complete study of the South Campus. This is a major undertaking and involves practical consideration of such things as existing utilities and possible changes of facilities, the number of levels forming terraces for complete or partial coverage of the area, etc. Consultation with other institutions such as St. Luke's Hospital, the Cathedral, St. Luke's Home and the Home for Old Men and Aged Couples is of the greatest importance. We must try to enlist their cooperation in maintaining their planning in fluid state until the best description of their required facilities can be determined so that the best possible overall plan may be produced. The importance of open spaces, the tying in of vistas and creating settings for the Cathedral and important buildings was stressed.

The architecture of the South Campus should be developed independently of existing architecture. There is no need for continuing the tradition of the old Columbia buildings. The South Campus will be an entity in itself and should represent the best obtainable expression of a modern urban university campus (Council Minutes, 15 January 1963, Central Files).

At its meeting of 5 February 1963, the Council endorsed:

Dean Colbert's proposal that a group of graduate architecture students do a study of the South Campus. It was stressed that this student study would in no way be a substitute for a full fledged professional study. The study would, however, have the effect of instilling an initial awareness in those who will have to be supplying the necessary data for any study of campus development (Council Minutes, 5 February 1963, Central Files).

37. Interview: Colbert by Author, 4 February 1981.

38. *Handbook of Student Regulations*, September 1961, Central Files.

39. Interview: Harper by Author, 25 June 1981.

40. Colbert to Kirk, 18 March 1963, Central Files.

41. In what could be construed as a criticism of Colbert's administration of the School, in January, 1963, eleven second-year students jointly enquired about admission to Yale University with the intention to transfer. The University first became aware of this when Paul Rudolph, then chairman of the department of architecture at Yale, wrote to President Kirk. See Rudolph to Kirk, 29 March 1963, Central Files.

42. On 16 February 1963, four days after Colbert's speech, Charles Rieger of the Faculty sent a memorandum of complaint to Colbert, with copies to Associate Dean Kenneth Smith, Jan Pokorny, Richard Boring Snow of the Alumni Association, and Members of the Faculty and Staff of the School. By early March, Jacques Barzun of the University administration was conducting interviews of students and faculty. On 3 April 1963, Colbert met with Kirk and offered his resignation.

43. Kirk to Smith, 3 April 1963, Central Files.

Stent, California. Graduating from M.I.T. in 1927, he joined the School of Architecture at Columbia as an Associate in Architecture in 1935, rising through the ranks to Professor in 1953, primarily teaching structural courses. He became Assistant Dean in 1957, and Associate Dean in 1962.[44]

The search for a new man from outside of Columbia to be Dean proved to be difficult and ultimately fruitless. Vincent Kling *(Columbia, 1940),* a University Trustee and an accomplished Philadelphia architect, pressed the matter of a new Dean with President Kirk, nominating I.M. Pei and Joseph Passonneau. Kling regarded Passonneau, then head of the school at Washington University in St. Louis, as the stronger of the two candidates. Kling listed three conditions which should be promised the new Dean:

1. The Architecture School and its leadership as the 'Mother Art' would be the keystone in the programming and ultimate physical housing of an Arts Center. The new dean, I think should be invited to lead this program.

2. The deanship should be projected with the understanding that the involvement of his leadership in architecture and planning would be concomitant on the Columbia campus…with his taking over the reins.

3. He should have adequate time, up to two years, if necessary, for unwinding his present commitments and yielding his devotion to duty at Columbia for five to ten years.[45]

Kling urged Kirk to present these conditions clearly to the candidates, and argued that if the Administration were ambiguous about the true role of the new Dean, "you will not be successful in attracting the No. 1 candidate."[46]

The Faculty of the School agreed with Kling's choice of nominees and enlarged the list to three: "Pei from the profession, Passonneau from the other schools, and [Victor] Christ-Janer from Columbia."[47] Jacques Barzun decided against Christ-Janer, and both Pei and Passonneau declined an offer to be Dean. Two conditions at Columbia negated attempts to attract a practicing architect to the Deanship: one, the new Dean would have to virtually abandon his professional practice to become a full-time administrator, and two, by longstanding policy, would not be allowed to accept a University commission, nor as matters stood, even to have an effective voice in matters of campus expansion. It can be suggested that the President and the Board of Trustees could have reversed the policy (as in time they did), and that they did not do so was detrimental to the School.[48]

While the search for a new Dean was underway, Acting Dean Smith faced the task of improving the sagging morale of the faculty and students in the wake of Colbert's resignation. One area where Smith was able to affect the School was in faculty appointments. Following Colbert's departure, five senior faculty and fifteen junior faculty did not or were not asked to return to the School. This allowed Smith to bring a number of new people to the School in the 1963–1964 academic year, including Lo-Yi Chan and Raymond Lifchez *(Columbia, 1957).*[49]

Smith also extended the work begun with the *Four Great Makers*

Kenneth Alexander Smith.
Photo: Columbia University.

44. Smith's curriculum vitae, Central Files.

45. Kling to Kirk, 5 December 1963, Central Files.

46. Ibid.

47. Smith to Kirk, 17 February 1965, Central Files.

48. See note 34.

49. *School of Architecture Handbook of Information, 1963–1964.*

symposium by convincing the President and the Trustees to confer upon Alvar Aalto an honorary doctoral degree. Smith observed that Aalto was among the greatest of modern architects, that the School had been criticized by some for not including Aalto in the original symposium, and that holding a convocation in Low Library for the degree-granting ceremony "would be of value to the School in showing we have not shut up shop in the interim period and might produce tangible results in the future." The convocation and dinner was held on November 30, 1964.[50]

As the Dean search proceeded through 1964, the idea began to emerge from various sources of a two-part administration, thus reiterating what the 1958–1959 Search Committee had advocated. Norman Hoberman, an Adjunct Associate Professor in the School wrote to Kirk advocating a Dean who would be the full time administrator of the school, and a chairman of the Architectural Department, who could remain a practitioner. Faculty like Hoberman began to indicate positive support for Smith:

I wish to state how effectively Acting Dean Smith has fulfilled the difficult position he has held during this transitional period. Whether it be teaching curriculum, student problems, or faculty relations, few architectural school deans could match the intimate knowledge he has of all the elements within the School. Were Dean Smith permitted to continue in his present position on a permanent basis, and were a chairman appointed either from the outside or on a rotating basis within the faculty, I am convinced that the future of the School of Architecture would be assured.[51]

While support was growing for a two-part administration for the architectural program, Charles Abrams was beginning to urge the establishment of an Institute of Planning, first within the School and ultimately as an independent entity at Columbia. At a meeting in January, 1965, attended by Jacques Barzun, Kenneth Smith, Percival Goodman, and Charles Abrams, Barzun created the threefold division of the School in order to head off Abrams' urging of an Institute of Planning, of which he wanted to be Dean.[52]

By February, 1965, the idea had been accepted by the Administration that Smith should be the Dean of a school divided into three divisions: architecture, planning, and architectural technology. Then a search began for a Chairman of Architecture. On February 16, 1965, Smith met with Edward L. Barnes, a distinguished New York architect, who declined the position because of the demands of his practice. Smith and Barnes discussed several alternate possibilities, including Henry N. Cobb, William Conklin, Ulrich Franzen, John Johansen, Elliot Noyes, Gerhardt Kallman, and Victor Christ-Janer.[53] In the end, none of these men was selected and Romaldo Giurgola *(Columbia, 1951)* was appointed the new chairman.[54]

On May 28, 1965, *The New York Times* announced that Kenneth Smith had been appointed Dean, effective July 1, 1965. The article further noted that "his selection ends a two-year search in which many of the nation's outstanding architects and architectural educators have been found to be unavailable," and it quoted Vincent Kling saying that "there is a terrific shortage of educators

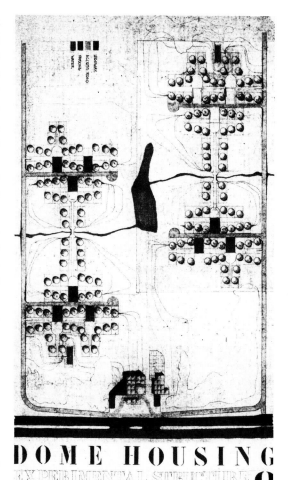

Dome Housing, 1967, Christopher Wadsworth *(1969)* and Michael Bissell *(1969)*.
Photo: GSAP Archive.

50. Smith to Kirk, 5 August 1964, Central Files.

51. Hoberman to Kirk, 11 May 1964, Central Files.

52. Barzun to Kirk, 29 January 1965, Central Files. See also, "Suggestions for the better administration of the School of Architecture," Barzun to Kirk, 20 January 1965, Central Files.

53. Smith to Kirk, 17 February 1965, Central Files.

54. Romaldo Giurgola was born on September 2, 1920, in Rome, Italy. After receiving a Bachelor of Architecture in 1948 from the University of Rome, he attended the School at Columbia as a Fulbright Fellow in 1949, receiving the M.S. in Architecture in 1951. After teaching at Cornell from 1952 until 1954, he taught at Penn from 1954 until 1967, starting a practice with Erhman Mitchell in Philadelphia in 1958. The firm placed second in the Boston City Hall competition of 1962, and in 1964, won the competition for the AIA National Headquarters in Washington, D.C., a scheme which was not constructed. In 1979–1980, his firm won the competition for the Australian Parliament House at Canberra. He was the Chairman of the Division of Architecture at the School from 1965 until 1971, and since has been Ware Professor of Architecture.

in architecture — and it's worse for deans than for anything else."
The article also announced the chairmen of the three divisions:
Giurgola in architecture, Charles Abrams in planning, and Mario
Salvadori in architectural technology.[55] Despite the implication
that the School had not been able to appoint the best man as Dean,
Smith's appointment indicated to Barzun that the School had
received the requisite "regilding with the real gold of a new plan, a
new dean, new heads of the divisions and expanded staff and
rationalized offerings within each."[56]

Soon, however, it became apparent that the two-part administration had drawbacks. While respected and even beloved as a
person, Smith was not perceived to possess an architectural
philosophy or pedagogical goals, and thus he administered the
School without really shaping it to a vision of his own. The
philosophical leadership fell to the chairmen who did not,
however, control the budget. Thus, the chairmen, who were the
sources of innovation in the program, had limits on their abilities
to enact changes involving budgetary expansion. Nevertheless,
because of Smith's essentially *laissez-faire* attitude toward
administering the School, the Faculty assumed a more important
role in its direction.[57]

Giurgola, in particular, acted as a magnet for a group of young
practitioners eager to become established in New York including
Giovanni Pasanella and Jaquelin Robertson, who had studied at
Yale, and Richard Weinstein, who had studied at Penn. And as a
consequence of being at the School, Giurgola opened a branch of
his office in New York, and one of his staff who came up from
Philadelphia with him, Robert Kliment, also began to teach at the
School. Giurgola and his young colleagues brought to the design
studios a discussion of architectural issues as they had evolved
under the direction of Louis Kahn at Penn, Princeton, and Yale in
the 1950's.[58]

The previous year, in 1964, Smith had hired Peter Prangnell
from Harvard to re-organize the first-year program, and he
brought with him to the School the ideas of the group of European
architects known as Team X.[59]

In the mid-1960's, the ideas of Team X, based at once upon the
enrichment of the formal language and an extension of the social
responsibilities of modern architecture, and those of Kahn, based
upon a search for the absolute fundamental aspects of architecture,
were easily the most advanced and the most inspiring. Thus, in the
architectural program at least, the years 1964–1968 were perhaps
as lively as any in the School's history.

The studio programs used in those years varied in complexity
from year to year as always, but in general they were based upon
real programs and sites rather than ideal programs and sites. A
first-year studio taught by Peter Prangnell, Theodor Rohdenberg,
and Nathan Silver worked on *A Mountainside Development for
Winter Skiing and Summer Recreation,* and on *A Residential Treatment
Center for Disturbed Children.* A third-year studio taught by Robert
Kliment and Richard Weinstein worked on *A Movie Theatre.* A
fourth-year studio taught by Alexander Kouzmanoff and Jaquelin

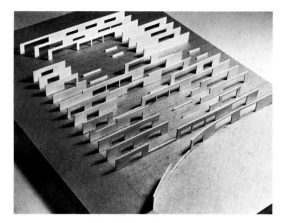

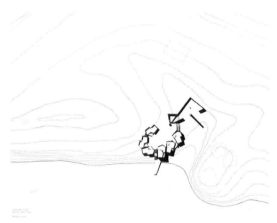

Top: Thesis Project, 1968,
Henry Altchek *(1968).*

Above: Sailing Camp, 1965,
Frances Halsband *(1968).*

55. *The New York Times,* 28 May 1965, p. 29.

56. Barzun to Kirk, 20 January 1965, Central Files.

57. Interview: Pokorny by Author, 20 August 1981.
Interview: R.M. Kliment and Frances Halsband by Author,
21 May 1981, GSAP archives.

58. Interview: Kliment and Halsband by Author, 21
May 1981.

59. Ibid.

Robertson worked on *An Urban College Campus* using a realistic, complex, and extensive program based upon the needs of Pace College in Manhattan. A graduate studio taught by Romaldo Giurgola worked on a development plan for Yorkville in Manhattan, an area stretching from 86th Street to 96th Street, from Fifth Avenue to the East River.[60]

The School published the third issue of *Program,* a student-produced journal founded "to provide analytical and creative criticism of architecture and planning, drawn from several fields of study: aesthetics, anthropology, economics, engineering, political science, and sociology, as well as from theoretical and realized work of architects and planners." As is often the case with student journals such as *Perspecta* at Yale, *Program* received "continued support and encouragement" from Philip Johnson.[61]

Charles Colbert had focused his attention on the one-year graduate program in architecture, with its three areas of concentration. By 1965, the program was enlarged to five areas of concentration: educational facilities planning and design, hospital and public health planning and design, urban design, restoration and preservation, and general design.[62] All through the 1960's, this program attracted good students to the School, drawn by the attractions of New York City, the short period of time, the possibility of independent study, and the resources of Columbia itself. Some of the graduates of the master's program during that decade are: John Fowler *(1959)*; Peter Eisenman *(1960)*; Michael McKinnell *(1960),* who designed the Boston City Hall with faculty members Gerhardt Kallmann and Edward Knowles; Cecil Steward *(1961),* who is Dean of Architecture at the University of Nebraska; Friedrich St. Florian *(1962),* who is head of the Rhode Island School of Design; Roger Sherwood *(1962),* who teaches at U.S.C.; Peter DaSilva *(1963)* and Lawrence Mason *(1964),* who practice in New York in the field of health care facilities; Norman Pfeiffer *(1965),* who is a partner in Hardy Holzman Pfeiffer Associates; and John Kurtich *(1968),* who is head of the Chicago Art Institute.

The undergraduate program also had graduates in the 1960's who have begun to distinguish themselves in practice. They include: Sanford Hirshen *(1959),* who teaches at Berkeley and who has worked on projects for migrant workers in California; Antoine Predock *(1962),* who has developed an important practice in Albuquerque, New Mexico; Daniel Solomon *(1963),* who has achieved great distinction in San Francisco; Robert Harper *(1964),* who is a partner in Moore, Grover, Harper; and Elizabeth Ericson *(1966),* who has developed a practice in Boston. Among the graduating members of the class of 1968, three have already distinguished themselves: Jaime Ardiles-Arce, who is a prolific architectural photographer; Henry Altchek, who is a graphic designer; and Frances Halsband, who practices in New York. More typical of Columbia graduates, however, is Sarelle Weisberg *(1966),* who works for the Port Authority of New York as an architect, thus continuing the long tradition of Columbia graduates who assume positions of responsibility in large offices in

Oasis, 1966, Douglas Engel *(1969).*
Photo: GSAP Archives.

60. See program statements, GSAP archives.

61. *Program,* (1964) Frontispiece, GSAP archives.

62. *School of Architecture Handbook of Information,*
1965–1966.

New York City, and who contribute more anonymously to the production of an organization.

In the 1960's, almost every institution came under critical review, and architectural schools were no exception. Change was in the air, and in March, 1967, *Progressive Architecture* reported on the "Revolution in Architectural Education," observing what were perceived to be new but what in fact were old issues: "arguments about whether to educate students more in basic principles or train them more in techniques, and arguments about whether to become a generalist or a specialist." The article also observed that the schools at Yale, M.I.T., and the University of Kentucky were implementing community projects to fully involve students in the social and constructional realities of architecture.[63]

If a "revolution" was actually going on, Columbia was not as involved as other schools. It can be argued that in the period from 1935 to 1959, the School had been on the periphery of discourse in both architecture and architectural education. Arnaud's long tenure was characterized by a resistance to change, while the epicenter of architectural education was at Harvard. Colbert's honest attempts to revitalize the School remained essentially stillborn because of his short tenure. Smith's tenure was characterized by the presence of relevant, contemporary ideas which originated elsewhere — at Penn, at Yale, and in Europe.

In 1968, however, the School attracted much attention. In the spring of that year, the School became enmeshed in traumatic events that on the surface at least were triggered by the University's attempt to build a new gymnasium in Morningside Park, thus exacerbating the unstable relationship of "town and gown" on Morningside Heights. While the immediate cause of the University-wide student strike in April of 1968 was the placement of the gymnasium, for the students in the School that was only symptomatic of a larger problem, one which had its roots in the expansion plans of the University.[64]

During the 1960's, the University began to consider the expansion of the original McKim, Mead and White campus. By 1966, what was described by the Advisory Council on Architecture as "the basic growth plans of the University" included six "interrelated and yet somewhat independent" areas:

A. *North Campus: 118th to 120th, Broadway to Amsterdam: This area will include future Engineering and Science facilities.*

B. *South Campus: 114th to 112th or 111th, Broadway to Amsterdam: This area will include future College housing and related facilities.*

C. *West Campus: 112th to 116th, Broadway to Riverside Drive: This area will include future graduate student and staff housing and probably, the new home for the School of Social Work.*

D. *East Campus: 115th to 120th, Amsterdam to Morningside: This area will include future buildings for Arts and Architecture, International Affairs, Political Science, and a graduate housing complex.*

E. *Outlying Campus: Medical Center; Lamont-Oceanographic*

63. "Revolution in Architectural Education," *Progressive Architecture*, 48 (March 1967), pp. 136-147.

64. Cox Commission, *Crisis at Columbia: Report of the Fact Finding Commission Appointed to Investigate the Disturbances at Columbia University in April and May 1968* (New York: Vintage Books, 1968).

Columbia University South Campus Study, New York City, 1963, Design team: Jack R. Cosner *(1963)*, Daniel P. D'Oliveira *(1963)*, Arnold G. Henderson *(1964)*, Richard E. Kaeyer *(1963)*, Kirby M. Keahey *(1963)*, David A. Millard *(1963)*, J. Daniel Spears *(1963)*, and Douglas Dean Telfer *(1964)*.

Research; Nevis-Physics Research; Alpine-Animal Care; Camp Columbia-Engineering.

F. Renovation of existing buildings.[65]

One criticism of the University's plans was the manner in which they were being formulated. By December of 1966, the University lacked a Comprehensive Plan for its development, and as an *ex officio* member of the Advisory Council on Architecture, Romaldo Giurgola wrote to Kirk about this:

In view of recent events which will greatly affect the growth of our University, it becomes urgent that an orderly expansion of the University's physical structure be planned. Short- and long-range objectives should be clarified, priorities established, a strategy formulated, and diversified efforts coordinated. As the building program gains momentum, it will become increasingly difficult for the participants in the Council to express sound opinions on the architectural validity of the buildings planned without a deeper knowledge of the general order of growth of the University.

May I take this opportunity to point out that the eventual contribution of the School of Architecture...should not be forgotten in reference to the work of the University Planning Office. Throughout the years the School has collected valuable material on the surroundings and experience in probing sites and may offer excellent skill in consultation and design work.[66]

The University continued to ignore the advice of its School of Architecture, and continued its plans for expansion without a Comprehensive Plan. In retrospect it is clear that the placement of the gymnasium was only a symptom of a more awesome spectre: that of a powerful institution operating without a clear and comprehensive understanding of its actions, and with what seemed to many to be an almost unchecked will to do as it pleased.

On April 24, 1968, Avery Hall was occupied by architecture,

65. Architectural Advisory Council Minutes, 3 May 1966, Central Files.

66. Giurgola to Kirk, 5 December 1966, Central Files.

planning, and preservation students, a defiant act which in the late 1960's seemed to be the only way to shock an institution enough for it to enter into a dialogue with its aggrieved constituents. What began as a challenge to University building policy quickly evolved into a challenge to the conventional process of architectural education. Many if not all the students in the School became dissatisfied and suspicious of the focus and content of architectural education, of the role of architecture, and of the values of the culture of which architecture is an expression. The occupation of Avery Hall led to a summer of introspection by students and faculty alike that was intended to produce a new vision of and a new structure for architectural education. Students expected to return in the fall of 1968 to a "new school of architecture." There were some important changes which are discussed in subsequent essays in this book, such as the increased participation of students in the administration of the School, and the increased presence of minority and women students and staff. But, nevertheless, it remains unclear today — thirteen years later — whether or not a fundamentally new and more relevant vision of architectural education itself occurred *at all* that summer, and if it did, the extent to which it had an effect upon the School, or even upon the participants themselves.

It's possible a little dose of history
May help us in unravelling this mystery.

W.H. Auden
"Letter to Lord Byron"[1]

Anatomy of Insurrection

Marta Gutman and
Richard Plunz

The year 1968 will take its place in the company of other important moments — 1848, for example[2] — as a catalyst for social unrest and insurrection. The strike at the Columbia School of Architecture in 1968, and the period of experimentation which followed it were an important contribution to that moment, but they were not borne exclusively out of the world events of that era. They also represented the culmination of a decade of dissatisfaction and unrest within the School. In addition, they can be traced back to the origins of the profession of architecture in the United States in general, and to the position of the Columbia School of Architecture in particular within this development.

The students in 1968 focused on the contradictions within the profession and School which had existed since their inception — most basically between responsibility to fulfill needs related to the welfare of the society as a whole and survival within the constraints of the American economic system. By 1968, many of those constraints seemed to be changing. The profession of architecture as an institution was founded at the height of unbridled nineteenth-century capitalism. By the 1960's it faced the issue of survival within a changing economic and cultural millieu, because, for example, the great social welfare programs of the 1960's pointed toward a kind of client quite unlike the wealthy individual or corporation. The students also focused on other social issues with long historical formation — for example, the physical development of the University, which began with the University's move to Morningside Heights at the turn of the century. In summary, discussion of the specific events of the strike and its aftermath cannot be isolated from two other sets of considerations: the origins of the School and its growth in relation to the problem of professional identity and social purpose; and the crisis which evolved in the 1960's specifically related to university building and expansion and to the quality and relevance of the educational programs of the School.

For a school of architecture in New York City, the issue of defining social purpose is probably more immediate than for schools located in more idyllic settings. As the American "metropolis," New York has harbored the most pervasive forms of wealth and poverty, presenting a broad range of possible social commitments and concerns. The architecture problems associated with wealth and poverty are quite different, and have led to contradictions in purpose and ideology within the profession. Given economic and cultural constraints, the profession of architecture, as an institution, was conceived with an identity on the side of wealth, without possessing the possibility for dealing adequately with the problems of the opposite end of the spectrum. The same can be said of schools of architecture.

A critical distinction must be made between the commitments

1. As quoted by Lincoln Kirnstein in "Lincoln Shelter," *The New York Review of Books,* 28 (August 13, 1981), p. 8. Kirstein's review of Edgar B. Young's book *Lincoln Center: The Building of an Institution* (New York: New York University, 1981) discusses the planning and architectural problems raised by the development of Lincoln Center which are similar to the ones faced by Columbia. The complete text of Auden's poem may be found in Edward Mendelson (ed.), *W.H. Auden: Collected Poems* (New York: Random House, 1976), pp. 76-100.

2. The revolutions of 1848 altered, among other things, the scale and shape of town planning reform. During the two previous decades liberal reformers tried to improve the industrial town by curing specific problems, primarily those of sanitation; more radical reformers tried to solve the problems by building model, at times utopian socialist, communities. In 1848 these groups joined forces briefly, but they did not transform the political revolution into a carefully constructed program for reform. Their failure brought conservative, popular governments into power — Napoleon III in France, Bismark in Germany, Disraeli in England — which consolidated the power of the centralized state to produce, in part, needed reform through large scale public works projects. This was the birth of neo-conservative town planning, examples of which include Hausmann's transformation of Paris, the Ringstrasse in Vienna, the alteration of the Barcelona grid and the vast plumbing and transportation systems which began to be constructed in London. For further information see Leonardo Benevolo, *The Origins of Modern Town Planning,* trans. Judith Landry (Cambridge, Mass.: The MIT Press, 1967), pp. 105-119; Leonardo Benevolo, *History of Modern Architecture,* vol 1: *The Tradition of Modern Architecture,* trans. H.J. Landry (Cambridge, Mass.: The MIT Press, 1971), pp. 61-63.

of the profession and schools as institutions and the commitments of individuals within them. Exceptions to institutional characteristics can always be found which create another level of professional contradiction. For example, Charles Follen McKim, businessman-architect, designed factory towns[3] which might be considered acts of social purpose in the interest of the worker. But towns also expressed the relationship of architectural practice to business-wealth which McKim helped institutionalize. For radicals of the 1960's, understanding this distinction between "institution" and "individual" became an important issue because it illuminated such problems as military involvement in Southeast Asia, university educational policies, and racism.[4] Institutions were understood to acquire characteristics independent of the sum of their individuals, which could be changed only through massive resistance. In the minds of the students, the Columbia School of Architecture was no exception to this rule by the 1960's.

By the mid-nineteenth century, the emergence of New York City as the American metropolis, with attendant signs of glories and miseries, pointed to the need for an architectural curriculum as an important step toward understanding the growing environmental problems of the city. In his Annual Report of 1857, George W. Morton, the City Inspector, called for the establishment of a college of architecture in New York City which would incorporate a clear social mandate, providing for:

the general diffusion of information as to the principles of hygiene, among the great mass of the population...for securing the united cooperation of architecture and agriculture, with the views of the medical profession, and for promoting from time to time, all those specific improvements which their resources, assisted by the chemistry and engineering of modern times may render it desirable to introduce.

In no such place can a college of architecture be founded with such advantage, as in a large city such as New York, where so much building is in progress, and from which improvements will naturally extend to the whole American continent.[5]

While Morton spoke not as an architect, but as director of the city's building bureaucracy, his proposal undoubtedly received notice by the American Institute of Architects, founded in New York City in the same year. Yet no professional school was founded in the city until 1881, when the Columbia course was established. Even though, by 1881, the social reform movement had made significant gains in the wake of the unrest and violence of the 1870's,[6] the relationship of the young profession of architecture and its schools to this movement conflicted with other concerns. These centered around the difficult issue of legitimizing a professional identity within the context of late-nineteenth-century American capitalism. An interesting example is the complicity of architects in setting design standards for the Tenement House Act of 1879.[7] That the act passed at all was a major breakthrough for reform, but the design standards which it enforced remained little better than the *laissez-faire* standards used by the city's real estate developers. It was a large scale architectural competition which set

3. Leland M. Roth, "Three Industrial Towns by McKim, Mead and White," *Journal of the Society of Architectural Historians,* 38 (December 1979), pp. 317-347.

4. The special summer 1968 issue of *Viet Report* on "Urban America in Revolt," commented extensively on the issue of institutionalization, relating it to the oppression of students. See in particular Peter Countryman, "The Professor as Policeman," *Viet Report,* 3 (Summer 1968), pp. 58-60.

5. George W. Morton, "Remarks," in *Annual Report of the City of New York for the Year Ending December 31, 1857,* (1858), p. 211. Aspects of the needs described by Morton and others are described in greater detail in Richard A. Plunz, *The Institutionalization of Housing Form in New York City: 1850–1950,* to be published as *Habiter New York: La Forme Institualise de l'Habitation New Yorkais,* by Pierre Mardaga Editeur, Brussells, 1981.

6. See in particular, Robert W. Bruce, *1877, Year of Violence* (Chicago: Quadrangle Books, Inc., 1970).

7. See Richard A. Plunz, *The Institutionalization of Housing Form.*

those standards. Even *The New York Times* echoed the widespread popular criticism, stating that "if the prize plans are the best offered, which we can hardly believe, they simply demonstrate the problem is insoluble," and that they "offer a very slightly better arrangement than hundreds of tenements now do."[8] Unlike *The New York Times,* the AIA had no objections. Such were the contradictions inherent to a profession struggling within the context of "liberal capitalism."

The identity of the American professional lobby for architecture grew out of engineering, beginning with initiatives like the founding of the AIA in 1857. By 1869, the American Society of Civil Engineers and Architects finally dropped "architects" from its title, presumably because competition from the AIA had caused architectural membership to dwindle. In these years, a struggle had transpired between engineers and architects over the power to protect the right to build. The issue was never formally resolved until 1915, when architects were finally given the right to grant professional privilege through examination and licensing in New York. In the split from engineering, the obvious and uncontested mandate for a separate profession of architecture was based more on aesthetic than on technical expertise. In general, the "art" of architecture was supported by the newly-rich. New York, which was the commercial center of the nation, became the nucleus of the new architectural expressions of wealth as well. Then, as now, the "art" of architecture bore little direct relationship to public service, or at least to the needs of Morton's "great mass." The aesthetic justification of the profession was further reinforced by the founding of The Architectural League of New York in 1881, coinciding with Columbia's first courses in architecture. It sought to unite Beaux-Arts architects with Beaux-Arts sculptors, painters, and artisans, rather than with structural and mechanical engineers or technicians.[9]

Frederick A. Schermerhorn, an engineering graduate of the School of Mines, was the Columbia Trustee who most adamantly supported an architecture program at Columbia. In general, he was typical of the kind of support which the new profession gained — a real estate entrepreneur and business associate of J.P. Morgan, with some tendencies toward cultural and philanthropic activity. He argued for the need for an architecture program in New York City, and for applying the prototype of the Ecole in Paris, via William Ware's experience in Cambridge. Schermerhorn also voiced a concern for providing a solid "scientific education," of the sort which presumably the School of Mines could provide. He appears to have envisioned a somewhat more utilitarian program than was to develop, which would have been more responsive to some of his own philanthropic interests. But the Columbia courses helped accomplish his goal of strengthening the profession, while reinforcing New York as the commercial and intellectual center for architecture.[10]

The stance of the Columbia program in relation to the issue of social purpose has been generally typical of other programs of architecture in the United States. But the Columbia situation does

Business School Protest, 1962.
Photo by Manny Warman.

8. "Prize Tenements," *The New York Times,* March 16, 1874, p. 6.

9. For further information see Plunz, *Institutionalization of Housing Form.*

10. F.A. Schermerhorn, "Proposal to Establish a Course of Instruction in Architecture in the School of Mines..." (New York: Columbia College, 1879).

appear to have harbored some unique contradictions most clearly related to its location in a city which represented the extremes of both wealth and poverty. For example, even during some periods when the program had become most conservative in its outlook toward social purpose, it still retained an unusually large number of politically progressive and activist faculty, even if they did not always influence the mainstream direction. Another contradiction involved Columbia's image. Located as it was, at the center of power, it has never been seen as the most important representative of the nation's highest elite.[11] Robert Moses, as a young Yale graduate, understood the sentiment well when writing his Columbia doctoral dissertation in 1912: the elite in public service would be drawn from Harvard, Princeton, and Yale.[12]

Model of the proposed Gym in Morningside Park, designed by Eggers and Higgins — Sherwood, Mills, and Smith.
Photo: *Columbia College Today.*

Columbia existed within a city whose fortunes rested on the tenement and the immigrant. To the extent possible, within the constraints of the same liberal capitalism which spawned tenement reform, the first two decades of the Columbia program under Ware's direction did entertain a certain discourse about the problem of social purpose, in the hope that in spite of its elitism, the program could still respond to the darker side of its social context. In 1891, Ware instituted a program which allowed professional draftsmen to enroll as special students in the school.[13] This program evolved into the night school, which still existed in 1968. But like the contradictions inherent to other such liberalizing efforts within the program, the night school tended to reinforce a stringent class structure, providing a first-class program for the day students, and a second-class program for those with less time or money.

In 1902, the School of Architecture was removed from the Faculty of Applied Sciences and granted independent status within the University, mirroring the split from engineering which had occurred in other aspects of professional development. Around the same time, the needs of the New York businessman-architect grew to dominate the School after Ware's retirement in 1902, symbolized by the coup of sorts when McKim began to influence the School's curriculum.[14] By then, the professional ideal in New York had been shaped in McKim's own image, melding the pedagogy of the Ecole with the aesthetic interests of American business. Architectural education was a critical ingredient of this strategy. The so-called "American Renaissance" was by definition an academically-dependent exercise, based on classical knowledge developed best through formal training. The Hastings and McKim *ateliers* were even located downtown in their offices (the third *atelier* remained in Havemeyer Hall). Even though McKim was interested in architectural pedagogy, his interest was more entrepreneurial than pedagogical. His ideas on education were subservient to a much broader commercial scenario, which as William Jordy points out, led to compromise.[15]

The influence of the businessman-architect began to call into focus conflicts of interest between professional practice and education — a dialogue which has remained in the School, sometimes as a positive force, and also depending on the chemistry of particular circumstances, as an unproductive influence on the de-

11. Gene R. Hawes, "America's Upper Class Colleges," *Columbia College Today,* 11 (Fall 1963), pp. 30-35.

12. Moses' stance is interpreted by Robert Caro, *The Power Broker* (New York: Vintage Books, 1974), pp. 52-55. See also Robert Moses, *The Civil Service of Great Britain* (Ph.D. dissertation, Columbia University, 1914).

13. William R. Ware, "Professional Draftsmen as Special Students in the School of Architecture," *The School of Mines Quarterly,* 18 (July 1897), pp. 422-429.

14. The reminiscences of Leopold Arnaud describe in some detail this situation in which A.D.F. Hamlin was named Acting Director. See also Theodore K. Rohdenburg, *A History of the School of Architecture* (New York: Columbia University Press, 1954), pp. 18-21.

15. William H. Jordy, *American Buildings and Their Architects: Progressive and Academic Ideals at the Turn of the Twentieth Century* (Garden City, New York: Anchor Books, 1976), pp. 344-349.

velopment and coherence of the program. Charges of negligence and opportunism against faculty and administration have recurred, beginning with Dean Austin Lord's somewhat tense tenure which ended in resignation due to outside professional commitments.[16] On the other hand, the school has also experienced insular periods of academic retrenchment,[17] without adequate exposure to new ideas — to the extraordinary degree that as late as 1958, it had a dean who discounted the importance of Frank Lloyd Wright.[18] It was this unstable relationship between professional and academic interests which was an important long-term cause of the 1968 strike.

Another of the important long-term causes of the strike involves the architectural plan for the University, designed by McKim in 1893 as the "architectural crown" of New York City.[19] It was to be the academic acropolis of Manhattan, removed from the problems of the older city to the south, and surrounded by Harlem to the north and east, which was then a middle class community. If the campus was to be the Acropolis, Broadway was to be the *Champs Elysees,* serving the University with housing, shops, and a social ambiance to rival that of Paris.[20] These images, which university officials still invoke today,[21] never fully materialized. Instead, real problems of poverty and crime gradually moved to the brink of the enclave, despite Columbia's efforts to stem the tide. Its expansionist policies toward the surrounding community in the 1960's, which went beyond the acceptable limits of business practice, became an important cause of the strike, especially within the School of Architecture.

In addition to the 1968 strike, there were two other significant periods in the history of the School when issues of the social purpose of the profession came into momentous question. The first period occurred in the early 1930's with the final demise of the Beaux-Arts curriculum and its abrupt replacement with the program developed by Joseph Hudnut. The second occurred in the early 1960's when Charles Colbert attempted to reform the curriculum. Like the curriculum developed after the 1968 strike, both previous experiments lasted only a few years, although their influence continued for longer.[22] The events of these three periods juxtaposed the interests of students, partially shaped by world events, with the failure of old curricula. And all involved conflict between old and new pedagogical ideals and between conservative and progressive political ideologies — much more than between young and old faculty or faculty and students.

The new Hudnut curriculum was preceded by the cataclysm of the Great Depression, which apart from the personal hardships involved, could only serve to underline for students the beleaguered state of the curriculum, which had become abstract and stale in contrast with the shattering realism of events in the outside world. Unrest in the School was most publicly displayed in April, 1932, within the context of a larger university-wide "riot" over student living conditions, and "free speech."[23] In what would prove to be a harbinger of 1968, architecture students seized Avery Hall. The immediate cause was a conflict with conservative stu-

16. Rohdenburg, *A History,* pp. 24-25.

17. The periods of the 1920's and 1950's appear to have been most retrogressive. An interesting collection of reproductions of student work from the 1920's exists in the Slide Library of the Graduate School of Architecture and Planning which bears out this assessment. Included are such projects as "A Campo Santo," "A Museum of Peaceful Arts," "An International Bank," "A War Memorial in Central Park," "A Triumphal Arch," and "Apartments for Millionaires."

18. Interview: Adolph Placzek by Diane Boas.

19. President Seth Low to McKim, 27 October 1895; in Charles Moore, *The Life and Times of Charles Follen McKim* (New York: Houghton Mifflin Company, 1929), p. 268.

20. Concern for the image of Broadway was not new. In 1853, just after Haussmann began the transformation of Paris, *Harper's Weekly* published a proposal to widen and construct arcades along Broadway, also called the Boulevard, from Union Square to the Battery. The article, which cited arcades from Paris, London, and other European cities as precedent, expected the design would relieve congestion, provide shelter, and turn the street into "the glory of New York." Though it was never built, the design also offers an early American example of the widespread influence of Haussmann's techniques which eventually altered the shape of major European and American cities. See "How to Relieve Broadway," *Harper's Weekly,*1 (December 19, 1857), pp. 808-809.

21. The Presidential Commission on Academic Priorities in the Arts and Sciences appointed by President McGill in 1979 found the ambiance of Morningside Heights not beneficial to the Columbia community, pointing to the desirability of making "a cultural center with some of the attraction of Greenwich Village, the animation of the Latin Quarter, the ethnic excitement of a Chinatown." See the report of the "Presidential Commission on Academic Priorities in the Arts and Sciences," (Columbia University, December, 1979), p. 18.

22. The two earlier periods were terminated by the resignation of the Dean, though the termination of the reforms after 1968 occurred somewhat differently. As well, the strike and its aftermath seem to have been considerably more momentous than the preceding disruptions in justification and method.

23. "2000 Students Take Part in 'Strike' Protesting Harris' Expulsion..." *Columbia Daily Spectator,* April 7, 1932, p. 1; "Two Mass Meetings Scheduled for Noon..." *Columbia Daily Spectator,* p. 1; "Riot at Columbia in Harris Protest," *The New York Times,* April 7, 1932, pp. 1, 14.

dents from outside the School, but no other university buildings were seized. Although the occupation lasted only a few hours, it was the strongest protest on the campus, indicating a dissent among architecture students which went beyond the normal limits. Boring supported the students' action, and he subsequently furthered his efforts to improve the School. But he was confronted with the new ideals of modernism, of which he had little understanding, and he had reached an impasse which prevented him from initiating the necessary degree of change.[24] Boring's resignation in 1933, due in part to advancing age, led to the appointment of Hudnut who was presented with the opportunity for far-reaching reform.

Hudnut's curriculum was characterized by choice and flexibility, by a new preoccupation with real programs, and by a stance toward social purpose. Hudnut's initiatives in housing and town planning courses were among the most important aspects of his tenure, and the structure of the design studios was entirely reformulated.[25] Hudnut's curriculum was significant as a leading attempt to create a comprehensive modernist alternative to Beaux-Arts pedagogy in the United States; and in many ways it may have been far more suited to American needs than the European-dominated programs which preceded it and would follow it. Hudnut represented a new kind of powerful personality in architecture at Columbia. The antithesis of the Beaux-Arts ideal, he had studied engineering in the Midwest before architecture at Columbia, and he never attended the Ecole in Paris. He belonged to a group of New York architects who were as concerned about social problems as business and aesthetics. None of them were involved with the promotion of modernism as the "high style" attempt to reinvigorate liberal capitalism in the mode of Hitchcock's and Johnson's "International Style." In fact, they were to question these stylistic initiatives as vigorously as they questioned the Beaux-Arts.[26]

Hudnut's "New Deal" in architecture was consistent with the radicalization of the profession of architecture during the 1930's and early 1940's. The School contributed to the role of New York City as one of the centers of national activity, which ranged from the formation of labor unions for architects and draftsmen, to the alternative professional publications, to alternative professional societies.[27] By the end of the 1930's, the School had a small but important legacy of faculty and alumni identified with progressive political activity. Their influence was felt indirectly in 1968. This legacy included older alumni such as Grosvenor Atterbury *(1892)*, I.N. Phelps Stokes *(1895)*, and Henry Atterbury Smith *(1893)*, who pioneered an alternative functionalist direction at the height of the Beaux-Arts,[28] a more recent generation of alumni such as Joseph Hudnut *(1917)* and Talbot Hamlin *(1914)*, and then contempary faculty such as Henry Wright, Carl Feiss, Eugene Raskin *(1932)*, Carol Aronovici, Sir Raymond Unwin, and Werner Hegemann. By the 1950's, the initial roster had gradually grown to include such personages as Percival Goodman, Mario Salvadori, Henry Churchill, Alexander Kouzmanoff, and James Marston

24. "Boring Sees Revolution in Architecture; Asks for Another Teacher in Report," *Columbia Daily Spectator*, October 10, 1932, p. 1. This article gives a strong indication of Boring's level of frustration.

25. Rohdenburg, *A History*, pp. 35-39; "New Method in Teaching Architecture," *Columbia Alumni News*, January 18, 1935. A clipping of this article may be found in the Columbiana Collection, Columbia University. See also Joseph Hudnut, "Blueprint for a University," *Weekly Bulletin, Michigan Society of Architects*, 18 (November 14, 1944), pp. 1, 4-7.

26. Within this context it is interesting to note that Hudnut used the word "post-modern" in 1945 not to denote stylistic anachronism, but to refer to questions he raised about the direction of modernism in the United States, especially the abrogation of its tenets of social purpose. See Joseph Hudnut, "The Post-Modern House," *The Architectural Record*, 97 (May 1945), pp. 70-75.

27. Labor unions included the Federation of Architects, Engineers, Chemists and Technicians and the Architectural Guild of America; *Shelter, Task* and *Technical America* were alternative technical publications; some alternative professional societies were the American CIAM, the American Society of Planners and Architects (A.S.P.O.), and the Architects' Committee of the National Council of Soviet-American Friendship. See also Plunz, *The Institutionalization of Housing Form*.

28. Grosvenor Atterbury's experiments with prefabrication at Forest Hills Gardens were extraordinary. Equally so was Smith's Mesa Verde housing in Jackson Heights, completed in 1926, together with the many studies which preceded it. See Plunz, *Institutionalization of Housing Form*.

Fitch. There were also important figures from related faculties, such as Meyer Shapiro in Art History, who participated in the programs of the school.

Hudnut managed to remove the Beaux-Arts curriculum in a matter of several months over the summer of 1933. He encountered opposition from alumni and faculty. Some of the most public opposition surfaced in the 1936 issue of *Pencil Points* in which Hudnut's advocacy of a "scientific" program concerned with the "enhancement of security and health," and "the happiness of populations," was treated as a threat to aesthetic integrity and historical inquiry. There was also notable public opposition from within the School which centered on the competition for the prestigious Perkins and Boring Fellowship in 1935. While the immediate controversy involved an interpretation of the rules of the competition, Hudnut was accused of opportunism in his initiatives at Columbia, and charges against him and other administrators and faculty continued[29] after he left to assume the Deanship at Harvard University. After Hudnut left for Harvard, the School settled down to a reinterpreted admixture of both Hudnut's reforms and the Beaux-Arts program which it had replaced.

The reports of the National Architectural Accreditation Board at the beginning and end of the 1950's sum up the situation of the School in that decade. In 1949, the report stated that "students are not producing outstanding architecture in their design problems," with "some sort of fire missing...without which all else may become flat, stale and unprofitable."[30] In 1959, the report was more subtle, pending selection of a replacement for Dean Leopold Arnaud, who had retired in 1958. The faculty was described as "competent but without particular brilliance in any specific field."[31] Other schools eclipsed Columbia's public image; not until the brief period following 1961, and finally 1968, would this condition change. The slender thread of social purpose in architecture remained in places, for example, in Percival Goodman's Master's Class. But it was not as evident as might be expected in spite of the personal convictions of many faculty. As a whole, very few architecture students were caught up in the emerging New Left criticism of 1950's culture, particularly political repression, even though New York City and Columbia fostered an important part of the movement, around figures such as Herbert C. Marcuse, C. Wright Mills and Paul Goodman.[32] The School was also very much outside of the post-war "high style" mannerist and commercialized reaction to the International Style which began in the 1950's, though some of its most public figures like Philip Johnson or Edward Durrell Stone were based in New York. Philip Johnson, for example, sought to develop an informal influence at Yale, in New Haven, beginning in the 1950's, rather than at Columbia, in New York. But even had he wished to develop a liaison with Columbia, his political past undoubtedly would have raised problems with those School faculty who leaned toward the left.[33]

The contrast between the relationship of Yale and Columbia to New York as a center of architectural activity is especially interesting. In spite of the fact that Columbia was at the epicenter, includ-

Rally outside of President Kirk's office — Sunday, April 28, 1968. Photo by Alan R. Epstein, courtesy *Columbia College Today*.

29. See H. Van Buren Magonigle, "The Upper Ground: Being Essays in Criticism," *Pencil Points,* 16 (January 1935), pp. 16-17. Information about the Perkins and Boring Fellowship dispute may be found in: Letter to the editor, *Columbia Daily Spectator,* February 12, 1935. The Columbiana Collection of Columbia University also possesses a mimeographed statement, dated received March 16, 1936, which outlines the accusations. It is attributed to Morris Lapidus *(Columbia 1931),* not the Morris Lapidus *(Columbia 1927)* who currently practices in Miami Beach.

30. Shaley W. Morgan, Secretary, National Architectural Accrediting Board, to Dean Leopold Arnaud, June 6, 1949, Central Files, Columbia University (hereafter Central Files.).

31. Elliot L. Whitaker, Secretary, National Architectural Accrediting Board, to President Grayson Kirk, March 11, 1959, Central Files.

32. A useful, brief history of this period at Columbia and in New York my be found in Irwin Unger, *The Movement: A History of the American New Left, 1959–1972* (New York: Dodd, Mead and Company, 1974), pp. 18-22.

33. Johnson has renounced his Nazi sympathies of the 1930's. They were controversial and well-known. Several persons interviewed for this essay provided detailed information. The journalist, William L. Shirer indicates the extent of Johnson's activity in *Berlin Diary* (New York: Alfred A. Knopf, 1941). See also Calvin Tomkins, "Forms Under Light," *The New Yorker,* 53 (May 23, 1977), p. 48 which mentions Johnson's work for *Social Justice,* and Paul Goldberger, "Philip Johnson: A Controversial New Vision for Architecture," *The New York Times Magazine* (May 14, 1978), pp. 26-27.

ing the professional media, *The New York Times,* various museums, professional alliances and other taste-making organizations, the School always remained slightly withdrawn from such activity. Arnaud, for one, took some pride in the fact that the School was not dominated by any one personality and that the faculty worked cohesively as a group, in which there were well-known members. For example, Talbot Hamlin and James Marston Fitch both taught architectural history and theory. Both were engaging personalities, but were not particularly interested in the kind of commercialization of style which the fashionable New York scene was beginning to revive in the 1950's. They supported a diverse range of interests which included social issues. Their emerging counterpart at Yale was Vincent Scully, whose interests were involved with the New York scene, especially the regrouping of architects which was occurring around the personage of Philip Johnson, and Johnson's interest in historicism, aestheticism, and monumentality.[34] In general, for two decades, until the mid-1970's, Yale was the academic mainstay of this movement, with its collection of buildings designed by "star" architects and its "star" faculty,[35] who sent many of their most aggressive students back to New York to further reinforce the new tendency.[36] Consistent with Robert Moses' vision in 1912, the Columbia students by and large remained in the background, not aspiring to the same combination of affluence, influence, and aestheticism. They participated in the emergence of the influence in America of another side of the reaction against the "International Style," more directly related to social purpose. A portion of this influence at Columbia came through the brief tenure of Dean Charles Colbert; and then slightly later, through the dissemination of new ideas drom Europe, most principally through the discourse emerging from the work of Team X, introduced by Peter Prangnell and others.

Charles Colbert *(Columbia, 1947),* a successful commercial architect in New Orleans, also had a more than cursory interest in education. He came to Columbia in 1960 with the clear intention of making Columbia's School of Architecture "the most contributive academic force in twentieth century architecture," more befitting its relationship to New York.[37] His emphasis contrasted with the Yale strategy, stressing "an academic and administrative climate allowing reasonable academic experimentation and opportunities for real community service projects."[38] He recognized that the Beaux-Arts pedagogy still very much underlay the curriculum, and like Hudnut before him, introduced "real" projects in an attempt to foster change. The first studio was involved with downtown Dallas, heavily funded by local Dallas businessmen and influenced by the urban renewal programs of that area.[39] Other similar enterprises ensued. He initiated public forums, the best known being the Great Makers Series[40] which considerably enhanced Columbia's public image.

His teaching philosophy included a strong committment to professional practice as a "moral pursuit," with the principle that "the first and only reason for architecture is people." He felt that "design courses should discourage the current extravagant emphasis

34. See in particular David McCullough, "Architectural Spellbinder," *The Architectural Forum,* 111 (September 1959), pp. 136-137; 191, 202.

35. For example see Walter McQuade, "Yale's Viking Vessel," *The Architectural Forum,* 109 (December 1958), pp. 106-111; "Design Jelled for Yale Art and Architecture School," *Progressive Architecture,* 43 (January 1962), p. 62; "Kline Science Centre, Yale," *Architectural Design,* 34 (April 1964), pp. 176-77; Ellen Perry Berkeley, "Yale: A Building as Teacher," *The Architectural Forum,* 127 (July – August 1967), pp. 46-53; William Jordy, "Kahn at Yale," *The Architectural Review,* 152 (July 1977), pp. 37-44.

36. Robert A.M. Stern's essay in *Oppositions* presents one kind of catalogue of the student work of many of Yale's successful New York alumni-practitioners. See Robert A.M. Stern, "Yale: 1950–1965," *Oppositions,* 4 (October 1974), pp. 35-62.

37. Quoted in Columbia University, News Office, "Press Release," January 25, 1968 (mimeographed); also see "A Direction," in Charles Colbert, *18 Talks* (New Orleans: January 1969), pp. 53-58.

38. Ibid.

39. Columbia University, School of Architecture, Master's Class, *Main Place: Dallas, Texas* (New York: School of Architecture, 1961).

40. Similar projects included a Study of Worcester, Massachusetts, Central Business Area; a Study and design of Camden, New Jersey, Neighborhood Schools; and a Study of New College, Sarasota, Florida. See Charles Colbert, "A Direction," *18 Talks,* p. 57. See also "Four Great Makers of Modern Architecture: Gropius, Le Corbusier, Mies van der Rohe, Wright" (New York: Da Capo Press, 1970). This is a verbatim record of the "Great Makers" Symposium held at the School of Architecture, March–May 1961.

on novelty of form and individual expression." He urged reconciliation of environmental disciplines, for example, between architecture and planning. He also argued for interdisciplinary cooperation within the University, and for strengthening of graduate level research. Finally, he felt that the architect could not afford to become more and more isolated from the expectations of the business entrepreneur, which would in effect make architecture a drafting service for the real architects of our time.[41] His ideas appear to have been molded by currents of post-Bauhaus humanism which characterized aspects of the thinking of such figures as Serge Chermayeff at Harvard, or William Wurster at Berkeley. But Colbert's reforms embodied severe contradictions, and as with Hudnut, the issue of opportunism and careerism underlay much of the criticism against him. The projects which he initiated came uncomfortably close to a form of professional practice, raising questions about a conflict of interest between professional and academic pursuits within the School. These charges were reinforced by the fact that the projects were isolated from the normal activities of the School, and largely isolated from the context of the School. For example, the problem of Dallas was viewed as having too little to do with New York City, and too much formulated by Colbert's professional connections. But whatever his weaknesses may have been, Colbert did present a cohesive philosophical alternative for the School, which if it had succeeded, might have created a "unique contributive force."[42]

On Tuesday, April 23, 1968, after tearing down construction fences around the gym site in Morningside Park, approximately 300 demonstrators, led by Students for a Democratic Society, and the Society of Afro-American Students, occupied Hamilton Hall, took Henry Coleman, Acting Dean of Columbia College, hostage and issued six demands.[43] Early Wednesday morning the white students left Hamilton Hall at the request of the black students and occupied the presidential offices in Low Library. By Thursday a total of six buildings were occupied including Avery Hall. After a series of unsuccessful negotiations and rising tension between pro- and anti-strike groups, the Administration asked the New York City Police to clear the buildings before dawn of April 30. A force of 1000 men brutally removed 700–1000 students.[44] The students, joined by 200 faculty, called a general strike, and the executive committee of the faculties of Columbia University requested the formation of a fact-finding commission, headed by Archibald Cox, then Dean of the Harvard Law School.[45] On May 17, New York City police removed forty members of the Community Action Committee which had occupied two apartments in partially vacant, Columbia-owned buildings. On May 22, students occupied Hamilton Hall again. The police removed them, and then, as they started to clear the campus provoked a large demonstration which was put down, again, with great brutality. Approximately 1000 students staged a counter commencement in June.

Initially the architecture students seized Avery Hall out of sympathy for the black students at Hamilton Hall, but they quickly

41. Charles Colbert, "The Future of Columbia's Architectural School," *18 Talks*, pp. 101-109.

42. Although the internal dynamics of schools are viewed from the outside with limited understanding, *Progressive Architecture* editorialized after Colbert's resignation in 1963 that he "*had* begun translating Columbia from a stagnant, old-line school into a more vital, contributing institution." See "Crisis at Columbia," *Progressive Architecture*, 44 (May 1963), p. 78. But Colbert may have succumbed to a variation on the "star" complex which existed at other schools by flying in such figures as Harwell Hamilton Harris and Ernest Kump to help implement his program — busy professionals removed from the School and New York. Indeed this problem only increased in the 1960's and was one of the contributing factors to the strike. Students resented Colbert's autocratic methods, but ironically, only five years later in 1968, they echoed many of his philosophical statements about education.

43. The building occupation culminated in a series of events during the spring of 1968 most of which the SDS organized to protest military recruiting on campus and University connections to the Institute for Defense Analysis. The construction of the gymnasium in Morningside Park was a secondary issue. The demonstrations prompted President Kirk to ban all indoor demonstrations on campus, but on March 27, 1968, the SDS defied the rule and students marched inside of Low Library. Six students, the "IDA Six," were placed on disciplinary probation, and on April 23, the SDS organized a rally at the sundial in front of Low Library which, in part, protested the disciplinary decision. Students went from this rally to the gym site where one student was arrested and then to Hamilton Hall which housed the administration of Columbia College. Dean Coleman was taken "hostage," and the students issued six demands which asked the university to grant amnesty for the original "IDA-Six," and those involved in the present protest; to stop construction immediately of the gymnasium in Morningside Park; to sever all ties with the Institute for Defense Analysis; to assure that future judicial decisions be made by student/faculty committee; to repeal President Kirk's ban on indoor demonstrations; and to drop all charges against all people involved in demonstrations at the gym site and on campus. See Columbia Strike Coordinating Committee, *Columbia Liberated* (September 1968), p. 6; and Cox Commission, *Crisis at Columbia: Report of the Fact Finding Commission Appointed to Investigate the Disturbances at Columbia University in April and May 1968* (New York: Vintage Books, 1968), pp. 89-105.

44. University officials expected that the police would outnumber students and easily overpower them. Cox Commission, *Crisis at Columbia*, pp. 163-167.

45. Numerous accounts of the student rebellion at Columbia have been written. The Cox Commission Report, *Crisis at Columbia*, and Roger Kahn's book, *The Battle for Morningside Heights* are among the more interesting. The *Columbia Daily Spectator* compiled major stories from its pages into a collection, "Crisis at Columbia: An Inside Report on the Rebellion at Columbia." *The New York Times* covered the events, but reporting in the *Village Voice* and the *Washington Post* provided more balanced accounts.

expressed a broad critique of University policy and architectural education.[46] They argued for the need for social responsibility on the part of the profession, for the replacement of the stagnant content and structure of architectural education, and against the quality of the architecture on campus and the University's arrogant policy toward its neighbors. Given a fragmented curriculum and a vacuum in the leadership of the School, students demanded and took control of their education. With some faculty and alumni support, they changed its structure into one which they believed was more democratic, would better train them to be socially responsible, and would correct the grievous errors of the University planning policy by offering practical experience in poor communities.

The questions the students raised about the nature of architectural education and practice, and the relations of the University to the community were part of a long tradition. Indeed, cracks in the walls of Columbia had provided a home for liberal reformers and radicals throughout the history of the School, if not the University. What was new, and what was important, about the 1968 rebellion was its shape, the scope of its criticism, and its intensity. These were due, in part, to larger questions about the nature of American imperialism, capitalism and racism which the civil rights, the anti-war, and the student movements raised with more and more passion as the decade of the 1960's progressed. This grew into a desire on the part of the New Left to examine the institutional base of American social problems which at Columbia and other universities meant questioning the consequent social policies of educational institutions. Though the tactics used by the students belong to a long history of civil disobedience and non-violent protest, they too grew out of various movements: the civil rights sit-ins; the protest marches and demonstrations against the Vietnamese War; and student demonstrations such as those staged at Berkeley by the Free Speech Movement. Many members of the New Left felt that the universities lost any claim to "academic immunity" once they became, as Columbia surely was, a part of the system of institutions which shaped the problem-ridden policies of American society.[47]

In addition, the rebellion took place during a traumatic series of events throughout the world, at a point when the Left and students felt that their actions could change, if not topple, governments. Just prior to the strike, the anti-war movement forced Lyndon Johnson to withdraw from the primary campaign for re-election to the Presidency while the campaigns of Eugene McCarthy and Robert Kennedy seemed to gather support by the minute. Alexander Dubcek led the Czechs into an experiment in democratic socialism, an experiment which was viewed as one of the most interesting and promising the world had yet seen. But, these hopes were quickly shattered by the Russian invasion of Czechoslovakia. In April, Martin Luther King was assassinated in what seemed a right wing plot to many liberals; his death sparked revolts and protest across the United States just weeks before the Columbia rebellion. During May, the period of the Columbia strike, stu-

46. Interview: Paul Broches by Marta Gutman and Harry Kendall, April 19, 1981; see also, Columbia University, School of Architecture, "Statement of Urgency" (mimeographed).

47. See Irwin Unger's discussion of the origins of the New Left in *The Movement,* particularly the Introduction and chapters I and II. Sheldon S. Wolin and John H. Schaar in *The Berkeley Rebellion and Beyond* (New York: Vintage Books, 1970) also offer an illuminating discussion of the student movement.

dents, especially those in France and Germany, manned barricades in the streets of major European cities; police and armies smashed these revolts. Just after the commencements at Columbia, Robert Kennedy was murdered. During the summer, when the School was trying to create a new curriculum, the Republicans nominated Richard Nixon as their candidate for President; during the trauma and violence of the Chicago convention, the Democrats nominated Hubert Humphrey, Johnson's Vice President. Nixon promised he had a "secret plan" to end the war; few on the left believed him, but his election seemed inevitable by the time the architecture students returned to Avery Hall in the fall.

On their own these events created a charged atmosphere at many universities. But at Columbia, as at other schools, the attitude of the Administration only aggravated the tension before, during, and after the strike. Though the Cox Commission lacked any sympathy for the confrontational tactics of the New Left, it unequivocally stated that the University failed to understand why the 1968 rebellion happened. In common with other institutions which experienced similar unrest, the Administration did not comprehend the extent of student opposition to the war in Vietnam; student support of the civil rights movement and the cause for social and economic justice among the nation's poor; and the growing belief that the policy of any institution which helped cause social problems should be changed.[48] The administration policy, which allowed military recruiting on campus, and its arrogant attitude toward the surrounding neighborhood, made the University, as others were, a target for student activist groups.[49]

The intensity of Columbia's rebellion also stemmed from deep-rooted dissatisfaction with the quality of education and campus life, and from the University's geographic location. Housing for faculty and students on or near campus was in short supply. The University displayed little concern for the problems of minorities on campus. An over-worked and under-paid faculty, unable to find housing nearby, was remote from student life.[50] The University's aloof, authoritarian attitude toward the students and faculty improved none of this. One dean's alleged statement became especially notorious:

A university is definitely not a democratic institution. When decisions begin to be made democratically around here, I will not be here any longer... Whether the students vote "yes" or "no" on an issue is like telling me whether they like strawberries.[51]

The denial of participation, the faculty detachment, the housing pressure, and the dissatisfaction with curriculum, created what the Cox Commission called a "lack of institutional confidence," on the part of students and faculty. This, accompanied by strong political beliefs, truly depressing world-wide events, and stubbornness on all sides created the explosive situation in 1968.

Most of the architecture students did not belong to the SDS; indeed, for the most part, older (average age was twenty-seven), white, middle class males seeking a second (professional) degree made up the student population. Some came to the School

"Strike" Spring 1968. Photo by Sid Slater, courtesy *Columbia College Today*.

48. Cox Commission, *Crisis at Columbia*, pp. 4-13, 19-21.

49. Ibid., pp. 12-13, 36-41.

50. Ibid., pp. 13-18, 21-24, 30-36, 41-53.

51. Herbert Deane, Vice-Dean of the Graduate Faculties, as quoted by Cox Commission, *Crisis at Columbia*, pp. 48-49. Dean's remarks were made in an interview published by the *Spectator;* he later charged they were "elliptically reported." See James S. Kunen, *The Strawberry Statement* (New York: Random House, 1969); and Cox Commission, *Crisis at Columbia*, pp. 48-49.

through the professional option program at Columbia College; some had served in the armed forces; some had worked in architectural offices.[52] Still they were among the first to occupy a building for when Dean Kenneth Smith asked them to leave Avery Hall on Wednesday evening, April 24, they refused and formed the "Avery Commune." As the Cox Commission stated, the building would not have been taken so quickly "without a much deeper sense of underlying grievance."[53] It was correct. Aside from the long-range causes of the "sense of grievance," the architecture students and faculty first began to criticize the University's architectural and planning policies and complain about their exclusion from a crucial role in that decision-making process early in the 1960's. Similarly, students and faculty stated their dissatisfaction with the structure and form of the educational system from the beginning of the decade. By 1968 the need for a socially responsible campus planning policy (and by implication professional practice) and the need for a socially responsible education merged to become the basis of the new curriculum.

In 1968 the University's architectural and planning policies ignited the student rebellion because its architectural and planning policy ignored the needs of its neighbors. During the late 1950's and 1960's the University escalated its acquisition of property on Morningside Heights and encouraged institutional expansion on the Heights. One part of its policy looked toward finding needed room to house a growing college-bound population. The other looked toward controlling the ethnic and class composition of Morningside Heights through building destruction and tenant eviction.

Admittedly the University needed space. Its problems with expansion were as old as the campus itself, because McKim's original plan could not be adapted easily to growth or change. The first major additions to the plan in the 1920's,[54] ironically guided by McKim, Mead and White, began to chip away at the integrity of the original plan, breaking the uniformity of the cornice line and the fenestration. Practicing "economic verticality," new buildings were built taller than before and with lower ceiling heights.[55] Still, similar materials, architectural style, and to some extent, urbanistic sensibilities linked the new campus architecture with the old. By the late 1950's and early 1960's these concerns disappeared: the University wanted space, and it wanted it as cheaply as possible. It made plans to expand the boundaries of the original campus to the east; it also signed, in the fall of 1961, a lease for land along the cliffs of Morningside Park on which it agreed to construct a gymnasium, a part of which it would share with the community. A post-war expansion drive[56] produced a series of banal buildings which delivered the final blow to the integrity of McKim's plan.[57]

But the University did not expand to meet simple needs for space. Rather, it was, as early as 1963, trying to create a white, upper middle class enclave on the Heights. To this end it supported three positions: no public housing between 110th and 123rd

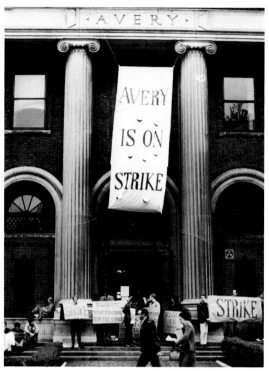

"Avery is on strike" Spring 1968. Photo: *Columbia College Today.*

52. Richard Rosenkranz, *Across the Barricades* (New York: J.B. Lippincott Company, 1971), prolog 2-3. Rosenkranz, a fellowship student at the Columbia Journalism School, joined the occupation of Avery Hall and wrote a controversial day by day account of it.

53. Cox Commission, *Crisis at Columbia,* pp. 110-111.

54. Buildings include Chandler, Pupin, Schermerhorn extension, and John Jay Hall. Butler Library was also built before World War II.

55. Frederick Woodbridge, "Buildings and Spaces, Past Present and Future," *Columbia College Today,* 10 (Fall 1962), p. 15.

56. The goal was announced as eighty million dollars in 1962; two hundred million in 1965. See "1959 — Columbia's Year of Expansion," *Columbia Daily Spectator,* December 18, 1959, pp. 1-2; Fred M. Hechinger, "Columbia Plans New Expansion," *The New York Times,* April 9, 1961, p. 1, 80; "Too many cooks, too few artists," *Columbia College Today,* 10 (Fall 1962), p. 1; Ada Louise Huxtable, "Expansion at Columbia," *The New York Times,* November 5, 1966, p. 33.

57. Examples include Ferris-Booth Hall, Carman Hall, Seely W. Mudd School of Engineering, the Law School, and Uris Hall, the Graduate School of Business.

Streets; the encouragement of institutional expansion on the Heights; and the removal of single-room-occupancy hotels north of 110th Street.[58] The process was not gentle, and in the same year, tenant groups began to picket President Kirk's house, protesting university expansion and tenant relocation.[59] *The New York Times* praised Kirk and the University for its "quiet" help in tenant relocation,[60] but the University was more concerned with amassing large amounts of property. By 1966 an estimate placed the worth of Columbia's rental property as sixty-one million dollars.[61] Jacques Barzun, the Provost, stated to a community meeting that the University wanted a "decent residential community,"[62] a goal with which few could disagree. This goal, however, was realized through the eviction of poor, black, white, and Hispanic tenants from newly purchased buildings which were then offered at subsidized rents to students and faculty.[63] This increased demand for the apartments, while generating volatile community resentment.[64] Little effort was made to relocate or provide social assistance to the original occupants because, as Barzun said, these were "technical problems we are not equipped to handle."[65]

This was matched by the beginning of a dramatic increase in the institutional presence on the Heights. In 1965 Columbia announced plans to construct fourteen major academic buildings and dormitories some of which were intended to stretch as far south as 110th Street.[66] In addition, the University tried to draw affiliated institutions, such as the School of Social Work and the College of Pharmacy into buildings on the Heights. The School of Social Work resisted but its argument, that a site in Harlem among the people it served would be more appropriate than a site on 113th Street, was not heeded. The College of Pharmacy failed to acquire a few of the buildings it needed to clear its site. Other institutions, such as the Bank Street College of Education and the Manhattan School of Music were lured to the Heights with financial incentives and loans.[67] Official figures stated that the move of the institutions displaced between 2000–3000 families, and protest, arguing that Bank Street only served as an "oasis" from integrated public schools, accompanied its move.[68]

There were disastrous urbanistic consequences. What had once been an economically, architecturally, and socially mixed community was on its way towards becoming an institutional wasteland. For example, the construction of the new buildings and the podium along Amsterdam Avenue destroyed the architectural and the social character of the street which was lined originally with small stores at the bottom of five and six story apartment buildings.[69] It also removed and did not replace needed community services. In *Death and Life of Great American Cities,* Jane Jacobs warned that this kind of monolithic development rather than the presence of mixed neighborhoods makes a community vulnerable to violent crime. But critics ignored these urbanistic problems until the late 1960's. Ada Louise Huxtable and Allan Temko guardedly praised the Law School building; Temko thought the podium was a sound approach to urban design. He even argued

58. Stanley Salmen, "Memorandum to the Trustees and President Kirk," as quoted by Columbia Students for a Democratic Society and Morningside Housing Committee of the Columbia-Barnard Citizenship Program in *Columbia and Urban Renewal* (mimeographed, 1968). Salmen's memo outlined the University's expansion policy in reference to Columbia's attempts to limit the number of low income units constructed on the Upper West Side. Salmen was executive director of Morningside Heights, Inc., the organization of Heights Institutions dominated by Columbia when he wrote the memo. He later became Coordinator of University Planning.

59. "Columbia Helping Evicted Tenants," *The New York Times,* October 20, 1963, p. 121; Robert Alden, "Neighbors Assail Columbia Growth," *The New York Times,* January 18, 1964, pp. 25-26.

60. Alden, "Neighbors Assail Columbia Growth," p. 25.

61. C. Richard Hatch, "Columbia: Pleonexia on the Acropolis," *The Architectural Forum,* 108 (July–August 1967), p. 73.

62. Jacques Barzun as quoted by Hatch, "Columbia," p. 73. Though seemingly mild, Barzun's statement angered those opposed to University policy, and strike publications often quoted from it. Rosenkranz, *Across the Barricades,* log. 191.

63. Written in 1966, the affiliation clause allowed the University to claim dormitory status for rooms and receive tax exemptions. Robert Keating, "Columbia Devours the Upper West Side," *The Village Voice,* 25 (May 19, 1980), pp. 1, 13-16.

64. "Architectural Students Join Columbia Strikes: Out of Chaos, Maturity," *Progressive Architecture,* 49 (June 1968), p. 45.

65. Barzun, as quoted by Hatch, "Columbia," p. 73.

66. Huxtable, "Expansion at Columbia," p. 33.

67. Hatch, "Columbia," pp. 73-73; Hatch notes that the Bank Street and Manhattan School of Music move to the Heights denied their "precious ideals" of playing an "important cultural function in their [original] working class neighborhoods."

68. Alden, "Neighbors Assail Columbia Growth," p. 25.

69. Hatch, "Columbia," p. 71.

that the University, at the time of McKim, ought to have purchased all of Morningside Heights to assure consistent community ·development.[70]

But direct examination of the social consequences of the University's expansion, particularly its foundation on the displacement of minorities, had begun. While Ada Louise Huxtable accepted the University's role as the "maker and shaper" of a large portion of Morningside Heights, she did say that it must do a better job because it had "proven inability...to see the environment as a whole and to recognize the need of highest level professional vision that threatens its development and the Morningside community with disaster."[71] Richard Hatch, the first director of A.R.C.H., Architects' Renewal Committee in Harlem, founded in 1964, published an attack on university policy in the *Architectural Forum*, "Pleonexia on the Acropolis." Criticizing the architectural character of the Columbia environment and documenting the University's expansion and its treatment of its neighbors, Hatch said that the University had no sense of public responsibility, that it was only interested in the fabrication of a "scholastic ghetto."[72] CORE, NAACP, and the City Human Rights Commission also attacked Columbia.[73] Stanley Lowell, a member of the Human Rights Commission, urged Columbia to "abandon its policy of near total reliance on tenant removal as a solution to social problems incidental to its expansion," and use a policy of social rehabilitation. Columbia responded that it was not a welfare institution.[74]

More than any other action or event, the planned gymnasium in Morningside Park symbolized the University's policy towards its neighbors. In exchange for the private use of public land, the lease negotiated between President Kirk and Parks Commissioner Robert Moses, provided that the University pay three thousand dollars rent a year. The University assumed all construction costs of a "double facility": offices and classrooms, and a gym on top for university use (85–88%); community facilities on the bottom which were slated for use by male, Harlem youth (12–15%).[75] Max Abramovitz *(Columbia, 1931)*, co-designer of the Law School building, takes credit for the concept of the gym, including its cross-section.[76] The gym presented a dull wall, lacking any architectural character; the view up from Harlem showed, approximately, a one-hundred-fifty-foot brick and concrete box rudely grafted onto the cliff and entered through a small door at the bottom.

Opposition to the gym was based upon the private use of public land, the lack of community involvement by the University in decisions affecting them, and the architectural character of the project, particularly the division of space given the low rent the University paid.[77] But it developed slowly. During 1961–65, while the University sponsored a nine million dollar fund raising drive, neighborhood opposition was minimal. According to the Cox Commission, there was even some sentiment that the rocky area of the park, as potentially beautiful as it was, could be put to better use as a recreational facility.[78] But some objections were raised. In 1964 *The New York Times* commented that "neglected

70. Temko and Huxtable did criticize the aesthetics of most of the new campus architecture. See Allan Temko, "A Brilliant Plan Gone Awry?" *Columbia College Today,* 10 (Fall 1962), p. 22; Huxtable, "Expansion at Columbia," p. 33.

71. Hatch, "Columbia," pp. 72-74.

72. Huxtable, "Expansion at Columbia," pp. 33, 34.

73. Ibid.

74. Stanley Lowell, Letter to Vice-President Lawrence H. Chamberlain, as quoted by Columbia Strike Coordinating Committee, *Columbia Liberated,* p. 9.

75. Cox Commission, *Crisis at Columbia,* pp. 76-77; "Four...Three...Two..." *Columbia College Today,* 9 (Fall 1961), p. 27; "Athletics at Columbia," *Columbia College Today,* 11 (Fall 1963), pp. 18-19.

76. Interview: Max Abramovitz by Richard Oliver, March 19, 1981, Graduate School of Architecture and Planning archives (hereafter GSAP archives). The partnership of Eggers and Higgins — Sherwood *(Columbia, 1936),* Mills, and Smith designed the building. Eggers and Higgins was the successor firm to that of John Russell Pope *(Columbia, 1894).*

77. Examples of criticism of the gym may be found in Ada Louise Huxtable, "How Not to Build a Symbol," *The New York Times,* March 24, 1968, Sect. II, p. 23; George Kelter, "Six Weeks that Shook Morningside," *Columbia College Today,* 15 (Spring 1968), p. 32; Cox Commission, *Crisis at Columbia,* pp. 78-79.

78. Cox Commission, *Crisis at Columbia,* p. 76; George Keller, "Six Weeks that Shook Morningside," p. 31. Keller hints the University chose the rocky slope to avoid displacement of Morningside residents, but such worries did not restrain future action. Robert Keating mentions numerous later examples in "Columbia Devours the Upper West Side."

park areas have been taken over by Columbia with the consent of the city. A running track, tennis courts, and a gymnasium are being constructed in these areas for joint public and university use," but the community has depicted the "park projects as land grabs."[79]

The situation began to change in 1965. From that year, when the Ad Hoc Committee on Morningside Park of the Parks and Playground Committee of the Morningside Renewal Council was formed, until 1968, the community raised objections to the proposed gym but expressed little hope of preventing construction.[80] They were joined by politicians, including John Lindsay, who issued a "white paper" on city parks during the 1965 mayoralty campaign which opposed the gym; Thomas Hoving, who as Parks commissioner in the Lindsay administration tried to convince the University to abandon the project; and State Senator Basil Patterson and Assemblyman Percy Sutton, who introduced legislation to repeal the act that allowed the University to rent public land, a tactic which proved a failure.

During these years the University and the community held meetings; in 1967 the University altered its position slightly. It still refused to share the entire facility, but it offered to build a swimming pool in the community's section of the building. Patterson chastized the University's attitude, but said little could be done, and the community should accept the offer because it improved the facility.[81]

Others disagreed and the Ad Hoc Committee gave way to the West Harlem Morningside Park Committee. This represented sixteen Harlem organizations, fifteen of which opposed the gym. Further and larger demonstrations occurred, but they proved fruitless and construction began unannounced on February 19, 1968. This sparked more protests which tried to halt the construction, and arrests were made of community residents and students. After the seizure and strike, the Trustees suspended construction indefinitely.

In evaluating the causes of the strike, the Cox Commission stated that the gym was essentially a fair "business transaction" and a "practical arrangement." However, university officials "utterly failed to grasp or if they did indeed grasp, utterly failed to acknowledge,"[82] that the proposed gym symbolized something far more serious: the University's failure to understand the problems of poverty and racism and its arrogant exclusion of the community from its planning policy. But as much as the gym was hated for these reasons, it came to be feared as a symbol of encroachment. For if Columbia were presented to Harlem as an Acropolis, then surely the gym could have become the gate, the Propylea of the complex on top of the Heights. Cruelly, though, since the gate did not give Harlem residents access up the hill, it was feared as the University's first step on a march that would ultimately invade and occupy West Harlem.[83]

Opposition from the "acropolis" joined community opposition to the gym proposal. Prior to the strike, support for the community stemmed from the University Student Council, the Citizenship

"The Gym must go" Spring 1968.
Photo: *Columbia College Today.*

79. Alden, "Neighbors Assail Columbia Growth," p. 25.

80. Description of the history of the gymnasium controversy may be found in Cox Commission, *Crisis at Columbia,* pp. 73-83; Columbia Strike Coordinating Committee, *Columbia Liberated,* pp.10-12; Huxtable, "How Not to Build a Symbol," p. 23; Ralph Blumenthal, "Columbia Scores Gym-Plan Critics," *The New York Times,* February 15, 1966, p. 31; Keller, "Six Weeks that Shook Morningside," pp. 31-32.

81. Ibid.

82. Cox Commission, *Crisis at Columbia,* pp. 83, 86.

83. Interview: J. Max Bond by Authors, June 24, 1981. Also many Heights residents shared Harlem residents' fear of Columbia's encroachment. Comments by Franz Leiter, a local Democratic politician, illuminate the extent of community resentment.

The gymnasium is only. . . a manifestation of. . . the whole uncoordinated, even legislatively, and unchecked expansion on the Heights and into the surrounding community. We have seen in the last seven years or so some 10,000 persons displaced from Morningside Heights. We have seen over 150 buildings taken by various institutions on the Heights, most of them by Columbia University. . . what was done. . . is really only part of the feeling that the people in the area have. . . that this large institution, which isn't subject to any of the usual pressures of society or. . . political pressures, . . . is just expanding, without any limit at all, without any means of imposing restrictions, or really without any procedures for the community to voice its opinion and to find anyone who will listen (As quoted by Cox Commission, *Crisis at Columbia,* pp. 86-87).

Council, the SDS, and the Graduate Student Council. However, the Cox Commission stated that there is little evidence that the gym was an important campus issue prior to the disturbance. Most people seem to have felt it was a *fait accompli*.[84] Even the *Spectator,* which was accused of biased, pro-strike reporting in April and May, supported the construction of the gym in an editorial on March 6 entitled "Enough is Enough."[85] But during the strike the situation changed rapidly. 4093 out of 6426 students asked said that they believed the gym construction should be stopped.[86] The faculty of Columbia College hastily passed a resolution urging the construction of the gym be halted on Wednesday, April 24, the day President Kirk's office was occupied. The architecture faculty was the only one to express an opinion before the strike. As mixed a political group as it was, it issued a unanimous resolution on March 27 asking the Trustees to reconsider the project.[87]

Within the School opposition to university policy toward the surrounding community grew out of dissatisfaction with the quality of new architecture being built on campus, and concern over the quality of the curriculum, faculty and administration. The circumstances under which Arnaud and Colbert left the school created a state of disorientation from which no school could be expected to recover readily. Pressure for curriculum reform gradually became linked to the interest in the relationship between architecture and social problems which grew out of government social programs sponsored by the New Frontier and the Great Society. It was a relationship not dissimilar to the connection between Hudnut's reforms and the New Deal. Although few architecture students were involved, the backdrop of activist politics of the New Left created an atmosphere sympathetic to dissent.

The quality of campus architecture generated the first public demonstrations of restlessness. In 1959 architecture students protested the quality of the design of Ferris Booth Hall, labeling it "bad Miami Beach Decor."[88] In 1961 the Seely W. Mudd School of Engineering was protested, and articles in the student newspapers criticized the new buildings.[89] The campus radio station asked Percival Goodman to comment on campus planning and architectural issues; Goodman agreed, but the University seized the tapes and prohibited their broadcast using the excuse that they feared Goodman had made libelous statements.[90] In 1962, having had no effect on campus policy, architecture students led by Alan Lapidus *(1963)* and Harry Parnass *(1963)* picketed the ground-breaking ceremonies of Uris Hall, the new building of the Business School. Designed by Moore and Hutchins, it was to be constructed on the site of the University's old gymnasium. The demonstration received nation-wide publicity.[91] James Marston Fitch joined the students' criticism along with other architectural critics and historians[92] and some faculty who joined anonymously to avoid violating the "code" of professional ethics.[93]

Impetus for this demonstration gained, undoubtedly, from protests which involved architects on campus and in New York. The "Ban the Bomb" movement had spread to the United States from Britain where it developed in the 1950's through the influence of

84. Cox Commission, *Crisis at Columbia,* p. 82.

85. Cox Commission, *Crisis at Columbia,* p. 89. Accusations of biased reporting may be found in George Keller, "Six Weeks that Shook Morningside."

86. Cox Commission, *Crisis at Columbia,* p. 89.

87. Robert Hardman, "Faculty of Architecture Asks Trustees to Reconsider Gym," *Columbia Daily Spectator,* April 15, 1968, p. 1; "New Columbia Gym is Opposed," *The New York Times,* April 16, 1968, p. 49. During the Spring of 1968, Alexander Kouzmanoff taught a studio in which students designed an Architecture School located on Morningside Drive and the south side of 116th Street, the area designated for the Columbia Fine Arts Complex. The complex had been slated originally for the Business School site but, despite Barzun's support, it was not built at either location. Kouzmanoff recalls the studio offered an opportunity for a dialogue on the problems of the architectural and planning policy of the University; these concerns prompted some students to design humanistic architectural connections between Columbia and Harlem which better used Morningside Park than the gym on which construction had just begun. Even though the studio roused student interest within the School, the issue of the gym did not concern many others, a situation typical of much of the University. Interview: Alexander Kouzmanoff by Plunz, Gutman, Kendall and Robert Lane, April 7, 1981.

88. As quoted by David Binder, "Columbia Is the Latest Target of Protests on Campus Designs," *The New York Times,* April 29, 1962, Sect. VIII, p. 1. Similar protests occurred at Princeton University and Trinity College. In 1960 Enrico Peressutti resigned in protest over Princeton's architectural policy.

89. Linda Bein, "New Buildings: Fifth Rate?" *The Columbia Owl,* 3 (November 22, 1961), pp. 1, 7; David Binder, "Columbia Is the Latest Target," Sect. VIII, p. 1.

90. Binder, "Columbia Is the Latest Target," Sect. VIII, pp. 1-2.

91. "Ground Breaking Ceremony Set for School of Business," *Columbia Daily Spectator,* April 13, 1962, p. 3; "Modern Architecture Hit by Reed, Picketers," *Columbia Daily Spectator,* April 18, 1962, p. 1; "Students Term New Hall Ugly," *The New York Times,* April 18, 1962, p. 18; "Architecture Protests Bring No Official University Action," *Columbia Daily Spectator,* April 26, 1962, p. 1; Binder, "Columbia Is the Latest Target," Sect. VIII, p. 2; Joseph Michalak, "Students Protest College Building Designs," *The New York Herald Tribune,* April 29, 1962, Sect. II, p. 5; "The Growing Campus," *The Columbia Owl,* 3 (May 2, 1962), p. 1; "Columbia Design Under Student Fire, *Architectural Forum,* 116 (June 1962), p. 9.

92. "Professor Joins Design Dispute," *The New York Times,* April 19, 1962, p. 33. Binder's article noted Blake's disapproval of Uris design; Henry Hope Reed criticized the building in a campus lecture, "The Ugly American Campus." *Columbia College Today* responded to the controversy by devoting the Fall 1962 issue to campus architecture. It included an editorial, "Too many cooks, too few artists," critical of building policy and Allan Temko's article, "A Brilliant Plan Gone Awry," which had few kind words for the new campus architecture. Katherine Kuh voiced her disapproval in "Art in America, 1962: A Balance Sheet," *Saturday Review,* 45 (September 8, 1962), pp. 30A-N.

93. Binder, "Columbia is the Latest Target," Sect. VIII, p. 2; Michalek, "Students Protest College Building Design," p. 5.

such people as Bertrand Russell.[94] It roused campus support during the winter of 1961 – 62 when faculty from fourteen universities and colleges in the New York area wrote "an open letter to President Kennedy and Governor Rockefeller" which critized the civil defense program, including the construction of fall-out shelters, and urged that the policy "be directed toward a positive program for peace with freedom." The faculty, connected to the School, who signed it were James M. Fitch, Percival Goodman, Alexander Kouzmanoff, Mario Salvadori, Stanley Salzman, and Meyer Shapiro.[95] During Christmas vacation, Columbia College and Barnard students joined others from Amherst, Oberlin, Smith, Illinois, Wisconsin, and Pennsylvania and picketed the White House in hopes that Kennedy would cease atmospheric nuclear bomb tests.[96] In addition, the protests over the demolition of Pennsylvania Station which occurred during 1961, helped legitimize the students' tactics.[97] The students' protests led to student proposals. In 1963 they presented a study of the South Campus to the Administration which grew out of a studio directed by Charles Colbert.[98]

Intelligent and progressive criticism of the Business School raised public questions about the aesthetic and urbanistic problems of the University's architectural planning policy. Students, contending that the production of such design would cause them to be thrown out of school, criticized the building for its backward-looking aesthetics, or "mock monumentality"; the lack of concern for sun control and light on a building whose major facade faced south; the failure to provide space around it; and the institutional imagery,[99] or what James Burns, an editor of *Progressive Architecture,* called the building when completed: the "scholastic model office building" which acclimated students to the business world.[100] Faculty broadened the scope of the students' criticism by questioning the exclusion of the architectural faculty from consultation on university projects and the lack of a serious plan for development and expansion.[101]

These issues and the growing trend towards student participation in university affairs to which they pointed, were ignored. The Administration, much as it shut its eyes toward the needs of its neighbors, shut its eyes towards aesthetic problems and defended Uris and other modern buildings.[102] William Platt *(Columbia, 1923),* a member of the Advisory Committee on University Architecture, presented the attitude of the committee, and by implication, that of the entire administration.

The committee had in mind a background building, not a unique design that would compete with present structures like Low Library. . . . It should not be the kind of building the architecture students have in mind. Rather it should be a nonentity, an efficient building that fits in. The committee did think [the design submitted] was adequate.[103]

Exactly why the University steadfastly resisted aesthetic criteria in its building strategies can be traced to the interests of the Board of Trustees. Yale, for example, was able to hire "star" architects, many from the ranks of its own faculty, and others associated in

94. Unger discusses the development of the nuclear disarmament movement in the first chapter of *The Movement.*

95. "An Open Letter to President Kennedy and Governor Rockefeller," *The New York Times,* December 19, 1961, p. 22.

96. "Bombs and Shelters," *Columbia College Today,* 9 (Winter 1961 – 61), p. 10.

97. The Pennsylvania Station protests became the occasion for some of the "best dressed" picket lines in New York including such figures as Philip Johnson, Aline B. Saarinen, and Paul Rudolph. The Action Group for Better Architecture in New York, the organization which sponsored the protests, made interesting proposals for the rehabilitation of the station, but the building was demolished in 1963. Even then its destruction galvanized support for the preservation movement. See "Penn Station Ruin Protested," *Progressive Architecture,* 43 (September 1961), p. 63; "Penn Station to Give Way to Madison Square Garden," *Progressive Architecture,* 43 (September 1961), p. 65; "Agbany Proposes Plan to Save Penn Station," *Progressive Architecture,* 44 (January 1963), p. 48; "Pennsylvania Station's Last Stand," *Architectural Forum,* 118 (February 1963), p. 3; "Pennsylvania Station: Finis," *Progressive Architecture,* 44 (December 1963), pp. 54-55.

98. Columbia University School of Architecture, *South Campus Study,* New York, 1963. Interestingly enough, the University administration resented, and then ignored, the students' studies. Interview: Charles Colbert by Richard Oliver, February 4, 1981, GSAP archives.

99. Allan Lapidus and Harry Parnass as cited by David Binder, "Columbia Is the Latest Target...," Sect. VIII, p. 2.

100. James T. Burns, Jr., "Uris Hall: An Opportunity Missed," *Columbia Daily Spectator,* May 8, 1964, pp. 1-2.

101. Colbert raised these issues with the administration. See also James M. Fitch's comments in "Professor Joins Design Dispute," p. 33.

102. "President Kirk Defends Columbia Architecture," *Columbia Daily Spectator,* May 7, 1962, p. 1.

103. William Platt as quoted by Binder, "Columbia is the Latest Target," Sect. VIII, p. 2. The media quoted Platt's statement frequently.

other ways with that school. But Columbia hired architects who were on the periphery of academic involvement and certainly not at the forefront of new ideas.[104] They tended to be connected to the University through business associations, reflecting a drawback of the proximity of Columbia to the center of American commercial power, of being too close for comfort. For example, Percy Uris, who was on the Board of Trustees, could through his financial contribution, influence the design of Uris Hall.[105] The Trustees settled for financial analysis rather than aesthetic analysis. As Ada Louise Huxtable pointed out, "programming, scheduling of needs, is mistaken for planning."[106] If severe cost restraints were indeed an issue, they could have been incorporated into open design competitions. Instead, architects were chosen by committee after initial design decisions had already been made.[107]

The opinions of the architecture faculty were unsolicited, except through a University Advisory Committee on Architecture, which had only "advisory powers," and was chosen to reflect closely the views of the Trustees. The Trustees refused to hire members of the architecture faculty, citing fear of conflict of interest. Yet Trustee Vincent Kling *(Columbia, 1940),* a prominent corporate practitioner from Philadelphia, told the striking students who had called from the Avery Commune, that he had every right to design Altschul Hall and McIntosh Center at Barnard, and that any conflict of interest on his part was not a problem. According to Peter Jackson *(Columbia, 1971)* who talked with Kling, he launched into the charge that the "faculty at Avery were so useless that they could never be relied upon to build anything, that the reason they were professors was that they couldn't compete in the real world with real architects, and the reason they couldn't compete was because they didn't know enough." He also related that Harvard and Yale were superior to Columbia because their students "did more drafting and talked less about politics."[108]

The students' interest in social problems and political change which so disturbed Kling developed in part from internal problems at the School. Most notably, the School suffered from poor teaching, the presence of many part-time, adjunct faculty with little commitment to education, tenured faculty with old ideas, and an out-moded curriculum. Dean Smith's cautious educational approach did not commit the School to a style, or formula, or an excessively structured curriculum. In and of itself, the approach did not cause problems, but when combined with budgetary restrictions and poor teaching, it generated criticism and student complaints.[109] To some extent, Smith's diligence and devotion to the School compensated for larger problems, as did his attempts to solve the prominent problems of too many part-time faculty and an out-moded curriculum. In retrospect though, little could be done without major, structural change. As Conrad Levenson *(Columbia, 1966)* recounted, it was only after the example of the 1968 strike that he realized the magnitude of the force needed to effect sweeping change.[110]

Peter Prangnell and Romaldo Giurgola *(Columbia, 1951),* both

104. See discussion of this problem in Temko, "A Brilliant Plan Gone Awry," p. 23; Michalak, "Students Protest College Building Designs," Sect. II, p. 5.

105. Temko, "A Brilliant Plan," p. 22; James T. Burns, "Uris Hall," pp. 1-2.

106. Huxtable, "Expansion at Columbia," pp. 33-34.

107. The procedure was swaddled in bureaucracy. In 1965, suggested plans went through the office of the Coordinator of University Planning; then to the Trustees' Committee on Development; then to the Dean of the involved School; then back to the Planning Office; then to the Trustees' Committee on Buildings and Grounds. At this point the site had been chosen, a schematic design proposed, and architects suggested. The design was then reviewed by the University Advisory Council on Architecture, established in 1956, whose membership included two practicing graduates of the School of Architecture, one member of its faculty, its Dean (or Chairman of the Division of Architecture), and the campus architect. This committee sent the plans, with a revised list of architects, to the office of Construction; the President made a final recommendation about selection to the Trustees' Committee for Appropriations. See Huxtable, "Expansion at Columbia," p. 34; Donald H. Shapiro, "CU Architect Talks About University Building Policy," *Columbia Daily Spectator,* May 2, 1962, pp. 1, 7; Binder, "Columbia Is the Latest Target," Sect, VIII, p. 1.

108. Peter Jackson as quoted by Rosenkranz, *Across the Barricades,* log. 182-83.

109. Interview: Conrad Levenson by Authors, June 24, 1981.

110. Ibid.

hired by Smith, introduced contemporary ideas into the School and began to solve the problem of little commitment to education. When Prangnell came in 1964, he was the only full-time design instructor. With the help of Ray Lifchez, he reorganized the first year program which he and Lifchez taught together until Prangnell left in 1967. Giurgola began to participate in the Columbia studios in 1965 and in 1967 was appointed as the first chairman of the division of architecture as part of a major revision of the administrative structure of the School.[111]

Prangnell introduced students to ideas shaped by Aldo Van Eyck and Herman Hertzberger, and to the Team X critique of modern architecture.[112] The first-year program stressed the connection between social systems and built form and drew on projects that referred to students' experience out of a desire to demystify the process of learning to design. For example, in the first semester concern with the formal language of architecture was augmented by the analysis of building in terms of program. The cultural context of architectural practice was introduced through assignment of a photo essay which documented a day in the life of a typical New Yorker. The second semester was devoted to a thorough study of a single building — a motel on a highway — from the perspective of formal and social criteria. Prangnell wanted students to think of the motel as an "oasis" and urged that the design address the processes of arrival, departure, and rest.[113]

The tepid intellectual atmosphere at the School, if not the entire University, provided fertile ground for interest in humanist ideas. Many students responded positively to Prangnell's search for a humanistic architecture, his dynamic teaching presence, and, some of them, to his politics.[114] Other teachers at the School, most notably Alexander Kouzmanoff, were similarly concerned with the issue of humanism;[115] he too was a devoted, influential, and very popular teacher. And, of course, the new campus buildings themselves began to educate students, for as strike and post-strike publications would comment, they provided little space for public appearance and social activity. Nothing could more insistently convince students that architectural form had to grow out of a concept of social structure.[116]

Most formally oriented students disagreed with Prangnell's method of analysis. They too criticized poor campus architecture, but they blamed formal issues of design and found more interesting ideas emanating from Penn and Yale, particularly the ideas of Kahn, Scully, and Venturi which the Giurgola group introduced to the School.[117] Romaldo Giurgola had taught at the University of Pennsylvania since 1958. He had completed several significant projects in the early 1960's and with his move to Columbia, he opened a Mitchell/Giurgola office in New York. He quickly introduced colleagues and associates to the School. In 1966 Jonathan Barnett, Giovanni Pasanella, Jaquelin Robertson, Richard Weinstein, and Myles Weintraub, in addition to teaching, publicized a study to be done under a grant through Columbia on ways to effect urban renewal through citizen participation.[118] Yale graduates, with the exception of Weinstein, who was from Penn, they were involved

111. Smith, an engineer who had taught at the School since 1935, divided the School into three divisions, with Charles Abrams as Chairman of Urban Planning, Mario Salvadori as Chairman of Architectural Technology, and Romaldo Giurgola as Chairman of Architecture. The revision of the structure of the School allowed experts with national and international reputations to shape different programs for the three divisions. Although the programs of the Divisions of Urban Planning and Architectural Technology are of great interest, the discussion which follows concentrates on the changes which occurred in the Division of Architecture. For further discussion of the revision of the School's structure, see "Columbia Revises Architecture School," *The New York Times,* May 28, 1965, p. 29.

112. For further information on Team X see Alison Smithson, ed., *Team 10 Primer* (Cambridge, Mass.: The MIT Press, rev. ed. 1968). The primer, originally published in 1962, influenced architecture schools other than Columbia; indeed students across the United States warmed to its critique of the modern movement which presented humanist, if sometimes utopian, architectural alternatives. The effects of the Team X critique on Peter Prangnell have been recounted in Peter Prangnell, "From Peter Prangnell," *Legacies of a Radical Era, Architecture at Columbia: 1968–80, Solicitea Messages to the Symposium* (mimeographed), 1980. Interview: Paul Broches by Gutman and Kendall; Interview: Chris Wadsworth by Authors, June 17, 1981.

113. Prangnell, "Statement from Peter Prangnell"; Interview: Broches by Gutman and Kendall.

114. Interview: Kouzmanoff by Plunz, et. al. Interview: Broches by Gutman and Kendall; Interview: Wadsworth by Authors; Rosenkranz, *Across the Barricades,* log 5.

115. The origins of Kouzmanoff's philosophy were different from Prangnell's, however. Kouzmanoff's formative years were at IIT before the war, and with Mathew Nowicki and the International Basic Economy Corporation (IBEC) afterward. Separated by a generation, Prangnell had studied at the Architectural Association in London before going to Harvard, where he was Aldo Van Eyck's teaching assistant.

116. CUSC, Social Atmosphere Committee, "The Quality of Life at Columbia: Ideas…Involving Architecture," Fall 1968 (mimeographed). This report, somewhat humorously, described the quality of student life. Comments, though, point out how poor architecture helped cause sterile campus life, and concrete suggestions for improvement were offered.

117. Interview: Robert Kliment and Frances Halsband by Richard Oliver, GSAP archives.

118. "Community Action," *Journal of the American Institute of Architects,* 66 (November 1966), p. 89.

with establishing themselves in New York, at that time through the Lindsay administration — principally the Office of Midtown Planning and the Urban Design Group. Some students found these connections exciting. Others found that they conflicted with teaching responsibilities.[119] Around the same time, Robert Kliment, who had worked for Giurgola since 1961, also began to teach at Columbia.

The new Yale/Penn group complemented many of the ideas of the existing faculty such as their interest in urban design.[120] But the strong influence in the design studios continued to come from the Team X approach toward urban design which dealt more with "infra-structure" than with traditionally defined building form.[121] Indeed, the influence of the Team X philosophy provided a powerful critique of the Yale/Penn group even though it also was involved with urban problems. The project of the Yale/Penn group for a development, forty-seven blocks long, over the Penn Central tracks on Park Avenue in East Harlem, was interpreted by some faculty and students as a formal exercise with little benefit to the community and whose main purpose was an exhibition at the Museum of Modern Art.[122] Hertzberger and Van Eyck were often guest critics at the School at student request and the work of James Stirling was well-liked.[123] In 1967 the students began publishing a school magazine, *Touchstone,* which the Team X philosophy strongly influenced.[124]

By 1967 it was clear that profound differences of opinion existed over whether formal design education should be integrated with social and political issues. The more conservative members of the Yale/Penn group believed that architecture schools ought to provide education in "professional skills." They believed that students should understand social issues, but they should learn about them in undergraduate school. Once skilled, a student could put his expertise to any use.[125] Others, Ray Lifchez and Herman Hertzberger among them,[126] saw the situation somewhat differently. Since architectural language was a public, social language there was no way to teach or understand it without understanding its connection to social structure. No technique could be value-free because there was no way to separate form from content. In an example that was cited during the hours of discussion that accompanied the occupation of Avery Hall, Hertzberger stated that he designed buildings for large capitalist companies but he tried to make them revolutionary by providing unsupervised places for social contact and political organization in them.[127]

Giurgola's presence at the School sustained this kind of debate, as it would sustain the discourse that produced a new structure and content for the curriculum after the seizure and strike.[128] But students lost an important ally when Peter Prangnell departed for the University of Toronto in 1967. On-going problems of a lack of strong leadership, poor faculty attendance, many out-moded courses, and students' growing realization that other schools provided a more coherent education fed student dissatisfaction.[129] Some students left. For example, the Class of 1969 graduated four or five members of the original class of thirty.[130] Others developed

119. Frances Halsband, in Richard Oliver's interview, comments on the positive aspects of this connection; for its problems see Columbia University, School of Architecture, "A Statement of Urgency," pp. 2-3.

120. The School of Architecture produced *Organization for Growth: A Study for the Harlem Community* in 1965. Percival Goodman and Alexander Kouzmanoff directed a study of the Hudson River, *Break-through to the Hudson River: A Plan for Yonkers to Peekskill* (New York: Columbia University School of Architecture, 1964).

121. Interview: Wadsworth by Authors; Exhibition materials, "Legacies of a Radical Era," Graduate School of Architecture and Planning, Columbia University, April, 1980.

122. The project was published in Museum of Modern Art, *The New City: Architecture and Urban Renewal* (New York, 1967), pp. 30-35. According to Max Bond, similar negative feelings were expressed by the community leadership of East Harlem (Interview: Bond by Authors).

123. Interview: Wadsworth by Authors.

124. Ibid.; Interview: Broches by Gutman and Kendall. Four issues of *Touchstone* appeared (1967–1968); issues 2 and 3 may be found in Avery Library.

125. Interview: Kliment and Halsband by Oliver, GSAP archives.

126. In 1967, Prangnell left Columbia to develop a fully-integrated five-year program at the University of Toronto.

127. Rosenkranz discusses these issues in *Across the Barricades.*

128. Interview: Broches by Gutman and Kendall; Interview: Bond by Authors.

129. Rosenkranz discusses these problems in *Across the Barricades.* They were similar to ones faced by other schools.

130. Interview: Wadsworth by Authors. This problem was not limited to the class of 1969. During these years students left the School for reasons which ranged from financial problems to dissatisfaction with the curriculum and administrative structure of the School. Increased trauma and awareness of the School's problems after the seizure and strike helped cause some students to transfer to other schools; others simply decided not to return to school at all. The "drop-out" problem occurred elsewhere at Columbia; indeed students left many other colleges and universities because they believed socially irrelevant higher education offered meaningless degrees.

an interest in activist politics and techniques of the New Left. Thus, students refused *en masse* to register for a required drawing course; the other faculty supported their action and the class requirement was dropped.[131] Students started to hold class meetings and elect class officials out of what the author of one post-strike leaflet called "fear of spending four years in Avery."[132] Students complained that some of the first year courses were too experimental, too formally oriented and that they lacked explicit connection with immediate social problems.[133] In addition the editors of *Touchstone* began to plan a conference on the need for social responsibility in architectural education and the profession. This was planned for May 1968; students from architecture schools along the East Coast would be invited.[134]

In the face of these complaints the administration of the School made some revisions, but avoided the drastic innovation and structural changes the program needed. The second and third semester studios became "vertical studios." No longer organized sequentially by year, a student could take studios in the order he or she preferred.[135] The program of one of the vertical studios, the Coney Island Studio, began to address the demand for social relevance in studio projects, by asking students to solve the planning and housing needs of an actual community. Working in teams of three and four, students examined planning issues in the first semester. During the second they designed housing prototypes.[136] They complained that the faculty still did not show up for studio criticism.[137] Two new teachers were hired, but tensions over the studio program and the administration only increased.

The number and nature of the different faculty-student alignments varied considerably during these years, but at the time of the building seizure, there were three general groups. There were, of course, students primarily interested in formal issues of design, who did not believe that "social relevance" was an important educational issue. During the building occupation, the traditional studio environment ceased to exist, and students who preferred that situation chose to work at home.[138] Then there were students who were interested in reforming the school, but who did not connect the issues of reform to larger political concerns. They did not join the occupation of Avery Hall, but were present on campus during the strike.[139] The third group made up about fifty per cent of the student body. This group was divided into those more concerned with the issues of humanistic design and those more concerned with larger campus and political issues. Members of this group occupied Avery Hall at the end of April.[140]

The occupation took place during a spring charrette for the Coney Island project, and the level of frustration was high. Two weeks earlier, Dean Smith, out of concern for the students' health, tried to close the building to prevent an all-night charrette. This angered students; when he announced that the building would close early on Wednesday, April 24, because of the unusual events on campus, they simply refused to let it happen.[141] At the beginning the building was not barricaded. Students and faculty were free to come and go as they pleased, though some faculty, for

131. The course was taught by Albert O. Halse. See "A Statement of Urgency, p. 2; Interview: Kliment and Halsband by Oliver, GSAP archives.

132. "A Statement of Urgency," p. 2.

133. "A Statement of Urgency," pp. 2-3; Rosenkranz, *Across the Barricades,* log 1-3.

134. Rosenkranz, *Across the Barricades,* log 5. Also, the Urban Action and Experimentation Program, directed by Harold Bell, helped formulate a two-million dollar low-cost, low-rent, low-rise housing project in East Harlem during this period. See Robert Hardman, "Architecture School Assists in Planning Housing for East Harlem" *Columbia Daily Spectator,* May 9, 1968, p. 1.

135. Interview: Kouzmanoff by Plunz, et. al.; Interview: Broches by Gutman and Kendall.

136. Columbia University, School of Architecture, "Coney Island" (mimeographed); Interview: Broches by Gutman and Kendall; Rosenkranz, *Across the Barricades,* log 2.

137. "A Statement of Urgency," p. 304; Interview: Kouzmanoff by Plunz, et.al.

138. Interview: Halsband by Oliver, GSAP archives.

139. Interview: Wadsworth by Authors.

140. Interview: Wadsworth by Authors; Interview: Broches by Gutman and Kendall; Rosenkranz, *Across the Barricades.*

141. "A Statement of Urgency," p. 4.

instance Alexander Kouzmanoff, were more welcome than others.[142] Most of the faculty, whatever their personal beliefs, viewed the student action with understanding, if not some sympathy and respect. An early decision was reached to ask the Avery Librarian Adolph Placzek to chain shut the doors of Avery Library to prevent damage to its world-renowned and priceless collection of architectural books and drawings, either from the students or eventually from the police.[143] By all accounts the students cared for the building, and there was hardly any damage to it.[144]

During the period of the building seizure students scrutinized the University's architectural and planning policy; indeed, one of the six university-wide student demands stated that the gym site in Morningside Park had to be abandoned. But at Avery the issues were of paramount concern because the majority of the students in the building were architectural, planning, and preservation students.[145] Study of alternative proposals for the gym site and the use of Morningside Park occurred during the occupation,[146] but discussion about how to make university policy more socially responsible took much time. Not surprisingly, the differences of opinion paralleled theoretical divisions in the New Left. One group insisted that social problems could only be cured by large-scale social, political and economic reform; thus students should concentrate on revamping the University's entire structure. The other, by far the larger in number, insisted that the problems were manifest in design and architecture; students, as potential architects, should concentrate on correcting social problems through architectural solutions.[147]

The theoretical divisions were never resolved but in an extraordinarily short time a new educational structure was conceived[148] which merged the need for curriculum reform with the concern for social issues. Called the "platform system," it came to be defined as

a broad area of interest proposed by one or a group of students and or faculty members who feel that the questions arising from the area of interest are architecturally significant and important enough to explore. A student's education in design consists of participation in a series of platforms, the order of which would correspond to his particular interest, development and abilities. The Platform System is founded on the belief that a student's education is most valuable when it is motivated by the relevance and significance of the issues which he is exploring.[149]

In its developed form the system encouraged architectural consideration of social issues and the structured examination of university policy towards the community. It allowed students to get hands-on experience in socially responsible practice.[150] And, it allowed students a formal role in the administration of the School.

The seizure of Avery Hall ceased when the police cleared the building early in the morning of April 30, but their actions across the campus helped prompt a call for a university-wide strike.[151] The School, where several faculty had been clubbed in their efforts to protect students from police, suspended classes. During this

142. Rosenkranz discusses student-faculty relations in *Across the Barricades*; Interview: Kouzmanoff by Plunz, et.al.

143. Interview: Kouzmanoff by Plunz, et.al.

144. Interview: Jane Bobbe by Plunz, July 10, 1981.

145. "Architecture Students Join Columbia Strikes Out of Chaos, Maturity," pp. 45-46; Ada Louise Huxtable, "Strike at Columbia Architecture School Traced to Anger Over Exclusion from Planning," *The New York Times*, May 20, 1968, p. 70; Rosenkranz, *Across the Barricades*, log 33-36, 42-48; Interview: Broches by Gutman and Kendall; Interview: Wadsworth by Authors.

146. Rosenkranz mentions these studies a number of times in *Across the Barricades*.

147. Interview: Broches by Gutman and Kendall; Rosenkranz discusses this issue throughout *Across the Barricades*.

148. Interview: Broches by Gutman and Kendall.

149. Columbia University, School of Architecture, "Week of Exchange in the New School of Architecture. A Collective Review of Platforms," 5-7 February 1969 (mimeographed).

150. During May 1968 students began to address campus planning issues. They participated in a "design-in" on the problems of the gym, and open student meetings were held with community groups. Students also prepared a position paper entitled "Towards Future Community University Cooperation." See "Architecture Students Join Columbia Strike Out of Chaos, Maturity," p. 45; Huxtable, "Strike at Architecture School Traced to Anger Over Exclusion from Planning," p. 70; School of Architecture, Striking Students and Emergency Committee of Morningsiders, "Joint Press Release," May 7, 1968 (mimeographed).

151. Cox Commission, *Crisis at Columbia*, pp. 162-167.

period, faculty, students and administration further developed proposals for the reorganization of the School. Three divisional councils with faculty and student representation were organized for Architecture, Planning, and Architectural Technology. An "executive council" was also organized with membership drawn from all three divisions. The Architectural Division Council in turn set up three subcommittees for curriculum, admissions, and University expansion. By the middle of May, the architecture subcommittee for the curriculum had begun the long and difficult task of formulating a new program based on the principle of the platform system,[152] a process which lasted all summer and was partially supported by Alumni funds and input.[153]

The formation of the Executive and Divisional Councils represented a major change in the governance of the School and raised opposition from conservative faculty. The Faculty Rules[154] which had previously been in effect, dating from 1964, provided for governance through a "Committee on Instruction," which advised the Dean on all matters of educational policy. It had no student representation, while the Executive Council which replaced it had five student members. Under the circumstances its powers went far beyond advisory status. The councils were intended to govern the School democratically, and were charged with the responsibility of reformulating the program. "Any programs formulated by the Divisional Councils and the Executive Council shall become the basis for the experimental operation of the School of Architecture and its Divisions."[155] The new system was officially approved by the faculty in April 1969 when the so-called "Interim Rules" which kept student representation intact were adopted.[156] This new democratic organization was technically illegal because the faculty and the students assumed power that the Trustees prohibited them from having.[157] Still the School operated under these rules for the rest of Smith's tenure as dean.

During the summer after the strike and seizure, students did not leave curriculum concerns behind. Many students left the School, some to use William Kinne Fellows traveling fellowships granted at the end of each student's second and third year. Paul Broches, a second year student at the time of the strike who worked for Hertzberger in Holland, recalls that much time was spent discussing the platform system.[158] Third year students sponsored a conference in Urbino during the last weeks of August. Each student contributed a small portion of his or her stipend to create the conference, which focused on problems of urban design, preservation and urban renewal. The conference developed further a similar initiative organized by students in Paris in 1967.[159] In addition, about twenty fourth-year students extended their thesis work over the summer. Assisted on a volunteer basis by faculty, many of their projects were related to Columbia and its environment.[160]

When the students returned they found a "new school of architecture."[161] The impulse was to make the program as open-ended as possible to allow "greater freedom for practical and academic advancement."[162] Still, it was structured. The first year program continued to be organized by the faculty; the second and

152. Columbia University, School of Architecture, *Bulletin of the School, Supplement* (mimeographed), "A Statement of Urgency," pp. 5-6; Columbia University, School of Architecture, "First Report of the Executive Council," September 25, 1968 (mimeographed).

153. The alumni donated $1000 to the effort; Conrad Levenson was appointed alumni representative to the Executive Council. Interview: Conrad Levenson by Authors.

154. Columbia University, School of Architecture, "Faculty Rules," 1964 (mimeographed).

155. Columbia University, School of Architecture, "Proposal Moved and Passed by the Faculty," May 17, 1968 (mimeographed).

156. Columbia University, School of Architecture, "Interim Rules for School of Architecture — adopted, Faculty Meeting," April 25, 1969 (mimeographed).

157. Columbia University, *Charters and Statutes* (New York: Columbia University, Edition of April 6, 1959 with amendments to November 2, 1970).158. Interview: Broches by Gutman and Kendall.

159. Interview: Wadsworth by Authors; Columbia University School of Architecture, "Urbino Planning '68, Workshop at Urbino, Italy," 25 August–14 September 1968 (mimeographed); and miscellaneous typed pages on Urbino conference.

160. Huxtable, "Strike at Columbia Architecture School Traced to Anger Over Exclusion from Planning," p. 70.

161. Romaldo Giurgola, "To the Students of the Division of Architecture," Fall 1968 (mimeographed).

162. Columbia University, School of Architecture, "Description of the Operation of the Platform System," Fall 1962 (mimeographed).

third years were arranged as vertical studios with the possibility of independent study; and in the fourth year, students produced a thesis. Students were expected to keep a visual and written log of their work which they would present at faculty "reviews" (as opposed to "juries" which were considered too competitive and authoritarian).[163] The council urged that ancillary courses be taught using problem-solving methods and that teachers encourage group and individual study. Structures and technology courses continued to be the only courses offered in sequence. The council also urged that a broader scope of expertise be made available to the students and that faculty be employed for varying lengths of time so that additional staff who could only be part of the School for a short period of time could still be used.[164] Attempts to recruit minority and women students, faculty, and staff began.[165] Architecture students were also urged to make their resources available for community use.[166]

The new system began "amid general enthusiasm, relief, reassurance, and pride that the diligent work of the student-faculty council had not been in vain,"[167] and, at its best, the "new school of architecture" encouraged students to accept social responsibility. When the University announced the appointment of I.M. Pei as university planner in the fall of 1968, the Committee on University Expansion produced guidelines which stated that the community had to be involved in the effort and offered planning advice. To his credit, Pei only accepted this position once the university guaranteed that it would abandon the gym project in Morningside Park.[168] But, even though he produced an interesting master plan, he refused to consider the A.R.C.H. and West Harlem Community Organization's suggestions for Morningside Park, one action, among others, which the Committee on University Expansion publicized.[169] In addition, architecture students and graduates in preservation, architecture, and planning founded Urban Deadline, a group which became a professional organization working in advocacy planning, rehabilitation, and other areas of urban need.[170] Through Urban Deadline, the Urban League sponsored a "street academy" program at the School in which schools were constructed in abandoned store fronts.[171] But, most crucially, as a position paper on community relations stated to incoming students in the fall of 1968, the School hoped that the platform system would become an avenue through which faculty and students would offer their services to the community.

In part, this succeeded. Richard Hatch offered a platform on university expansion in the fall of 1968, but more popular were the Real Great Society platforms sponsored by Max Bond, an adjunct faculty member and then director of A.R.C.H.[172] Unlike A.R.C.H., which was a professional group providing technical assistance to community residents, the Real Great Society was a community group directed by Richard Rinzler *(Columbia, 1968)* which provided social programs in East Harlem. It welcomed the opportunity to give students experience (and gain their aid) in solving architectural problems of East Harlem residents[173] which ranged from designs for a community center in East Harlem, to an

163. Columbia University, School of Architecture, "Description of Students' Log," (mimeographed).

164. Columbia University, School of Architecture, "Architectural Divisional Council Position Paper on Courses," (mimeographed), p. 2.

165. Max Bond offered a platform in which students designed a program of minority recruitment. Interview: Bond by Authors. See also Columbia University, School of Architecture, "The Black/Puerto Rican Student/Faculty and Administrators' Organization," June 1971; rev. ed. July 1974 (mimeographed).

166. Columbia University, School of Architecture, Division of Architecture, "Position Paper on Community Relations." (mimeographed).

167. Tony Schuman, "The Platform System," *Touchstone 4* (1968).

168. Keating, "Columbia Devours the Upper West Side," p. 13.

169. School of Architecture, Committee on University Expansion, "Community and Student Participation in Morningside Heights Planning," January 13, 1969 (mimeographed), p. 6; Alan Feigenberg and Saul Rosenfield, "Morningside Park North: Proposals for Community Discussion," prepared for the Architects' Renewal Committee in Harlem and the West Harlem Community Organization, May 1969 (mimeographed); "Committee on Columbia Expansion," *Touchstone 4* (1968).

170. Rosenkranz, *Across the Barricades*, epilog 1-4; "Latest from Columbia," *The Architecture Forum*, 129 (July/August 1968), p. 40; Paul Broches, "Urban Deadline," *Touchstone 4* (1968).

171. "Latest from Columbia," p. 40; Paul Broches, "Urban Deadline."

172. Schuman, "The Platform System."

173. Interview: Bond by Authors.

addicts' rehabilitation center, to a minimum rehabilitation cooperative housing project, to a vest pocket park in East Harlem. For example, in the design of the East Harlem Center, students made a counter proposal to one offered by the Department of Social Services "which accomodates...an emerging political and social body;...a building which invites community control for a community organization which wants to control its own affairs."[174]

Still, most of the platforms were more typical studios with programs oriented toward issues of adaptive reuse, advocacy planning, and other contemporary urban problems. They ranged from Alexander Kouzmanoff's platform on the problems of urban transportation to the masters' class study of adaptive reuse proposals for the Brooklyn Navy Yard which Percival Goodman directed.[175] In an "education platform" which offered the study of the "physical and social relationship between school and community and meaningful...transfer [of] these objectives into built form," students used sites and proposals of the Education Construction Fund or they suggested their own which ranged from a program using a site in Fort Washington to a Gulf Service Station renovation.[176] Robert Kliment offered a platform in which students proposed their own program. In the fall one student studied the conversion of a small Morningside garage into a community center.[177]

The strike also improved the situation of minorities and women within the School, at least for a period of some years. At the time of the strike, there were only three minority students in the School. By the fall of 1969, fifteen new minority students were registered, and by the fall of 1972 forty-one minority students had joined the School with considerable effort due to some resistance within the School.[178] Minority representation on the faculty and administrative staff also improved from none in the mid-1960's to a fairly consistent level of five or six full or part time faculty and staff throughout the 1970's. In addition, in 1968 an Assistant to the Dean for Minority Affairs was appointed and the Black/Puerto Rican Student/Faculty and Administrators Organization was founded.[179] Both organized recruitment efforts and remained active during the 1970's.[180] As for the status of women, enrollment within the architecture program increased substantially in the 1970's, to approximately one-half of each class. The number of women faculty also increased toward the end of the decade.

But the success of the new structure, as with any system that is founded on participatory democracy, depended on the commitment of its participants, and that waned quickly. As early as the Fall of 1968, student attendance at council meetings dropped and students were charged, by other students, with apathy and complacency.[181] At the close of the first semester of experimentation, Tony Schuman *(Columbia, 1970)* stated that "the major weakness [of the platform system] is consistent apathy of the students [and their refusal] to tie the school and the system together."[182] During that semester the faculty made interesting and innovative initial presentations, but soon after they failed to provide critical and dynamic leadership. Most did not openly oppose the system; but

174. "Week of Exchange in the New School of Architecture: A Collective Review of Platforms"; "Real Great Society Planning Studio," *Touchstone* 4 (1968); Tony Schuman, "RGS-UPS: Cooperative Rehabilitated Housing," *Touchstone* 4 (1968).

175. "Week of Exchange in the New School of Architecture."

176. Ibid.

177. Interview: Broches by Gutman and Kendall.

178. The authors do not wish to present an overly positive view of the situation of minorities. Gains frequently required a hard fight, and the situation of minorities remains a complex and frustrating one. For figures see "The Black/Puerto Rican Student/Faculty and Administrators' Organization," pp. 9-14.

179. Ibid., pp. 11-12.

180. Ibid.

181. "A Statement of Urgency," p. 10.

182. Schuman, "The Platform System."

most did not aggressively seek to make it work. They soon fell back "into fairly traditional academic situations, even to the extent where scheduled periodic reviews were deemed necessary to prevent a complete breakdown in studio communications."[183] The burden was left up to the students, a strategy which eventually produced failure, especially with the loss of continuity as the original student leadership graduated. By 1970, after only two years of struggle to implement it, the platform system showed signs of disintegration.

Specific controversies fed the erosion. Many students who did not participate in the initial formation of the platform system tended not to have the same desire to channel the freedom of choice, which the system offered, into a cohesive curriculum for the entire School. More and more students began to pursue individual interests, which helped fragment studio concerns. In addition, the contrasting nature of studio work raised considerable question about individual student abilities. The more traditional platforms produced more traditional work — drawings, models, and analysis — but the work of the more socially oriented studios mixed construction experience, writing and design proposals. Since the latter studios addressed sociological and political issues, and students spent much time analyzing programs and issues of planning, the work, at times, did not reach a polished, formal resolution. This led to charges of poor design ability, but the more traditional platforms and the Real Great Society studios attracted talented students equally.[184] It also appears that more formally oriented faculty did not like these projects because they could not be evaluated simply according to formal principles. In addition, they disapproved of students spending time in "store fronts" rather than in Avery, because the store front did not present an environment which was "abstract" enough for proper learning.[185]

As the platform system weakened, a period of struggle began, lasting for several years, over the structure and content of the design studios. Studio faculty who joined the School reinforced the debate through their diverse points of view. For example, Ada Karmi, who began teaching in 1969, lent support to the basic premises of the platform system, especially its concern for urban problems. On the other hand, Robert A.M. Stern, who began teaching in 1970, held a critical view, offering programs which were more limited to formal and stylistic issues.[186] Other new faculty, such as Anthony Pangaro, were sympathetic with the concern for urban problems, but felt that student efforts should be more structured. The changes in emphasis and structure of the platform system pleased some students, but many others, especially minority students, were outraged. By 1973, the Black/Puerto Rican Student/Faculty and Administrators' Organization had become one of the most organized channels of criticism of the new direction.[187]

The disintegration of the platform system was also reinforced by a swing to the right in American politics. Elected by the new conservative sentiment, Richard Nixon withdrew support for Kennedy and Johnson era social programs involving architects, and the generally conservative 1970's sublimated the social com-

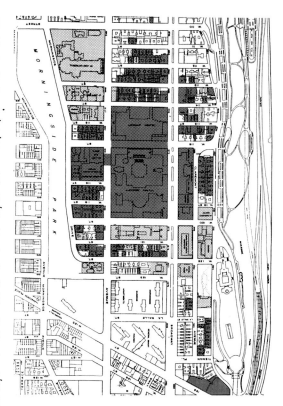

Present landholdings of Columbia and other institutions on Morningside Heights, 1981, a composite map based on the I.M. Pei plan of 1969, and later research by Peter Marcuse and the authors. Photo: Marta Gutman and Richard Plunz.

183. Ibid.

184. Exhibition Materials, "Legacies of a Radical Era"; Interview: J. Max Bond by Authors; Interview: Kliment and Halsband by Oliver, GSAP archives.

185. Interview: Kliment and Halsband by Oliver, GSAP archives.

186. Notable was Stern's housing option entitled "'Gimme Shelter': or Learning to Love the Upper Middle Class," which caused considerable controversy among students and faculty.

187. Details of the controversy surrounding the changes in emphasis were discussed in telephone interviews by the Authors with the following persons: Aris Tee Allen, Jr., Stanford Britt, Elaine Carter, Lia Gartner, Michael Kirkland, and Anthony Pangaro. See also: Interview: Bond by Authors; Interview: Broches by Gutman and Kendall; Interview: Kouzmanoff by Plunz, et.al.; Interview: Wadsworth by Authors.

mitments of the profession. Concommitantly, radical chic lost its glamour. Indeed, Tony Schuman, perhaps somewhat ironically, wondered in the fall of 1968, to what extent participation in the Real Great Society programs stemmed from philosophical commitments or just "represented fashionable involvement or assuaged...a personal hang-up."[188] Thus, for a number of reasons, interest in architectural solutions to social problems declined, and by 1971, the class as a whole was noticeably less interested in improving University-community relations and in studying the University's planning policy.[189] Recruitment efforts of minorities were also reduced as nation-wide interest waned in minority representation in the architecture profession. Ultimately, the loss of political conviction ground the platform system to a halt, and the new dean, James Stewart Polshek, appointed in 1972, replaced it during the first years of his tenure.

The power of the demands of the students and concerned faculty for a more relevant education and a more socially responsible campus architecture and planning policy made some long term changes. However tenuous the gains of minorities were, the position of women definitely improved. The quality of the architecture on the Columbia campus also improved substantially since the 1969 Trustees decision to involve architecture faculty in commissions and decision making. In that year, Alexander Kouzmanoff was commissioned to begin studies for the Avery Library Extension. Somewhat later, Giurgola began work on the Fairchild Life Sciences building. The selection of Dean James Stewart Polshek also represented a continuing commitment to the need for change at the School. The first years remained unstable, but Polshek quickly cemented a new, productive relationship with the University administration and hired needed new faculty, among them a group of full-time teachers, professionally committed to education and to rebuilding the Columbia program. The remaining influence of the Yale and Penn schools was reduced by a dialogue which developed between representatives of the Princeton-Cornell Schools and a post-Team X ideology.[190]

One of the most persistent problems dating from the strike has been related to the rules of the School. At stake has been the balance of power between the Dean, the Faculty, and students in decision-making. There was some pressure to reconsider the "Interim Rules" which were in effect since April, 1969, without approval by the Office of the Provost. By April 1972, a permanent set of rules was adopted by the faculty, but not until after considerable controversy which, like in 1968, centered on the representation to the Committee on Instruction. Provision for student representation remained, but a voting membership for the Dean was added. None of the previous rules granted this privilege because the committee was advisory to the Dean. Again, the Office of the Provost never approved the rules, presumably because the student representation was still considered a momentous precedent. As a result, the 1964 rules are still legally in effect, but are not followed.[191]

As one placard in the 1962 Uris protest implied, it will be a

188. Schuman, "The Platform System."

189. Interview: Wadsworth by Authors; Interview: Levenson by Authors.

190. These influences are discussed in some detail by Kenneth Frampton and Alessandra Latour, in "Notes on American Architectural Education," *Lotus,* 27 (1980/11), pp. 5-39. Many of these faculty were within the liberal political tradition of the School and so continued to explore aspects of humanism and issues of social purpose. But, while much of the debate had taken place in the storefronts and the streets of East Harlem just a few years earlier, it moved up the hill to the Columbia studios where formal issues structured social concerns more than they had previously. The most important evidence of the continued concern for social issues in the School has been the constant interest in housing as a discipline which bridges architecture, planning and preservation.

But, on many social issues, the stance of the School has moved substantially away from the beliefs of the strike and seizure sympathizers. For example, in 1973 the night school program was abolished, ending the problems of "a second class program for second class students." But, this also ended a long history of opportunity for students with fewer financial resources. At the same time, when the four year Bachelor's program was changed, as it was at many other schools, to a three year Master's, it increased the amount of time students had to spend to earn a professional degree. And, while interest in the relationship of architectural form and social purpose still exists among students, many limit their discussions to formal issues.

191. Columbia University, Faculty of Architecture, "Stated Rules of the Faculty of Architecture," April 25, 1972 (mimeographed). The implementation of the 1972 rules has been somewhat lax, including the procedures for organization of the Committee on Instruction. Other troublesome ambiguities are related to the duties and powers of the Chairperson and the Program Directors.

hundred years before the architectural legacy of the 1960's will be erased, with even recent heroic efforts destined to remain in its shadow. The simple strategy of building "star" buildings is not enough, as the fate of the Yale Art and Architecture building dramatically demonstrated. The University will never again be so brazen as to claim public parkland for itself; indeed the gym was eventually completed by 1974, woven into the original McKim complex. But the decades-old conflict with the Morningside Community remains as heated as ever. The Pei Plan made well-considered provisions for Columbia to try to heal some of the past injustices to the community,[192] but it was never followed. The University now admits that it used Pei to placate the community after the strike, and it had no intention of following the recommendations.[193] Indeed, many argue that the situation is now worse than before because the University, having learned from its previous experience, has become shrewder and better skilled in its real estate operation.[194] Even some of the new architecture is not exempt from the debate. As sophisticated a building as the East Hall Dormitory by Gwathmey/Siegel might well be described as brutal and inconsiderate, especially the spectre of the twenty-three story light-colored wall which it presents to Harlem.[195] As before, its construction required tenant eviction and building destruction, this time to provide housing for graduate students and faculty. Like much else connected to the social issues the 1960's brought to the forefront, indeed, much else connected with the history of the School, the dormitory evokes contradictory responses of relief and anger. Relief because at least the building is not in the park. Anger because it represents the tenacity of the problems that still remain to be solved.

It may be difficult for architects to integrate social commitments with other professional concerns, but, as we have seen, interest in this issue has surfaced throughout the history of the School, appearing most notably in the 1930's and 1960's. When the concern for social purpose in architectural education and practice erupted in 1968, it culminated a decade of growing unrest within the School over educational and campus planning issues, unrest which also mirrored problems endemic to American higher education. The explosion produced the platform system which, like Hudnut's earlier curriculum, plunged the School into a needed experiment with systematic reform. It represented one of the most radically innovative architecture curricula to be produced by that era. Students were encouraged to search for architectural solutions to social problems, and acting within the "spirit of the age," they claimed a share in the reins of leadership. One may question, perhaps with just cause, the School's failure to establish a more rigorous educational structure and its dependence on participatory democracy, given the speed with which student and faculty initiative disappeared. But, whatever its structural failings, the system voiced concerns for an architecture of humanism which strove to address the architectural needs of all strata of society.[196]

192. I. M. Pei and Partners, "Planning for Columbia University: An Interim Report," Submitted March 9, 1970.

193. Keating, "Columbia Devours the Upper West Side," p. 13.

194. Ibid., pp. 13-16; Clyde Haberman, "Columbia: The Good/Bad Guy Landlord," *The New York Times*, January 31, 1981, Sect. II, pp. 1, 6.

195. Keating, "Columbia Devours the Upper West Side," p. 13, 14; Michael Sorkin, "On Building Blocks," *The Village Voice*, 26 (April 8–14, 1981), p. 91.

196. The authors wish to express their appreciation to the following persons: Wiebke Noack, who assisted in all aspects of the preparation of this essay, and whose prodigious research was especially crucial; Harry Kendall and Robert Lane whose initial research helped launch this effort; Diane Boas who collaborated in making several of the interviews; Kenneth Frampton and Richard Oliver who gave editorial advice. In addition we would like to thank the following persons who consented to be interviewed: Averna Adams, Aris Tee Allen, Jr., Jane Bobbe, J. Max Bond, Jr., Stanford Britt, Paul Broches, Elaine Carter, James Marston Fitch, Lia Gartner, Percival Goodman, Michael Kirkland, Alexander Kouzmanoff, Conrad Levenson, Anthony Pangaro, and Christopher Wadsworth. We also thank Richard Oliver for making available information from his interviews of Max Abramovitz, Charles Colbert, Frances Halsband, and Robert Kliment, transcriptions of which are in the GSAP archives.

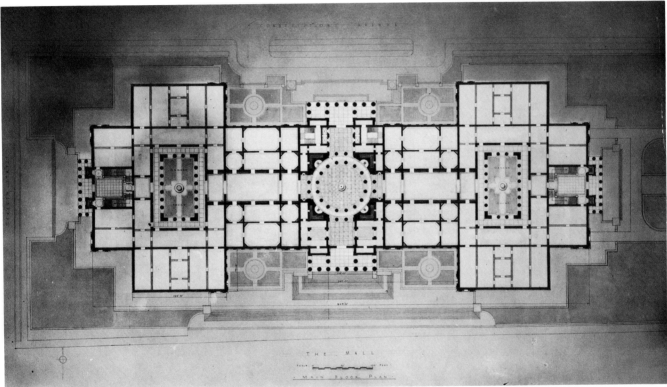

The National Gallery of Art, Washington, D.C., 1940, John Russell Pope *(1894)*. Drawing by Otto Eggers.
Photo by Peter A. Juley, courtesy of The Eggers Group.

Above left: Irving Trust Company, One Wall Street, New York City, 1932, Voorhees, Gmelin, Smith & Smith: Perry Coke Smith *(1923)*. Photo: Haines, Lundberg, Waehler.

Left: Stephen Wise Free Synagogue, New York City, 1941, Block & Hesse: Walter Hesse *(1913)*.

Above right: Addition to the New York Stock Exchange, 1923, Trowbridge & Livingston: Samuel B.T. Trowbridge *(1886)* and Goodhue Livingston *(1892)*. Photo by The Byron Co., courtesy of The Museum of the City of New York.

Above left: Stuart Building, Lincoln, Nebraska, 1926, Ellery Davis *(1911).* Photo: Davis, Fenton, Stang, & Darling.

Left: Longue Vue House, New Orleans, 1939, William A. Platt *(1923).* Photo: William Platt.

Above right: St. Regis Hotel, New York City, 1904, Trowbridge & Livingston: Samuel B.T. Trowbridge *(1886)* and Goodhue Livingston *(1892).* Photo: The Museum of the City of New York.

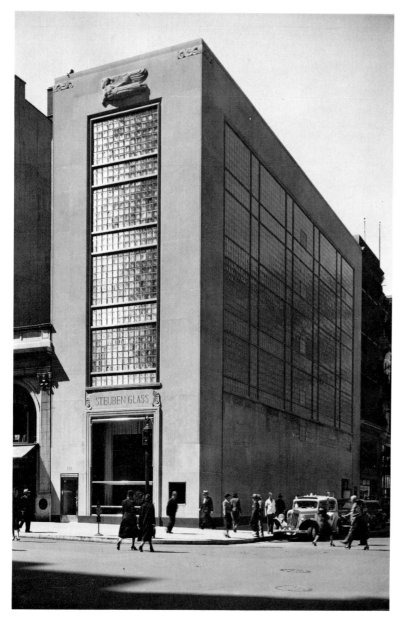

Above left: The Corning Building, New York City, 1937, William A. Platt *(1923)* and Geoffrey Platt *(1930)*. Photo: Geoffrey Platt.

Left: Soldiers and Sailors Monument, New York City, 1902, Stoughton, Stoughton and Duboy: Arthur A. Stoughton *(1888)*. Photo: The Museum of the City of New York.

Above right: Church of Christ Scientist, New York City, 1950, C. Dale Badgeley *(1925)*. Photo by Gottscho-Schleisner.

Right: Metropolitan Square (Scheme A), New York City, 1929, Benjamin Wistar Morris *(1894),* Avery Archive.

Below: Australian Parliament House, Canberra, 1980, Mitchell–Giurgola Architects and Thorpe Architects: Romaldo Giurgola *(1951).* Photo: Mitchell–Giurgola Architects.

Above: Library and Humanities Building, State University of New York, Stoneybrook, 1974, Jan Hird Pokorny *(1940),* in joint venture with Damaz & Weigel. Photo by Norman McGrath.

Middle: St. Vincent Hospital, Portland, Oregon, 1980, Naramore Bain Brady & Johanson: James O. Jonassen *(1965).* Photo by Dick Busher.

Below: La Guardia Airport, New York City, 1965, Harrison & Abramovitz: Max Abramovitz *(1931).* Photo by Ezra Stoller, ESTO.

Opposite page.
Above: 9-G Cooperative, New York City, 1968, Edelman & Salzman: Judith Edelman *(1946).* Photo by George Cserna.

Right: Bridge Apartments, New York City, 1964, Brown & Guenther: George D. Brown, Jr. *(1931).* Photo: Brown, Guenther, Battaglia & Seckler.

Left: Restoration of the Jasper Ward House, New York City, 1981, Meadows/Woll Architects: Robert Meadows *(1968),* Michael Jackson *(1980),* Julia Gersovitz *(1980)*; Center for Building Conservation: Harry Hansen *(1979),* Theodore Kinnari *(1979),* Raymond Pepi *(1979),* and Mark TenEyck *(1979).* Photo by Michael Devonshire/CBC.

Above left: The United States Pavilion, Expo '70, Osaka, Japan, 1970, Geiger Berger Associates: David Geiger *(1967)*. Photo: Geiger Berger Associates.

Above right: Daniel Freeman Memorial Hospital, Inglewood, California, 1976, Bobrow/Thomas and Associates: Michael L. Bobrow *(1963)*. Photo by Julius Shulman.

Left: St. Michael's Hall, Dormitory, Minneapolis, Minnesota, 1963, Hansen and Michelson: Valerius Leo Michelson *(1952)*. Photo by Shin Koyama.

Opposite page.
Above: Pickering Wharf, Salem, Mass., 1978, ADD, Inc.: Wilson Pollock *(1968)*. Photo by Steve Rosenthal.

Left: Domaine Chandon Winery & Visitors Center, Yountville, California, 1980, George T. Rockrise *(1941)*. Photo by Joshua Freiwald.

Right: Bonniers Shop, New York City, 1948, Warner-Leeds: Charles Warner, Jr. *(1938)*. Photo by Lionel Freedman.

Above left: House VI, Cornwall, Connecticut, 1976, Peter Eisenman *(1960)*. Photo: Peter Eisenman.

Middle: Alden B. Dow Office, Midland, Michigan, 1935, Alden B. Dow *(1931)*. Photo by Balthazar Korab.

Below: Kinney Residence, Westchester County, New York, 1979, Ricardo Scofidio *(1960)* with Elizabeth Diller. Photo by Ricardo Scofidio.

Above right: A Country House, 1980, Moore, Grover, Harper: Robert Harper *(1964)*. Photo: Moore, Grover, Harper.

Opposite page.
Above: Caribe Hilton, San Juan, Puerto Rico, 1950, Oswaldo Toro *(1937)* and Charles Warner, Jr. *(1938)*. Photo by Ezra Stoller, ESTO.

Below: Dorr-Oliver, Inc., Stamford, Connecticut, 1960, Sherwood, Mills & Smith: Thorne Sherwood *(1936)*. Photo by Joseph W. Molitor.

Above left: House on Nantucket Island, 1979, Bissell & Wells: Michael Bissell *(1969).* Photo by David Franzen, ESTO.

Left: "Snowflake House," Bear Valley, California, 1973, Donald MacDonald *(1963).* Photo by Karl Reik.

Above right: Glover Street Condominium, San Francisco, 1981, Daniel Solomon *(1963).* Photo by Joshua Freiwald.

Above: Harriet Newhall Center, Mt. Holyoke College, South Hadley, Mass., (restoration of and addition to a 19th-century house), 1980, Elizabeth Ericson *(1966).*
Photo by Edward Jacoby.

Left: Billings Forge (extended use), Hartford, Connecticut, 1980, Smith Edwards Architects: Tyler Smith *(1969).* Photo by Roger V. Dollarhide.

Empire State Building, New York City, 1931, Shreve, Lamb & Harmon: William F. Lamb *(1906)*.
Photo by Peter B. Kaplan.

Opposite page.
Above: Pedro Albizu Campos Park, New York City, 1969, Urban Deadline: Alain Salomon *(1969)*.
Photo: Alain Salomon.

Below: Greenacre Park, New York City, 1971, Goldstone, Dearborn & Hinz, associated with Sasaki, Dawson &
DeMay: Harmon Goldstone *(1936)*. Photo: Goldstone & Hinz.

Top: Improvements to the Queensborough Bridge, New York City, 1979, Palmer & Hornbostel and Gustav Lindenthal: Henry Hornbostel *(1891)*. Photo by Richard Oliver.

Above: Downtown Urban Renewal Project, Wilkes-Barre, Pennsylvania, 1978, Bohlin Powell Larkin Cywinski: Bernard Cywinski *(1966)*. Photo by Joseph Molitor.

Opposite page: Orchestra Hall, Denver, Colorado, 1974, Hardy Holzman Pfeiffer Associates: Norman Pfeiffer *(1965)*. Photo by Norman McGrath.

Pepsi-Cola Building, New York City, 1960, Skidmore, Owings & Merrill: senior designer, Natalie DuBlois *(1944)*.
Photo by Ezra Stoller, ESTO.

Pacific Heights Townhouses, San Francisco, 1979, Daniel Solomon *(1963)*. Photo by Joshua Freiwald.

Spear House, Miami, 1978, Arquitectonica: Laurinda Spear *(1975)*. Photo by Robert Lautman.

Top: Byland Solar House, Fayette, Missouri, 1980, James McCullar *(1967)*. Photo: James McCullar.

Above: Swan House, Atlanta, Georgia, 1927, Hentz, Adler & Shutze: Philip T. Shutze *(1913)*.
Photo by Richard Oliver.

Top: Boston City Hall, 1962–69, Kallmann, McKinnell & Knowles: Michael McKinnell *(1960)*.
Photo by Steve Rosenthal.

Above: Y.W.C.A. Building, Kingston, New York, 1979, R.M. Kliment and Frances Halsband *(1968)*.
Photo by Norman McGrath.

La Luz Community, Albuquerque, New Mexico, 1973, Antoine Predock *(1962)*. Photo by Joshua Freiwald.

Opposite page:

Above: Apartment, New York City, 1975, Armstrong/Childs Architects: Leslie Armstrong *(1966)*. Photo by Robert Perron.

Below: Greene Street Cafe, New York City, 1980, Siris/Coombs Architects: Peter Coombs *(1971)* and Jane Siris *(1971)*. Photo by Roger Bester.

Above: Missouri State Office Building (extended use of Louis Sullivan's Wainwright Building), St. Louis, 1980, Mitchell-Giurgola Architects: Romaldo Giurgola *(1951)*. Photo by Sadin/Karant.

Right: Restoration of the Woolworth Building, 1975 – 81, The Ehrenkrantz Group: Theodore Prudon *(1972)*. Photo by Theodore Prudon.

As the School of Architecture at Columbia University celebrates its first centenary, it also marks a program in historic preservation which is the first of its kind founded in the nation and one of the first in the world.[1] It is today the largest American program.[2] Although sponsored by a school of architecture, the program has from the first been interdisciplinary, accepting students with undergraduate degrees from all the adjacent areas (landscape architecture, archaeology, art and social history, the physical sciences, geography: it has even had a few students from law, journalism and business administration). Although a number of American universities now offer comparable programs of study, Columbia was for many years the only School to offer a separate degree — the Master of Science in Historic Preservation.

HOW DID THIS DEVELOPMENT COME ABOUT?

As the founder of the program, and until 1978 its director, it might be productive for me to discuss the background of this program. Its beginnings were modest enough — a one-semester seminar in historic preservation to which a number of specialists active in the field were invited to give a single lecture each. The subject matter of the seminar course, even during these early days, was holistic, interdisciplinary as were the students accepted for registration. This was a purely pragmatic response to the problem as I then understood it.

The idea of such a program had begun gestating for several years and represented my own dismay at the widening environmental disasters of the post-World War II years — especially as the real consequences of the urban renewal programs became increasingly apparent. There was no conscious antiquarianism in these initial feelings; having myself escaped the results of a Beaux-Arts education and several years of work in architectural offices engaged in the design of "period" houses, I was still prejudiced against historic preservation as late as 1948.[3] Jane Jacobs seminal book *The Death and Life of Great American Cities* did as much as anything to persuade me to begin to look at cities as living organisms, not inert tissue which architects and planners could manipulate at will, each according to his own private standards of good design.

For many people of my generation, the post-war development of cheap and rapid air travel had made repeated trips to Europe suddenly feasible. As a consequence of such experience, it began to dawn on me around 1958, that the survival of the monuments which I had been visiting was no mere accident. Odd as it now seems, it had not previously occurred to me that these monuments — the Tower of London and Westminster, Notre Dame and Carcassone, the Roman Forum and Pompeii — were the visible evidence of a great invisible system of curatorial institutions, some of them, like the French *Service des Monuments Historiques,* over a century old. It is a measure of the isolation of architects from their own historic roots that this discovery came as such a surprise.

From the perspective of the past two decades, which have witnessed the maturation of the whole field of historic preserva-

A Short History of Historic Preservation at Columbia University

James Marston Fitch

1. A comparable program was established that same year (1963) at the School of Architecture of the Middle East Technical University at Ankara in Turkey.

2. 78 students currently enrolled in a two-year course of studies.

3. In the first edition of my book *American Building: The Forces that Shape It* (Boston: 1948), I saw Colonial Williamsburg as "the secret weapon" of reactionary forces. "Whatever the intentions of its founders, this project has done more to stultify and corrupt American taste than any (other) single event in our history, the Columbian exposition possibly excepted" (p. 141).

tion, it is easy to see that the appearance of formally-structured courses in historic preservation, like ours at Columbia, would be inevitable. Such academic training had not been necessary in Europe because the national institutes of historic preservation had long ago set up their in-house systems of work-and-study apprenticeships for young professionals who wished to enter the field. This was, and still is, the optimal way in which to train preservationists because it integrates theory and practice. But, in the mid-1960's when the Columbia program was beginning, no comparable institutional apparatus existed in the United States; nor did it seem very likely that one would appear in the near future.[4] Hence, there seemed no alternative to academic training for the American preservationist. It was in these circumstances that I suggested the initiation of such a program at Columbia.

THE CULTURAL CONTEXT OF THE COLUMBIA PROGRAM

It is important that we remember the cultural context into which this new academic program was to be inserted. Throughout its formative years, the American preservation field, unlike the European, had been dominated by laymen — antiquarians, connoisseurs, history buffs, amateurs (i.e., people who did the work for love, not money). These circles had little or no contact with professional architects and urbanists and even less reason either to like or to trust them: architects and planners were often the agents of the forces which were intent on wiping out the very buildings which the preservationists were battling to save.[5] In short, historic preservation was a field of activity dominated by citizens who stood completely outside government, unaided by the professionals and untouched by academia. The profession as a whole played no role whatever in the movement before the early 1970's. This was paradoxical, to put it mildly, since all the great American architects in the period between the two Chicago Fairs of 1893 and 1933 were historicizing eclectics: that is, their practices were built on producing facsimile reproductions of the very buildings which were being everywhere destroyed. There is no evidence that any of them saw any connection between the two aspects of the problem. They studied old buildings, both here and abroad, but only to plagiarize them, never to preserve them: Richard Morris Hunt; McKim, Mead & White; Carrere & Hastings; Delano and Aldrich; Arthur Brown; Charles A. Platt — that constellation of eclectics for whom Henry Hope Reed coined the term "American Renaissance." They travelled to photograph and sketch; at home they built up large libraries of plates and measured drawings which both principals and draftsmen learned to copy with precision.

It is true that they sometimes incorporated fragments of old buildings in the new constructions. Julia Morgan employed some of William Randolph Hearst's indiscriminant purchases at San Simeon; Addison Mizener had a huge cache of antiques at Palm Beach; Hunt used odd bits of imported panelling in The Breakers. This sort of cannibalizing reached an apex in the museum vogue of the 1920's for "period rooms" when entire rooms were removed

4. The Heritage Conservation and Recreation Service, created by President Carter in 1978, would have been the nucleus for such an American agency. But it was eliminated by President Reagan in one of his first acts in office. This suggests that it may still be some years before we have this much needed keystone for an effective program for the protection of our national artistic and historic patrimony.

5. It is true that a few architects were actively associated with the preservationists: Charles S. Peterson, as founder of the Historic American Buildings Survey, waged a decades-long fight to preserve the records, if not the fabrics, of historically significant old buildings; Orin Bullock as a practicing architect was personally responsible for the restoration of a number of important buildings; and archaeologists like James L. Cotter played an active role in saving such historic sites as Jamestown.

from houses to be installed in art museums in Boston, New York, Detroit and Kansas City. Dyed-in-the-wool preservationists were opposed to this method of "saving" old buildings. But it was not an issue which attracted much attention in architectural circles.

The ideological space between professional architects and amateur preservationists grew steadily wider in the decades after 1929. In Europe the collapse of Imperial Germany in social and economic chaos had served to discredit every aspect of the old order, including its architectural establishment. It was in the resulting vacuum that the Bauhaus and the Modern Movement leapt into ascendancy. A decade later, the process was repeated on this side of the Atlantic. The October 1929 crash and the savage Depression which followed it brought American ruling circles into serious disrepute; and the architects were not immune from the opprobrium which overtook their patrons. Thus, the Modern Movement with the Bauhaus and the International Style inundated America like a tidal wave. Washed away was the lordly country estate and the lofty Georgian townhouse, the lavish country clubs and huge metropolitan churches. And gone with them were the eclectic idioms in which they were designed.

Almost all the old masters of historicizing eclecticism had passed on by the time that civilian construction resumed after World War II. Bertram Goodhue had died in 1924; William Rutherford Mead in 1928; Thomas Hastings in 1929; Charles Platt in 1933; John Russell Pope in 1937; Chester Holmes Aldrich in 1940; Ralph Adams Cram in 1942; Paul Cret in 1945; Arthur Brown in 1957. Almost alone among his generation William Adams Delano lived on until 1960.

But the disrepute which historicizing eclecticism had brought down upon the profession seems to have had no impact upon the preservation movement itself — perhaps because that movement had always been intent on preserving the past, not on copying it. Despite this isolation, the movement had grown steadily in size and power throughout those decades. It was, of course, "the little old ladies in blue hair and tennis shoes" who had first absorbed the lessons of European efforts to protect the artistic and historic patrimony. And it was they who had taken the first steps toward organizing and institutionalizing the protection of the American heritage in such pioneering ventures as the Association for the Preservation of Virginia Antiquities (1888), the Society for the Preservation of New England Antiquities (1904), and the Society for the Preservation of Long Island Antiquities (1924). The amateurs won their first great victory with the establishment of the Colonial Williamsburg Restoration in 1929. And as a corollary of this organizational growth, there followed a growing number of accomplishments — historic districts in Philadelphia, Annapolis, Savannah and Providence all were established in the late 1940's and early 1950's. The ascendancy of the preservation movement was capped by the creation by the Congress of the National Trust for Historic Preservation in 1950.

It has been the historic preservation movement which has played a fundamental role in altering the attitudes of the profession toward old buildings. It has been the movement which made the past respectable. Moreover, in the past decade or so, it has made *all* the past respectable — not merely the high style, urbane idioms of Federal and Greek and Gothic Revival, but also Stick Style and Queen Anne. It is the historic preservationists, with their steadily expanding understanding of what is historically significant, who have led the drive to designate such buildings as the Chrysler Building (1930) and Radio City Music Hall (1932) as historic landmarks. And the umbrella of significance has been extended horizontally as well, to cover new building types hitherto ignored — log cabins, mining towns, railroad stations, and gasoline stations.

This altered climate of opinion has made possible profound changes in attitude *within* the profession (it might, indeed, be argued, that it was this re-evaluation of our architectural past, forced upon us by the rising prestige of the preservationists, which laid the groundwork for the current wave of Post-Modernism). In any event, when the Columbia program first began in the mid-1960's, we faced the distrust of the preservation movement *and* the more or less genial contempt of the architectural profession itself.

THE FORMATIVE YEARS

The beginnings were modest enough. Not only was there no staff, no funding, no physical facilities: there was, even more importantly, no curriculum nor any prototypes on which to model one. We had to begin literally from scratch. Several things seemed clear to me, however, from my study of the European experience:

(1) The program had to be interdisciplinary. European preservation practices made it apparent that a wide range of professionals had to collaborate if the work was to succeed — architects, landscape architects, archaeologists; art and cultural historians; engineers and physical scientists.

(2) A second consideration was that, with students coming from such diverse fields, a synoptic interdisciplinary course would have to teach them to work together — to develop a common conceptual approach to the task; shared methodologies for dealing with it; even a common language for describing it. Instead of the usual pattern of graduate studies, in which the student "learns more and more about less and less," we had to visualize a curriculum in which the preservation student would learn more and more about more and more. The success of the program seems to have vindicated this policy. From four students in 1965 the program has grown to seventy-eight enrolled in the 1980–1981 academic year.

(3) The Columbia program would have to be "artifact-centered," not only because it was in a school of architecture but also because an urgent requirement was for a cadre of trained professionals who could not only research, write about and criticize historic structures but also actively intervene to preserve them for posterity.

From the start, the program has had several innovative, not to say unorthodox, dimensions. These have included: programmed, expense-paid field trips for the entire class; laboratory work in

Richard Goldsborough, mason, artisan, and RESTORE graduate, demonstrating stone carving techniques during a RESTORE field workshop session. Photo by Jan C.K. Anderson.

conservation; required internships; and, of course, the presence of an extra-mural faculty of visiting lecturers. Initially, we had a permanent faculty of one and he, in a very real sense, an auto-didact in preservation.[6] The first step was the introduction, in 1964, of a Seminar in Historic Preservation, offered as an elective to matriculated students in architecture. This seminar was designed to give the student a panoramic over-view of the field (as things turned out, it also served as a kind of theoretical armature around which a yet-to-be-developed program would evolve). The seminar was designed as a structured series of lectures in which specialists would delineate the interfaces between their own work and that of the preservationist.

This format of a class taught wholly by visiting lecturers might have been considered as a mere expedient — a means of collecting an extraordinary faculty at very limited costs — and so initially it was. But it soon proved to have much more significance: it was, in effect, the beginning of "a university without walls." It offered an interdisciplinary faculty which no single university could have afforded or have kept fully at work, even if affordable, since most of these men and women devote only a small portion of their academic time to preservation per se.[7]

It was under such constraints that we began the preservation program. But it required several years of incremental additions, in terms of establishing new classes and acquiring new instructors, to establish the nucleus of a program. Initially, it was a 32-credit course of two semesters. Architectural students who enrolled in the program were awarded the M.S. in Architecture. Students with other undergraduate backgrounds were awarded the Certificate in Historic Preservation. This was an anomalous situation which we were able to correct only in 1974, when we initiated the present two year course of study, open to all qualified applicants. This new program, which led to a new degree, the Master of Science in Historic Preservation, was approved by the New York State of Regents in the same year. The unified course of study was identical for all students but those without course work in architectural history or proficiency in drafting and sketching were required to make up such deficiencies.

A STEADILY EVOLVING CURRICULUM

The Columbia curriculum has always had two components — a "warp-and-weft" of generalizing and specializing course work. The first category has aimed at raising the literacy and competence of every member of the class to the highest possible common denominator in the history of architecture, decorative arts, and landscape. These classes are required for everyone. The second category of specializing classes are designed to permit the individual student to develop skills in areas of his own choice: design; historical and archaeological research; building materials conservation; preservation planning. Preparation of the thesis is naturally in this second area.

THEORETICAL PARADIGMS FOR PRESERVATION TRAINING

On the basis of my own experience at Columbia and elsewhere, I think that the field has reached that level of development where

6. Thanks to Dean Kenneth Smith, I was permitted gradually to shift more and more of my time from teaching in the Department of Architecture to administration and teaching in the evolving preservation program.

7. Such a program of visiting lecturers would not have been possible, at least in the early years, without the generous and on-going support of a number of organizations: among them have been the Edgar Kaufmann Charitable Foundation, the J.M. Kaplan Fund, the Lila Acheson Wallace Fund, the Samuel H. Kress Foundation and, more recently, the National Trust for Historic Preservation.

It should be noted that these lectures were carefully sequenced and structured. They were repeated annually, usually with the same lecturer to guarantee continuity. A single lecture on a given subject — e.g., Bunting on New Mexican architecture, McKee on early American masonry — was often expanded to three or four. A number of them subsequently were developed into entire courses — e.g. decorative arts, archaeology, historic landscapes. Jacques Dalibard, program director for the years 1977–78, introduced the valuable method of systematizing some of the more specialized subjects into concentrated, two-week-long "mini-courses" — a technique which it is hoped the new administration will revive. The variety and richness of their contributions is suggested by this cumulative list up through the spring of 1977:

(1) Pre-industrial domestic environment: Rita Adrosko, Smithsonian Institution, *Pre-Revolutionary domestic textiles;* Helen Bullock, National Trust, *Pre-Revolutionary fireplace cookery;* R.O. Cummings, Brooklyn College, *Refrigeration and the Natural Ice Industry;* Samuel Dornsife, Williamsport, Pa., *19th century American wallpapers, drapery, and upholstery;* Sam Edgerton, Jr., Boston University, *Early American Stoves and Furnaces;* Jan Frank, Ann Arbor, Michigan, *Pre-industrial cuisine, diet and cooking;* Virginia Partridge, Cooperstown Museum, *Care and Maintenance of pre-industrial household textiles;* L.S. Russell, Ontario National Museum, *Domestic lighting before gas and electricity.*

(2) Early American building materials and structural systems: Abbott Cummings, Jr., Society for Preservation of New England Antiquities, *17th and 18th century wooden buildings of New England;* Bainbridge Bunting, University of New Mexico, *Mud masonry buildings of the Southwest, pre-history to the coming of the railroad;* Robert Fitchen, Colgate, *Early Pennsylvania barns;* Margo Gayle, Friends of Cast Iron Architecture, *American cast iron industry;* Harley McKee, Syracuse University, *Early American masonry;* Charles S. Peterson, Philadelphia, *Metals in early buildings and Early New World concretes.*

(3) Preservation and Maintenance of Early Landscapes: Rudy Favretti, University of Connecticut, *American pleasure gardens;* Albert Fein, Long Island University, *Olmsted, Central Park and the American urban landscape;* Carleton B. Lees, N.Y. Botanical Garden, *Horticultural development in 19th century America;* Elizabeth McDougall, Dumbarton Oaks, *Historical evolution of the pleasure garden;* Robert Harvey, University of Iowa, *Restoration of vanished landscapes.*

(4) American regional architecture: Carl W. Condit, Northwestern University, *Development of the Chicago Skyscraper;* John L. Cotter, National Park Service, *Architecture and Urbanism of Jamestown, Virginia;* Henry W. Glassie III, University of Indiana, *Folk architecture of Appalachia;* Bernard Lemmon, Tulane University, *Architecture of New Orleans: 1717–1861;* John Stevens, Old Bethpage Village, *The Dutch architecture of New York State;* Samuel Wilson, Jr., New Orleans, *Evolution of the New Orleans house types;* Samuel Simmons, Charleston, *Charleston architecture: 1721–1861;* Clay Lancaster, *Architecture of Nantucket.*

(5) Curatorship of the Historic Patrimony: Leopold Adler, Historic Savannah, Inc., *Preservation in the City of Savannah;* Frances Edmunds, Historic Charleston Foundation, *History*

some theoretical paradigms are both possible and necessary. The broad outlines of this philosophy can be seen in the pioneering program now in being at Columbia.

One limitation of all American academic programs is that, by their very nature, they can offer little or no "hands-on" or "on-site" experience to the student. Nor is there as yet anything approaching a national program of apprenticeship or internship. Thus each student is required to fend for himself — an unhappy situation in the best of circumstances. This problem, already serious, will grow steadily more pressing as the volume of work increases. Lacking any centralized program by the Federal government, some alternative internship system will have to be evolved.[8]

If European and American experience up-to-date is any index, most restoration/preservation projects will be of governmental or institutional nature. This suggests that most graduates of historic preservation programs will work as civil servants or institutional employees rather than as free-lance professionals. It is easy to visualize some architects developing a private practice in the area of architectural conservation;[9] but most architects, like most historians or archaeologists, are likely to function in curatorial or administrative capacities in specialized institutions. Precisely what functions they will discharge — administration, research, legislation, curatorial, or educational — will depend upon both training and temperament. At the present time, the entire American field is still fluid, in the process of becoming institutionalized: thus it offers an unusual range of opportunities for the imaginative and energetic newcomer.

It is obvious that any broad national program of preservation and restoration will require the training of a large force of journeymen in the traditional building crafts as well as technicians in modern building technology. In the first category would be carpenters, cabinetmakers and woodcarvers; plasterers and masons; painters, paperhangers, seamstresses and upholsterers, etc. In the second category would be plumbers, steamfitters and electricians; heating, cooling and ventilating craftsmen; etc. It is also apparent that, to work effectively together, these individuals, too, must share a common understanding of the special problems of preservation both among themselves and with the professionals in the field. Yet, today there is no consensus on what relationships, if any, should exist between academic programs for training professional preservationists, and vocational programs for training craftsmen in traditional building trades. Obviously, the professional will profit greatly from "hands-on" experience in workshops and construction sites. So, too, would craftsmen benefit from academic coursework in architectural history and decorative arts. Both would profit from laboratory experience and lectures in such subjects as stone disease or the pathologies of timber construction. Perhaps we should visualize an educational program with parallel academic and vocational tracks in which cross-overs would be permitted to any student who is able and willing to operate at both levels.[10]

of the preservation movement in Charleston; James M. Massey, Historic House Association, *Management problems of the historic house;* Richard M. Candee, Old Sturbridge Village, *Management of outdoor architectural museums;* James M. Deetz, University of Rhode Island, *Innovative Interpretation at Plymouth Plantation;* Diane Pilgrim, Brooklyn Museum, *"Period" rooms in the fine arts museum;* Sabina Wright, Historic Annapolis, Inc., *The preservation and restoration of the Paca House and Gardens in Annapolis.*

(6) Archaeology: John L. Cotter, National Park Service, *Salvage archaeology in Philadelphia;* James W. Deetz, University of Rhode Island, *Principles of archaeology;* Robert Vogel, Smithsonian Institution, *Industrial archaeology;* Stanley Smith, University of South Carolina, *Historical archaeology.*

(7) Conservation: Bernard Feilden, York, England, *Conservation and consolidation of the masonry at York Minster;* Lawrence Majewski, Institute of Art, *Conservation of Frescoes and Mosaics;* Sheldon Keck, Cooperstown Museum, *Conservation of American painting;* Martin Weaver, Canadian Park Service, *Diseases and treatments of wooden structures;* Perry Borchers, Ohio State University, *Photogrammic Recording of Buildings;* Meredyth Sykes, Canadian National Parks, *Computerized Surveys and Inventories of historic resources.*

The field trips have been made possible by using our pro-rata share of the William Kinne Fellows Travelling Fellowship funds. They enabled the class to make from five to ten field trips each year, visiting such *historic towns* as Salem, Boston, Quebec, Albany, Philadelphia, Baltimore, Annapolis, Washington, D.C., Charleston, Savannah, and Beaufort; *outdoor architectural museums* such as Plymouth Plantation, Old Sturbridge Village, Bethpage Village, Richmondtown, Cooperstown, Williamsburg, Philadelphia; *museum houses* in Boston, Annapolis, Mt. Vernon, Monticello, Charleston, Savannah; *conservation laboratories* in Philadelphia, New York, Harper's Ferry.

Always artifact-centered, the preservation program has recently begun to develop a program in *architectural conservation.* Under the leadership of Prof. Norman Weiss, himself a chemist with extensive experience in conservation of masonry and paints, we have installed a conservation laboratory and are now offering regular lab classes.

8. The only programs approaching a national scope are the excellent summer survey teams of the Historic American Buildings Survey and the Historic American Engineering Record, both departments of the National Park Service. These surveys employ small teams of architects and historians for 10-week periods to measure and document a wide range of projects all across the nation. They constitute an excellent introduction to this aspect of the field and deserve to be enormously expanded. An optional solution, proposed by the author, is for the creation of a nation-wide consortium of schools which have programs in historic preservation. The Consortium would, among other things, administer a national program of subsidized internships for graduates of the member schools. Each intern would be assigned to appropriate non-profit projects in archaeology, museology, restoration, etc., for a stated period.

9. The French *Service des Monuments Historiques* has resolved this somewhat anomalous situation by employing architects both as full-time civil servants and as free-lance consultants working on special government projects for an individually negotiated fee.

10. Cervat Erder, head of the Restoration Department of Middle Eastern Technical University in Ankara, Turkey, suggests that, in countries like Turkey where highly skilled craftsmen may be semi-literate, training in both classroom and workshop should form an integral whole.

In the Western world, the training of craftsmen in traditional, pre-industrial crafts is even more neglected than is the professional training of preservationists and conservationists. Indeed, at the end of 1977, there were only two centers offering a structured training program in the traditional building crafts.[11] Such young workers as are entering this very important area are doing so on a personal, ad hoc basis, picking up what training may be assimilated by observation and apprenticeship in small, scattered restoration projects. Their search for training is not made any easier by the attitudes of building trades unions which tend to severely restrict apprenticeship and employment in their respective fields. This attitude is, of course, a reflection of the attitude of the entire construction industry towards the problems of retrieval and recycling of the built world. In an industry in which unemployment has recently been chronic and high, there is still little comprehension of the potential economic importance of this field. Yet preservation and conservation projects — unlike conventional new construction with its emphasis on labor-saving technologies — is by definition labor-intensive rather than energy intensive. Even now, few architectural firms have begun to specialize in this type of work: thus it is not surprising that few contractors with any expertise are to be found.

Ironically, most of the young people who are becoming traditional craftsmen seem to come from middle-class families. Most of them tend to be college graduates who see the crafts as one channel of escape from the routinized tracks of business and the professions. This is actually a significant cultural phenomenon. Working class youth is notable for its absence, showing a class prejudice against any sort of hand labor (with its connotation of sweaty armpits and dirty hands) and its bias in favor of the clean quasi-white collar activities of the service industries.

In America, at least, the trade unions seem to share a prejudice against the old, the used, the handmade. Even craft unions like carpenters, masons and plasterers (which might be expected to see in historic preservation new areas of employment for their members) have so far displayed no interest in it. On the contrary, in most communities in which there have been sharp battles for the preservation of historic buildings or districts (Boston, Providence, Savannah), the building trades unions have usually been solidly on the side of those projects which threatened them (new highways, airports and industrial construction). It is apparent that the environmental crisis will have to be much more mature before a wide recognition of its implications will be shared by the working people of the world who currently see the massive application of technology as the unique road to material well-being; and who regard aluminum, air-conditioning and glass as the iconography of this state of being.

None of which alters the fact that we must have training centers for the traditional building crafts. As long as preservation was limited to work on a few isolated great houses or monumental buildings, it was possible to find the necessary craftsmen, usually older and retired workmen who had had such apprenticeship

RESTORE field workshop session, joined by the Local No. 66, Pointers, Cleaners and Caulkers apprentices. Norman Weiss, senior RESTORE Lecturer, and Robert Meyer of Brisk Waterproofing of New Jersey, demonstrating various cleaning procedures. Photo by Jan C.K. Anderson.

11. Two such programs have recently been initiated. One is sponsored jointly by the Municipal Arts Society and Local 66, International Union of Bricklayers, both of New York City. The other has been initiated by the Durham Technical Institute of Durham, N.C.

training in their youth, before their crafts had been transformed by the massive application of mechanization to every branch of the field. Exactly what form such a training program will take is a matter of conjecture. It will almost certainly have to be governmentally-initiated or foundation-financed, at least initially.

Viet Nam War Memorial, Washington, D.C., 1980, Mary Pepchinski *(1982)*.

James Stewart Polshek. Photo by Pat Tine.

History VII: 1968–1981

Susan M. Strauss

When James Stewart Polshek was appointed Dean in 1972, the School was in a period of rather self-conscious reassessment in light of the events of 1968 and the intervening four years. Although Kenneth A. Smith, who had been appointed Acting Dean following the resignation of Charles Colbert in 1963 and Dean shortly thereafter,[1] had seen the School through the turbulent events of the spring of 1968, the School had not emerged unscathed. In a word, it was a shambles. Reorganization was imperative, since the very existence of the School was threatened. The events of 1968 are insufficient in themselves, however, to explain the state in which Polshek found the School. Problems had been smoldering at least since the mid-1960's, and the general discontent and self-consciousness prevalent among American youth, which exploded in the spring of 1968, if nothing else, drew attention to the situation. The composition of the Faculty — an inconsistent and uncoordinated group whose members for the most part pursued their individual philosophies of architecture and of architectural education, many of which were severely outdated — the non-systematic nature of the curriculum, and Smith's non-interventionism had set the scene. The 1968 strike and the events immediately following merely catalyzed what clearly was an inevitable deterioration. Afterwards, though, there was no turning back: neither could the School be returned to its previous state, nor could the disillusionment and dissatisfaction that had surfaced in the spring of 1968 be ignored. But there were no clear directives to emerge from the immediate situation, and indeed this was to be expected. The students and Faculty clamored for a re-

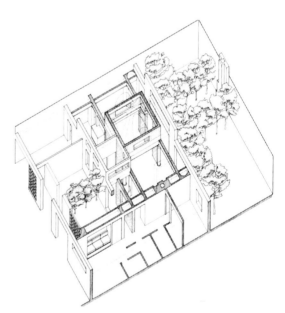

A House Made of Parallel Walls, 1979, Frank Arvan *(1982)*.

1. Kenneth A. Smith to William J. McGill, 18 November 1970, Central Files, Columbia University (hereafter, Central Files).

structuring of the architecture curriculum and a re-evaluation of architectural education generally: the watchwords were relevance and responsibility — both social and individual.

The formulation of Interim Rules for governing the School, the introduction of student participation in School decisions, new curriculum options, issue-oriented platform studios, experimental urban action programs, community-oriented learning and service opportunities' for students, and an aggressive minority students admissions policy, although of significance in themselves, must be considered rather minor changes in the absence of a broad framework for future development. And, in light of the tension, apathy, and disunity prevailing in the School, which in fact had led to its predicament, agreement on a long term plan for rebuilding the curriculum would not have been forthcoming were there not a strong hand to initiate and implement it.

Which is not to say that Smith had not contributed in an administrative capacity to the development of the School. During Smith's tenure, the School was reorganized under three divisions: architecture, architectural technology, and urban planning. The curriculum was enlarged, and a new Institute of Urban Environment had been created. While Smith was perhaps the ideal Dean to sit out a student strike, in that he paternalistically encouraged the students to air their grievances, for a number of reasons, he was not the one to attempt to restructure a confused department.[2]

In November 1970, approximately six months after the National Architectural Accrediting Board (NAAB) had granted only provisional accreditation,[3] Smith asked that he be allowed to resign as soon as a suitable replacement could be found.[4] His tenure was to have continued until August 1974. Smith was approaching mandatory retirement age, and in a realistic appraisal of the situation, he stated:

I am making this suggestion now because I feel that in view of the problems [to be] faced by the School and the University in the next few years, the School should be headed by a man who can provide continuity over a longer period than I have remaining.[5]

While there does not appear to have been much explicit pressure on Smith to step down, the pressure implicit in the need for reorganization must have been a factor in his decision.[6]

One wonders to what extent the NAAB report influenced Smith's decision to seek early retirement and the University's willingness to accept it, particularly in light of the criticism levelled at the administration of the School. The NAAB maintained that out of five major problem areas identified in its 1965 report — administrative apparatus and rules, space deficiencies, faculty salaries, instruction in design, development in relation to geographical and institutional resources — the first three remained largely unsolved in 1970.[7]

Notwithstanding the improvement in certain areas, a number of additional problems and deficiencies were identified including: a lack of planning with respect to overall institutional development concept and program manifested by uncoordinated planning and

2. Smith essentially adhered to a *laissez-faire* philosophy respecting the operation of the School. The Chairmen of the various divisions retained a free hand with respect to curriculum and educational philosophies, while Smith reserved control of the budget.

3. In spite of the deficiencies, the NAAB voted to accept the recommendation of its Visiting Committee and to grant accreditation to the Bachelor of Architecture program for a normal five year term subject to specific stipulations requiring evidence within a maximum of two years that significant progress had been made in removing major deficiencies to which the report referred (*Report of the National Architectural Accrediting Board,* May 1970, Central Files).

4. Smith to McGill, 18 November 1970, Central Files.

5. Ibid.

6. McGill expressed his appreciation of Smith's overture in a letter:
We are in for five years or more of intense self-examination accompanied by occasional trauma. I do not believe that this time is going to be easy for any of us and I am especially grateful for young willingness to let new leadership emerge in the School of Architecture before your own retirement becomes mandatory. Accordingly, I shall ask Vice President Kusch to proceed immediately with the construction of a Search Committee for a new dean (McGill to Smith, 4 December 1970, Central Files).

7. The report of May 1965 had recommended that "as soon as possible, a strong and highly motivated administrative leadership should be acquired." While the report of May 1970 commended Kenneth Smith's recruiting efforts, which resulted in a number of distinguished persons being designated Chairman and key professors (including Giurgola and Salvadori), adding leadership quality and diversity of academic strengths to the School, ti also pointed to "continuing evidence of serious administrative weaknesses and ambiguity in the governance of the School, perhaps due as much to failings of the 'system' as to the fault of any particular administrative or academic leader." In addition it criticized the Interim Rules for not having clarified areas of responsibility or points of accountability in the governance of the School. The 1965 report had recommended that space deficiencies in the architecture school be alleviated as soon as possible. In 1970, the NAAB commented that no real progress had been made in rectifying the serious overcrowding situation and the inadequacy of space and facilities. The 1965 report had insisted that salaries of the Faculty be increased to a scale comparable to those of other institutions of similar stature and reputation. The 1970 report observed that salaries of faculty members remained at an inadequate level and compared unfavorably with those of other graduate degree granting institutions. On the other hand, two areas were commended in 1970 as having been greatly improved since 1965. In response to the 1965 recommendation that a design sequence with respect for detail and educational significance be organized and initiated, the 1970 report indicated that the "sequence indeed offers a balance between architectural detail and a purposeful involvement in relevant architectural and educational issues" and accorded Columbia "strong relative distinction in terms of its design studios." Secondly, the 1970 team observed that much had been done since 1965 to improve the School's programs and to take advantage of its enviable location in New York City (*Report of the NAAB,* May 1970, Central Files).

administrative procedures; underuse and misuse of faculty resources; administrative ambiguity resulting in a general lack of authority commensurate with responsibilities, in a lack of accountability and an excessive amount of ineffective administrative and committee activity, and in questions respecting the proper jurisdiction and responsibilities of the Dean's office; lack of effective interaction between programs within the School and across the University; and lack of viable posture toward research and advanced educational needs in architecture.[8]

The report also called attention to the fact that evidence of continuing unrest was quite widespread in part because "the causal factors of '1968' have not been removed," and significantly, "the sense of community and of collective responsibility was missing in the Columbia School of Architecture to a very marked degree."[9]

More than any other single event, the search for a Dean tested the University's commitment to architectural education and its willingness to make good on a number of promises it had made as a result of the 1968 strike, particularly with respect to student participation.[10] Although it was hoped that the new Dean would prove to be a catalyst whereby many of the problems plaguing the School could be resolved, at the same time there was a desire to eliminate the Interim Rules prior to the designation and to present the new appointee with a firm framework in which to carry out his responsibilities.[11]

By March 1971, Ivar Berg submitted to McGill a slate of nominees for the Search Committee, determined as a result of consultations with faculty members, students, alumni, and representatives of all architecture constituencies connected with the School.[12] In mid-April, the President first apprised the prospective members of the Committee of their individual and collective responsibilities[13] and asked Alexander Kouzmanoff, Professor of Architecture, to chair the Committee.[14] The thirteen members included seven Faculty, four students and two alumni; three of the Faculty, one of the students and one of the alumni were minority group representatives.[15]

On behalf of the President, Polykarp Kusch, Vice President and Dean of Faculties, advised that most importantly, the Committee must be thorough in its search. He charged the Committee with submitting a list of three names ranked in order of preference and stressed that a Dean should be appointed as early as possible and preferably before July 1, 1972. Although the President retained the final word in the selection of a Dean, he would not normally exercise such power without the concurrence of the Faculty of the School and of the Search Committee.[16]

While the Committee embarked upon its appointed task, a move was afoot to thwart the selection of a Dean. Citing the advantages of shared resources and the saving of manpower, and appealing to the interface of the disciplines and the necessity for the University to contract, Cyril M. Harris, Professor of Electrical Engineering and Architecture in the Department of Electrical Engineering, suggested that the search for the Dean be discontinued immediately, that the position of Dean be abolished, and that the

8. Ibid.

9. Berg assessed the realities of the situation at hand. From his points, it becomes clear that Dean Smith's resignation may have been desirable on grounds other than those concerning continuity of administration:

(1) There is a little bit of trust among some of the faculty in each other;

(2) Some of the white students are placid but most are hypercritical of the faculty and all are critical of the Dean;

(3) The Dean, not the students, runs the School, the difficulty with which is that he does it very badly and often cynically;

(4) The Black Faculty-Student Organization is an incredibly well-organized, hard bargaining, politically sophisticated and exceedingly embittered group;

(5) A significant number, though not all, of the latter's complaints are justified (Berg to McGill, 19 March 1971, Central Files).

10. In January 1971, on the advice of Dean Smith, Thomas K. Dahlquist, President of the Columbia Architectural Alumni Association, suggested to McGill that the alumni of the School be involved in the selection of Smith's successor and in the definition of the Dean's role and the School's structure and direction (McGill to Smith, 13 January 1971, Central Files and Dahlquist to McGill, 9 January 1971, Central Files). On behalf of the President, Ivar Berg stated that the participation of the Alumni Association would be much appreciated and indicated that a representative would be invited to an upcoming meeting of the Faculty and students at which time Berg would address some of the issues, opportunities, and procedures relating to the search for a new Dean (Berg to Dahlquist, 27 January 1971, Central Files).

Student participation in the selection of the Dean did not proceed without some confusion. At one point, the students, represented by James B. Straw, Chairman of the School's Executive Council, Terry Tornek, Chairman of the Planning Division Student Faculty Council, and Nancy Laleau, Student Senator of the School, accused the President of scheduling a meeting at which time the faculty representatives would put forth preliminary proposals affecting the School's operational policies. Their objections to such a meeting turned on the following two points: that the proposals had not been presented and discussed with the student body or its official representatives, and that the Chairmen of the Planning and Architecture Divisions were out of the country and therefore not available for guidance. The letter to McGill had been signed by eighty-six students. Berg assured the students that no such meeting had been contemplated and reiterated that they would be involved in the search for the Dean and would have full opportunity to comment on any position papers that emerged from the informal 'smokers' held by the Faculty. Thereupon, Berg urged Dean Smith to call a meeting of students and faculty members in order that he might outline search procedures and specify issues facing the School. Whether or not such a meeting as that to which Straw, Tornek and Laleau referred had in fact been planned is irrelevant, the important point being that the students continued to be somewhat uneasy in the face of what could have been a routine bureaucratic procedure designed to exclude their participation. They therefore demanded that their participation in the selection process be guaranteed.

11. Smith to McGill, 16 December 1970, Central Files.

12. Berg to McGill, 19 March 1971, Central Files. The idea of the Search Committee was not received with overwhelming enthusiasm even though its necessity clearly was not disputed. Berg had assessed the difficulties entailed in coordinating the group and in steering it toward a common goal. A skeptical attitude toward the Search Committee was not exclusively an administrative phenomenon. Warren Dougherty, the Student Representative for the Urban Planning Divisional Council, questioned the advisability of the Committee in light of the difficulties encountered the

School be incorporated within the School of Engineering and Applied Science with an administrative structure similar to that of the Henry Krumb School of Mines.[17] Ironically, it had taken twenty-one years after its founding in 1881 for the School to come of age as an independent and autonomous entity within the University system, and in 1971, a proposal would have it return to its original status![18]

By early December 1971,[19] the Search Committee had nominated three men for the Deanship: O. M. Ungers, Sy J. Schulman and James Stewart Polshek[20] — an academician, an administrator and a practitioner with teaching experience respectively. While such a characterization may be overly simplistic, each candidate, by virtue of his professional orientation, represented a distinct direction the School might take. James S. Young, Deputy Vice President of the University, was charged with interviewing the three candidates and transmitting his evaluation to McGill.[21]

J. Max Bond Jr., then an Associate Professor of Architecture, had asked Polshek to consider the Deanship.[22] Due in part to his involvement with his practice, Polshek was not particularly enthusiastic about becoming engulfed in University administration; nevertheless, he consented to explore the situation.[23] From the point of view of the University, if Polshek, who was well-connected in the New York architectural community, were to be designated, the appointment would attract notice in the profession and would "raise both internal and external expectations about the University and School"[24] — both of which were sorely needed. Clearly, the appointment either of Ungers or of Schulman would not serve the University in the same way. Then too, with students clamoring for greater "relevance" in their architectural education, especially with respect to design, the appointment of a designer to head the School, it was hoped, would quell some of the dissatisfaction.

In Polshek's view, the architectural profession was at a critical point. The necessity for it to take stock of and to validate itself had never been more imperative. Such redefinition would not be effected by the profession per se but by architectural education, the role of which would be to develop a new generation of architects responsive to reconceptualization of the architect's function. In opposition to Ungers' view that the disjunction between the architecture schools and professional practice could be eliminated only by the School's catching up with modern practice, Polshek contended that architectural practice must be reformed by supplying a new breed of architect. Polshek stressed the academic and practical advantages to Columbia's being located in New York City — a constant theme throughout the history of the School.[25] Polshek's most identifiable weakness was presumed to be his having no direct experience with university administration; even so, he was not a complete stranger to the operation of a school since he had had teaching experience at Yale and at Cooper Union.[26] In addition, his office experience was expected to stand him in good stead with respect to procedural matters in the School. On the basis of the high standards that he set for himself, it was assumed

previous year by a similar committee charged with selecting a Chairman of the Division of Urban Planning (Dougherty to Berg, 15 February 1971, Central Files).

13. McGill to the prospective members of the Search Committee for the Dean of the School of Architecture, 16 April 1971, Central Files.

14. The other members of the Committee were: Professor Victor G. Alicea, Carl Anthony, Professor Max Bond, Carl Brown, Peter Brooks Combs, Thomas K. Dahlquist, Professor Sigurd Grava, Professor Charles Hamilton, Louella Long, Richard Nichols, Professors Jan H. Pokorny and Danforth Toan (Ibid).

15. Uncertain of exactly how to proceed with the search and of what exactly was understood by a reorganization of the School, the Search Committee addressed a number of questions to the President dealing with: determination of the prospective dean's salary, the spatial expansion of the School, a prospective School of Urban Studies, the expansion of the School's budget to cover new appointments, increased use of the resources of the School for the University's architecture and planning problems, and projected growth of the School.

16. Kusch to McGill, 21 May 1971, Central Files.

17. Harris to McGill, 27 November 1971, Central Files.

18. McGill assured Harris that although the search would not be discontinued, Harris' advice would be held for future consideration.

19. Young to McGill and Theodore de Bary, 24 January 1972, Central Files.

20. Even before the formal invitations had been extended to the nominees for the Search Committee, communications respecting potential candidates for the Deanship had been brought to the attention of the President. In March, Harold Bell, Chairman of the Urban Planning Division, had suggested that Lloyd Rodwin's name be placed before the Search Committee (Bell to Berg, 8 March 1971, Central Files). In April, Chester Rapkin, Professor of Urban Planning, advised that Deans Kusch and Berg had met with Jaquelin Robertson and had considered him eminently qualified for the position. Rapkin subsequently requested that Robertson's name be brought to the attention of the Search Committee (Rapkin to McGill, 1 April 1971, Central Files). Other names presented to McGill for forwarding to the Search Committee were: C. Richard Hatch, Bertram Bassuk and Vernon Robinson (Bassuk to McGill, 25 May 1971, Central Files, and Lowell Brody to Berg, 13 May 1971, Central Files).

The circumstances surrounding the nomination of Robinson, who had been the coordinator of the School's Urban Action and Experimentation Program, were unique. McGill had been inundated with letters endorsing Robinson for the Deanship. McGill had speculated that either Robinson or an individual acting on his behalf was waging an organized campaign. On August 9, 1971, he received confirmation from Frederick Johnson. Johnson had been the Project Director of the Stryker's Bay Community Action Project in 1967–68, supervising Robinson, who had been Training Director. The origin of the campaign was the Black/Puerto Rican Faculty/Student Organization operating out of an office on the fifth floor of Avery Hall. Hiram Jackson, Assistant Dean for Minority Affairs in the School and spokesman for the organization, had circulated a memorandum to potential supporters of Robinson requesting that they send a letter of recommendation to McGill by July 30, 1971. Jackson enclosed a model to be used in developing the letter of support.

The model stressed Columbia's unique position with respect to its environs and the inherent and complex social concerns and responsibilities, and the advantages to the appointment of Robinson including his already being within the University system as co-director of the Urban Action and Experimentation Program and specifically his being that Polshek would demand quality performance from both students and instructors, that he would take a rather strong interest in the academic matters at hand, and that he would be able to withstand the various pressures entailed in restructuring the School, including the not-so-subtle pressure to disband the School altogether.[27]

Having eliminated Ungers as a candidate, in part for his proven inability to deal with dissatisfaction among students while at the Technical University in Berlin, Young recommended that the President confer with Polshek and Schulman.[28] Young's "own preference put[s] Polshek ahead of Schulman, despite the unknowns, because...we ought to try first for something more than a manager to reclaim our School."[29] In analyzing first the nominations for the Deanship and second the actual selection, it becomes clear that, all things being equal, Polshek represented the most prudent choice. His appointment entailed the greatest risk but also the greatest chance for success. The candidates for the Deanship must be considered in light of the fact that the necessity for reorganization was considered a foregone conclusion: paralleling other times in the history of the School, the selection of a Dean coincided with a need for radical revision.

On March 16, 1972, Polshek was named to succeed Kenneth Smith as Dean effective July 1, 1972. Born in 1930, Polshek completed his undergraduate education at Case Western Reserve University in 1951. In 1955, he received a Master of Architecture degree from the School of the Arts, Yale University. The Department of Architecture in the School of the Arts was then under the leadership of George Howe; Louis Kahn served as Polshek's studio critic in his final year. Following employment in the office of I.M. Pei and Partners, Polshek won a Fulbright Fellowship in 1956 that enabled him to study new developments in prefabricated housing in Denmark. Upon his return, he was employed by Ulrich Franzen and Associates. His own firm, established in 1962, first received international attention in 1964 with the designs for two major textile research buildings in Japan for Teijin Limited.[30]

Polshek's commitment to rebuild Columbia's damaged reputation by means of a sound program of development and his commitment to integrate architectural education and practice are evident in the conditions he placed on his acceptance of the position. The six conditions defined in very broad terms the scope of Polshek's authority and responsibility and thus established basic guidelines according to which he would reorganize the School:

(1) Because he felt that it was important to make a physical impact and in order to make the Dean's office a more prominent place, Polshek requested a grant of $50,000 to effect physical changes to the School. Physical improvements would symbolize the general restructuring of the School;

(2) Polshek requested that the Avery bequest for the extension of Avery Library be liberated. The President and the Trustees had refused to allow the funds to be used for their assigned purpose

black. McGill promptly confronted Robinson, who confirmed that the campaign had indeed been organized. Despite the fact that Robinson acceded immediately to McGill's demand that the campaign be extinguished on the grounds that it was highly undignified and would prove to be counterproductive, the minority students and faculty members had made clear their dissatisfaction with the operation of the School. Even McGill was forced to comment that "it appears that there are few subtleties in the selection of the next Dean of Architecture." There seem to have been no further complications as a result of the Robinson incident. Needless to say, Robinson was not considered a legitimate choice.

21. Young commented on O.M. Ungers, a tenured faculty member at Cornell:

The overriding task of an academic dean in his [Ungers'] view is to liberate architectural training and education from the beaux arts tradition. Entrenchment of this tradition in the schools of architecture has resulted in turning out architects who are more competent as designers and aestheticians than they are as creators of habitats, the essential function of the practicing architect.

Ungers' position regarding students' understanding of the social and political sphere informed his general attitude toward architectural education. He maintained that as the scope of architectural activity broadened, it would be the task of architectural education to ensure that students acquire knowledge respecting the social, political and economic forces at work in the modern world. Ungers' approach was sympathetic to planning as well as to architecture, and his focus with respect to Columbia appears to have been curricular reform and integration of the School with other schools and departments in the University. An obvious difference between the philosophies of Ungers and of Polshek turned on the relation between academics and professional practice. Ungers' approach enjoined the full-time faculty member from continuing his professional practice on the basis of a conflict of interest, although adjunct faculty members were permitted to continue practicing. Contrarily, in Polshek's view, a design professor's continuing to practice would enhance his ability to teach and to evaluate design in the studios. Indeed as one of the conditions of his accepting the Deanship, Polshek would insist that he be allowed to continue to practice. Young feared that Ungers would work most effectively in a fairly stable and untroubled school, one with firm directives as to how architectural education could best keep pace with the vicissitudes of modern life, rather than at Columbia, where disunity and confusion were rife. Furthermore, Ungers' ability to handle the different factions at Columbia was questionable in light of the way he had dealt with dissatisfaction and unrest as Professor and Dean of the Faculty at the Technical University at Berlin.

Sy J. Schulman, a professional planner and a member of the Urban Planning Faculty, was as much an administrator as Ungers was an academician. He had a strong reputation for dealing with politically difficult problems, but appeared to Young to be somewhat apathetic toward new approaches in the intellectual direction of the School. Young feared that Schulman did not have a clear conception of what would be entailed academically. While Schulman emphasized planning as the means to integrate architecture and technology, his concept of planning seems to have been abstracted from the realities of the social and political spheres.

As he [Schulman] sees it, contention is endemic to the confrontation between art and technology that takes place in schools of architecture; it is the role of planning to bring the two together, both in the educational process and in real life practice. He is skeptical of the view that social or economic trends make reforms in architectural education necessary, and believes that the Columbia School of Architecture has continued to perform fairly well even without the kind of leadership that is desirable.

Consistent with Schulman's *laissez-faire* attitude toward the leadership of the School and with his view that the

Above: Perspective of Alberti's Sant' Andrea, 1981, Marcus Gleysteen *(1983).*

Left: Weekend retreat for a Labor Union, 1979, Peter Schubert *(1982).*

until the administration was confident that the School was on the road to recovery;

(3) On the grounds that the character of the Faculty would determine the character of the School to a great extent, Polshek needed to be able to attract new instructors. To this end, he requested that he be granted a sum equal to the salaries of four faculty members whom he felt contributed little to the educational framework, in order to hire new teachers. The four instructors would remain on the Faculty but would have reduced teaching responsibilities;

(4) Integral to his attitudes about architectural education was the idea that a practitioner should head a school of architecture. Following from this, Polshek asked that he be allowed to continue to practice;

(5) In keeping with his view that the School should be intimately involved with the physical planning of the campus, Polshek requested that he be named publicly and in writing as special adviser to the President for planning and design. Further, he requested that he have the right to develop lists of architects and planners who might be considered for commissions on the Columbia campus. As such, Polshek was named Adviser to the President for Physical Planning and Development. In order to avoid any conflict of interest, Polshek suggested that neither he nor anyone in his office would undertake any commission for the University for a fee. In contrast, it was agreed that appropriate members of the Faculty and other prominent architects could be retained to execute designs for the University;

(6) Polshek asked that the central administration support his in-

intellectual quality and educational direction of the School were satisfactory, Young was doubtful that Schulman would take initiative in matters of academic policy. Rather, Young anticipated that Schulman would either rely heavily on selected faculty advisers or would allow the educational apparatus to take care of itself. Young commended Schulman's pragmatism in that it presaged an aggressive posture with respect to the interests of the School and it would lend expertise and considerable political savvy to its management. Nonetheless, Young feared that Schulman's low level of concern for the academic aspects of the position could not but represent a "retreat from challenge" (James S. Young to McGill and De Bary, 24 January 1972, Central

22. Interview: James Stewart Polshek by Richard Oliver, 6 July 1981, transcription in Graduate School of Architecture and Planning archives (hereafter, GSAP archives).

23. Ibid.

24. Young to McGill and de Bary, 24 January 1972, Central Files.

25. Ibid.

26. Interview: Polshek by Oliver, 6 July 1981, GSAP archives.

27. Ibid.

28. Young to McGill and de Bary, 24 January 1972, Central Files.

29. Ibid.

30. In 1972, just prior to assuming the Deanship, Polshek received his first AIA Honor Award for the New York State Bar Association Center in Albany, New York — one of the first national design awards to a structure combining new building design with historic preservation. Polshek resigned as First Vice President and President-elect of the New York Chapter of the American Institute of Architects upon accepting the Columbia position (Memorandum: Polshek to Author, 10 August 1981).

tention to make the program in architecture exclusively a three year graduate course.[31]

The administration agreed to meet all of Polshek's conditions. A number of important architects have executed or will execute buildings in New York City as a result of Columbia's patronage and Polshek's arrangement with the University.[32]

In September 1972, Polshek began to act on his commitment to replace the Bachelor of Architecture with the Master of Architecture degree program. He appointed an ad hoc committee of Associate Dean David Glasser, Assistant Dean Loes Schiller, and former Dean Kenneth Smith to explore the possibilities.[33] Polshek's commitment was based in part on the increasing numbers of applicants who already had earned undergraduate degrees — a fact that seemed to substantiate a belief that architecture, like medicine and law, should be a post-graduate professional discipline. In addition, applicants who had undergraduate degrees in fields other than architecture or environmental design were expected to broaden and intellectually enliven the School and ultimately the profession. Polshek maintained that the graduate degree program would be more beneficial to students who eventually planned to teach and would bring Columbia in line with its sister schools of architecture including Harvard, Yale, Penn, M.I.T. and Princeton, which already had made the switch.[34]

In defense of a shorter program, the Faculty agreed that "aside from making our program more in keeping with our sister schools, there is a strong case for introducing a shorter, more intense, program and getting our students out into practice."[35] Although the institution of the Master's program would shorten the program in terms of years spent at the University, the focus on design would be intensified since a minimum level of competence in the liberal arts could be presupposed of all students entering with an undergraduate degree. A compelling and highly practical reason for a shorter program turned on the high cost of educating architects and on the inevitably rising tuition.

According to the original plan, any student entering with an undergraduate degree would receive a Master's upon completion of the architecture program, and any student with only two years of college training would receive a Bachelor's degree. The provisions were to be retroactive.[36]

Most important for Polshek and his long range plans was the fact that there was no precedent at Columbia for a three year curriculum in architecture. The move would necessitate not a reorganization, but a complete investigation, articulation and implementation of a new program. The complete overhaul including new faculty members, new courses and a new determinative philosophy would have been more difficult, if not impossible, to implement successfully were it necessary to retain the existing degree framework.

The plan to develop the program in architecture as a post-graduate professional course would facilitate the elimination of the Evening Program in Architecture, which Polshek counted as one of his primary objectives.[37] The Dean felt that while the program

31. Interview: Polshek by Oliver, 6 July 1981, GSAP archives.

32. Two of the most recent of these are James Stirling's new Chemistry building and Gwathmey/Siegel's East Campus dormitories. Despite discussions in 1973 on conflicts of interest deriving from the retention of faculty as professional advisers, precipitated in part by Alexander Kouzmanoff's having been selected to design and execute the extension to Avery Hall, Polshek has stood firm on his commitment to tap faculty resources whenever possible. In addition to Kouzmanoff's selection, which predated Polshek's arrival, Romaldo Giurgola, Chairman of the Division of Architecture until 1970 and presently Ware Professor of Architecture, was selected to design and execute the Fairchild Science Center. Robert Stern completed Greene Hall for the Law School — an interior redesign. Tim Wood and Michael Mostoller executed a remodelling of Lewisohn Hall, Robert Kliment and Frances Halsband *(Columbia, 1968)* remodelled Hogan Hall and are currently at work on a design for a new computer science center, and Lo Yi Chan of Prentice, Chan and Olhausen designed the new East Asian Library. Richard Dattner and Associates was retained to execute a new athletic complex at Bakers Field. Cain Farell and Bell are designing a new Rare Book Library within Butler Library, and Henry Altchek *(Columbia, 1968)* has been retained to design a new campus graphics system.

33. Minutes of meeting of the Faculty of Architecture, 19 September 1972, Central Files. The issue of graduate education had been considered previously. In a letter of 1935 focusing specifically on a replacement for Dean Joseph Hudnut, C. Grant LaFarge made patently clear that the idea was in the air. Further, LaFarge's emphasis on Columbia's unique location and resources, and on the Dean's being in sympathy with the role of graduate education reiterates themes that remain constant throughout the evolution of the graduate school:

The choice of a man to be Dean of course will be influenced by what the future policy of the School is to be. I take it that it is our aim to make this a progressive, perhaps finally a graduate school. That is evidently what Harvard intends to do, and there is even better reason for a graduate school at Columbia than at Harvard. This may be briefly stated, for the moment, as being that inasmuch as a graduate school should be a sort of laboratory for mature development and for research it not only should benefit from the prestige and resources of a great university, but would best be situated where it may command the lessons and the stimulus of the completest metropolitan life and have available the richest field of professional ability. The finger points at Columbia and New York City.

This is not the moment to argue the desirability of graduate schools; let it suffice merely to say that the need definitely exists.

A graduate school being then the contemplated aim, it is clear that the man to head that school as Dean should understand this problem, be in sympathy with it, possess the ability to handle it. One guarantee of that ability is his record of accomplishment in conducting a school (C. Grant LaFarge to Frederick Coykendall, 9 July 1935, Central Files).

34. Memorandum: Polshek to Author, 11 August 1981.

35. Summary of Issues for Special Faculty Meeting to be held 21 November 1972, 6 November 1972, Central Files.

36. Minutes of meeting of the Committee on Instruction, 1 November 1972, Central Files.

37. Interview: Polshek by Author, 10 August 1981.

was touted as being one of the more democratic aspects of the School — enabling less privileged, but talented students to get a degree — in fact, this was not the case. At best, the evening classes were filled with architects that were practicing in offices and merely taking a few courses or a design studio. At worst, the Evening Program had become a "dumping ground" for weaker students and was leading to a two-class school. This two-class character ran counter to the contention that the program represented one of the most democratic aspects of the School. In the absence of matriculated candidates for the degree and on the basis of the poor quality of the program, which in large part was determined by the calibre of the students, the expenditures of time and money could not be justified. Nonetheless, on the basis of the "democracy" argument, certain of the Faculty (especially those teaching in the program) initially opposed efforts to tamper with the program. In the end, though, Polshek was able to convince all concerned to phase out the program by 1972–73.[38]

However, because at least one of the factors that had caused its coming into being — namely, the inability on financial grounds of some students to attend daytime classes and to devote full time to their studies — remained relevant, the Ad Hoc Committee on the Evening Program and the Committee on Instruction recommended that a Work and Study Program be developed beginning in 1973–74. To accomodate the Work and Study students, mandatory courses and a maximum of electives would be scheduled for late afternoon and evening hours.[39]

With the Evening Program abolished and the Faculty adamant about the need to reorganize the Division of Architecture, the Faculty Senate voted unanimously to institute the Master of Architecture degree program beginning with the 1973–74 academic year.[40] It was highly unlikely that the University administration would reject the implementation of a Master's program requiring one hundred credit points to be distributed over three years. However, as an indication of the level of dissatisfaction with the existing program, the Faculty insisted that in the event the graduate program were not approved, at the least, the Bachelor of Architecture curriculum would be revamped.[41] The name change to the Columbia University Graduate School of Architecture and Planning, which not only reflects the School's being exclusively a graduate institution granting graduate degrees but also awards equal status to the planning program, was approved by the Trustees in June 1973.[42] The degree and name changes were symbolic of the objectives of the new administration. Also in June, the Bachelor of Planning degree, which had not been granted in at least ten years, was eliminated.[43]

Changes to the curriculum and to the Faculty during Polshek's tenure have been many and have been directed toward intellectually revitalizing the School, particularly the Master of Architecture program. As a means of expanding the Faculty and secondarily of providing instruction in architecture for undergraduates when the School became exclusively a graduate institution, in 1974, an architecture major was introduced in Columbia College. The con-

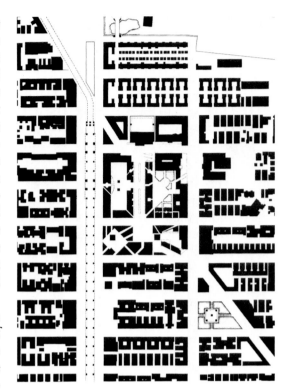

Above and opposite page: Community Club, 1978, Steven Elmets *(1979).*

38. Ibid.

39. Minutes of meeting of the Committee on Instruction, 1 November 1972, Central Files.

40. Minutes of meeting of the Faculty Senate, 1 February 1973, Central Files.

41. Minutes of meeting of the Committee on Instruction, 1 November 1972, Central Files.

42. Minutes of meeting of the Trustees, June 1973, Central Files.

43. Minutes of Faculty meeting, 20 February 1973, Central Files.

cept was not new: Columbia followed the lead of Yale, Penn, and Princeton, among others. The scheme allowed those teaching only part-time in the graduate school to fill out their full-time load in the College. Robert A.M. Stern (B.A., Columbia, 1960 and M. Arch., Yale, 1965), at that time a controversial first year critic, became the first departmental representative for the major.[44]

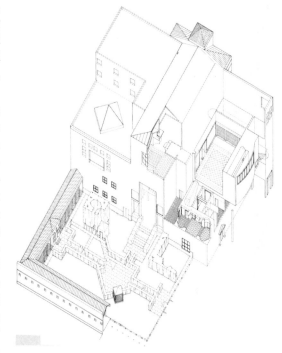

When he became Dean, Polshek observed a lack of cooperation among the Faculty, manifested by each member pursuing his own course according to his own philosophy, an imbalance between full and part-time faculty members, and a certain degree of factionalism. There was no sense of community or collective responsibility among the Faculty or the students; indicative was the fact that rarely if ever did the students work in the studios or the instructors in their Avery offices.[45] The School had taken on the character of a commuter institution. All of this was possible because of Dean Smith's laissez-faire administration and the general apathy prevalent at the time. Consequently, a first objective was to change the composition of the Faculty and in so doing, to expand it. Not all of the early decisions were popular, and to a certain extent, the Dean operated under an "ends justify the means" rationale and perhaps could be accused of being somewhat overzealous in his desire, albeit an admirable one, to accomplish a great deal in a short period of time. Polshek's strategy was two-pronged: first to work within the structure of the existing program to replace faculty members whose effectiveness he felt had waned,[46] and then to bring in younger and more innovative instructors to help determine the need for, and then to effect monumental changes to the curriculum. Polshek outlined two basic criteria for recruitment:

The first is that the [teacher]...be capable of giving the most sensitive individual attention to the students in an effort to encourage them to both discover themselves and to expose their work to the critical view of others...The second criterion...is that the faculty member possess those attributes of scholarship which one normally expects from a member of a university community. Implicit in this second quality should be a basic loyalty and commitment to the university as a force for positive social change.[47]

With respect to the reorganization of the School, the issues and effects of changes to the Faculty and to the curriculum have increasingly become intertwined. Polshek was well aware that in the absence of a strong Faculty to administer it, the most highly systematized curriculum would not be successful, and conversely, in the absence of a coherent, well-organized curriculum providing a constant framework, the ultimate strengths and capabilities of the individual instructors could not be tapped. Thus, it is impossible to separate the faculty members and their individual philosophies from the curriculum as it now stands. The Dean's appointments were not intended to fill existing positions and to continue instruction in architecture as it had taken place in the past. On the contrary, in light of the chaotic state in which Polshek found the School, new teachers were expected to revamp entirely instruction

44. Memorandum: Polshek to Author, 11 August 1981.

45. Interview: Michael Mostoller by Author, 12 August 1981.

46. An outstanding example was the program in architecture directed exclusively by Victor Christ-Janer. Polshek considered the program as being economically and academically counterproductive with respect to his larger plans for the School; he was committed to phasing out the one-year program.

47. Five Year Plan of the Graduate School of Architecture and Planning, 24 July 1974, Central Files.

in design. Along with this would come a reorientation in the teaching of history and theory to respond specifically to design courses, which were considered preeminent.

Kenneth Frampton, a central figure in this endeavor, was Polshek's first appointment to the Faculty. Despite his recently having been tenured at Princeton, Frampton had expressed a desire to relocate to New York; Polshek offered Frampton a significant role in the reorganization of the School. Not only did he perceive Frampton as "a great magnet for bright young people," but in that many of their interests coincided, Polshek saw Frampton as an ideological ally. In addition, Frampton had a special interest in architectural education, had followed its recent development quite closely and was well known in academic circles. Thus, through his recommendations and his recruiting efforts, Frampton was instrumental in determining the configuration of the Faculty.[48]

Polshek and Frampton shared the view that although it was desirable that faculty members hold diverse philosophies of architecture, common to all should be the commitment to represent a clear pedagogical approach and a firm dedication to teaching. Indicative of this commitment to diversity were the first few appointments: Klaus Herdeg, Michael Mostoller and Richard Plunz. Herdeg, who at the time was being considered for tenure at Cornell, had adopted, in general outline, a post-Corbusian formalist position developed at Cornell with Colin Rowe. Antithetically, Mostoller and Plunz, both of whom were trained at RPI (where the architecture program was structured generally on Team X ideologies and methodologies), adhered to a position according to which the socio-cultural and technical organization of the urban fabric was stressed.[49]

The antithesis manifested in the first few appointments was fortuitous. According to Polshek, the essential strengths of the core group of design instructors, which had been expanded by three new permanent members, and of the School generally, resided and continue to reside in the diversity of philosophies, objectives, and ambitions, and in the balance between practitioner and theoretician, between the interest in the social implications of architecture and its aesthetic dimensions.[50]

Herdeg was engaged specifically to organize and to implement the first year design program along the lines of the one he had developed at Cornell. Organized on a strict pedagogical basis, the underlying principle entailed the necessity for a systematic and rigorous first year, emphasizing both basic skills and theoretical principles in order that all students would be prepared for the more advanced design sequence.[51] The first year was predicated on the students' having had no prior training in design; thus it was intended as a great equalizer. In their relatively "abstract" first term, students were occupied exclusively with exploratory exercises of a formal nature. The projects were not buildings, and no programs were issued; analysis and description of the problem were stressed. Because more and more entering students have backgrounds in design, and because Herdeg no longer retains sole responsibility, the course has changed somewhat. Less time is spent on purely

48. Interview: Polshek by Oliver, 6 July 1981, GSAP archives; and Interview: Polshek by Author, 11 August 1981.

49. Interview: Kenneth Frampton by Author, 11 August 1981.

50. Interview: Polshek by Author, 11 August 1981.

51. Interview: Mostoller by Author, 12 August 1981. Polshek's teaching experience at Cooper Union and his own student work under Eugene Nalle at Yale in 1951–52 had convinced him of the necessity of a pedagogically sound first-year design course. Thus, in the first year of his term, Polshek had formed a team including William Todd Springer, Sean Sculley, John Gaunt and John James, whose attitudes toward the importance of rigorous first year training were in line with his own. Appropriately, Springer, Sculley and James had taught at Cooper Union. A number of criticisms were leveled at this relatively abstract course, not the least of which hinged on the fear that Polshek would "sacrifice the architecture of humanism for the architecture of craft," and that he was going "to turn Columbia from a great general education university into a polytechnic" (Memorandum: Polshek to Author, 10 August 1981; and Interview: Polshek by Oliver, 6 July 1981, GSAP archives).

formal exercises, and two building design projects have been introduced. The principles upon which the course is based remain fundamentally the same, that is,

through a combination of 'limited objective' and 'real' problems, it exposes a number of complex issues and investigates methods of analysing and describing these. The tool of analysis is explored not only as a way of judging built architecture, but also as a means of testing design decisions and developing solutions. The problems introduced to students during this semester deal with the richness of the processes of making architecture through an emphasis on discovery; a series of problems provide the vehicle for the learning process, each, in turn emphasizing a different cluster of the following architectural issues: form/space; symbol/meaning; construction/implementation; use/activity.[52]

During the second term of the first year, the two major design problems are intended to introduce the ideas of social and physical context and to prepare the student for his third term investigation of housing typology.[53]

Similarly, when Michael Mostoller was hired away from Harvard, he was asked to coordinate a program for second year design work.[54] At first, the two terms of the second year were a coordinated sequence under one instructor. It was not until Richard Plunz became the Chairman of the Division of Architecture in 1978 that the first and second semesters in each of the first two years began to be organized independently. In consonance with the stress on urban issues at RPI, Mostoller organized the second year accordingly. From the outset, the second year focused on housing. Whereas the intent of the first year was to define architectural attitudes and approaches, that of the second year was to establish a discipline of design. Housing was considered to be "ideally suited to this endeavor as it combines urbanistic and social phenomena."[55] While the quality of public space was stressed, solutions were predicated on "an investigation of the nature of residential life and the generation of a suitable form for the dwelling and its 'group.'"[56]

The first term problem introduced the idea of typologies. The second term of the second year evolved as a link between the highly structured introduction to design in the first three terms and the more individualized and ad hoc final year. As such, the work was intended to build upon past experience by introducing new material and by enabling the student to place his design experiences within a broad context for future development. The program has evolved to include the following major issues:

the building in the context of existing built form in the urban environment; the building in the natural context and the issue of landscape design; the program as an instrument of architectural expression, particularly with regard to the use of circulation patterns to inform both internal and external organization; the relationship of community structure to architectural form; the development of architectural style in the process of form-synthesis and the articulation of architectural detail as an extension or elaboration of architectural intentions.[57]

Shades and Shadows study, 1981, Margaret Tasker *(1983)*.

52. "Tradition: Radical and Conservative," *Precis,* 2 (1980), p. 6.

53. Interview: Mostoller by Author, 12 August 1981.

54. Frampton had recommended Mostoller and Plunz on the basis of his knowledge of R.P.I. and its teaching methods. He considered it to have a more engaged, systematic and methodical program in architecture than any other school in the country. While at Princeton, Frampton had attempted unsuccessfully to recruit Mostoller, who had invited Frampton to R.P.I. to visit in 1966, and Robert Winney (who was a professor of Mostoller's and of Plunz's at R.P.I. and continues to teach there). Upon Frampton's arrival at Columbia in 1972, he advised Polshek to employ Mostoller and Plunz.

55. *Precis,* p. 10.

56. Ibid., p. 10.

57. Ibid., p. 15.

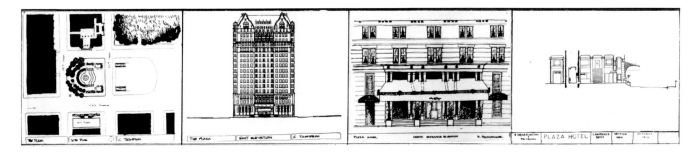

The organization of the first two years coincides in that in each, the first term adheres fairly strictly to a given theme while the second term is looser and is concerned with application of the principles. From the first, the reorganization of the second year was intended to allow the four critics and the students some independence while working together on a common theme. Presently, the first year reflects this same intent, although originally Herdeg had retained almost complete control.[58]

The final year traditionally had been the loosest of the design studios and continued that way largely because senior instructors, who were for the most part more varied in their positions, continued to administer it. The fall curriculum has focused on the design of the city and endeavors to confront both urbanistic and architectural issues as two facets of the same problem. Resolution of questions respecting the interface between urban design and architecture is the pedagogical objective of the studio. The second term has been organized conceptually to allow students to pursue advanced design projects that respond to their specific areas of interest. Programs are developed by the students or by members of the Faculty or both and reflect the diversity of interests in the School. Students usually work in studio groups.[59]

The balance between a concern with image and formal reality on the one hand, and considerations of a socio-cultural nature on the other has been maintained over the years, although modified slightly. Urban concerns, which have been central to the "RPI line" also have been dealt with by faculty members Jon Michael Schwarting, Steven Peterson, Barbara Littenberg and Timothy Wood, who adhere to a kind of *Collage City* approach along the lines developed by Fred Koetter and Colin Rowe.[60]

When finally the guidelines for organization of the design curriculum had been substantially articulated, the Program Council began to focus on history, theory, and construction courses that would complement the design studios and would provide historical, philosophical, and technological frameworks for the teaching of design.

The first year course, "Principles of Architectural Design," entails executing drawings and constructing models of canonical works irrespective of historical context. Analysis of these works in terms of proportion, scale, and order is accomplished in conjunction with lectures. Predicated upon the existence of universal principles, the course explores a general range of architectural examples in order to discover such principles. Fulfilling a need in the

Above, opposite and following page: "Leporello" composite analytic drawing of the Plaza Hotel,1974.

58. Interview: Mostoller by Author, 12 August 1981.

59. Ibid.

60. Interview: Frampton by Author, 11 August 1981.

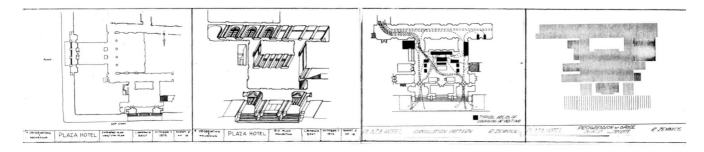

second year complementary to that fulfilled by "Principles" in the first, is "Comparative Critical Analysis of Built Form," a course that Frampton had begun to develop at Princeton. Whereas "Principles" stresses formal considerations, "Comparative Critical Analysis" emphasizes cultural, ideological, and historical specificity. The course is conducted as a seminar in which students compare and contrast pairs of buildings with reference to details and to the hierarchical configuration of their constituent parts. Analysis of spaces proceeds on the basis of public, private, semi-public, and service uses. The purpose is to give the student some understanding of the ways in which and the extent to which architecture can be made to embody meaning.[61]

The courses in principles of architecture are to be taken in conjunction with history courses, taught not as straight architectural history, but organized around specific issues and attitudes corresponding to issues encountered in the studios. "Thresholds in the History of Architecture" was introduced in 1979 to coincide with first year work; the two semester course covers the history of modern architecture through the nineteenth century. "Twentieth Century Architecture I and II," developed by Mostoller and Frampton for second and third year students, endeavor respectively to consider specific issues in an historical way and to present theoretical platforms and recent history from an architectural standpoint. As such, the first two years in the School have evolved to include a "course package" — a studio course with a supplementary theory course, a history course, a structures, and a construction course. During the third year, students may elect history seminars. In his first year at Columbia, Plunz, who had been teaching at Penn State where his research on indigenous architecture and his interest in housing had resulted in two important publications,[62] introduced a unique on-site research course to study indigenous Turkish architecture.

Polshek's intention to develop a Faculty with wide ranging philosophies rather than one with a single ideological or pedagogical stance was facilitated by his inheriting a rather diverse group of instructors. Ada Karmi-Melamede occupies a unique position in her concern with very large scale urban structures, which frequently accommodate a variety of uses. Alexander Kouzmanoff has a strong interest in public buildings, his work exhibiting a sort of late modern movement style. Adopting a "late Philadelphia" position akin to that of Venturi, Moore and Vreeland, Romaldo Giurgola often employs thin screen-like facades and diagonally

61. Ibid.

62. Interview: Mostoller by Author, 12 August 1981. In 1970, Plunz published *Mantua Primer: Toward a Program for Environmental Change,* and in 1973, *San Leucio: Traditions in Transition.*

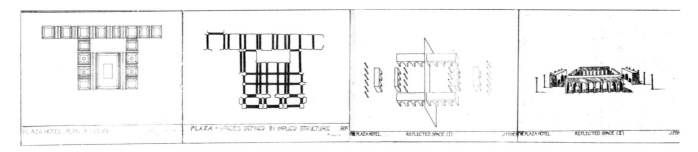

PLAZA HOTEL PLAN, REFLECTED   PLAZA - SPACES DEFINED BY IMPLIED STRUCTURE   RF   THE PLAZA HOTEL   REFLECTED SPACE (I)   J FISHER THE PLAZA HOTEL   REFLECTED SPACE (II)   J.FISH

articulated planning devices. While it is not a regularly given course, "Exercises in Style," in which the student is expected to design the same house in four different historical modes over the course of the semester, seems to represent Robert A.M. Stern's position as a teacher. He is perhaps more concerned with stylistic devices and the uses of history than anyone on the Faculty, and in terms of his own design work and writing, he has played a significant role in the articulation of a post-modern aesthetic.

In sum, the architecture program develops sequential and topical relationships among the six terms of design, taking the student progressively from simpler to more complex challenges, from individual buildings to urban design. Design courses are supplemented with complementary history, theory, and construction courses.

In 1971, Kouzmanoff, a highly respected senior design faculty member, succeeded Giurgola as Chairman of the Division of Architecture. That the established length of the Chairman's term was three years complicated matters for Polshek. If he were to act according to precedent, which dictated that the Chairman had jurisdiction over curriculum, it would be two years before a change of Chairman would enable Polshek to implement his own ideas. Therefore, Polshek and Kouzmanoff, who was not by nature particularly enthusiastic about administration, worked out a rather unconventional arrangement according to which the Dean assumed many of the Chairman's responsibilities and the Chairman assumed a larger teaching role. Thus, Polshek began to fulfill President McGill's mandate to renew the architecture program administratively and intellectually.[63]

Kouzmanoff's three year term ended in the spring of 1974. The Dean, impatient to overhaul the program, wrote an open letter to the Chairman, the Divisional Council and the School generally in which he rather naively but unequivocally stated that commencing in the fall of 1974, the Chairmanship would cease to exist, and the Chairman's administrative duties would be absorbed by the Dean's office. Polshek further stated that he would appoint a director for each of the three years of the program. Polshek thought the scheme was feasible; yet, within one hour of the letter's being made public, the Dean was summoned to the sixth floor of Avery where he was met by an angry crowd of students and a number of faculty members. The substance of their complaint was that a co-terminus Dean and Chairman on the model of the Princeton

63. Memorandum: Polshek to Author, 12 August 1981.

and Yale architecture schools was unacceptable. Polshek therefore named Kouzmanoff Chairman for another three-year term.

By the end of Kouzmanoff's second term in 1976–77, the School was in very good order. New faculty members were working well with the original core group; applications were at an all-time high, and the reputation of the architecture program had achieved national prominence. Polshek appointed a Committee to seek a Chairman for the upcoming three years. He intended to pull back from an active role in the Master of Architecture program and to turn leadership over to other faculty members.

The Search Committee, composed of instructors as well as of students, decided not to consider candidates other than members of the Columbia Faculty of Architecture. After considerable debate, they recommended that Richard Plunz become the Acting Chairman for one year with a mandate to strengthen and regularize administrative procedures and curriculum. A year later, the Dean named Plunz Chairman for the remaining two years of the traditional three-year term. During this period, Steven Peterson, Mary McLeod and Lauretta Vinciarelli became full-time instructors. Plunz's administration improved the management of the Division but made few intellectually substantive changes. In 1980, Max Bond, who had just been appointed by Mayor Koch to the New York City Planning Commission, was elected Chairman, and a series of major curriculum changes was initiated. In Bond's first year, two more full-time women were added to the faculty roster: Susanna Torre and Barbara Littenberg. Both Plunz and Bond were committed to the importance of social content in the architecture program.[64]

Faculty appointments must be understood in light of the specific framework for development of the Columbia program. Symbolic of Polshek's desire to negate the past and to place his own stamp on the School, was his rewriting the description of the degree program in architecture that appears in the School catalogue. He characterized the Master of Architecture program in terms of three primary matrices: the perceptual, the constructional and the cultural. The matrices effectively define the orientation of the program. The constructional matrix, which focuses on technology, and the cultural matrix, which concerns the social, political, and economic exigencies of design, would be subordinated to the perceptual matrix, which deals with design and constitutes the core of the curriculum.[65] The clarification was intended to respond to students' confusion respecting the proper relation between architectural and social aspirations. The catalogue describes the program's commitment to a value system encompassing both social reform and excellence in design.[66]

As a means of defining educational objectives and of introducing changes to the curriculum, Polshek revived the Master of Architecture Divisional Council. Further, Polshek created two other divisional councils: Urban Planning and Historic Preservation. The separate Councils were to make recommendations to the Committee on Instruction, which would then forward these to the Faculty for final action. The initial meetings of the Architecture

64. Ibid.

65. *Catalogue of the School of Architecture, 1973–74.*

66. Memorandum: Polshek to Author, 12 August 1981.

Council were indicative of the enthusiasm for the return of participatory administration: meetings often continued for two days,
often over weekends. Specific plans for curriculum reorganization
were submitted, subsequently debated and finally revised on the
basis of both the students' and the Faculty's contributions.[67]

One of Polshek's first administrative acts was to name Loes
Schiller Assistant Dean for Admissions, Financial Aid and Student
Records; he also nominated her to the Faculty. Polshek's appointment of Schiller, who was the second woman to be designated
Dean in the University, was a practical as well as a symbolic gesture. The appointment recognized Schiller's administrative
abilities and at the same time was a symbolic commitment to the
importance of increasing the number of women students in
the School.[68]

In the first few years, measures instituted by Polshek were not
always met with enthusiasm by the Faculty. In fact, in the late fall
of 1972, a group of senior professors, who remembered Charles
Colbert quite clearly, complained to McGill that Polshek's
methods were of concern to them.

Around the same time, Polshek asked for the resignations of
Associate Dean David Glasser (who was succeeded by Professor of
Structural Engineering Charles Thurston) and Assistant Dean
Robert Speaks on the basis of irreconcilable differences. Polshek
was firmly committed to the special needs of minority students
and earlier had created a position of Assistant Dean for Minority
and Urban Affairs. Robert Speaks, a black urban planner, who had
graduated from the School and was a holdover from the old
Black/Puerto Rican Student/Faculty group originally headed by
Vernon Robinson, was the first incumbent. The Dean appointed
Elaine Dowe Carter to succeed Speaks and expanded her role to
include an active involvement in the affairs of the Urban Planning
Division; Ghislaine Hermanuz succeeded Carter. Arverna Adams
presently occupies the position. All three women performed invaluable services for the School and its minority community —
strengthening ties between minority students and the Dean's office. On this same point, one important factor in the appointment
of Max Bond as Chairman of the Division of Architecture was to
underscore the continual importance of recruiting more black and
Hispanic faculty and students.

While one may argue the merits of one method over another, the
School began to make a marked comeback even in the first years of
Polshek's administration. Within two years, applications to the
School for the Master of Architecture degree had increased by one
hundred fifteen percent, even when applications to other architecture schools had remained relatively constant. Admission of
women increased, and the geographical distribution of students
widened.[69] This was particularly notable considering that the profession was entering one of the worst economic periods since 1930.
The reasons for the revival were several: attending school in New
York City had gained in popularity; the School had formally become a graduate school and thus had begun to attract students
from a wide variety of disciplines; Polshek was a well-known

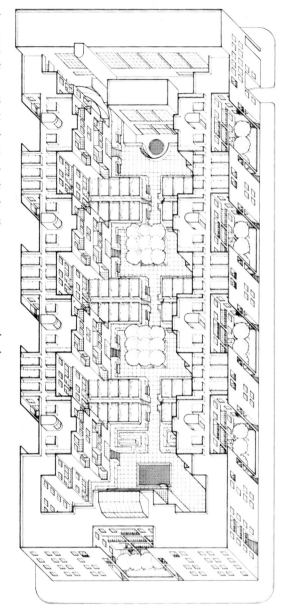

Above and opposite page: Perimeter Housing,
1979, Margaret Walker *(1981).*

67. Ibid.

68. In the fall of 1970, the Master of Architecture program
had a total of 109 men and twenty-four women, and the
applications of men and women were considered and acted
upon separately. Although in 1972–73 the totals for the
program were seventy-eight men and thirty-three women,
seventeen men and seventeen women entered the first year
Master of Architecture class, a first in architectural
education. By the fall of 1980, the totals in the Master's
program were ninety-nine men and seventy women, while
the total School population numbers 197 men and 169
women (Memorandum: Loes Schiller to Author, 14 August
1981).

69. Memorandum: Polshek to Author, 11 August 1981.

practitioner; newly appointed instructors for the most part had established reputations and therefore would be a drawing point for the School; and other schools, particularly Harvard and Yale, had been on the decline. Finally, faculty members had begun to participate more frequently and enthusiastically at design reviews at other schools, thereby spreading word of a renascence at Columbia.

When Percival Goodman, who with his brother Paul had written *Communitas: Means of Livelihood and Ways of Life* in 1947 and who had been influential in the School as Director of the two-year Urban Design program, retired at the end of Polshek's first year, lack of leadership for the program provided a first opportunity for sweeping change. A period of uncertainty ensued during which time Polshek relied primarily on visiting professors for instruction, and condensed the program into one year as a "holding action" to allow time to explore its relationship to planning and architecture generally and to build a Faculty that would reconceptualize the program. Finally, in 1974, Alexander Cooper, a member of the Urban Design Group under Mayor Lindsay, who had recently been appointed to the City Planning Commission, was hired to direct the program. Cooper and Stanton Eckstut (hired shortly thereafter) reformed the program from one that had been design-oriented to one that dealt primarily with planning, zoning, land use, and economic development.

The increasing importance of preservation and restoration precipitated Polshek's efforts to strengthen the program in historic preservation and to integrate it more fully into the School. In anticipation of the need for professionals in the field, James Marston Fitch, critic and historian, had formulated a graduate course of study in restoration and preservation of historic architecture. Fitch served as the Director from the inception of the program in 1964 until his retirement in 1977. The Columbia course is the oldest training program of its kind in America. Originally granting only a certificate, the program was expanded to two years duration and presently grants a Master of Science in Historic Preservation. Following Fitch's retirement, a search committee, comprised of representatives of the students, the Faculty and the small but powerful Preservation Alumni, unanimously selected Jacques Dalibard as Director. Dalibard had received a Master of Science in Architecture, Restoration and Preservation from the program in 1971. At the time of his appointment in 1977, he was a member of the Canadian Commission to UNESCO and the Chairman of CORTS in Canada. Polshek gave the new Director an enlarged budget, enabling him to expand the Faculty; in line with a belief that a comprehensive education in historic preservation must include conservation and planning in addition to history and design, two full-time faculty members were added. Norman Weiss, a well-known conservation chemist from M.I.T., and Christine Boyer, an historian with a PhD in Urban Planning (who was transferred from the Planning Faculty), together with David DeLong and William Foulks, both of whom are architects and historians, constituted the core Faculty.[70]

70. Ibid.

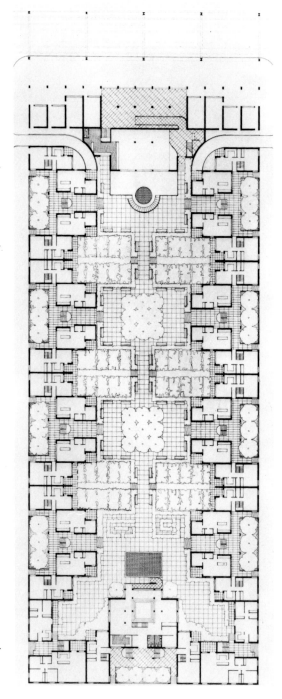

For personal reasons Dalibard resigned in the late summer of 1978. Robert McNulty, who had recently left the NEA, was designated Acting Director while a new Search Committee was activated. Late in the spring of 1979, William Murtagh, the Keeper of the National Register, was appointed. His two-year stay was uneventful, and in May 1981, he accepted a position with the National Trust. Rather than convene a Search Committee, Polshek appointed David DeLong as permanent Director with a mandate to energize the program and to re-integrate it with the School.[71]

The schism between the division of architecture and that of preservation traces to Professor Fitch's elegantly articulated antagonism toward modern design — an attitude proceeding from what Fitch perceived as the architect's insensitivity toward history generally and existing architecture specifically. Polshek collaborated with DeLong and Plunz, then Chairman of the Division of Architecture to develop a blueprint for a joint degree program between Architecture and Historic Preservation. Although Preservation alumni vigorously opposed the move, the Preservation students enthusiastically supported it. In 1979, this program was approved by the University Senate.[72]

The Division of Urban Planning proved to be the most difficult for the Dean to administer and to improve. When he assumed responsibility for the School in 1972, Polshek found a demoralized Division. Charles Abrams had been the dynamic and influential Chairman until his death in 1970. Only two senior faculty members remained: Sigurd Grava, a relatively young professional planner and engineer, and Chester Rapkin, an influential and conservative planner. Rapkin left for Princeton in 1973. The remainder of the Faculty was very young, and almost all were recent graduates of or current PhD candidates in the Columbia program. Interest in the Urban Planning program was virtually non-existent among the members of the Faculties of Architecture and Urban Design, many of whom questioned the very existence of the program.

Recognizing the study of housing to have been particularly strong at Columbia, Polshek believed that could be the focal point around which to build a new program. Still, a leader for the program was needed. A nationwide search was initiated. One of the candidates, Peter Marcuse, was an attorney who had received a PhD in Urban Planning from Berkeley and was the son of Herbert Marcuse, a name that carried considerable import. His reputation was impeccable, and after a trial semester, Marcuse was hired as the new Chairman of the Urban Planning Division, in which capacity he served from 1973–74 through 1978–79. During this period a

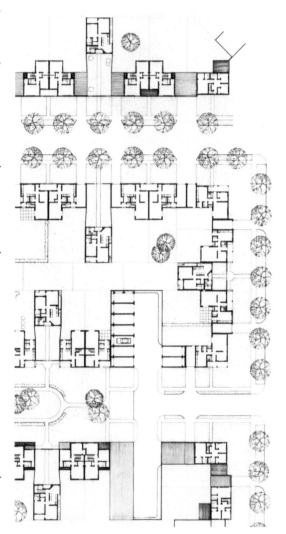

Above and opposite page: Subway Suburb, 1978, Roger Seifter *(1978).*

71. Memorandum: Polshek to Author, 11 August 1981.
72. Ibid.

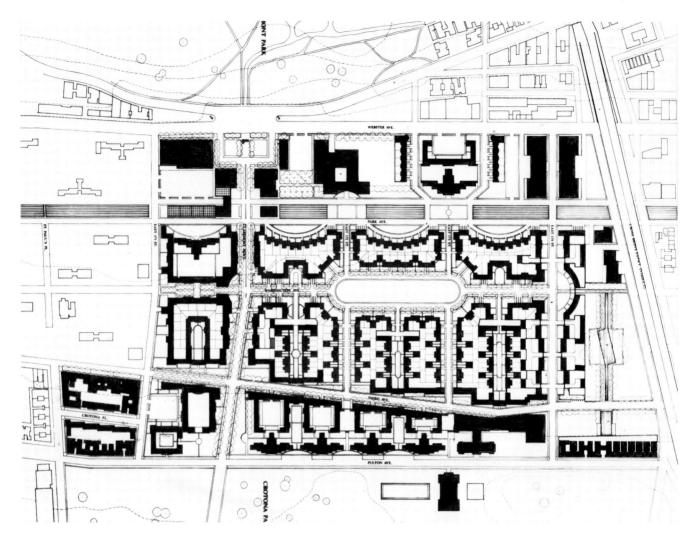

cohesive new Faculty was hired, but the shift toward policy analysis and theory and away from an orientation toward professional practice served to weaken what otherwise would have been a strong program. Also, the fragmentation into other sectoral interests such as public health and social policy further weakened the program. In an effort to accelerate the shift from policy planning to physical planning and to integrate the Urban Planning Division more fully into the School, Elliot Sclar was appointed Chairman in 1979.[73]

Another course of study that emerged directly from the Master of Architecture program was that in Health Services Planning and Design, which had been established by Charles Colbert in 1960. When Polshek became Dean, the one year Master of Science program was operating out of the apartment of Robert Chapman, an adjunct professor. Despite its relatively informal status, the program had in its early years prepared some of America's most prominent Health Service administrators, as well as specialists in the design of health care facilities. In a first effort to reinforce the program, Polshek appropriated a studio on the fifth floor of Avery and provided an office/seminar room for Chapman. Also, Chapman was accorded full-time status on the Faculty. After Chapman

73. Ibid.

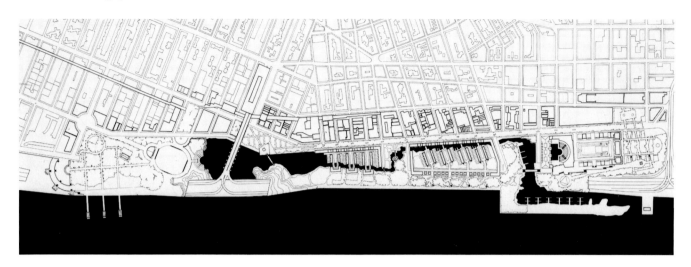

left in 1974, George Mann, a Columbia graduate who had been running a similar program at Texas A&M, came to Columbia to direct, and when he left a few years later, William Parker, an architect and graduate of the program, took over. Unfortunately, a national surplus of hospital rooms and the dwindling number of government programs in the health services resulted in fewer and fewer applicants, and the program finally was phased out in 1978.[74]

The governing apparatus of the School, including the locations of power and responsibility, the means of implementing rules, and the rules themselves, has proven to be rather unconventional. Ever since 1968 and the institution of the Interim Rules, the government of the School has not been sanctioned by the University. As such, Polshek has not in fact been bound by any rules, although for the most part he does abide by the Interim Rules. In 1980, Polshek suggested that rules be proposed and sent to the University Council for approval. In what appears to have been a vote of confidence, the Faculty agreed unanimously that the existing adhocism was preferable to a rigid set of rules. Thus, although the Committee on Student Performance and a committee for the hiring of studio instructors, for example, are organized on an ad hoc basis, care is taken that all interests in the School are represented.[75]

Beyond specific curricular changes, in 1979 the School began to publish a student edited journal entitled *Precis* after years of inactivity in this area. *Precis* has evolved as a vehicle for discussion primarily of students' designs and for the presentation and criticism of issues in architectural literature.

A Center for Advanced Research in Urban and Environmental Affairs administered by the Office of the Dean replaced the Institute of Urban Environment and the Urban Action and Experimentation Program. Projects supported by the Center are academically related and "have as their central objective the revival of humane values in planning policies and environmental design as they affect both the public and the university community."[76] The Center supported research by Herdeg and Plunz: Herdeg to write a

Westesy Housing Complex, 1979, William Fellows *(1979)*.

74. Interview: Loes Schiller by Author, 18 August 1981; and Memorandum: Polshek to Author, 12 August 1981.

75. Memorandum: Polshek to Author, 12 August 1981.

76. Five Year Plan of the Graduate School of Architecture and Planning, 24 July 1974, Central Files.

polemic on Gropius and Harvard, entitled *The Decorated Diagram,* and a monograph on Islamic architecture; and Plunz to complete a work on Turkish vernacular architecture and a biography of Serge Chermayeff. The benefits of the Center are twofold: it enables individuals to publish, and because they are supported by an organ of the Columbia School of Architecture, their publications serve to enhance the School's reputation.[77]

Polshek resurrected the Wednesday lecture series, which is so structured that various practitioners, theoreticians and historians may speak on subjects of their choosing. In addition, he returned the Mathews Lectures from the Metropolitan Museum to Columbia, as much for the educational advantages to the students as for the publicity attaching thereto.[78]

Pursuant to a request by McGill, Polshek had submitted a Five Year Plan in July 1974. At the time, Polshek had acknowledged that the document was optimistic; however, he believed that the objectives could be met, and when met, "Columbia can at long last possess in its midst a Graduate School of Architecture and Planning superior in every way to those presently existing in any of our sister institutions."[79]

Themes of the report recalled those underlying the century long evolution of the School and of architectural education in general: specifically, bridging the gap between the University and the profession at large; utilizing the University's resources including its unique location in New York City; and developing a broad program that would train students to understand formal considerations in architecture and also to cope with the practical demands of professional practice. The educational intentions for the five year period were expected to "redefine and ultimately to redirect the energies of the profession without fundamental disruption of its traditional humanitarian base." It was concluded in the Five Year Plan that "a basic academic and administrative goal of the School is to move toward a situation where all programs support and reinforce one another."[80] Today, that remains a relevant, though not yet fully realized, goal.

77. A more recent initiative is the Dean's plan to establish a six million dollar endowment to support the Center for the Study of American Architecture. To assist him in this he has formed a small advisory committee consisting of Ada Louise Huxtable, Henry Russell Hitchcock, Vincent Scully, I.M. Pei, Phyllis Lambert, Edgar J. Kaufmann and Adolf Placzek. Catha Rambusch has been made the Director of Development. The Center will have an Executive Committee consisting of its Director, the Dean, the Avery Librarian, the Chairman of the Division of Architecture, the Director of the Historic Preservation Program and four at-large faculty members. Its activities will focus on architecture, town planning and landscape architecture of the past and present in America and will include a fund for the acquisition of American drawings and other materials for Avery Library. It will support funded research in the conservation of American architecture and will hire resident junior and post-doctoral scholars as well as practitioners taking time off to pursue special studies. A publication program is projected and will ensure a wide distribution of the work of the Center (Memorandum: Polshek to Author, 10 August 1981).

78. An endowment from Charles T. Mathews *(Columbia, 1889)* initiated the Charles T. Mathews Foundation Lecture Series, which were begun in 1935. Among the lecturers who have participated in the Series are: Joseph Hudnut (1935); C. Grant LaFarge (1936); Leopold Arnaud (1937); Talbot Hamlin (1939); Everard Upjohn (1942); Meyer Schapiro (1946); Sumner Crosby (1948); Kenneth Conant with Emerson Swift (1952); John Mundy (1965); Whitney Stoddard (1967); Henry R. Hitchcock (1971); Nikolaus Pevsner (1972); George Collins, Henry Millon and James Ackerman (1973); Alfred Frazer (1974); Spiro Kostof (1976); Paul Mylonas (1976); and Vincent Scully (1977).

Originally presented as a series of ten public lectures on a topic in mediaeval architecture and held at the Metropolitan Museum of Art, currently the series is constituted of four to six public lectures held at Columbia, followed by a series of tutorials open to students of the Graduate School of Architecture and Planning.

79. Five Year Plan for the Graduate School of Architecture and Planning, 24 July 1974, Central Files.

80. Ibid.